AF754113

The Historic Fort Worth Stockyards

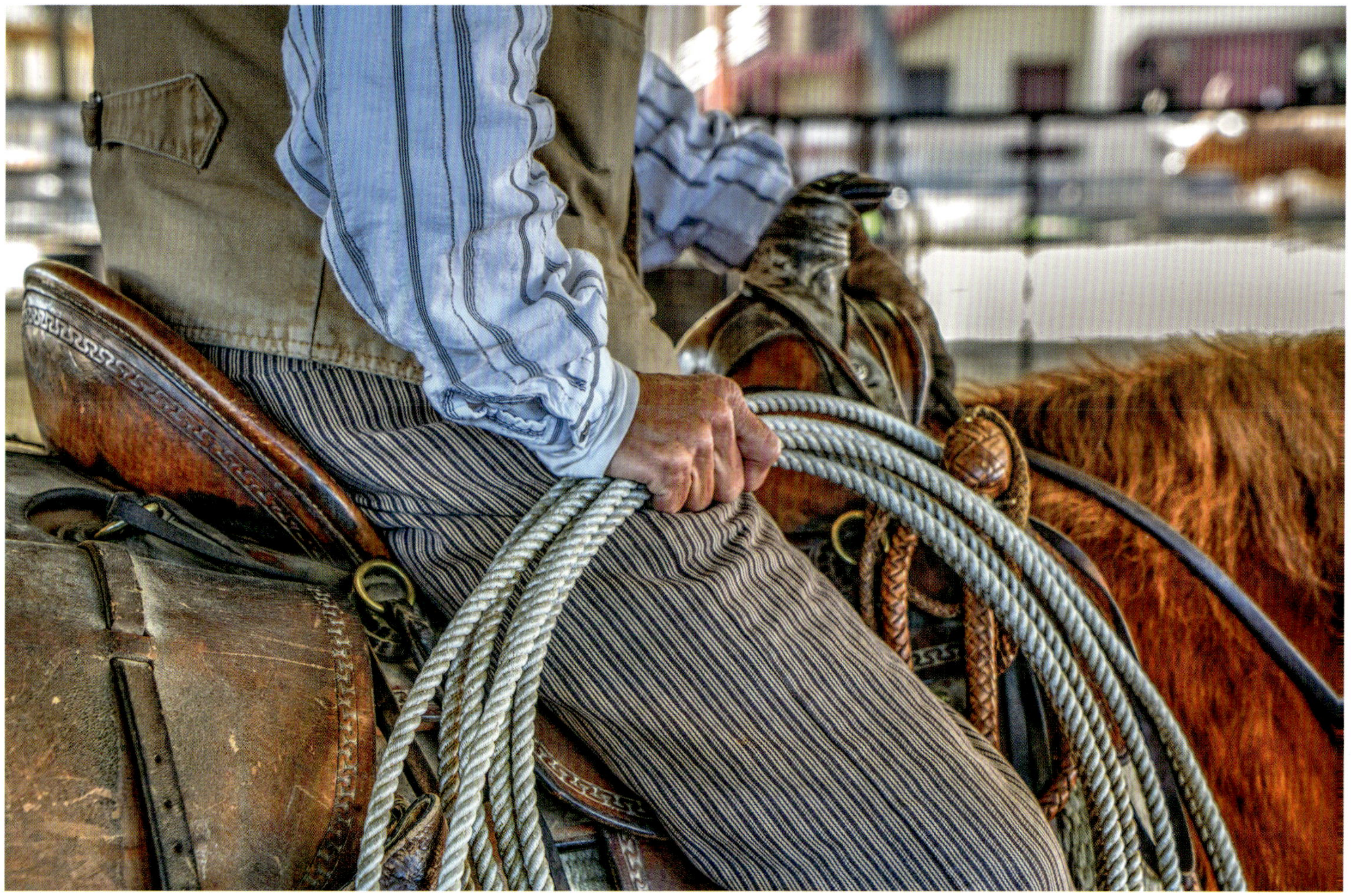

Nancy and Ted Paup Ranching Heritage Series
Paul H. Carlson & M. Scott Sosebee, General Editors

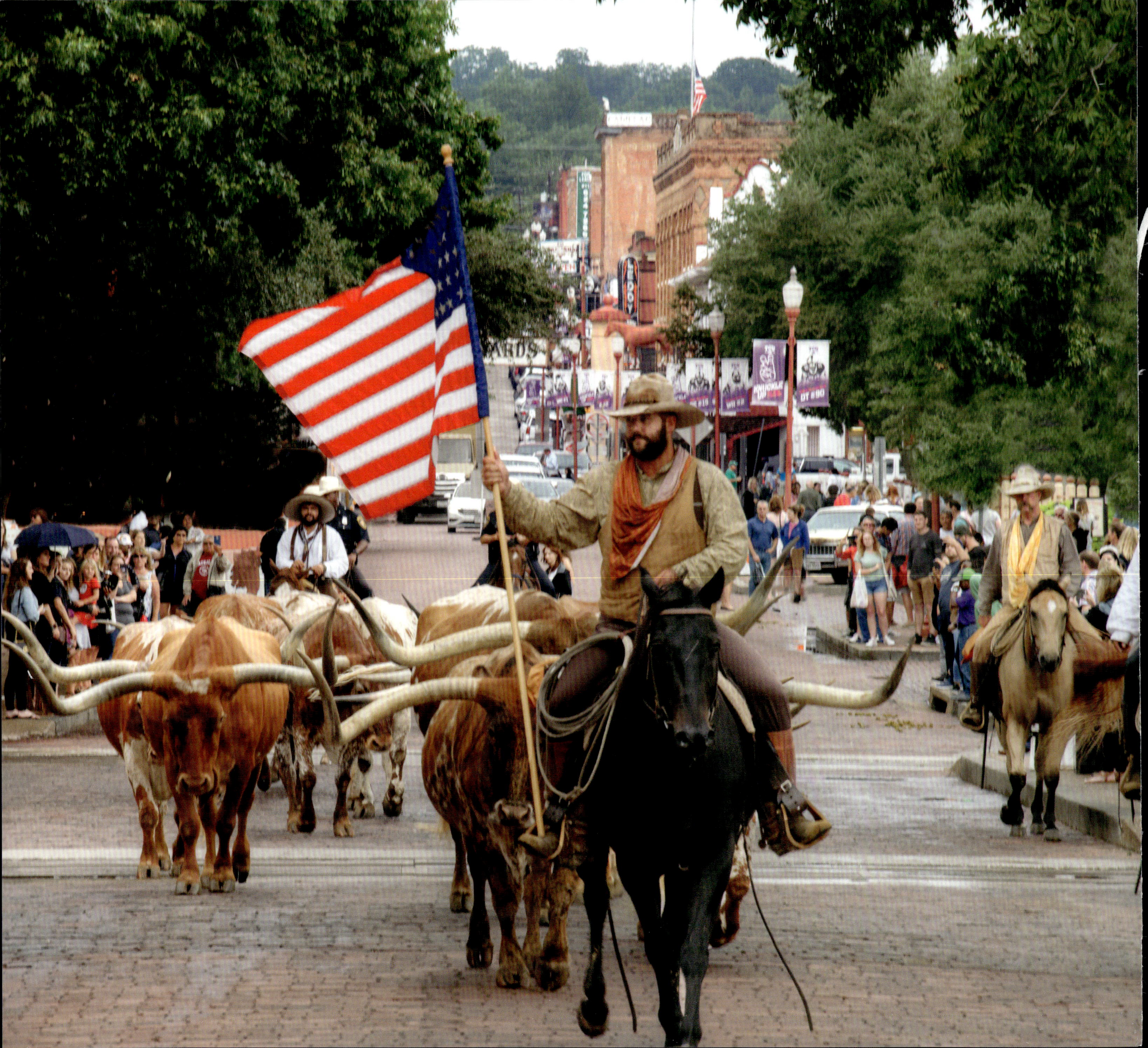

The Historic Fort Worth Stockyards

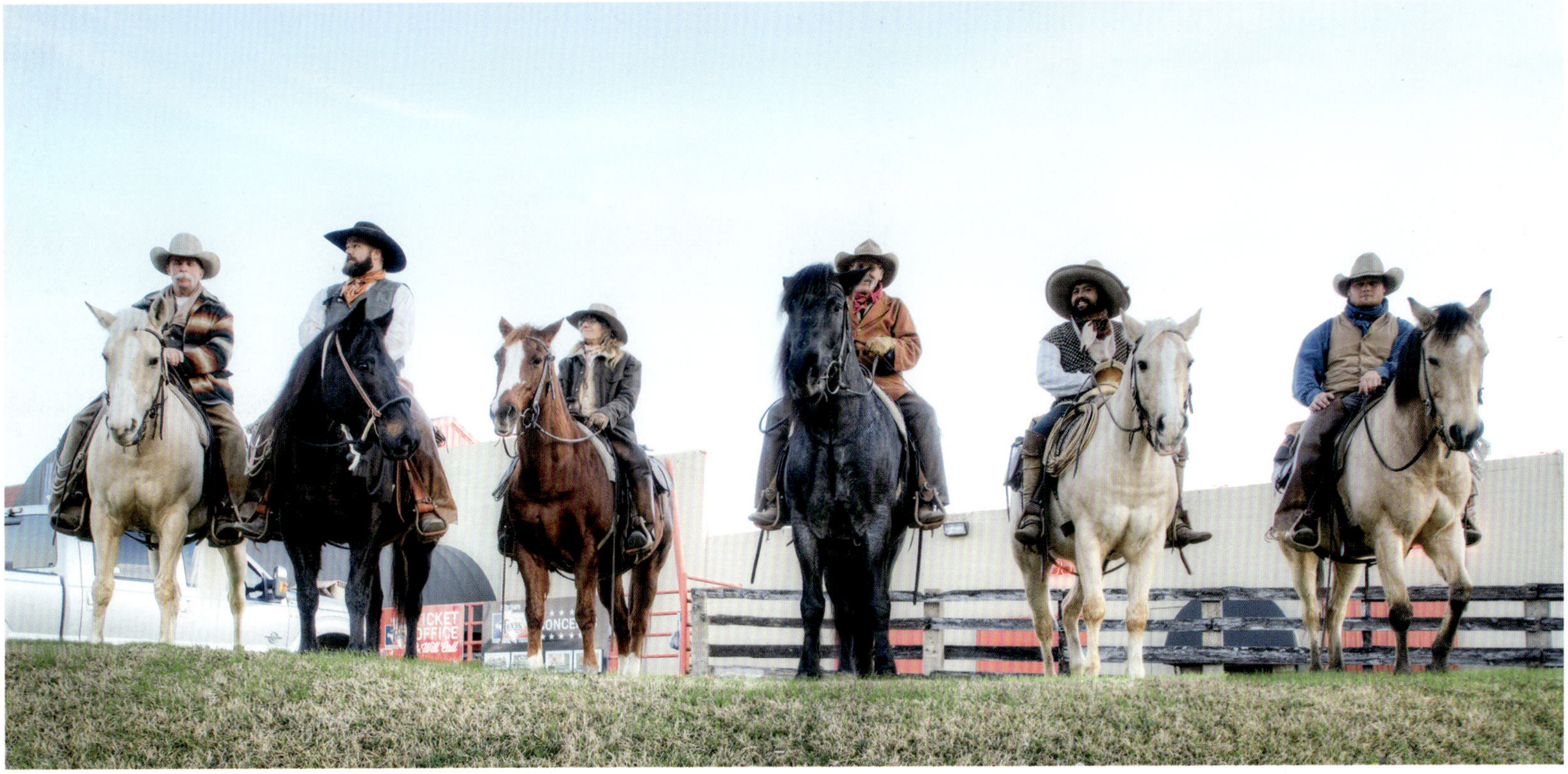

J'Nell Pate   Photography by Carolyn Brown

TEXAS A&M UNIVERSITY PRESS   COLLEGE STATION

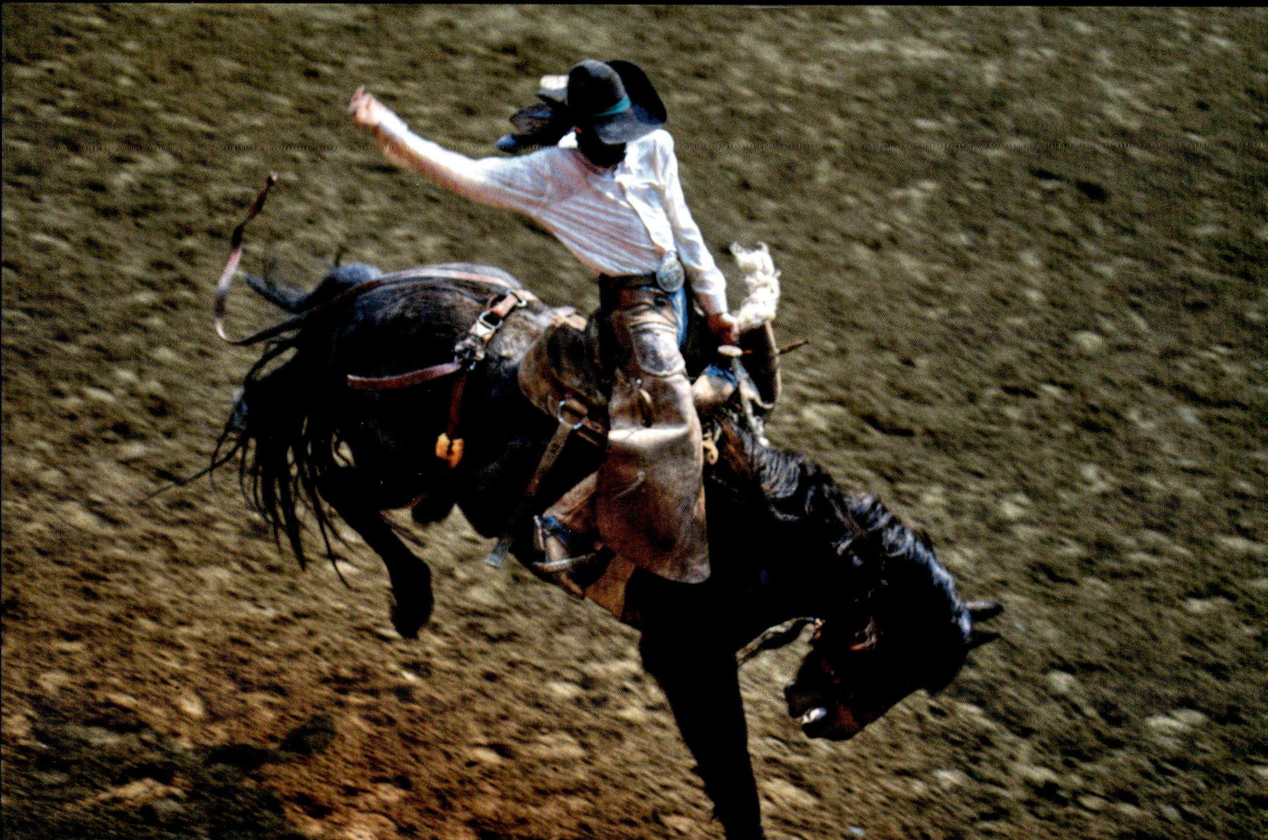

Copyright © 2022 by Carolyn Brown
and J'Nell Pate Barnes

All rights reserved

First edition

This paper meets the requirements
of ANSI/NISO Z39.48–1992
(Permanence of Paper).

Binding materials have been
chosen for durability.

Manufactured in China through
Martin Book Management

∞

LIBRARY OF CONGRESS CATALOGING-IN-PUBLICATION DATA

Names: Pate, J'Nell L., author. | Brown, Carolyn, 1936– photographer.
Title: The historic Fort Worth Stockyards / J'Nell Pate; photography by Carolyn Brown.
Other titles: Nancy and Ted Paup '74 ranching heritage series.
Description: First edition. | College Station: Texas A&M University Press, [2021] | Series: Nancy and Ted Paup ranching heritage series | Includes bibliographical references and index.
Identifiers: LCCN 2021036710 (print) | LCCN 2021036711 (ebook) | ISBN 9781623499242 (cloth) | ISBN 9781623499259 (ebook)
Subjects: LCSH: Stockyards—Texas—Fort Worth—History. | Livestock—Texas—Fort Worth—History. | Fort Worth (Tex.)—Buildings, structures, etc.—Pictorial works. | BISAC: PHOTOGRAPHY / Subjects & Themes / Regional (see also TRAVEL / Pictorials) | PHOTOGRAPHY / Subjects & Themes / Historical
Classification: LCC F394.F7 P374 2021 (print) | LCC F394.F7 (ebook) | DDC 976.4/5315—dc23
LC record available at https://lccn.loc.gov/2021036710
LC ebook record available at https://lccn.loc.gov/2021036711

To my husband, Fred Barnes,
who was very helpful during the entire process.
—J'Nell

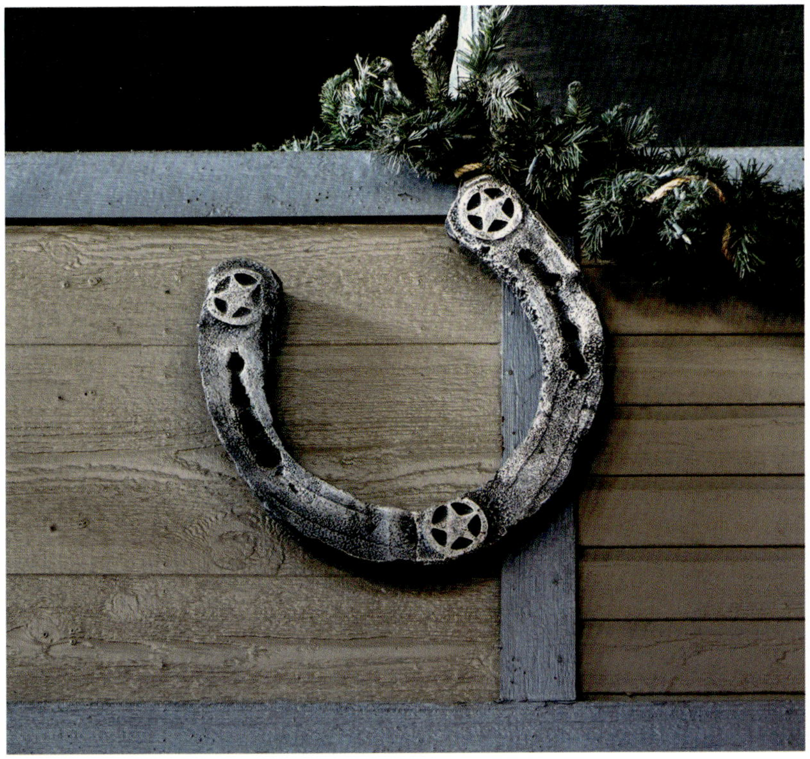

The Advancement Board of Texas A&M University Press dedicates this book to the memory of Joann Seely (1941–2020), wife of longtime board member Charlie Seely '55, beloved member of the Fort Worth community, and a true inspiration to those she met.

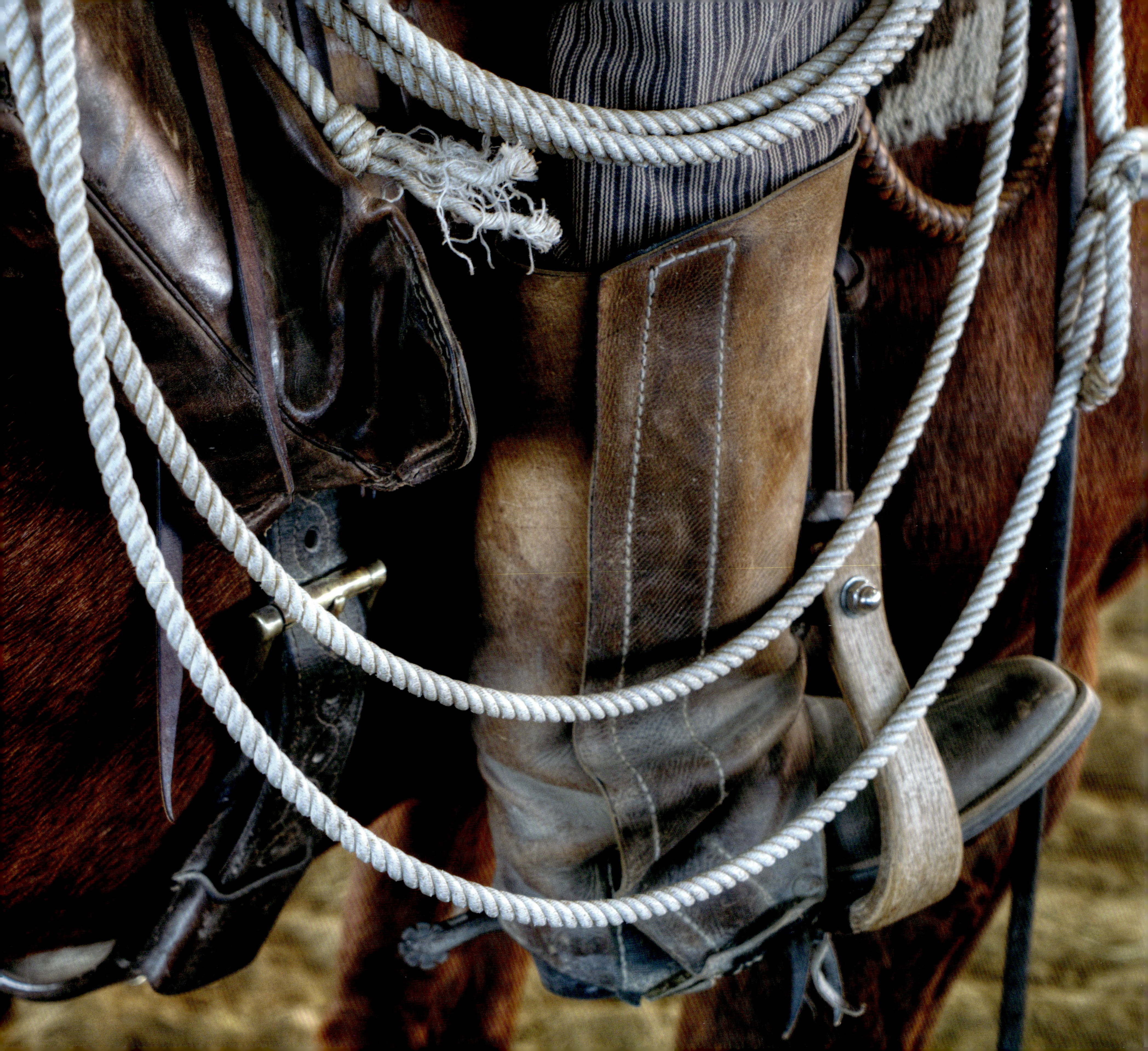

Contents

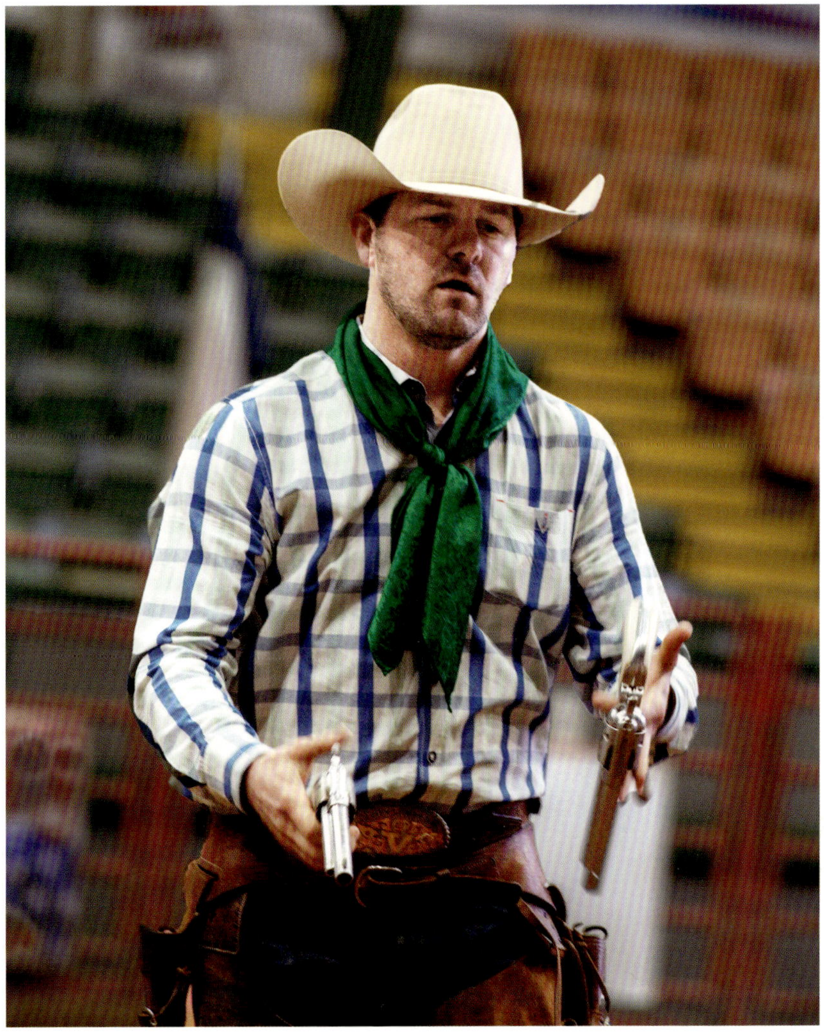

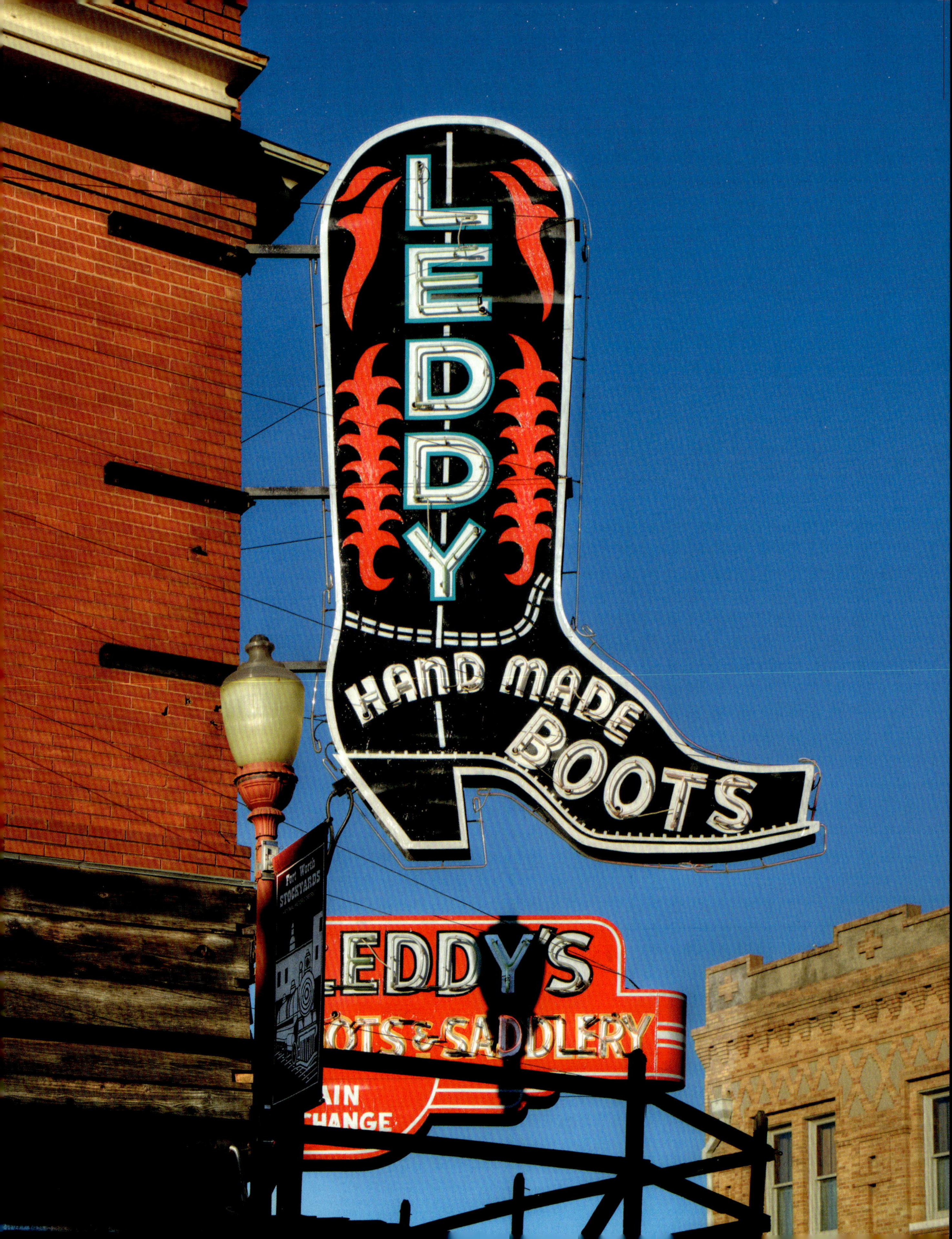
LEDDY
HAND MADE
BOOTS
Fort Worth
STOCKYARDS

The Historic Fort Worth Stockyards

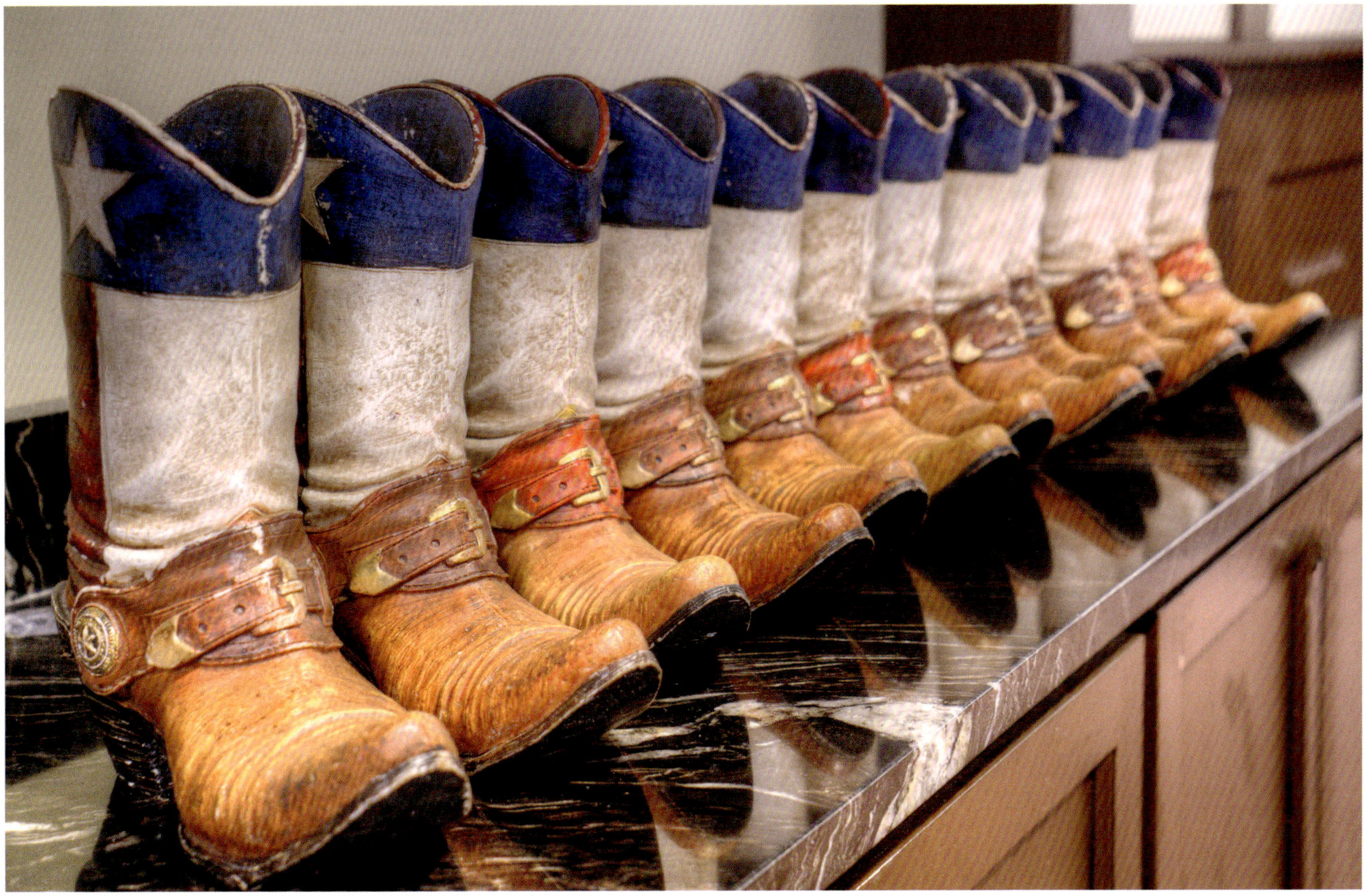

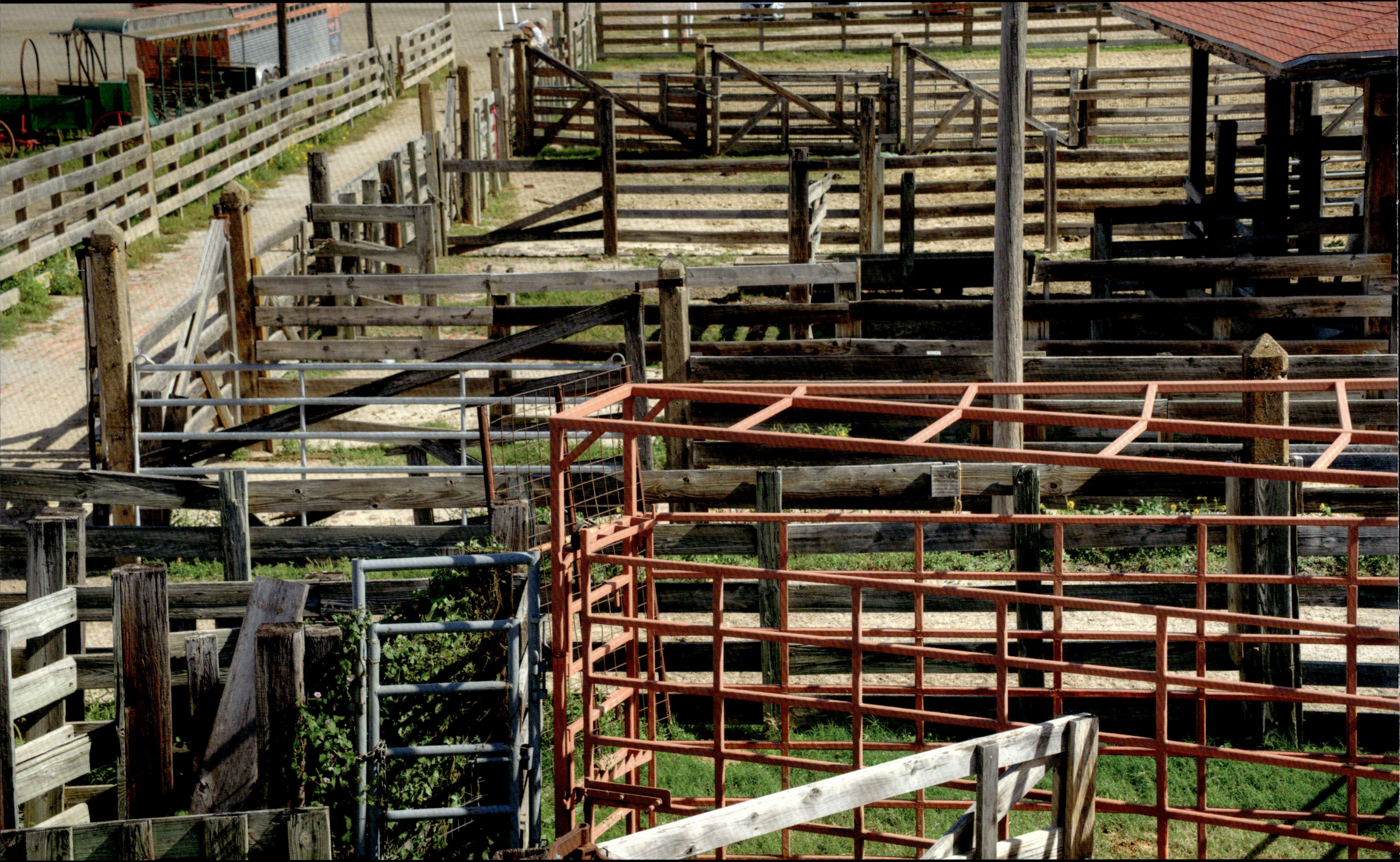

CHAPTER 1

Early Background

The mighty Fort Worth Stock Yards, ultimately the largest in the entire Southwest, began because of a couple of unfortunate incidents and a misunderstanding. A wealthy Boston businessman, Greenlief W. Simpson, with his lawyer, William Johnson, came to Fort Worth in October 1892 and visited what then was the small Union Stock Yards north of downtown.

The unfortunate incidents were that heavy October rains caused several washouts, and then a railroad strike allowed more livestock than usual to be placed in the yards the day the two Boston men visited. The fledgling stockyards had only enough pens to handle 150 railroad cars of cattle, not the 500 carloads that overflowed the yards that day. Thus, Simpson looked over at Johnson and said amazingly, "This is *some* market!" As a result of this misunderstanding, they invested immediately.

"Some market" it eventually would become, but Simpson and his Boston neighbor, Louville V. Niles, whom he persuaded to invest with him, faced a few years of struggle first. Local Fort Worth citizens already had exerted years of hard work and struggle to turn their only asset—thousands of cattle from South Texas passing through each spring—into jobs and businesses for the little settlement on a bluff overlooking the Trinity River.

South Texas ranchers by 1865 began rounding up the herds of Longhorns that ran wild and multiplied during the Civil War. They learned that cattle selling for three or four dollars in Texas brought forty to fifty dollars in northern markets. Walking them to market on a long cattle drive thus became the short-term solution. When the Kansas-Pacific Railroad reached Abilene, Kansas, in 1867, it became the chief cattle market for Texas herds. The herds came up the trail through Fort Worth.

The maze of stockyard livestock pens spans over fifty-four hundred square feet. Visitors can follow an overhead walkway to view the historic labyrinth of wooden pathways.

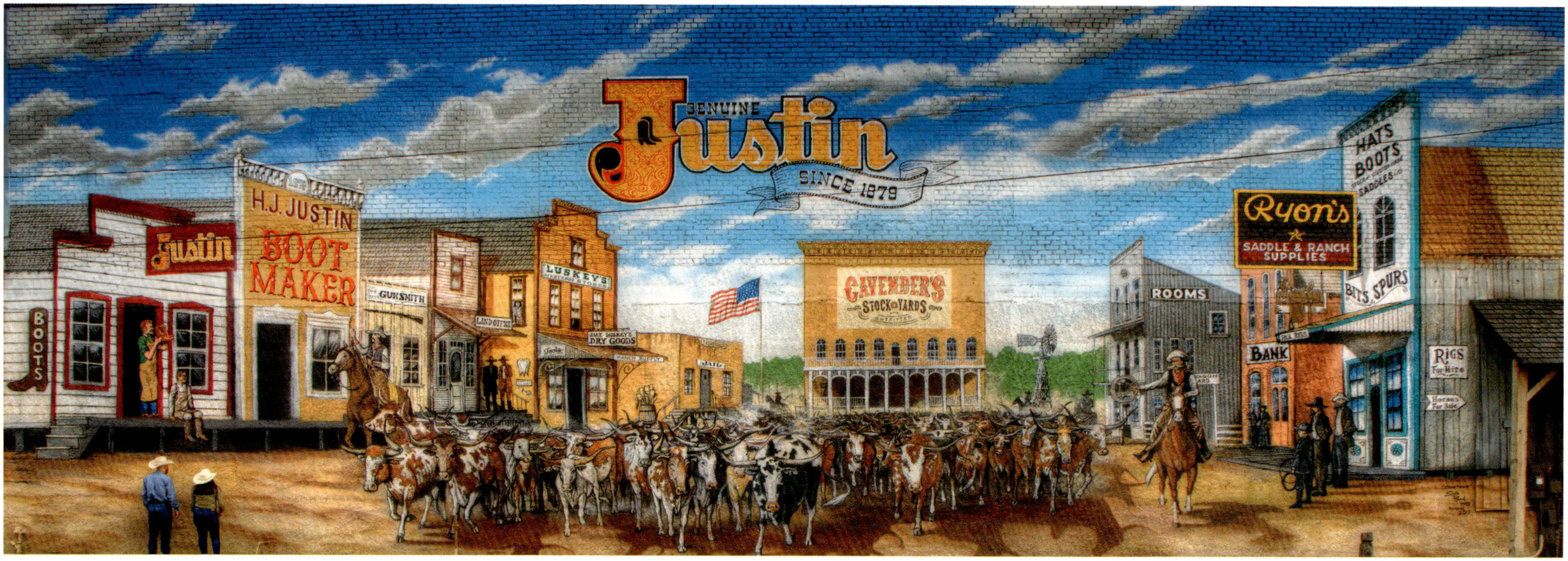

The Justin Boot mural facing Northeast Twenty-Third, adjacent to Main Street, was painted by Western artist Stylle Read in 1993. It depicts a perfect stockyards business district with Cavender's Boot City in the center. Two people are standing to the left.

Fort Worth leaders wanted stockyards, a meat-processing plant, and a railroad to create a market in their city. As early as November 1858, local leaders tried to induce the Houston and Texas Central and the Southern Pacific Railroads to come to Fort Worth, but nothing happened. The few residents of Fort Worth in 1875 suggested that a packing plant be built in their town. Businesses that slaughtered animals in earlier days packed the meat in barrels of salt brine, from which the name "meatpacking plant" arose. Those facilities being built by the late nineteenth century shipped meat first in iced-down railroad cars and later in refrigerated cars. However, the term "packing plant" remained in use.

A railroad first became a priority for the citizens of Fort Worth, however. The editor of the *Fort Worth Democrat* newspaper, Buckley B. Paddock, optimistically included a map on the front page of his June 26, 1873, edition showing seven railroad lines from several North Texas cities heading into Fort Worth as the hub. Other newspaper editors or writers began to make fun of Paddock and his map, saying that it looked like a tarantula. His and the city's high hopes for a railroad at that time failed because of an 1873 recession, or panic, as people called it then. Population dropped from four thousand to less than one thousand in only a few months.

Fort Worth businessmen did not give up. By 1875 Major Kleber M. Van Zandt enlisted help and talked to the Texas and Pacific Railroad officials, who said they could buy rails on credit but had no money to do the grading. The Fort Worth businessmen agreed to do that. In October 1875, they created the Tarrant County Construction Company, of which Van Zandt became president. The state of Texas offered a land grant of sixteen sections to the railroad for each mile of track laid, but created deadlines.

Fortunately, the state extended the deadline a couple of times but finally issued an ultimatum. Unless the railroad began serving Fort Worth by the day in 1876 that the first legislature of the new constitution adjourned, the state would reclaim the right of way.

Stories are told about a state representative from Fort Worth, who, though ill, did his best in the legislative chambers to delay the closing of the session by a day or so. Meanwhile, work continued around the clock on the railroad track for the last few days the legislature met; workers did not stop to sleep and were kept awake by the women bringing coffee and food to them. When a telegram from Fort Worth arrived in Austin stating that the tracks were down, only then did their valiant state representative cease his delaying tactics. At any rate, the first railroad arrived in Fort Worth at 11:23 a.m. on July 19, 1876, with the legislature still in session. A twelve-piece band and a huge crowd greeted the train. Fort Worth had its railroad; cattle soon filled the cars.

John F. Swayne gets the credit for owning the first load of cattle ever shipped out of Fort Worth; twenty-three head left on September 6, 1876. He sold them for a little over ten dollars per head. That same month the Texas and Pacific Railroad began building cattle pens near its tracks to hold cattle for shipment. Drovers coming north from South Texas saw the opportunity either to sell their cattle in Fort Worth or put them on a railroad car and send them northward rather than walk them the rest of the way. However small, Fort Worth had its first stockyards.

The population of Fort Worth tripled from approximately two thousand to six thousand people within ninety days of the arrival of the railroad. The number of saloons

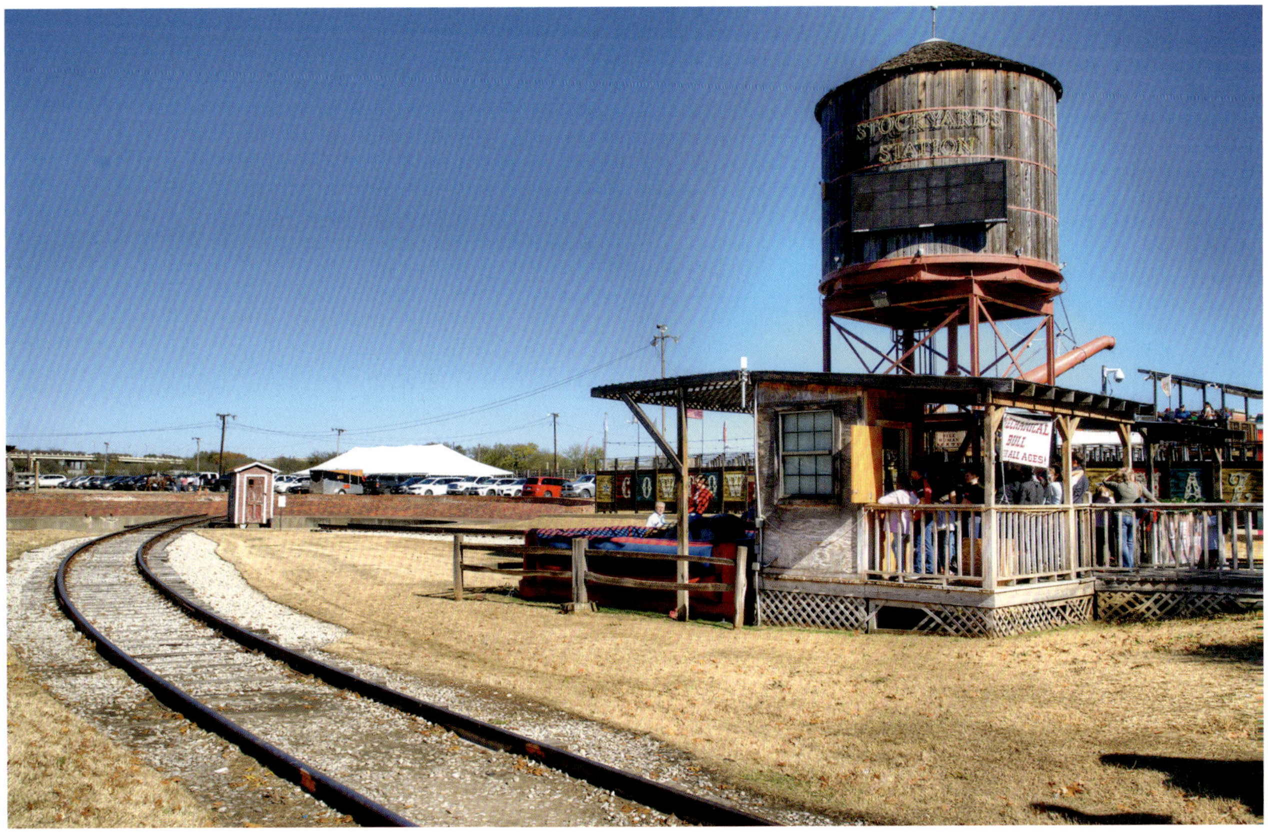

The railroad track leading into the stockyards business area was used for Puffy, a vintage locomotive owned by Southern Pacific Railroad, built in 1896. Due to mechanical requirements and engine and equipment changes, it is presently being reconditioned.

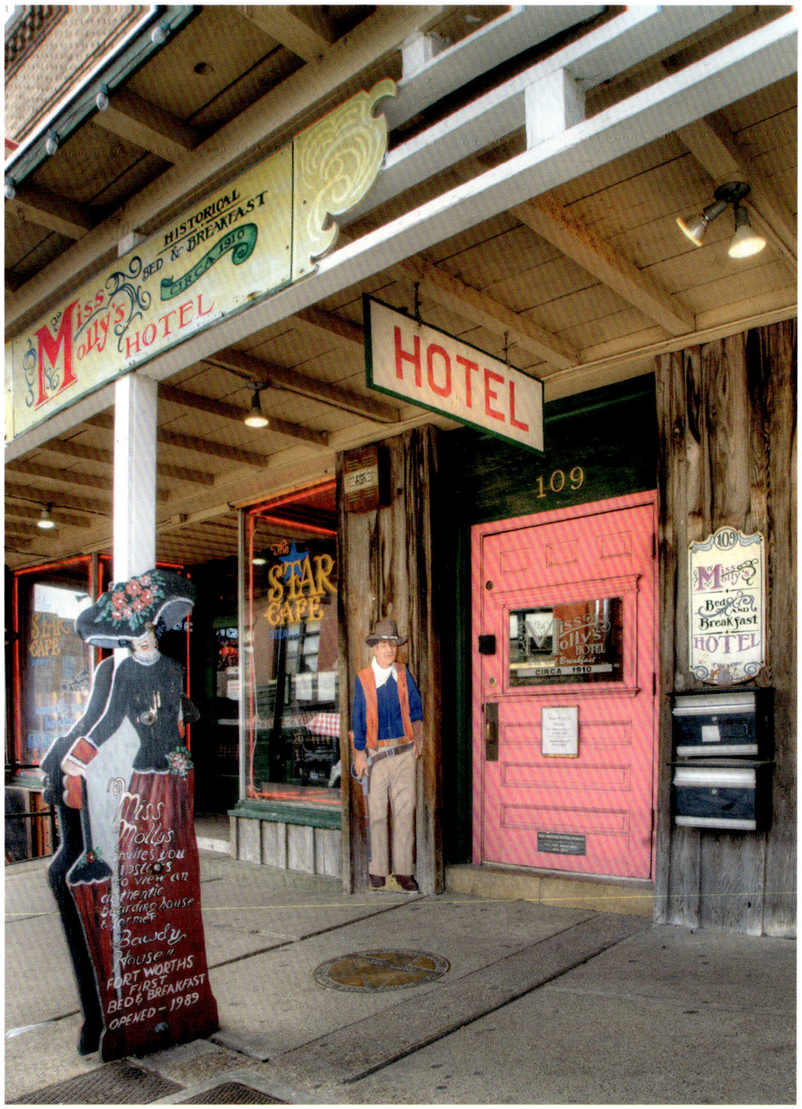

At various times a boardinghouse and bordello, Miss Molly's Hotel now offers an authentic "Old West" experience to overnight guests of the stockyards.

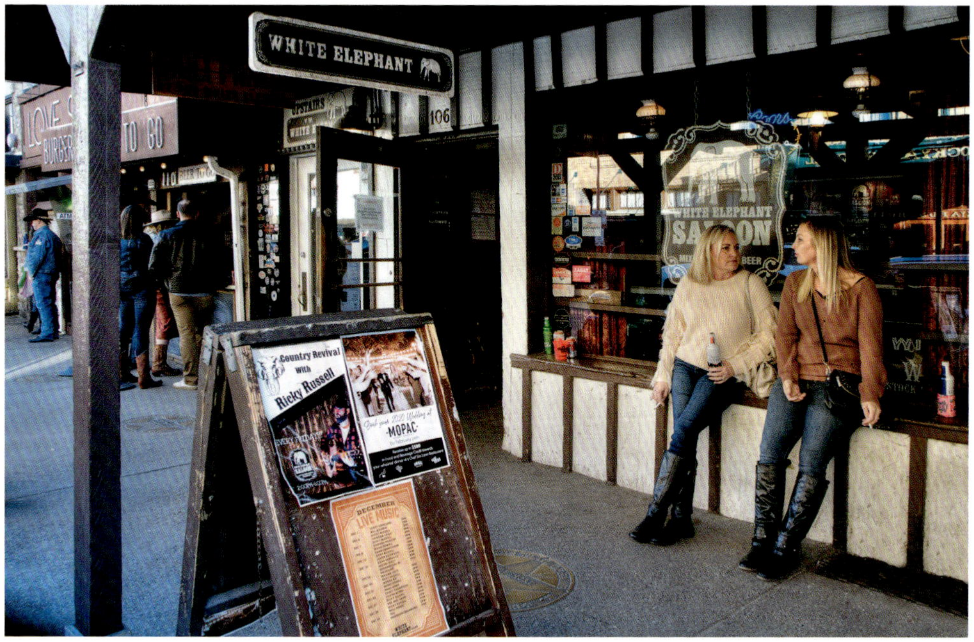

Formerly named the Woodhouse Building (1931), this art deco building later became known as the White Elephant Saloon, dating back to the 1800s. It was used in the filming of the CBS television series *Walker, Texas Ranger.*

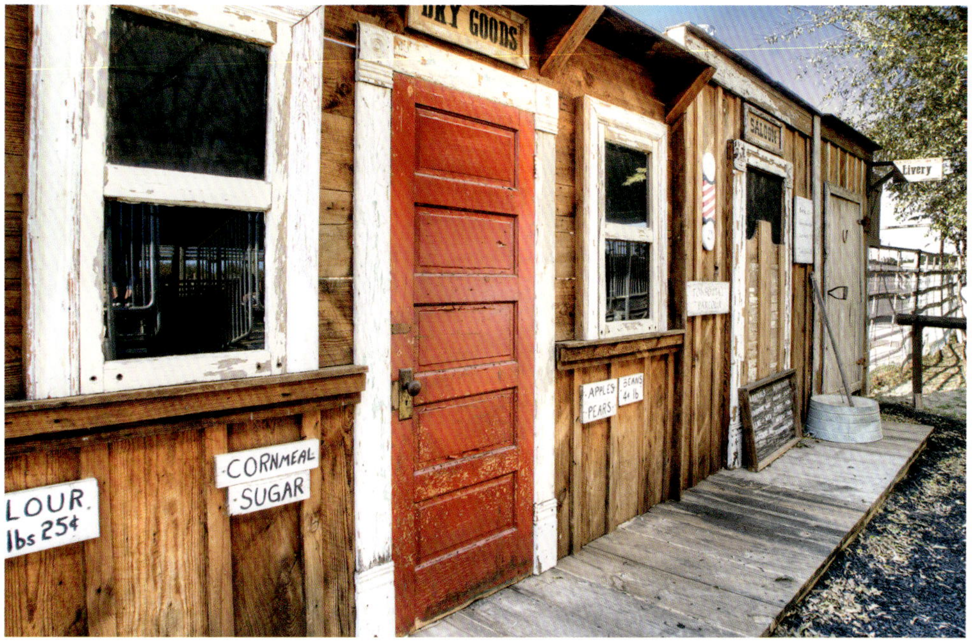

The popular Educational Program area is faced with an enchanting replica of an early Western village. Weekly, drovers and their horses gather to present programs on early cattle drives and horse husbandry for schoolchildren and tourists.

more than tripled as well to at least thirteen—the Waco Tap, the Headlight Bar, the Tivoli Saloon, the Occidental, Our Friends, the Red Light, Our Comrades, the Beer Garden, the Bon Ton, the Cattle Exchange, the Horse Head, the White Elephant, and the Trinity.

Unfortunately, all of the herds that came through Fort Worth did not sell at the new stockyards. Some owners shipped them out by rail, but the railroad did not always have enough stock cars to handle them. More important, the drovers could still walk their cattle to Kansas more cheaply than shipping by train. Even so, all the activity allowed Fort Worth to acquire its first commission company, a branch of one of the largest in the nation, Hunter, Evans. A commission company sold a farmer's or rancher's animals at the stockyards for him.

Attempts to create profitable meatpacking plants in Fort Worth continued through the 1880s but failed even as more railroads arrived. Promoters built various stock pens near the railroads at the south end of Fort Worth. A gunfight took place in March 1886 south of downtown at a place called Buttermilk Junction as strikers tried to keep the trains from moving.

By the mid-1880s the long drives through Fort Worth dwindled to nothing, so the only way for Texas farmers and ranchers to sell their livestock became the fledgling market that promoters developed in Fort Worth. After numerous failed attempts, Fort Worth businessmen chartered Union Stock Yards on July 26, 1887, but they were not ready to receive stock until midsummer of 1889. The following year the directors of the new Union Stock Yards met and formed the Fort Worth Dressed Meat and Packing Company to be located near a new stockyard north of downtown. (In these early days folks spelled "stockyards" as two words, "Stock Yards," in their writings.) In 1890 investors rechartered the packing plant as the Fort Worth Packing Company, and finally Fort Worth could slaughter meat locally. However, the two new facilities faced problems. Trail driving ceased in the mid-1880s, and local farmers and ranchers did not provide sufficient cattle and hogs for the local packing plants to make a profit.

Despite the struggles at the new stockyards, the city began growing rapidly, with the population more than tripling again, from 6,663 in 1880 to 23,076 by 1890. Beef production increased by 51 percent in Texas in that decade. Another reason for the huge population increase is the result of a phenomenon that swept the entire United States beginning in the 1880s. Huge numbers of central and eastern Europeans left their homes in Czechoslovakia, Hungary, Croatia, Greece, Italy, Yugoslavia, and other countries to seek jobs in America. When they learned that they could receive more money in a week in America than it took a year to earn in the "old country" and that the cost of fares on ships declined, they saw no reason to stay in Europe. Historians called this the "new immigration," contrasting with the "old immigration" that settled the East Coast in the eighteenth and nineteenth centuries, with newcomers seeking farms in the Midwest. Historian Frederick Jackson Turner wrote that by the 1890s the frontier was ending, leaving less free land to be claimed. This meant that most new immigrants flocked to big cities for jobs.

Consequently, most of the participants in the new immigration sought jobs in cities in the Midwest: Chicago, Kansas City, St. Louis, Cincinnati, and Fort Worth. Because slaughtering animals and operating railroads at the time represented the two biggest businesses in the United States, jobs became plentiful in these industries. Often immigrants from the eastern European countries took ships to Galveston and then boarded a train heading directly to Fort Worth for homes and jobs at the new meatpacking plant or the stockyards.

Mike C. Hurley, who took over as head of the Fort Worth Packing Company in April 1892, realized that the local meatpacking business needed help against the large Chicago firms that could manipulate livestock prices and railroad rates. The local packing plant needed more money than Fort Worthians could supply. Hurley thus

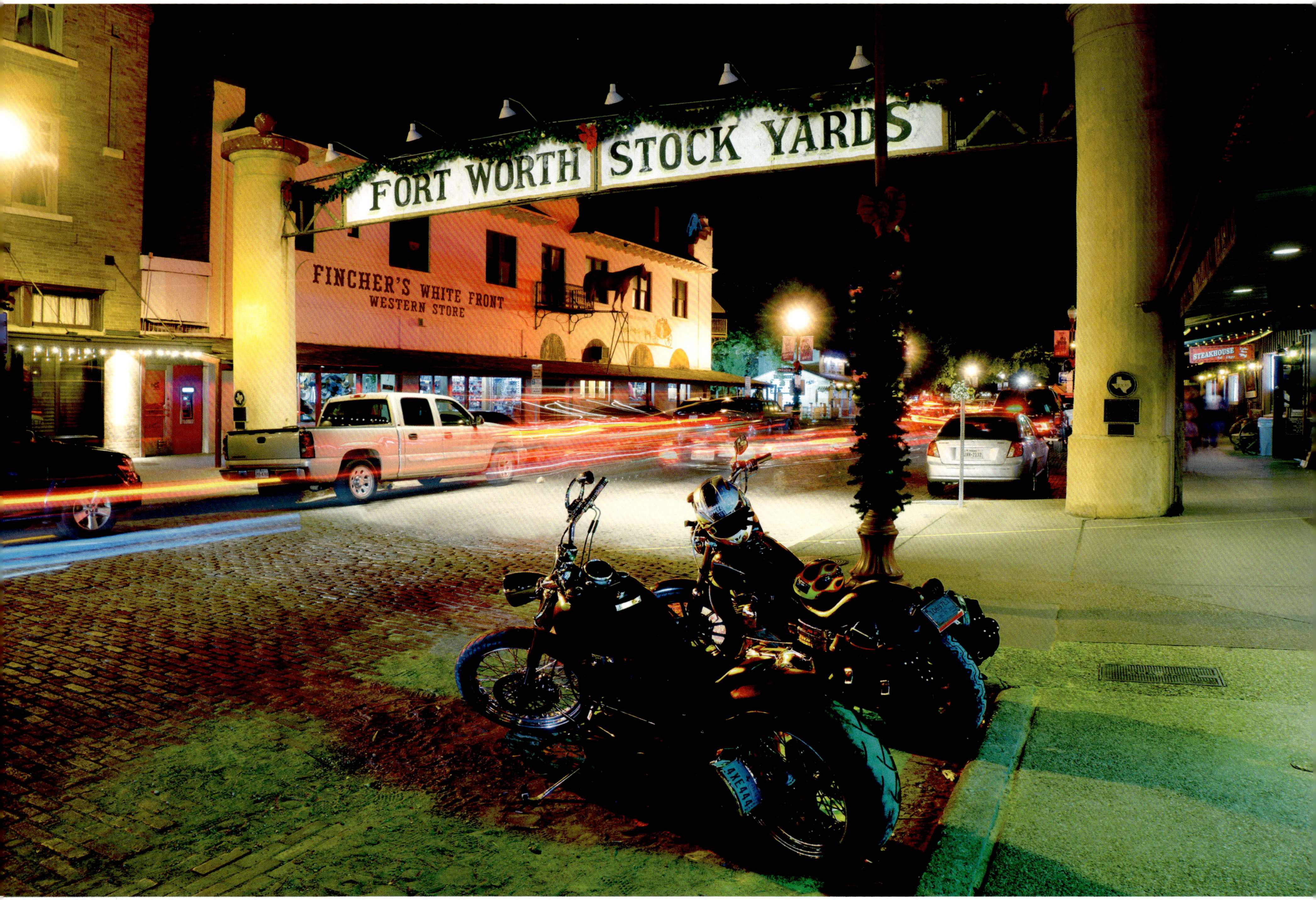

Visitors enter the main part of the Fort Worth National Historic District on Exchange Avenue and pass under this archway, built in 1902, which serves as the official entrance to the historic stockyards area. The name "Fort Worth Stock Yards" was later changed to "Fort Worth Stockyards.

became the person who traveled to Boston to interest a wealthy capitalist in investing. He invited Greenlief W. Simpson to visit during the last week of October 1892, when he and his lawyer witnessed all those cattle pens bursting with bawling animals.

Simpson, formerly a trustee of the Bay State Cattle Company of Boston, had sold out. When the local Fort Worth people involved in the packing plant talked to Simpson, their business was in so much trouble that the owners offered to sell both the packing plant and Union Stock Yards below cost. When learning of the deal, local citizens urged the sale and subscribed forty thousand dollars to the present owners, knowing that they needed to keep the two facilities open until a sale could be made.

Simpson attended a meeting of the Cattle Raisers Association of Texas in the spring of 1893 and told the group that if they shipped their animals to Fort Worth, he would pay them fifty cents a head more than they had been getting at Kansas City, where most of them had been going. Consequently, many of the producers signed pledges to sell to Simpson. The cattlemen at the meeting even voted to move their headquarters from Jacksboro, Texas (sixty miles to the northwest of Fort Worth), believing that Fort Worth was the coming market.

Simpson chartered a new company, the Fort Worth Stock Yards Company (he spelled "Stock Yards" as two words) in West Virginia, where tax laws for corporations proved more favorable than in Texas. Among new di-

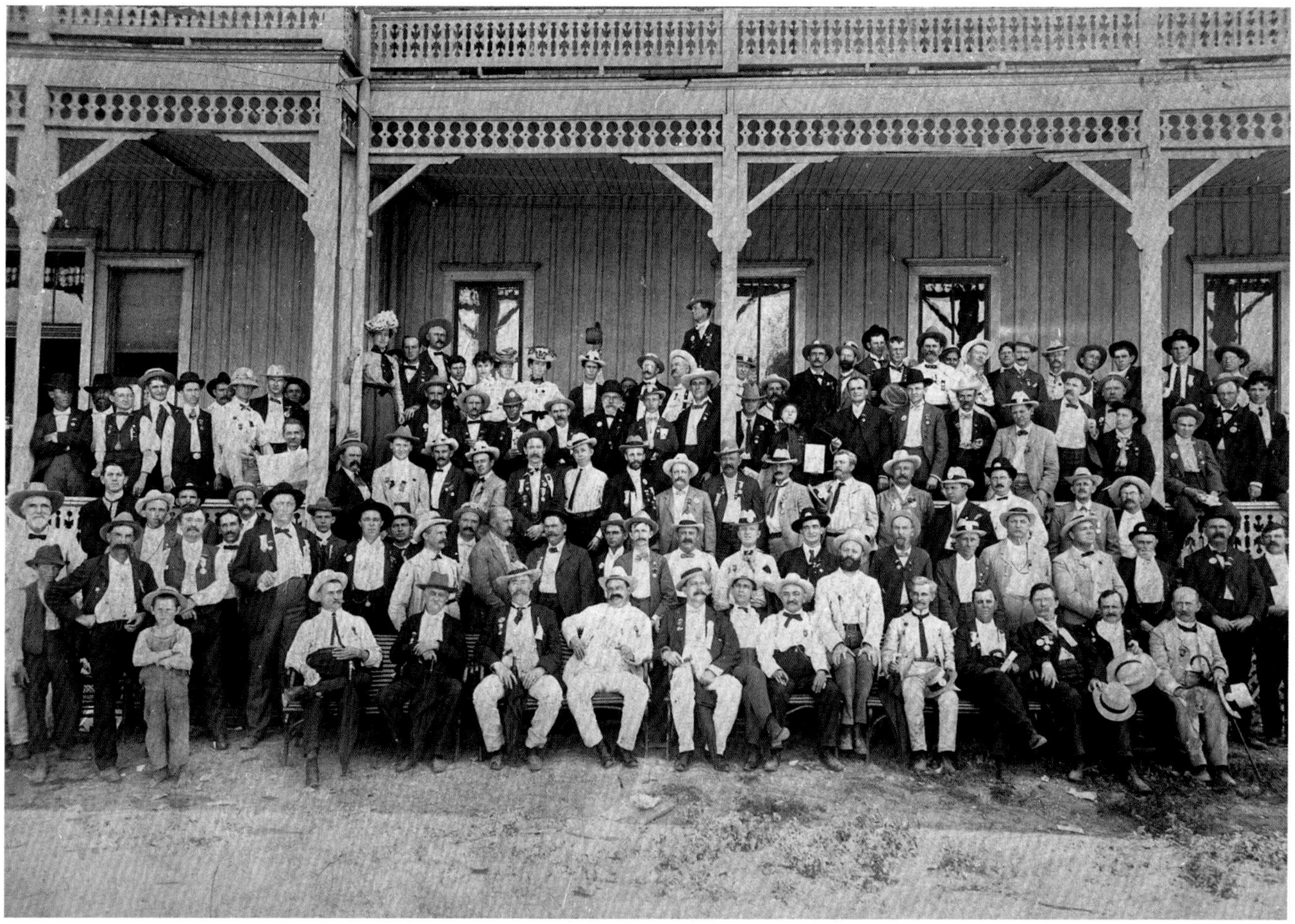

Texas Cattle Raisers met at the stockyards not long after the original Exchange Building was erected. Note the handful of women in attendance. Courtesy of Fort Worth Stockyards Collection, University of Texas at Arlington Libraries.

rectors who joined with him was Louville V. Niles, who in Boston had been president of the Boston Packing and Provision Company.

Charles C. French began working as a public relations agent for the Fort Worth Stock Yards Company almost from the beginning. His job was to make contact with livestock producers on their ranches to encourage business for the stockyards. Early in 1896 he talked about the need of more cattle receipts with rancher Charles McFarland of Weatherford. McFarland suggested a fat stock show to draw business. As French later related the conversation, he confessed that the idea did not much appeal to him because the stockyards had no fat stock to exhibit. However, McFarland promised to bring a couple of loads from his herd and to persuade other ranchers to do the same. The two men agreed to do it if they could raise money for some prizes, such as hats, spurs, bridles, boots, and saddles.

Stockyards manager W. E. Skinner liked the idea and arranged the stock show to coincide with the Cattle Raisers convention to take place in Fort Worth in March 1896. A few cattlemen brought animals from their herds. No hogs or sheep were exhibited. To dampen spirits, a sleet storm took place the evening before the show. The cattle, tied under trees along Marine Creek, looked "a pitiable sight" with ice on their backs in the morning. However, as often happens in Texas when a bit of snow falls in March, the sun came out. By noon, the ice had melted, and the show went on. The Fort Worth Stock Yards Company held another show that same year, October 12–13, 1896, when the National Live Stock Exchange held its eighth annual convention in Fort Worth. With hogs and sheep added, it became a much larger show.

Numerous cattlemen joined together and took an important step on October 24, 1901, when they agreed to work with officials of the Fort Worth Stock Yards Com-

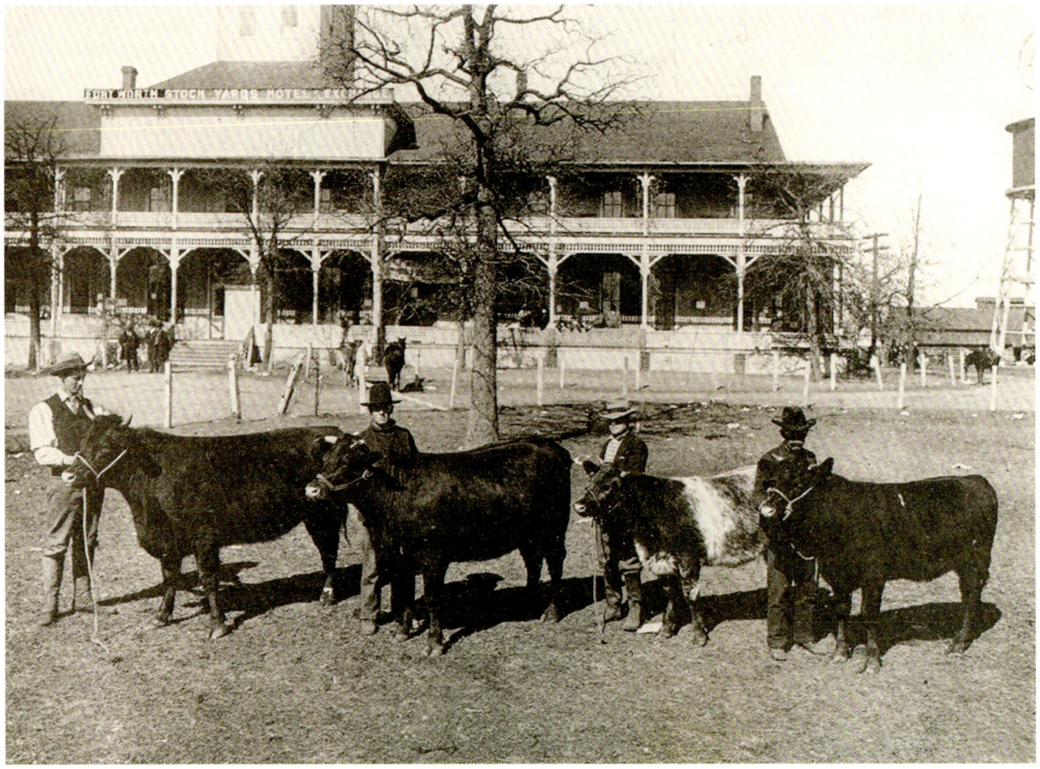

This wooden Livestock Exchange Building existed prior to the one built in 1902 that is still in use. Courtesy of North Fort Worth Historical Society.

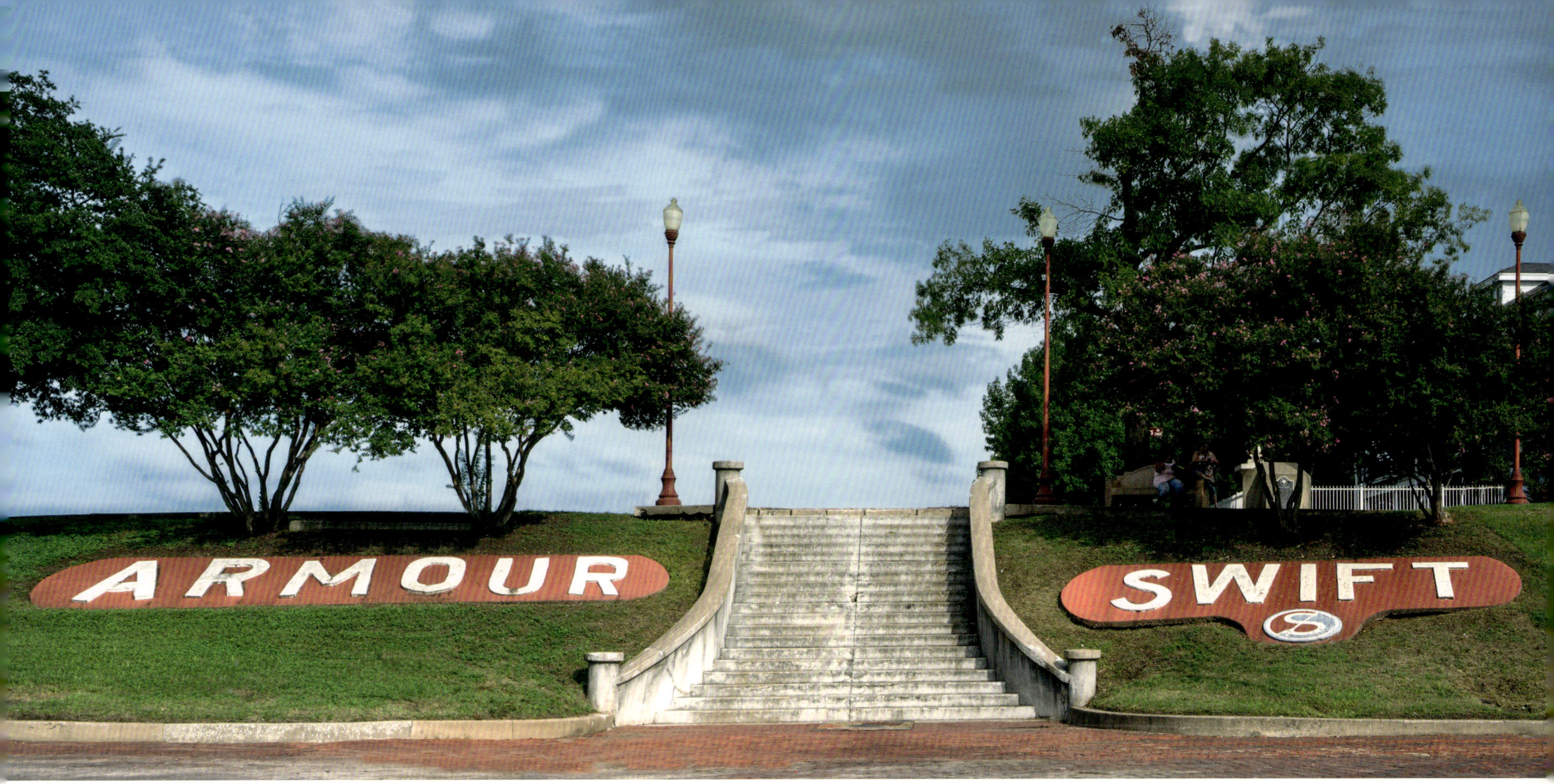

A magnificent stairway, framed by Armour and Swift signs, introduces the once-vibrant Armour and Swift meatpacking companies that covered the land beyond the steps. The annual A&M Midnight Yell takes place in September from these steps.

pany and commission firms at the market to incorporate the Fort Worth Livestock Exchange to be housed in the large office building of the stockyards company. Most stockyards created exchanges to promote their market so that members could enforce needed rules.

The year that Armour and Swift, the top two meatpackers in the country, came to Fort Worth, 1902, ranks as a red-letter date for the city. Local leaders knew that with the presence of these two companies, Fort Worth finally—after a quarter century of trying—would become a stable and wealthy livestock center. City businessmen actually raised fifty thousand dollars for each of the two meatpacking companies to induce them to come. They also gave the two companies the land on which to build their plants, approximately twenty-two acres for each.

As soon as Armour and Swift arrived, more construction occurred. Each became a one-third owner of the yards, and Greenlief W. Simpson and Louville V. Niles retained the final third. The owners began construction of a new Livestock Exchange Building, the one still in use today as an office building and museum. Armour and Swift were part of a Big Four nationwide group of meatpackers that many called a meatpacking trust. The other two large ones in 1902 were Morris and Cudahy.

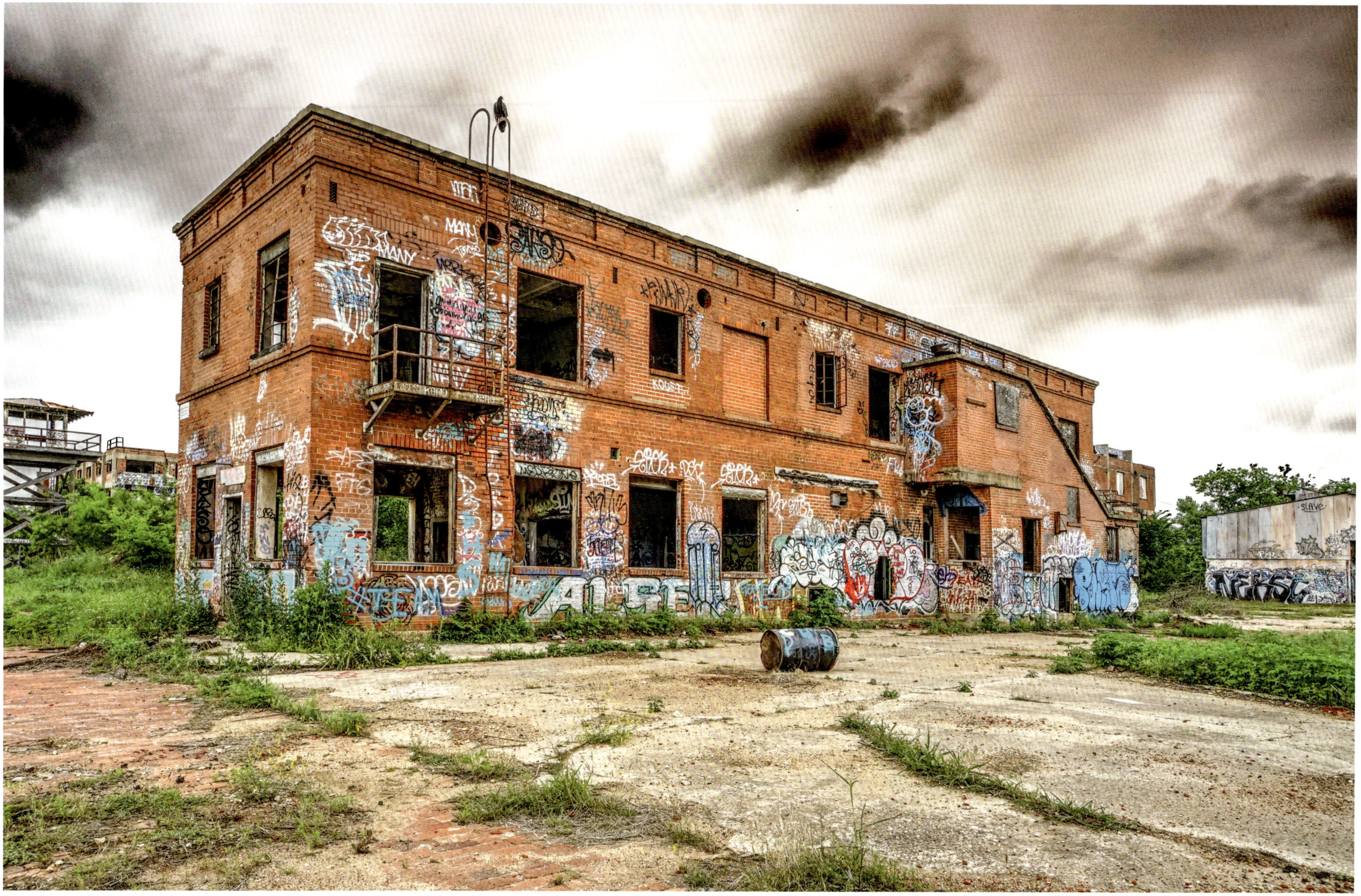

In 2016, the Laboratory Building at the Swift meatpacking plant was one of two structurally sound structures to save when others were demolished after being abandoned in 1971. The buildings were constructed from Acme brick made in Bennett, Texas.

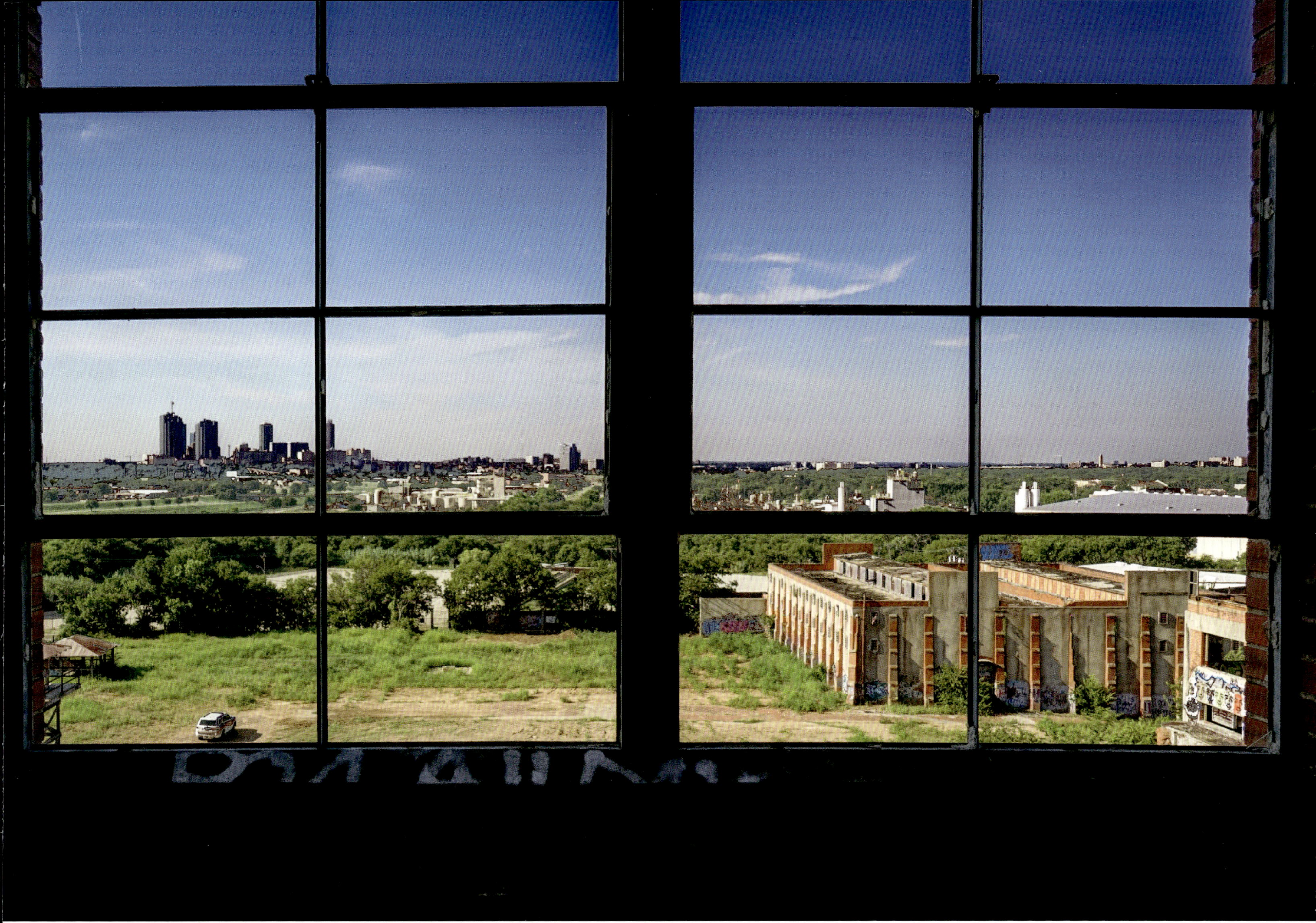

A view through a high window from one of the Swift meatpacking buildings frames the Swift Fertilizer Building and a faraway view of the city of Fort Worth. The building where the photo was taken was later torn down to make room for new development.

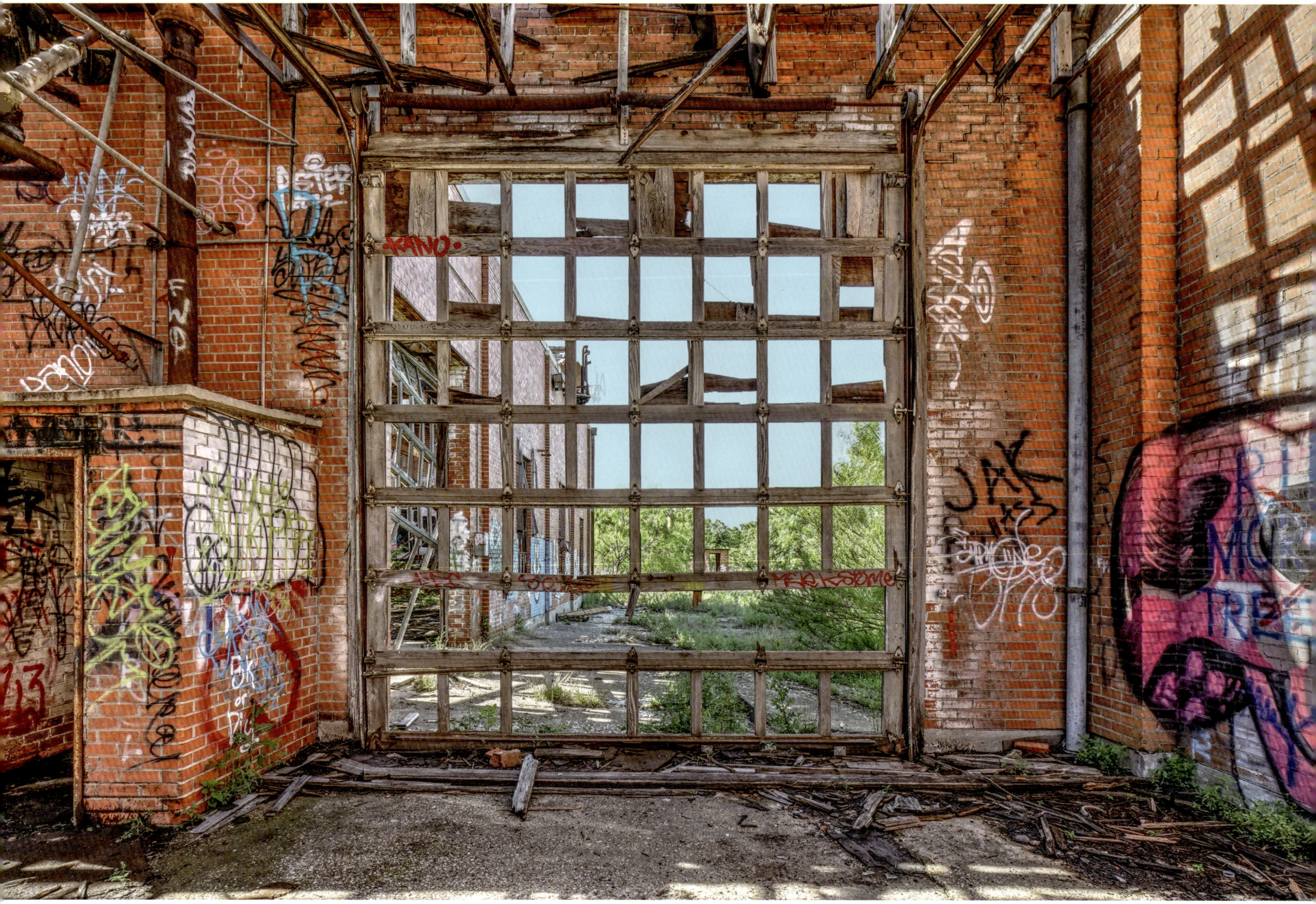

Ground was broken for the Swift plant in February 1902, and several buildings opened for operations in November. Five rail lines were extended to the plants. This area is what remains of a garage. This building was demolished in 2016.

The move to Fort Worth became a good one for the two large meat giants, and they were eager to come. Texas, New Mexico Territory, and Indian Territory (present Oklahoma) together produced one-fifth of all cattle in the United States. Because it cost the packers from three to five dollars to transport a beef steer from the Texas ranges to Chicago, Kansas City, or St. Louis for slaughtering, it would pay packers to relocate near the raw material. The new company agreed to establish a bank, a townsite company, and any other businesses "as are usual at stockyards."

In the spring of 1902, J. Ogden Armour became president of the reorganized Fort Worth Stock Yards Company; Edward Swift, vice president; and Greenlief W. Simpson, second vice president. Andrew Nimmo served as secretary-treasurer, and W. O. Johnson, Simpson's lawyer since at least 1893, became assistant secretary. W. B. King took over as general manager on February 15, 1902, at a monthly salary of $375. Officials planned for groundbreaking ceremonies during the Cattle Raisers Association of Texas meeting in Fort Worth in March. Workers cut down a large tree on the banks of Marine Creek, site of the first stock show, to make room for the packing plants. They also filled in the east branch of the creek and diverted the water to the west. Construction of the two new packing plants began March 13, 1902.

An Armour official told the story many years later that in 1902 representatives of Armour and Swift tossed a coin for the choice of locations. Swift won and naturally chose the site closer to downtown. This disappointed Armour because its employees would have to walk farther from the trolley line, and Armour horses would have a longer haul from Fort Worth to the plant. Soon the Armour men got even. When they started to excavate for their plant, they uncovered a fine gravel pit. Swift had to buy all of the sand and gravel for its building from Armour.

Workers leveled the old hotel and exchange building that local businessmen had erected in 1889 for the Union Stock Yards. Workers soon completed new ones. New stock pens for the Fort Worth Stock Yards Company then covered a forty-acre tract west of the packinghouses. All eventually would be covered with brick, most of which came from Thurber, Texas. Workers laid out the brick in various patterns, some diagonal, some perpendicular.

The packing plants opened formally on March 4, 1903, during the annual fat stock show. Among the speech makers, S. S. Conway, superintendent of the Armour plant, expressed no doubt about Fort Worth's becoming a second Chicago. "The packing plants are now in a position to handle all the cattle, hogs, and sheep that can be shipped here," he said. The Armour plant claimed to be the "best equipped packing plant in the world." At the

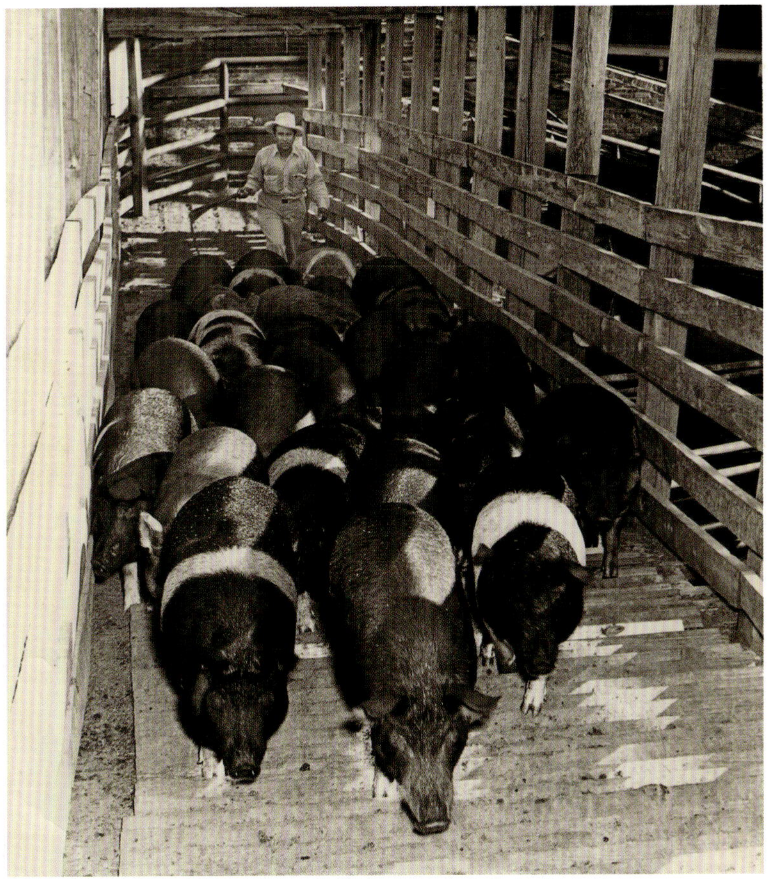

A stockyard worker drives hogs in a narrow chute on their way to slaughter. Courtesy of North Fort Worth Historical Society.

time it had a daily capacity of fifteen hundred cattle, three thousand hogs, and fifteen hundred sheep.

The big packers called themselves pioneers in the assembly-line technique and said that Henry Ford, who later claimed the credit for assembly lines, gained his inspiration from packinghouse methods. Actually, the packinghouse was a "dis-assembly line" because the animal carcass kept getting smaller as it traveled through the process.

When the new $125,000 Spanish-style, tan, stucco exchange building opened in April 1903, it housed a stockyards office, the Stockyards National Bank, and offices for five railroads and twelve commission companies. Two white marble staircases in the inner gallery led to a common landing on the second floor. A big marble fountain in the lobby spurted water upward and would refresh many a sweating stockyards worker on sweltering summer days. A dining room on the north ran the width of the building. A post office and a telegraph office also served the stockyards workers and patrons.

In the first ten months of business, the two packers bought 265,279 cattle, 128,934 hogs, and 40,160 sheep. This brought six million dollars into the local economy. Armour and Swift succeeded where others before them failed in Fort Worth because they were large enough to handle the thousands of head that came through the yards; they met their obligations promptly, and in cash, and they obtained the trade of other Texas cities. Armour and Swift could meet the price competition, whereas the earlier packing concerns did not.

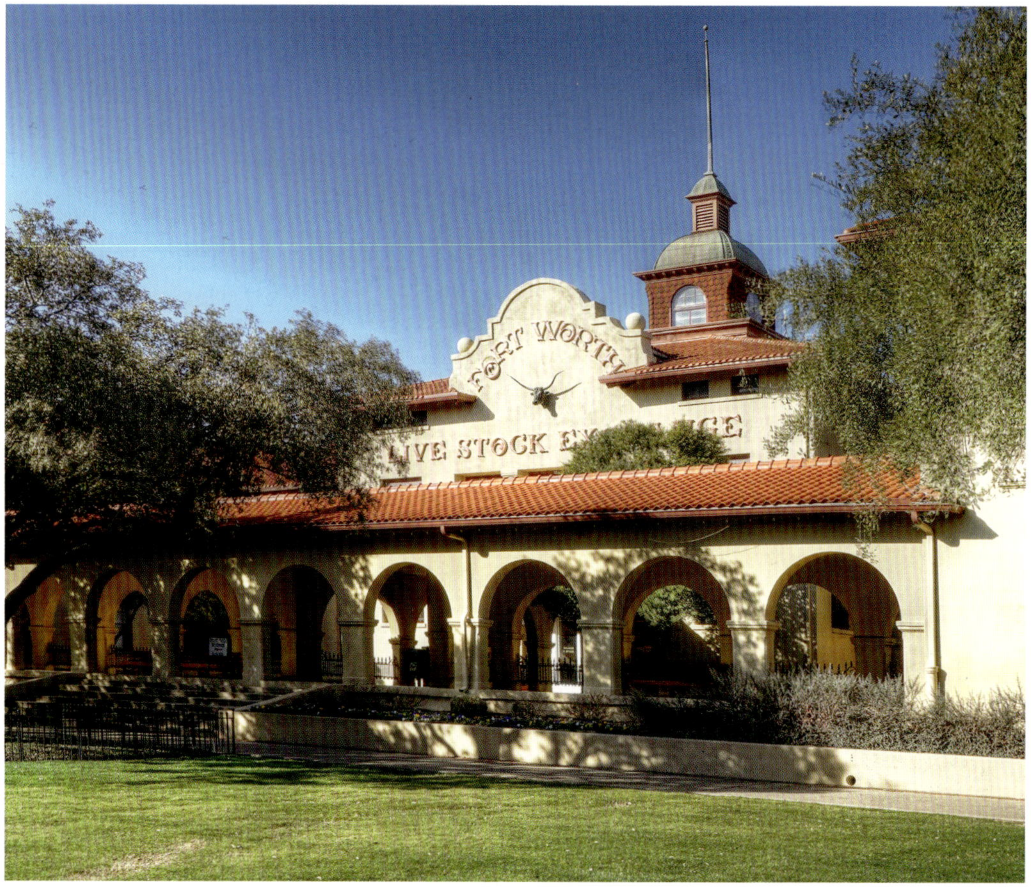

The Livestock Exchange Building was erected in 1903 as an office for cattle traders, once known as "The Wall Street of the West." It now houses the North Fort Worth Historical Society Museum, featuring historical information and artifacts related to the development of the Stockyards Historic District.

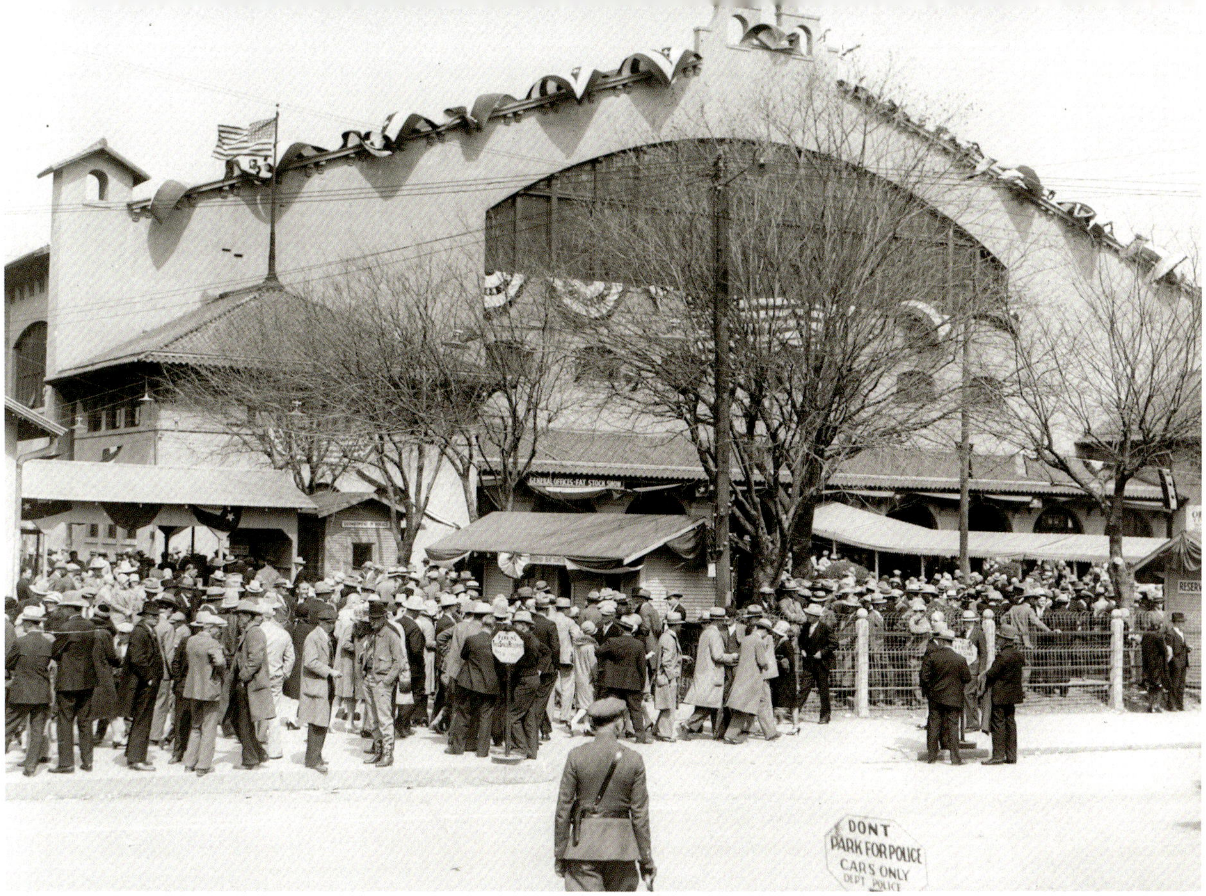

Cowtown Coliseum, constructed in 1908, hosted many events, including the first indoor rodeo. Courtesy of North Fort Worth Historical Society.

Cowtown Coliseum is located in the heart of the stockyards. It has a rich history steeped in rodeo and the Wild West. Programming featured the world's first indoor rodeo, and to this day the coliseum holds the only year-round rodeo every Friday and Saturday.

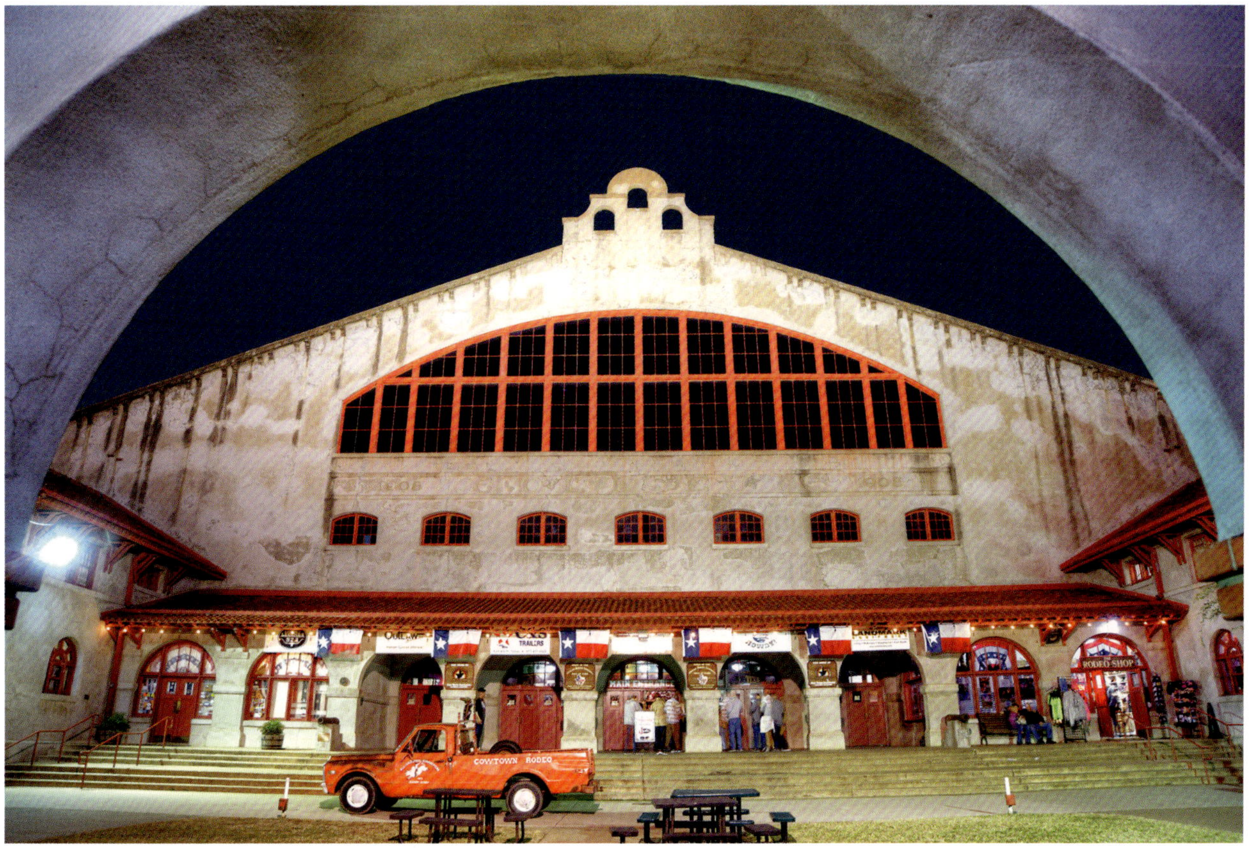

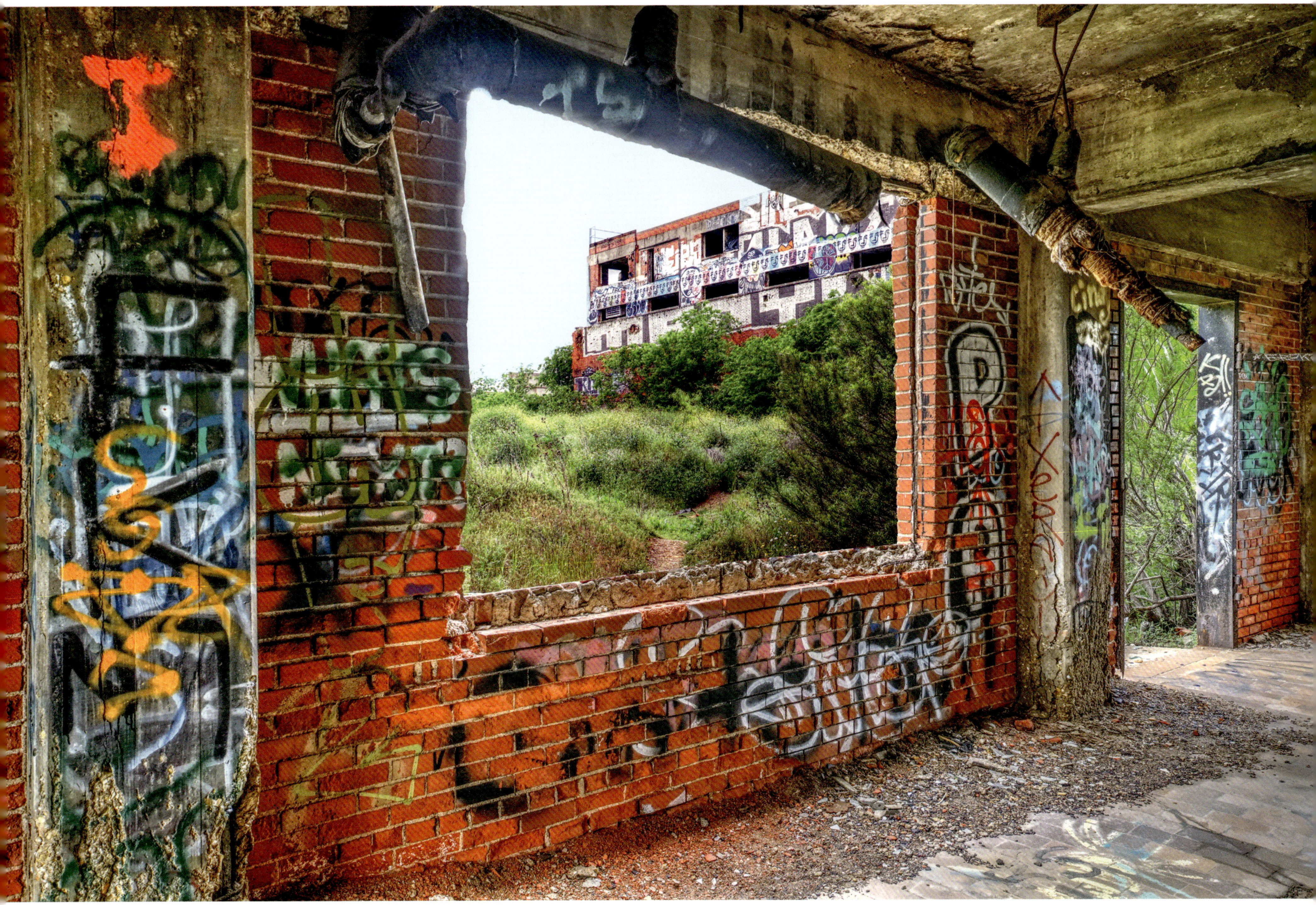

The Swift meatpacking plant, located at 600 East Exchange Avenue, opened for operations on November 1, 1902, and closed in 1971. The remaining structures were brightly decorated by graffiti artists until most of the buildings were demolished in 2016 to make room for new development.

Besides each owning one-third of the Fort Worth Stock Yards Company, the two great meatpackers jointly owned two-thirds of the Reporter Publishing Company, the Belt Railway Company, the Stockyards National Bank of North Fort Worth, the Fort Worth Cattle Loan Company, and the North Fort Worth Townsite Company. The latter company bought thirty-four hundred acres north of the stockyards area, the present Diamond Hill Addition. The name probably was chosen because the man heading the surveying team was a retired British army officer who had been wounded on Diamond Hill in South Africa during the Boer War.

By April 1904 the area around the stockyards and packing plants had grown from an open prairie with a few scattered houses in a loose community called "Marine" to a town of five thousand people. Paddock's "tarantula map," which brought ridicule back in the 1870s, became a reality, for shortly after the turn of the century, twelve railroad trunk lines reached Fort Worth. The railroad's switchyards soon handled one and a half million cars annually. The packing plants of Swift and Armour drew nearly all the cattle of West Texas to Fort Worth for sale. Businesses throughout the city grew. Ranchers' wives came along with their husbands and shopped in Fort Worth. In addition, the city soon became one of the leading grain-storage and milling centers of the Southwest. Pharmaceutical firms sprang up to combat livestock disease. Cattlemen's associations moved their permanent homes to the city. Fort Worth's livestock industry became "the catalytic agent that propelled Fort Worth toward industrial greatness."

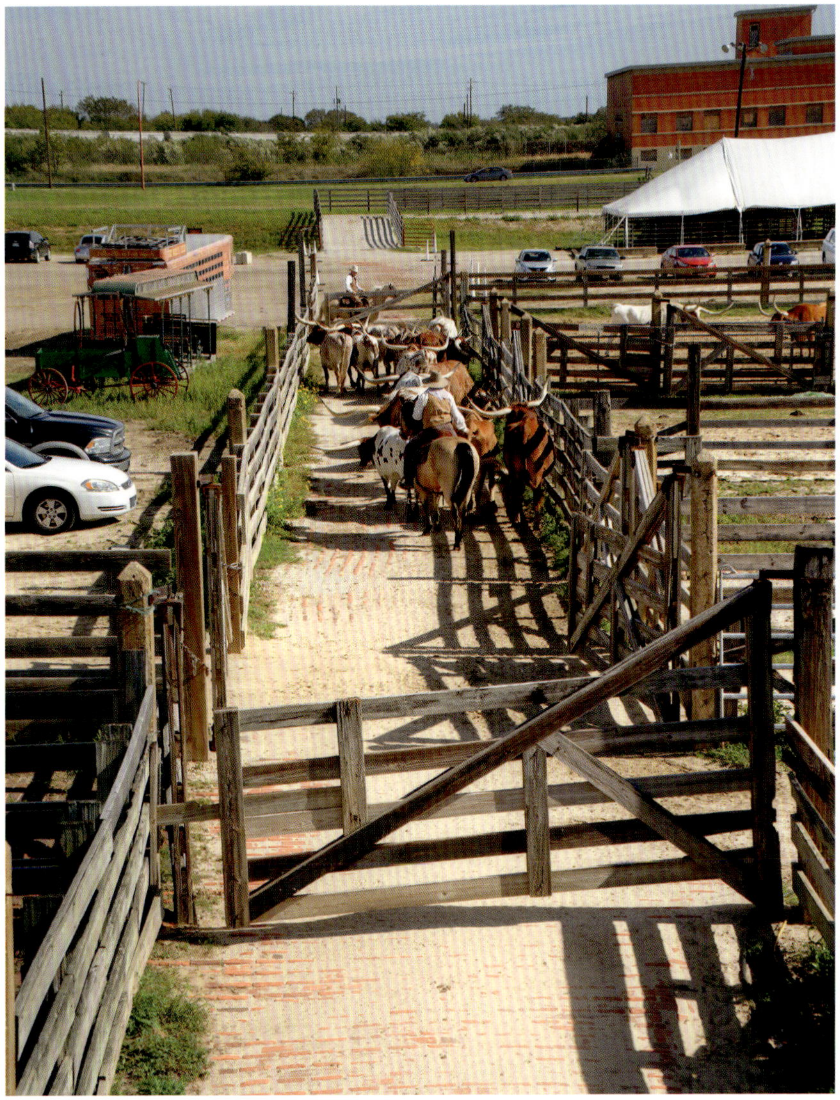

The first cattle pens were built along with the Livestock Exchange Building and the Swift and Armour meatpacking plants as early as 1902. They are made of wood, with poured-in-place corner posts. The floors are paved with Thurber brick.

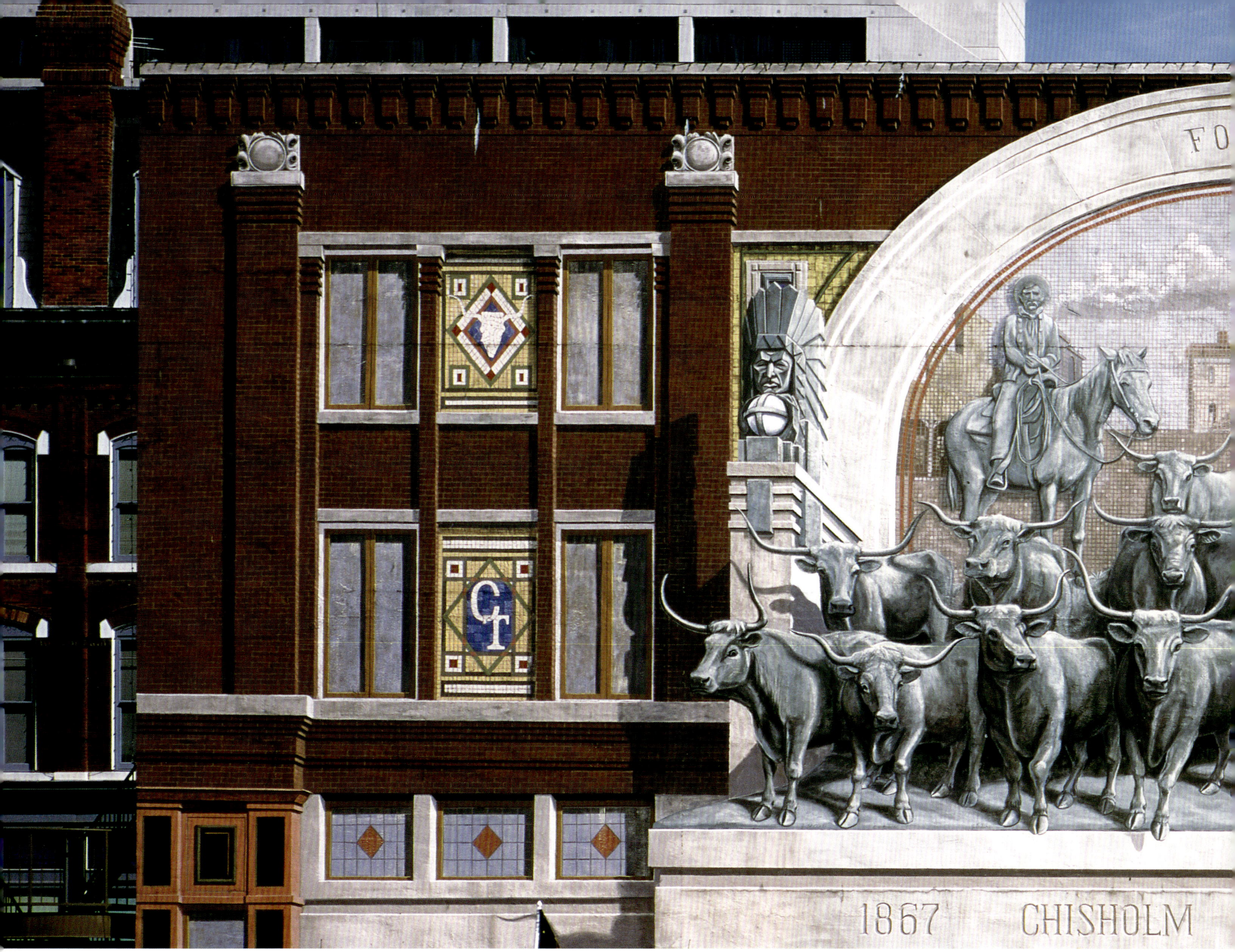

The Chisholm Trail Mural Building, built in 1902, is located in Sundance Square in downtown Fort Worth. The mural was painted by artist Richard Haas in 1985 after the building was reconditioned. The mural and fountains surrounding it attract many tourists and residents to the area.

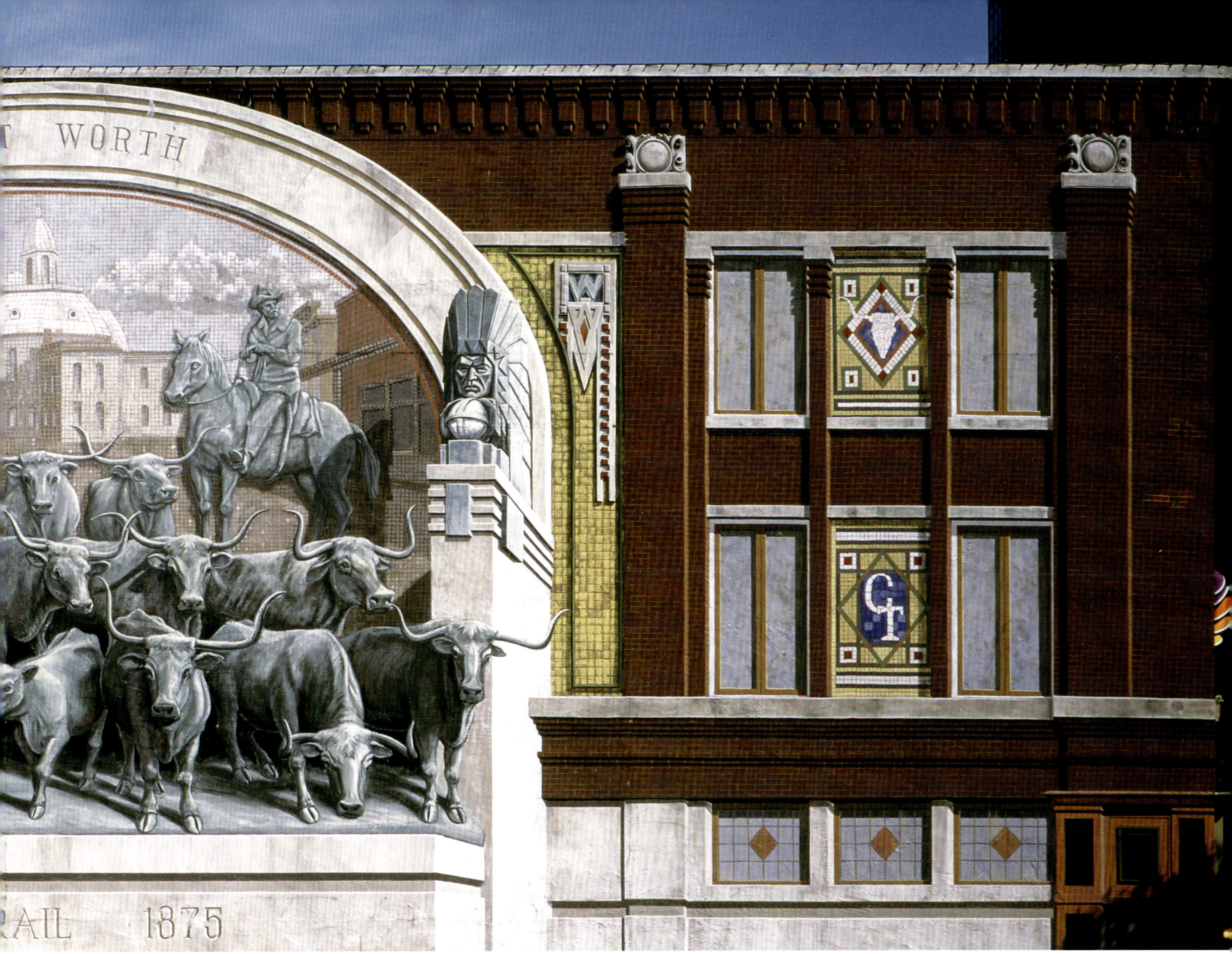
WORTH
RAIL 1875

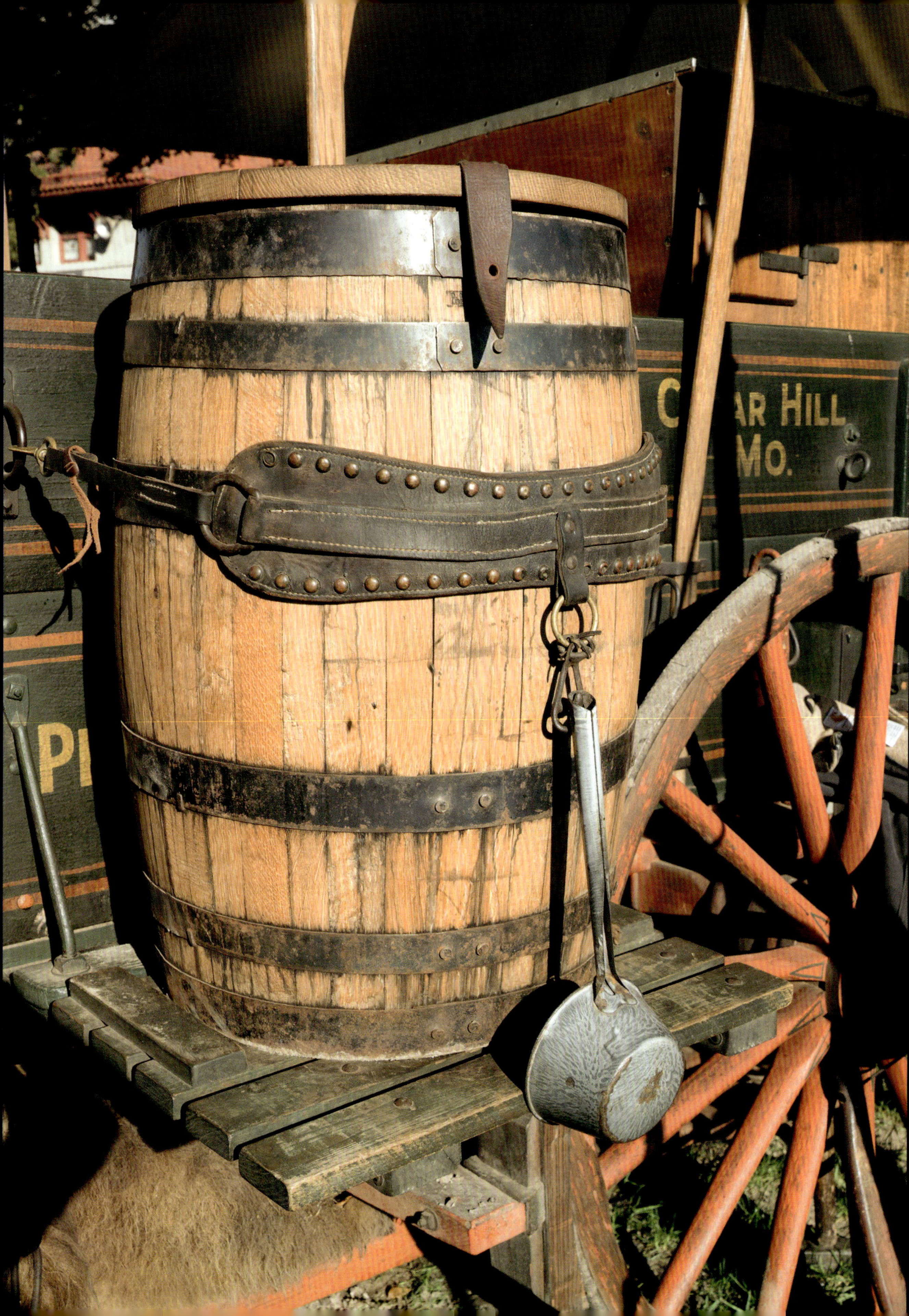
AR HILL
MO.

CHAPTER 2

Highlights from the Past

The arrival of the two biggest meatpacking giants in the country, Armour and Swift, did more than just raise hopes high. Fort Worth citizens' hopes soared sky high. Even the giants believed that their new plants in Fort Worth might surpass the mighty stockyards in Chicago in livestock receipts. Optimism prevailed. As a result, word spread across the Atlantic to Europe that plenty of jobs existed in America, especially in the various stockyards. In mid-America major cities such as Omaha, Cincinnati, Kansas City, St. Louis, St. Joseph, Sioux City, Chicago—and now Fort Worth—needed many workers. Livestock and the railroads that carried them became the largest business in America in the 1890s and continued into the twentieth century. All those Texas cattle that traveled up the trail in the early days now arrived in stockyards by rail. The stockyards needed many workers to meet the demand.

Often groups of young immigrant men dressed in their various European-style clothing traveled directly by ship to Galveston, Texas; boarded a train; and headed immediately to the Fort Worth Stock Yards. From an electric streetcar that stopped at the corner of Main and Exchange Avenues, they disembarked. They eagerly looked eastward down Exchange Avenue toward the Armour and Swift plants. The stockyards area began booming, and not just from young, eastern European immigrants looking for jobs. Americans living in small towns near Fort Worth moved to the city as well.

One day early in 1906, local businessmen accepted an invitation from the stockyards to witness an experiment of a substance that might become more efficient for

A water barrel and tin cup are displayed on a vintage chuckwagon on the grounds facing the front of the Livestock Exchange Building during the annual Red Steagall Day event.

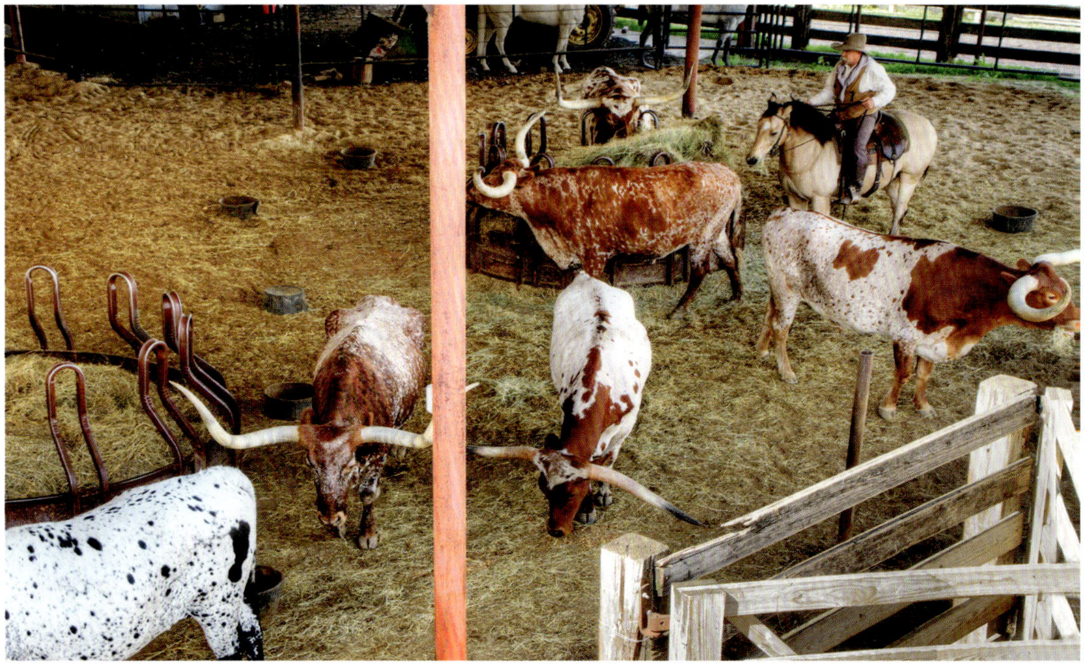

A drover patiently watches over Longhorn cattle as they feed between daily trips down East Exchange Avenue. The first cattle pens were built in 1902.

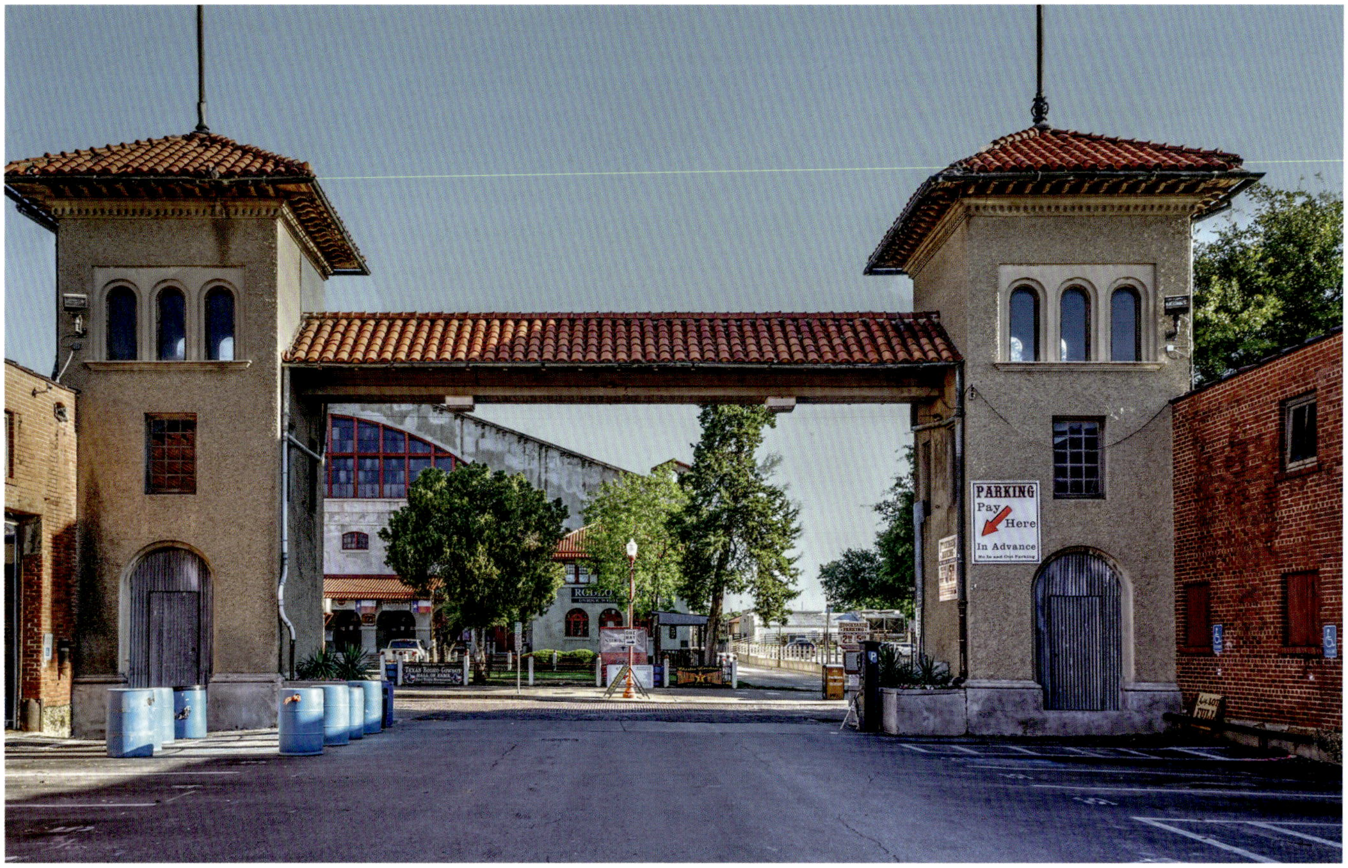

The Horse and Mule Barns, built in 1911, are located within the Fort Worth Stockyards Historic District. This view is from Mule Alley, looking through the historic entrance, facing the Cowtown Coliseum.

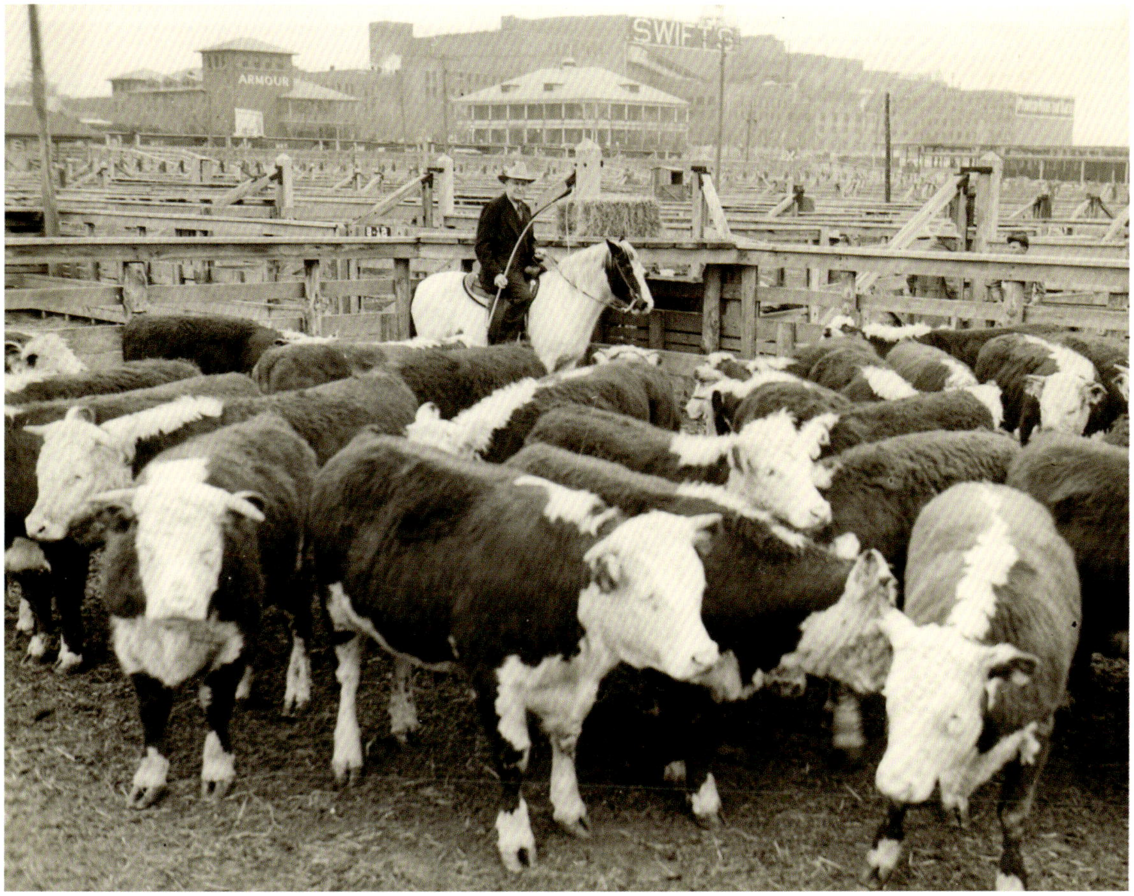

Behind the Hereford cattle can be seen pens, the early Exchange Building, and the Armour and Swift meatpacking plants. Courtesy of North Fort Worth Historical Society.

heating than coal or fuel oil alone. One of the onlookers, a young man named Amon G. Carter, who later became very prominent in Fort Worth, came to the event to see something new. At the experiment Carter encountered two newspapermen, A. G. Dawson, a correspondent for the *Dallas Morning News*, and D. C. McCaleb, city editor of the *Fort Worth Record*. Not conversing about the subject at hand, heating, the three men talked newspapers. On the spot they agreed to form a new newspaper in Fort Worth and call it the *Star*. Carter had been selling things for years, even before age eleven, when he left home after his mother died and his dad remarried. He knew he could sell advertising for the new newspaper. The men shook hands over their deal and later set it in motion. Three years later they bought out the *Telegram* and merged the two papers, thus creating the *Star-Telegram*, which still exists in the twenty-first century.

The heating experiment involved pouring fuel oil over dried cow chips. Most of the crowd decided it would never take hold as a new means of heating homes or businesses because of the smell. Years later Jerry Flemmons wrote a biography of Amon Carter, telling the story of the meeting of the three men. He wrote that the *Star-Telegram* was the only newspaper ever conceived and founded in a stockyards "over a pile of burning cow manure."

In the first decade of the twentieth century, after more than twenty years of struggle to create prosperous stockyards and packers, Fort Worth and the livestock industry began to boom. On Exchange Avenue one could find eight to ten saloons, two or three eating houses, a couple of

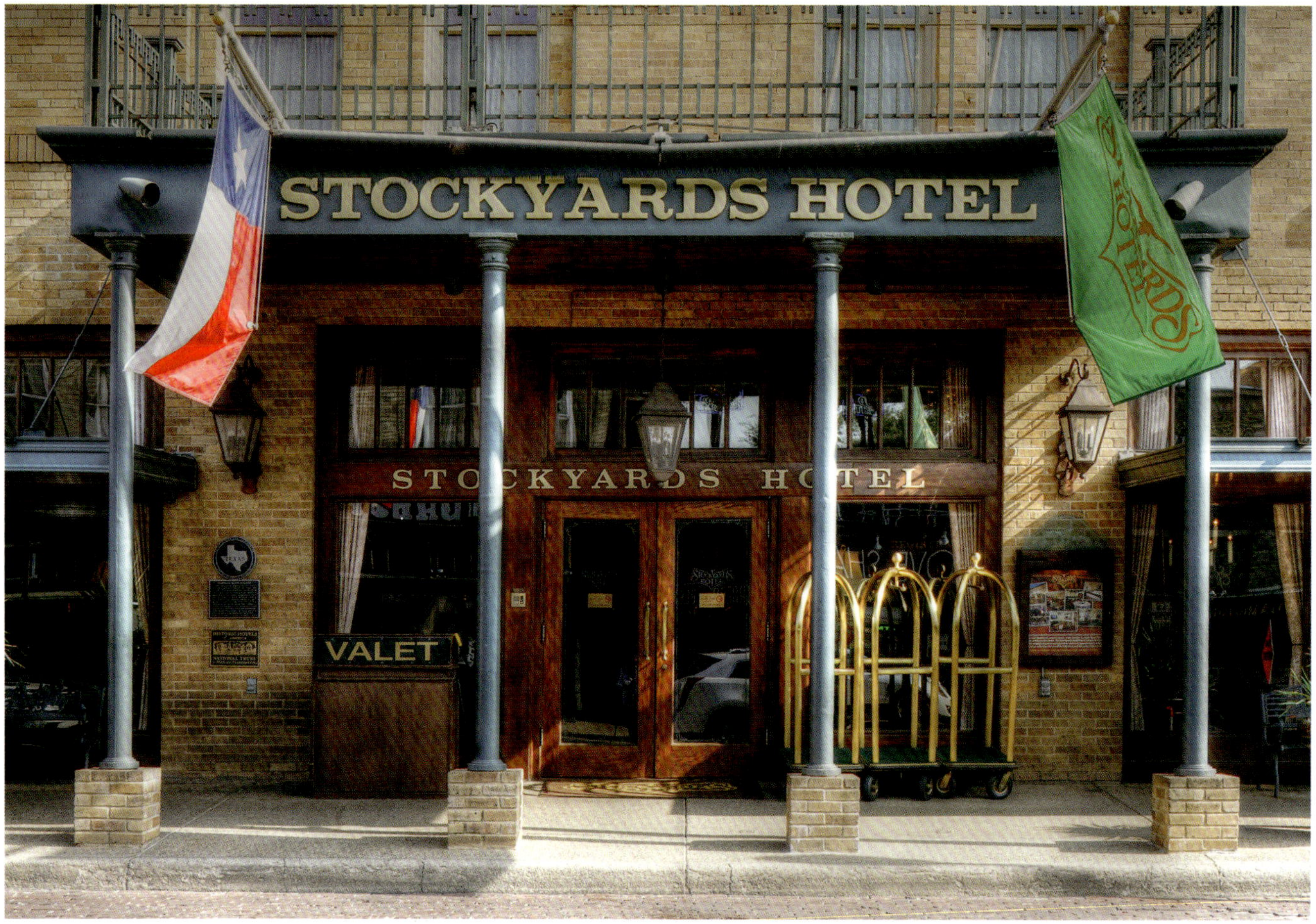

The Stockyards Hotel (lobby shown at right) has a long history, welcoming guests since 1907 and housing celebrities, including Tanya Tucker, Trisha Yearwood, and Willie Nelson. The Bonnie and Clyde room is the actual room occupied by Clyde Barrow and Bonnie Parker in 1933.

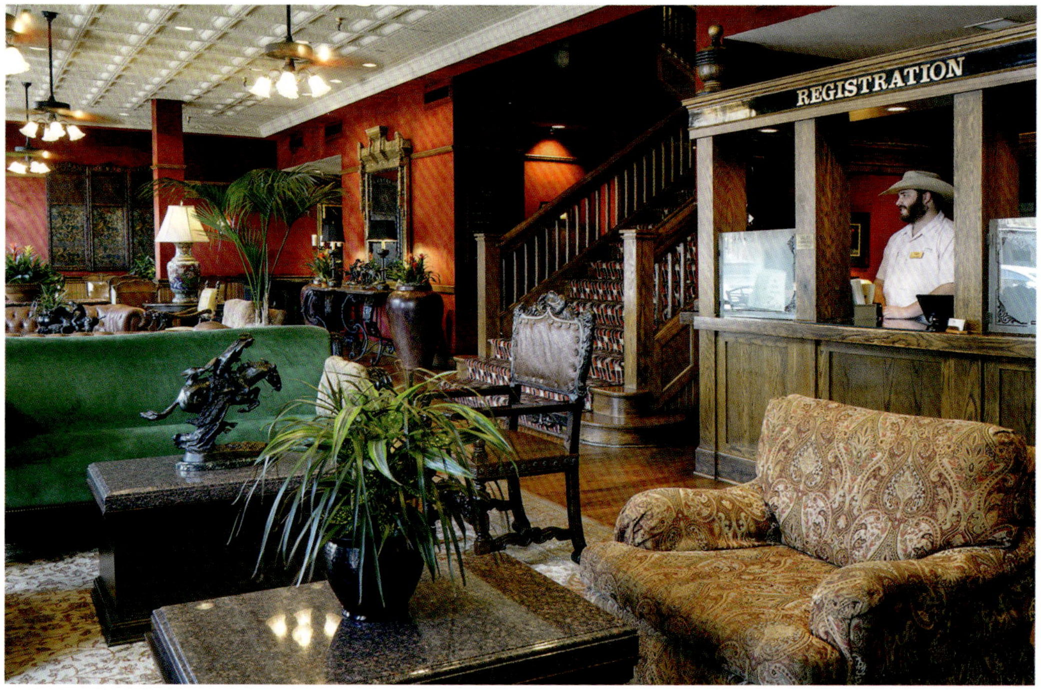

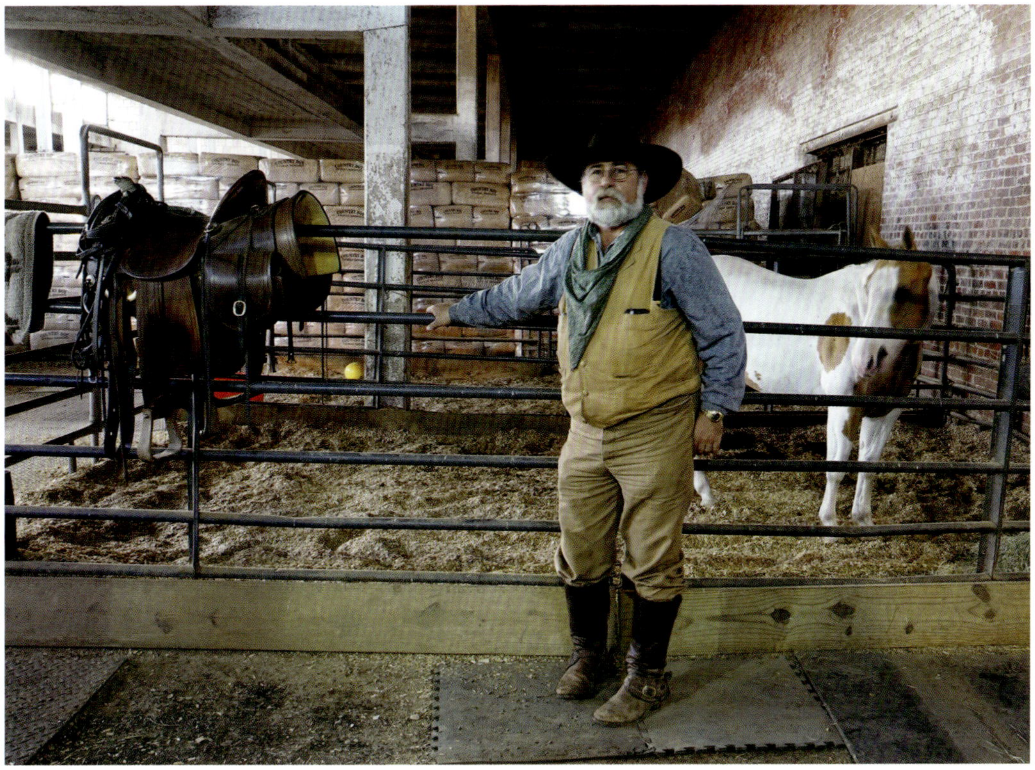

Dewayne Waldrup, operations supervisor and drover, stands between a saddle and horse where horses were housed and groomed in the historic Horse and Mule Barn.

hotels, and two dry goods stores, all within a few blocks of each other. The dining room in the Exchange Building stayed busy because commission firms gave free meal tickets to ranchers and herdsmen who came to the stockyards with livestock.

Newcomers to the stockyards only needed to turn right on Exchange Avenue if coming north from downtown to see the action a block away. Wooden horse and mule barns stood on the south side of the street, and the two-story Spanish-style Exchange Building faced them on the north. North and east of the Exchange Building stretched the newly constructed, brick-floored pens that had a capacity of twenty-four thousand animals. Railroad tracks separated the pens from the huge Armour and Swift plants, located farther east. The Armour sign painted on the west wall of the Armour refrigerator building stretched four hundred feet long and eighty feet wide to be the largest sign in the state of Texas.

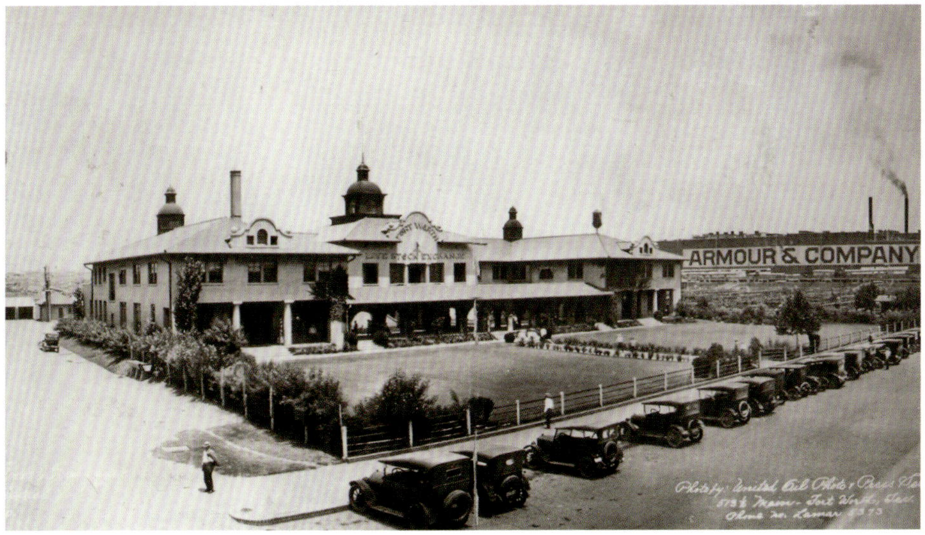

The Livestock Exchange Building welcomes its visitors in their 1920s vehicles. Courtesy of North Fort Worth Historical Society.

Before the first decade of the twentieth century ended, more commission companies needed offices, so the stockyards company constructed them out of the large dining hall that formerly occupied the entire north part of the lower floor of the building. Ten commission companies quickly moved in.

The way that the major stockyards worked was that first, a farmer or rancher who wanted to sell his animals at the stockyards would consign (turn them over) to a commission agent or commission company to sell for him because, by knowing the market better, the agent could get the best price for the animals. The stockyards company never owned any animals; it simply provided a place for the buying or selling to occur and charged for keeping the animals in a pen and feeding and watering them until they were sold. Someone later called this arrangement a "livestock hotel," and stockyards nationwide occasionally used the term. The commission agent then sold the animal or animals either to the meatpacking company or to a dealer or speculator who planned to fatten them up for resale.

J. Ogden Armour wanted the Fort Worth Stock Yards to be larger than those in Chicago because the big packers like Armour did not own the Chicago stockyards; the Vanderbilts did. For that reason, Armour promoted Fort Worth as a new, booming market. By March 1910, five meatpackers besides Armour and Swift maintained buyers on the Fort Worth market: Morris, Cudahy, Schwarzschild and Sulzberger, Independent Packing Company, and Dold Packing Company. As a result, from 1900 to 1910 Fort Worth again almost tripled its population, from 26,688 to 73,312. Perhaps it was bragging, or maybe that so many new residents came to work in the yards, but the company put up a huge sign across East

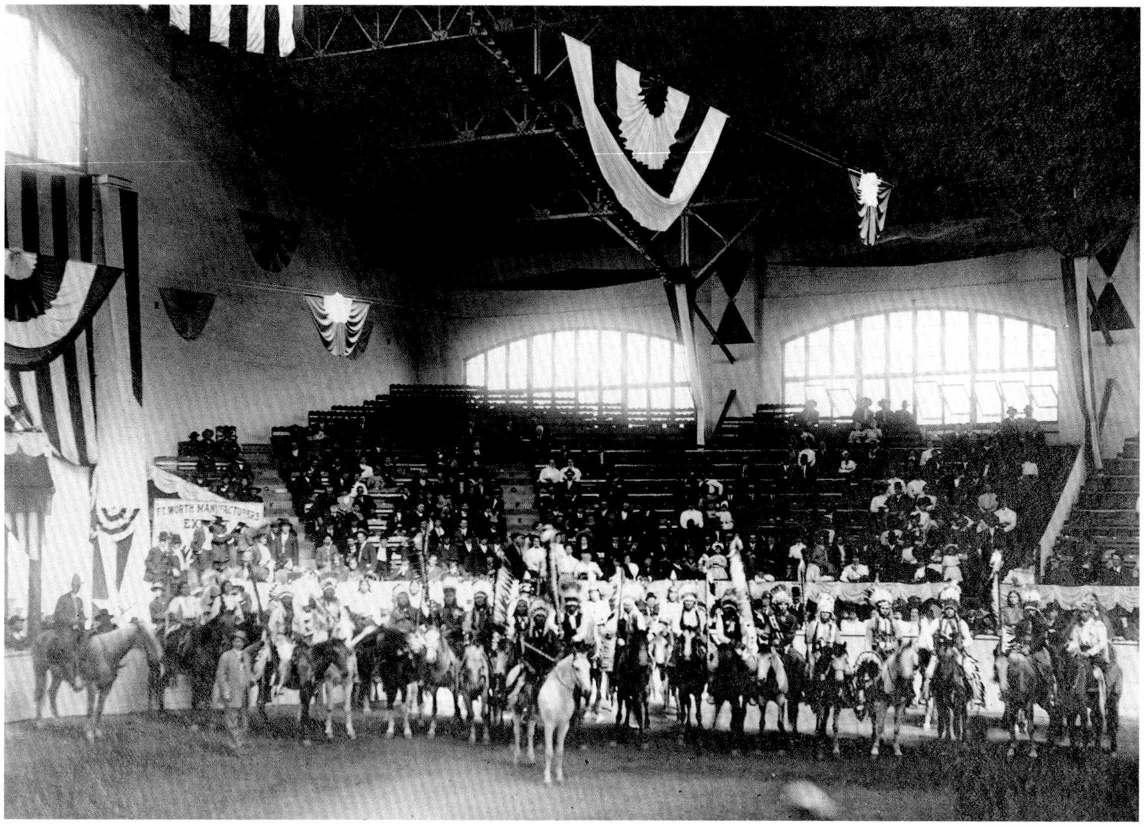

Quanah Parker and his tribesmen appeared at the 1909 event inside the coliseum. Courtesy of North Fort Worth Historical Society.

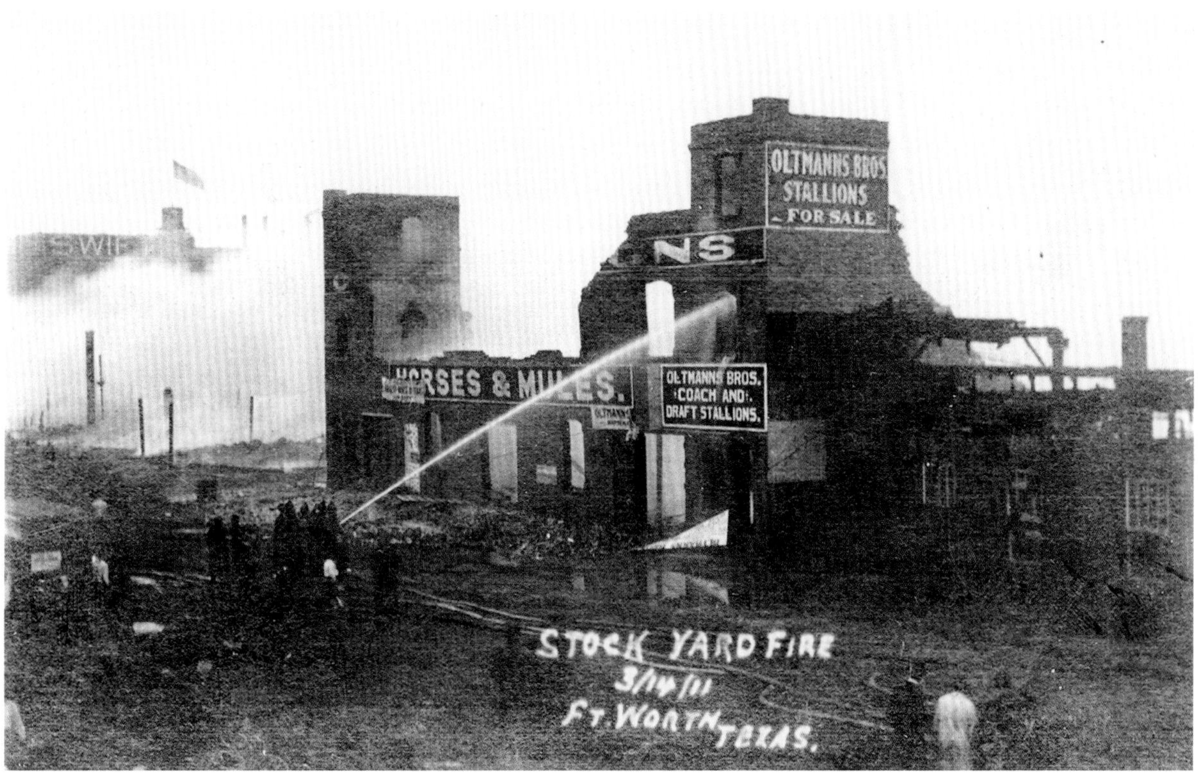

The Horse and Mule Barns burned in 1911 and were rebuilt. Courtesy of North Fort Worth Historical Society.

Exchange Avenue that read "Fort Worth Stock Yards" in 1910, which remains to this day.

Niles and Simpson, jointly the one-third owners of the Fort Worth Stock Yards Company, came from Boston nearly every year to visit the stock show and to check up on their investments. On March 14, 1908, they and other visitors witnessed the first indoor cutting-horse contest ever held under electric lights.

Other distinguished guests during the early years of the Fort Worth Stock Yards included former US president Theodore Roosevelt. The Annual National Feeders and Breeders Show being held at the stockyards provided the occasion for Roosevelt's visit and speech to the five thousand people who gathered in the three-year-old coliseum at 9:00 a.m. on March 14, 1911. Unfortunately, on that very day a fire destroyed the horse and mule barns, killing between five hundred and six hundred horses, a hundred hogs, and an unknown number of sheep. Nevertheless, Roosevelt congratulated the people of Fort Worth on their livestock market. Receipts of animals in all categories were growing, even those of hogs.

The decade from 1910 to 1920 became a profitable one. An Armour official at the end of 1914 cited Fort Worth, Kansas City, St. Louis, and Chicago as major markets in the United States. Fort Worth officials proclaimed the local market the largest horse and mule market in the world from 1915 to 1917 during World War I because of the many foreign governments that bought animals for use during the war as cavalry mounts or even food. The number of horses or mules shipped from Fort Worth by June 1916 totaled one hundred thousand, for which local dealers received eleven million dollars. In that same year market officials boasted that more than a billion dollars had been paid for livestock at the Fort Worth market since 1903. The packing plant employees and other workers at the yards earned a combined three million dollars in wages each year, and the market employed forty-seven hundred people.

The year 1917 set records for the local market that would stand for nearly thirty years. During World War I Armour and Swift both enjoyed army contracts. Daily receipts often surpassed 350 railroad cars full of animals. Both cattle and hog receipts each reached over one million in 1917. Fort Worth became the third largest in cattle, and the cattle industry represented the largest business in Fort Worth.

Making a success of Fort Worth as a livestock market attracted the assistance of prominent Fort Worth citizens because everyone would benefit. *Star-Telegram* publisher Amon Carter became active in the effort to publicize the local stockyards. He earned the name "Mr. Fort Worth" because he promoted his city so much. By 1917 his newspaper reached a circulation of sixty thousand, mostly in Fort Worth and West Texas. The *Star-Telegram* became the largest newspaper in Texas and held that distinction for four decades.

One idea to promote the local market came from the Fort Worth Chamber of Commerce, on which stockyards officials served prominently. They and the *Star-Telegram* always urged West Texans to ship to the Fort Worth market. The chamber used its influence to call representatives from West Texas to meet in Fort Worth on December 21, 1918, to form plans to organize. Representatives from thirty-seven counties heard the manager of the chamber make a motion to create a West Texas Chamber of Commerce. The visiting representatives adopted the suggestion unanimously, knowing that it would benefit them. The new chamber would be good for Fort Worth and its major industry—the Fort Worth Stock Yards.

The new chamber discussed mutual agricultural and livestock problems but also received encouragement from Fort Worth to participate more fully in the annual

A view from the north at the 1922 Fort Worth Fat Stock Show. Courtesy of the Clemons Collection, University of Texas at Arlington Libraries.

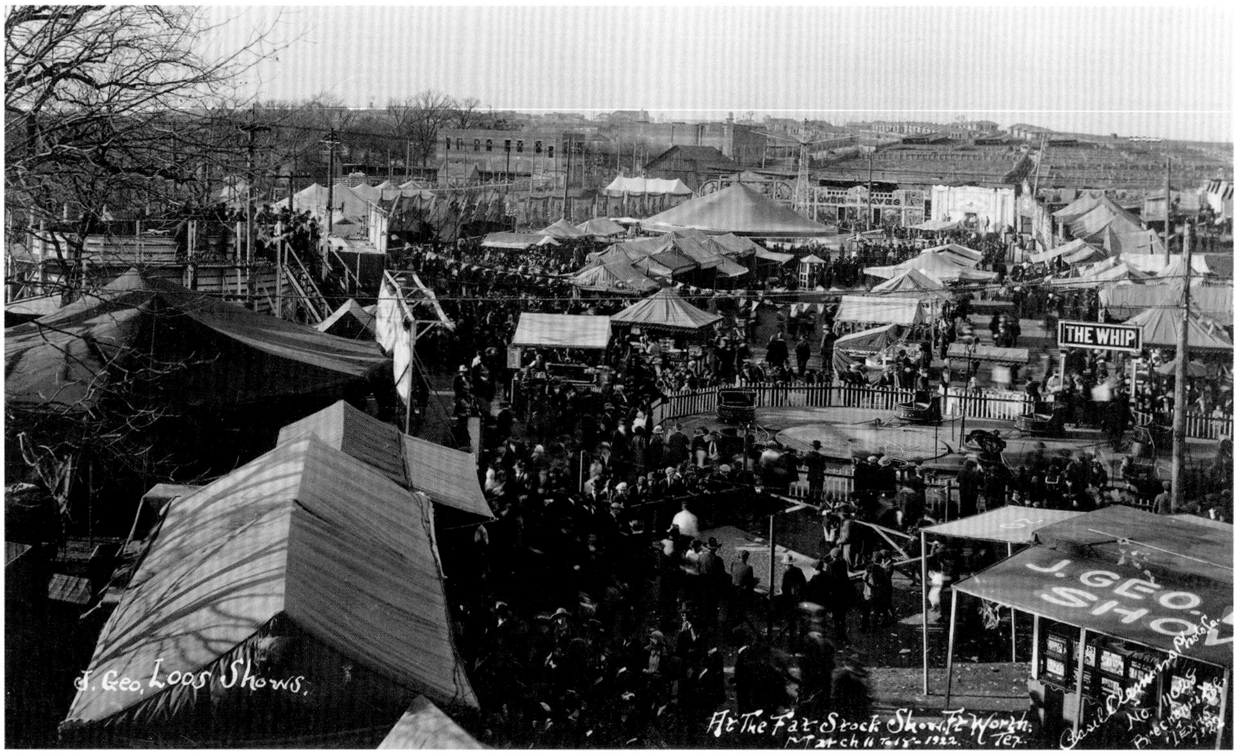

fat stock show. Amon Carter always reported activities of the show in the *Star-Telegram*. Beginning with the show's origin in 1896, the stockyards company subsidized it but ended that practice in 1911. For a time the show struggled to pay expenses.

Wild West shows became popular, and the stock show officials decided to stage such an event to draw larger crowds. The first one took place in 1916 when they invited Joe Miller of the 101 Ranch in Oklahoma to put on a show. Zack Mulhall and his daughter Lucille brought a Wild West show to the coliseum. Lucille, a bronc rider, became a featured attraction, and some claim that the term "cowgirl" began with her. The show featured bronc riding, steer riding, and bulldogging but paid all the hired performers the same fee since it was more a demonstration than a competitive show. Either by the time of this 1917 performance or shortly thereafter, officials changed the name to Southwestern Exposition and Fat Stock Show. Late that same year Ray McKinley, editor and publisher of the *Daily Live Stock Reporter* and *Sunday North Fort Worth News*, lunched with Marion Sansom, stock show president, and A. B. Chase, manager of Armour and Company in Fort Worth. McKinley suggested that monetary incentives or competition would bring out the best in the

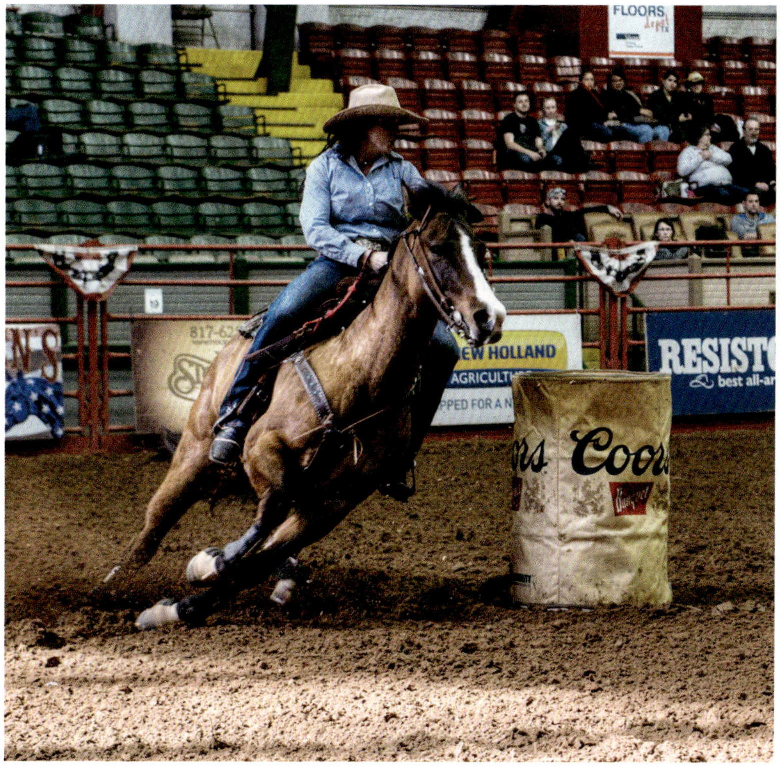

The world's only year-round rodeo happens every Friday and Saturday night at 8:00 p.m. in the historic Fort Worth Cowtown Coliseum. The two-hour Stockyards Championship Rodeo maintains a strong commitment to visitors looking for an authentic Western cowboy experience.

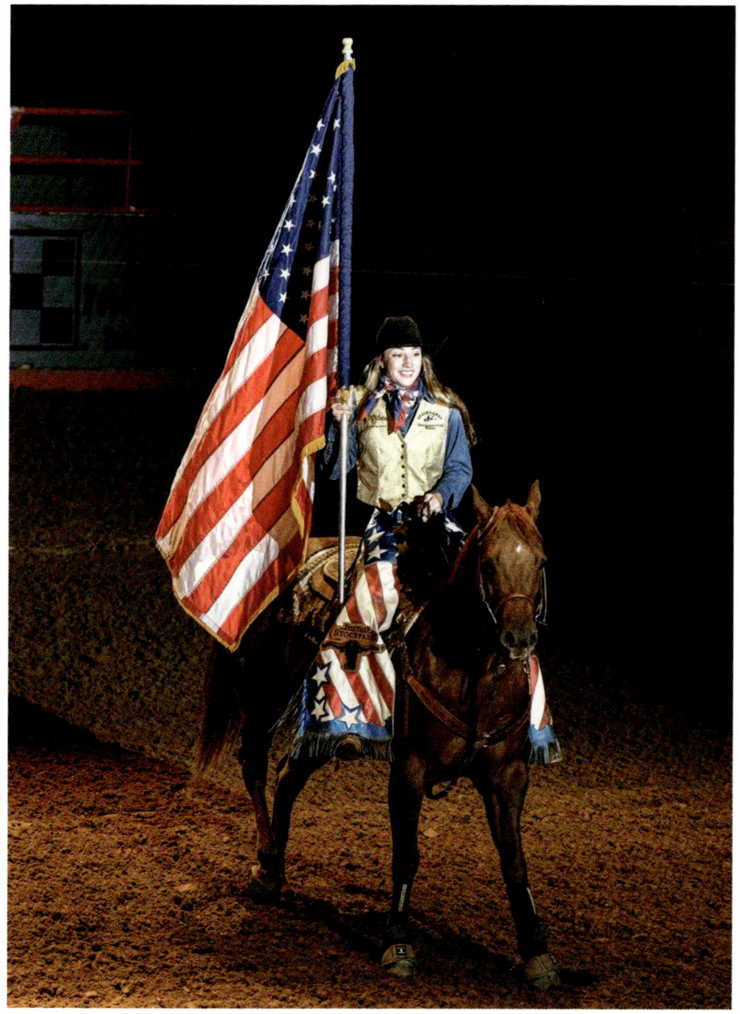

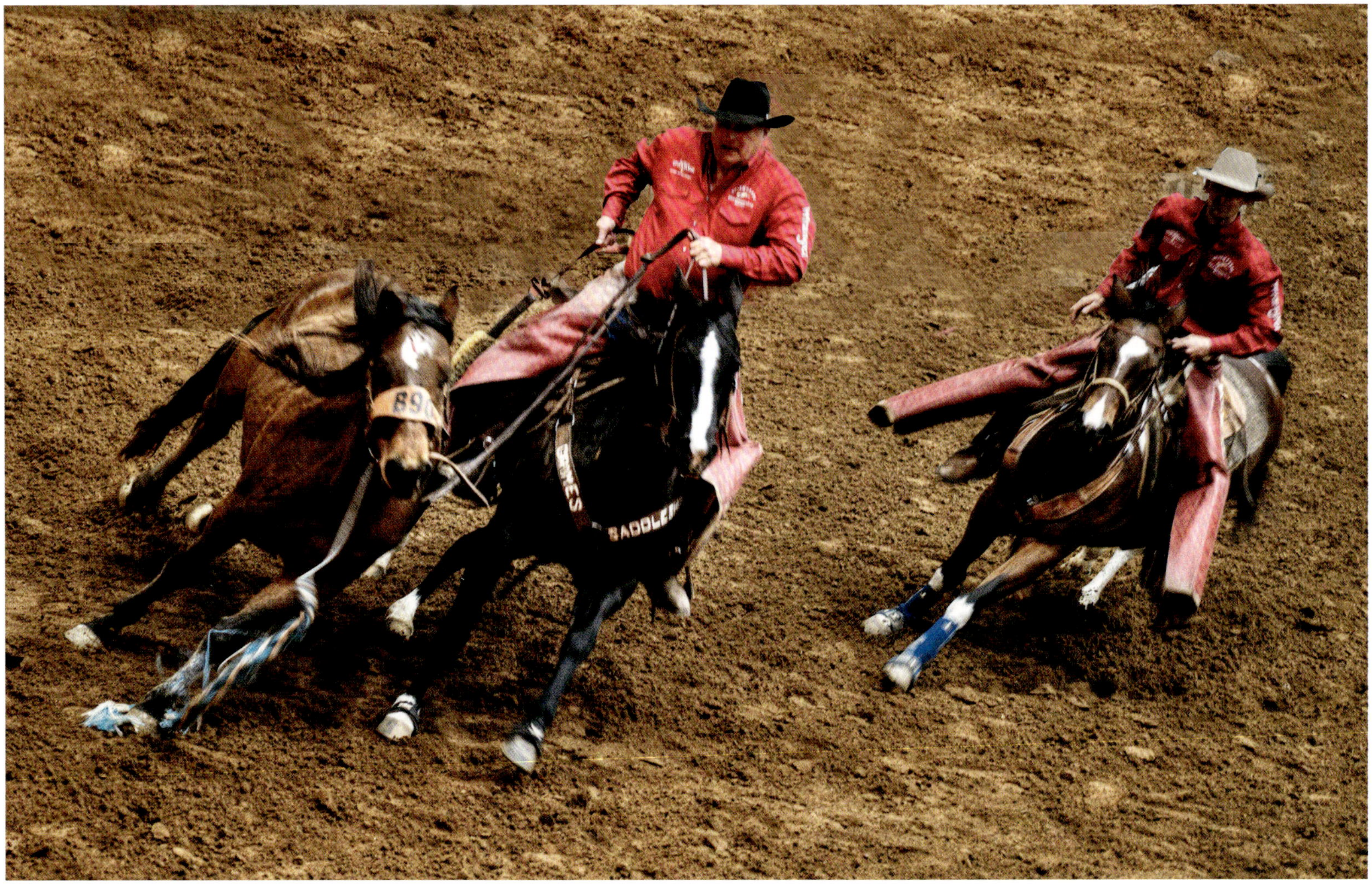

Two cowboys bring in a bronc that has thrown his rider at the Cowtown Coliseum.

Wild West show performers, and such a contest should be added for the 1918 show. A committee later met to work out the details and make it different from the Cheyenne "Frontier Days" and Pendleton's "Roundup."

Claude Hamilton, a member of the committee, mentioned a Spanish word meaning "to encompass or encircle" used frequently by cowboys to mean a roundup, cow work, or horse breaking. He pronounced it "Ro-DAY-o." A member of the committee asked how it was spelled. Hamilton went to the blackboard and printed "RODEO." Buck Sampson, son of Marion, spoke up and said, "That spells RO-dee-o." The men liked the name and called their show "The Rodeo of the Southwestern Exposition and Fat Stock Show." The show on March 11–16, 1918, with its rodeo, became the largest cattle show ever held southwest of Kansas City. An estimated twenty-three thousand people attended, and it made history as the first indoor rodeo.

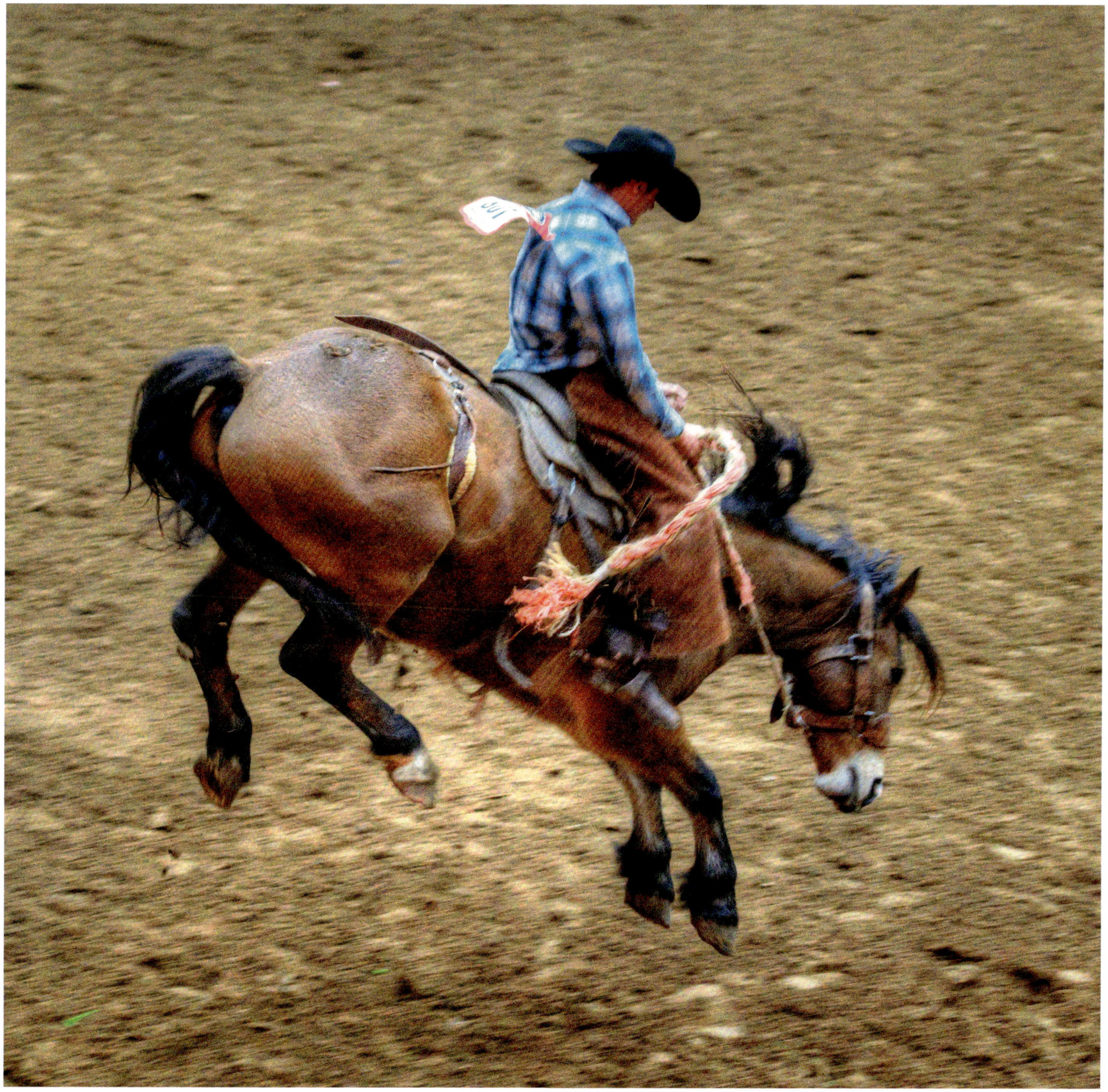

Bronc riding, either bareback-bronc or saddle-bronc competition, is a rodeo event that involves a participant riding a bucking horse that attempts to throw or buck off the rider. Originally based on the necessary horse-breaking skills of a working cowboy, the event is now a highly stylized competition that utilizes horses that often are specially bred for strength, agility, and bucking ability.

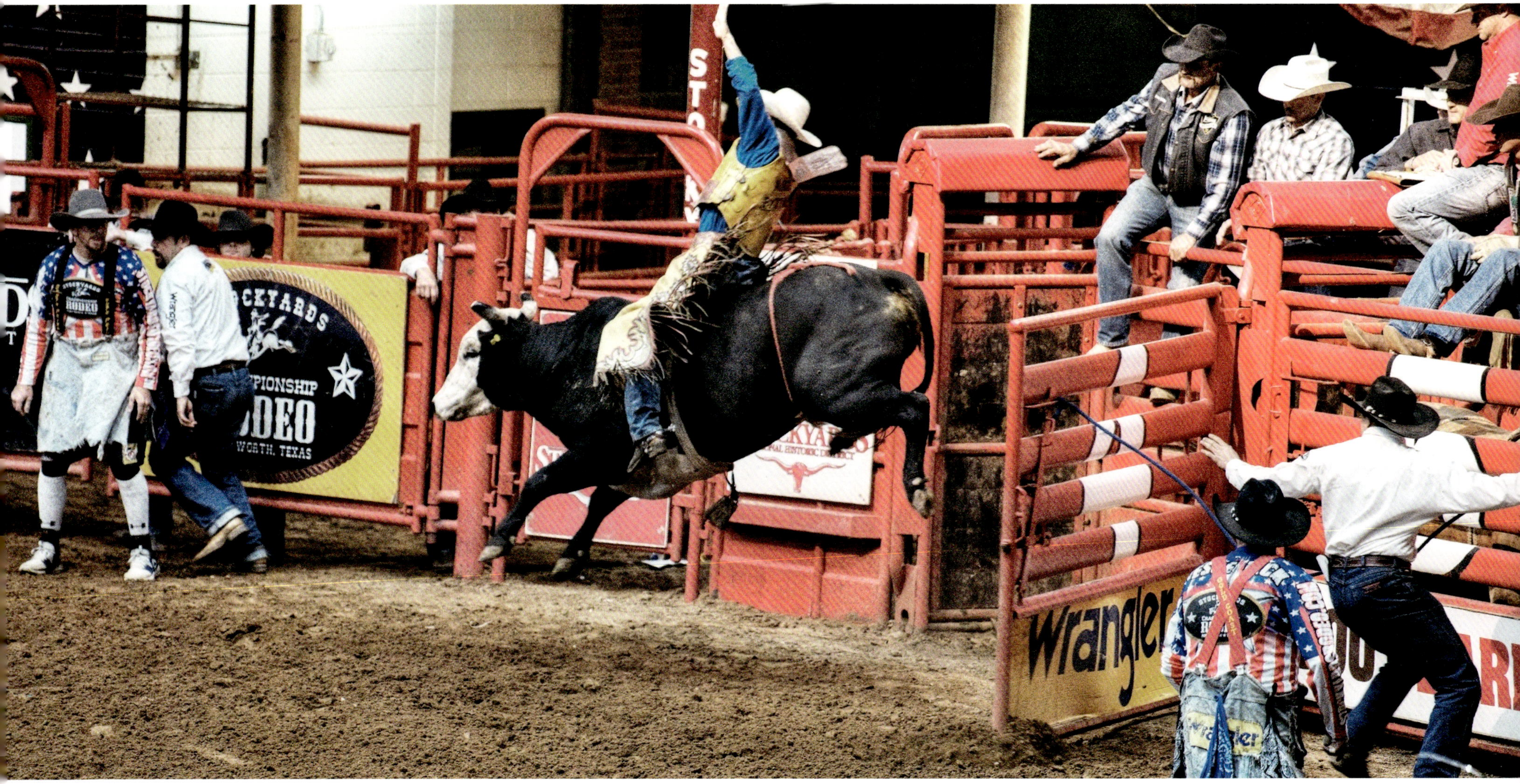

Bull riding is a rodeo sport that involves a rider attempting to stay mounted on a bucking bull while the animal tries to buck the rider off. American bull riding has been called "the most dangerous eight seconds in sports."

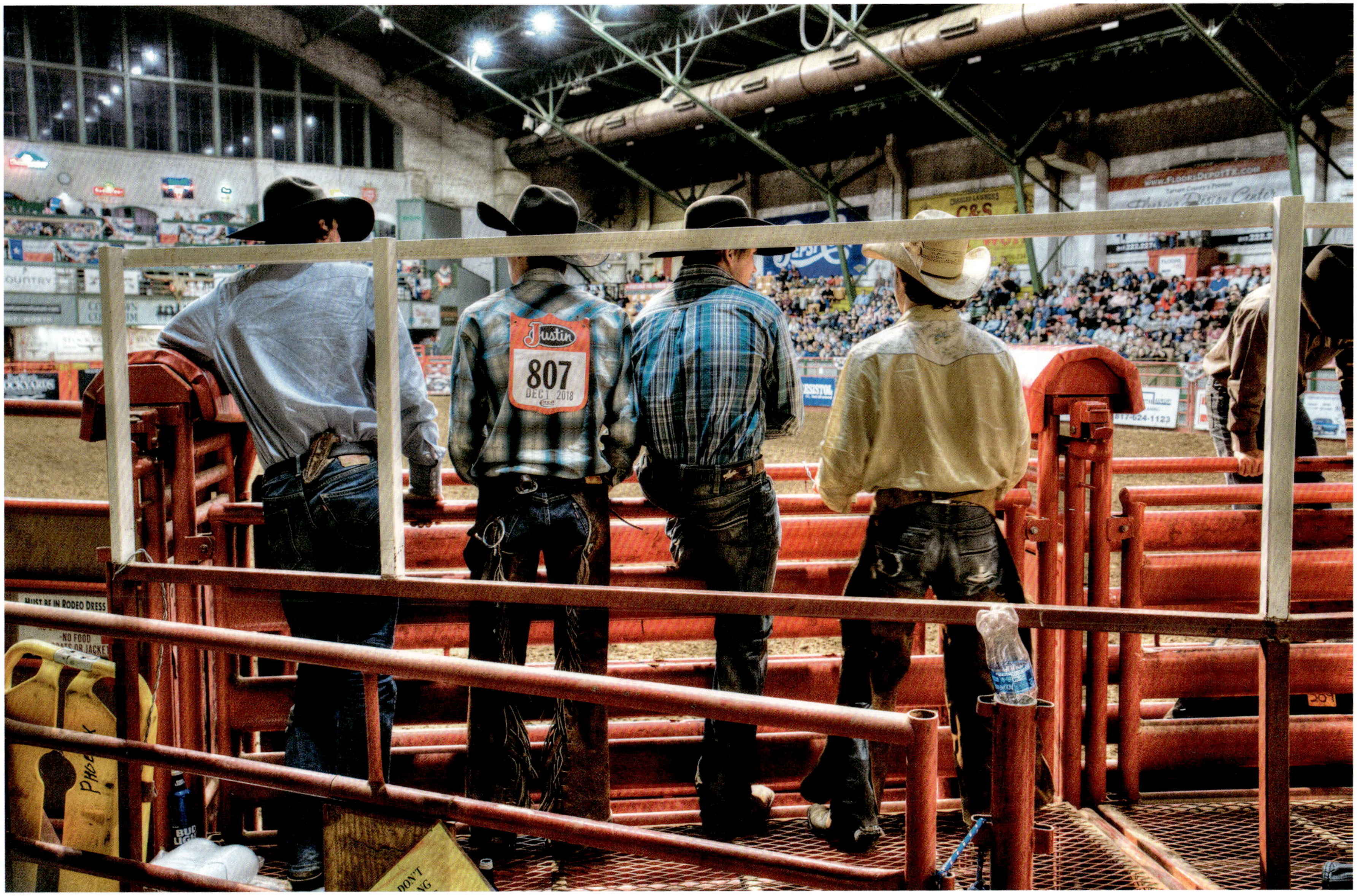

Contestants await their turn to ride a bucking bull at the Cowtown Coliseum weekly rodeo.

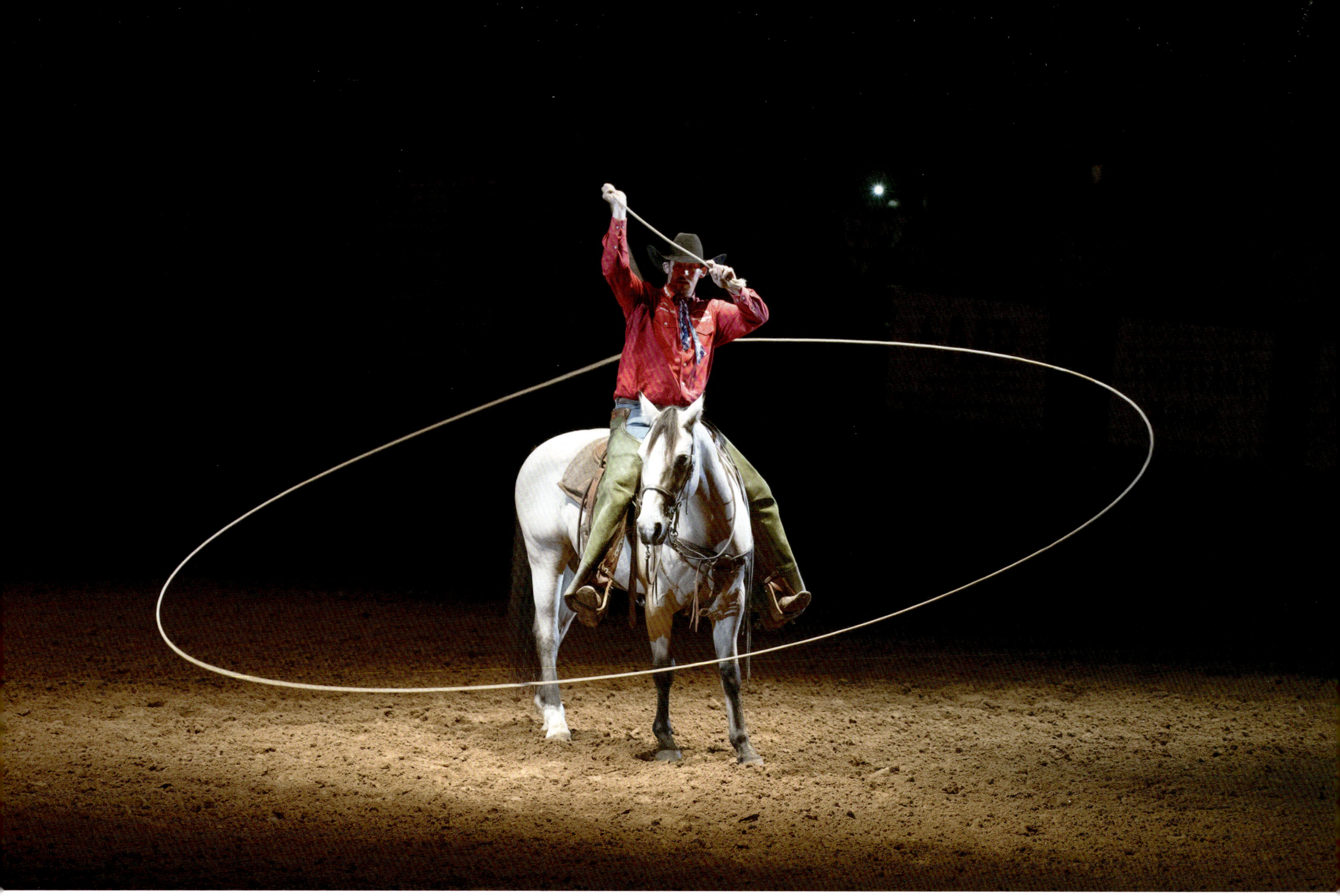

An artist performs lasso tricks, mounted on his very patient horse, at the Cowtown Coliseum during a rodeo event.

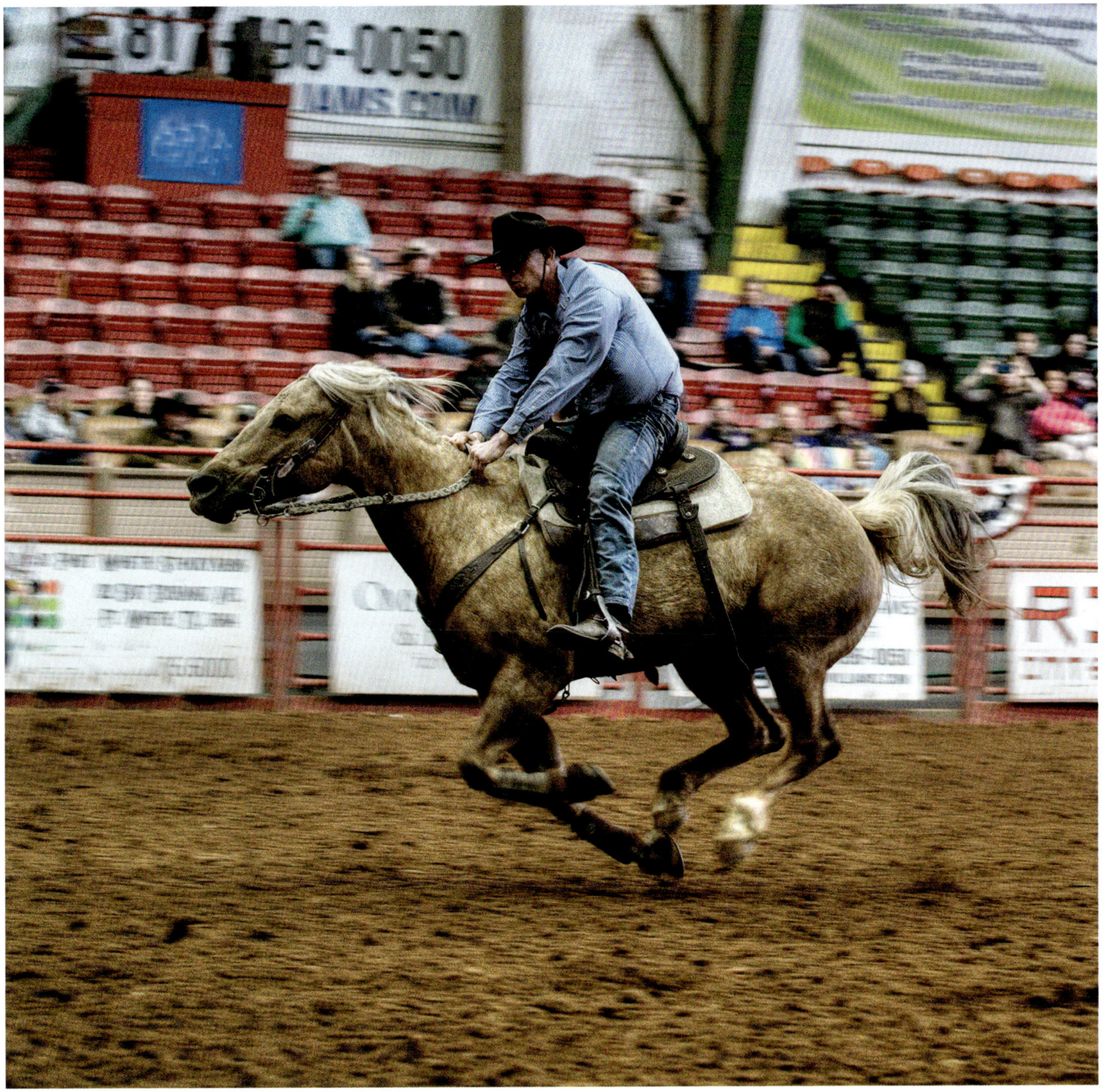

A steer wrestler and his well-trained horse sprint across the earthen floor at the Cowtown Coliseum.

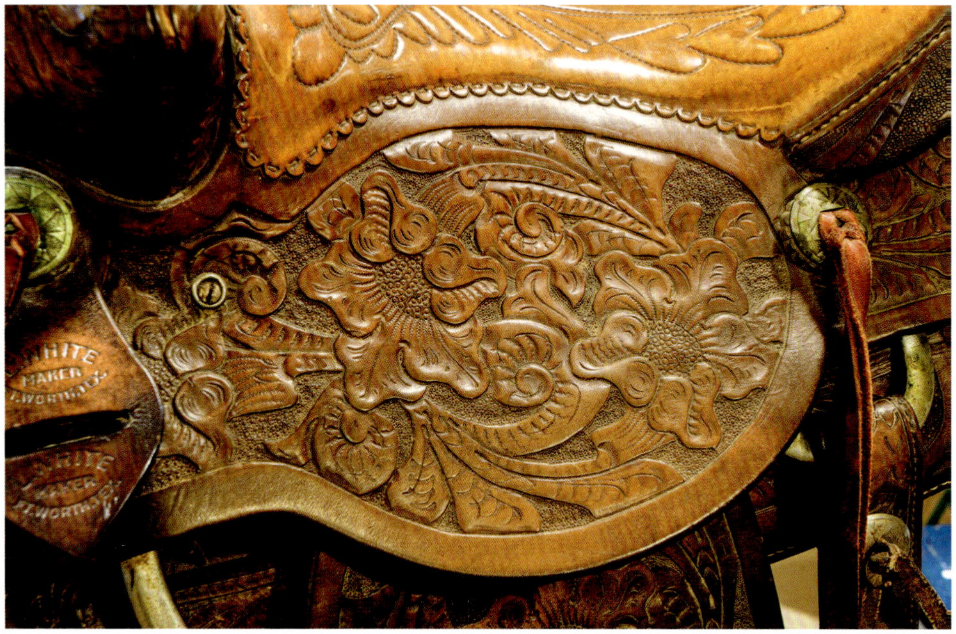

This hand-tooled saddle was made by prominent Fort Worth saddle maker L. White. This detailed photo reveals the beautiful craftsmanship. It can be seen at the Stockyards Museum, located in the Livestock Exchange Building.

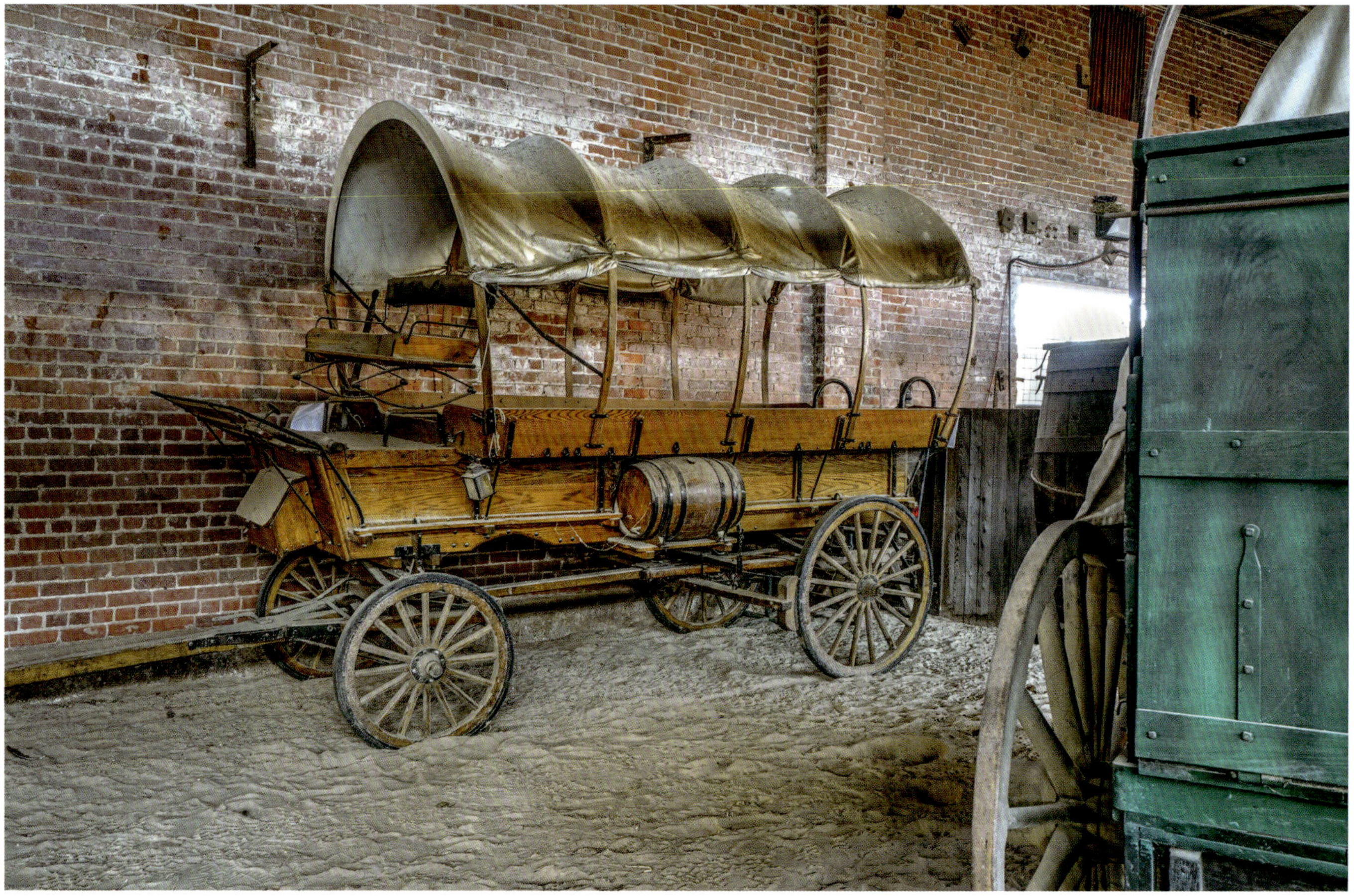

One of several vintage wagons with wooden wheels was safely stored in the historic Horse and Mule Barns.

Indeed, mushrooming growth represented the major theme of the first decade of the twentieth century for the Fort Worth Stock Yards. Local market officials fully expected the growth to continue and for more of the Big Five packers to build packing plants locally. They would be disappointed. The need for more hog receipts at the yards was the apparent problem. The hope was that if more hogs were brought to the stockyards, so would more meatpacking facilities. The leading notion of the day was that a packinghouse could not run on beef alone. Fort Worth businessmen in November raised one hundred thousand dollars to offer to an additional meatpacking company if it would build a plant in Fort Worth. No takers responded. The men later gave the hundred-thousand-dollar bonus to a smaller company. The large companies complained that there were not enough hogs at the Fort Worth market for their slaughtering needs.

Charles C. French, promotional agent for the Fort Worth Stock Yards Company, told of a conversation with a Big Five packer, Nelson Morris, in Chicago. He urged Morris to build a packing plant in Fort Worth. Morris asked, "How soon will you have hogs enough?" French had begun work as the promotional agent for the Fort Worth yards in 1896. As a young man he left his home in Pennsylvania and came to Texas to trail cattle northward in the 1870s. Then he handled cattle sales for three commission companies from 1888 to 1896, when he helped organize the first fat stock show in Fort Worth. During 1900 to 1902, things were slow, and he had to work for a commission company for a while. At the stockyards promoting cattle sales became his main job. Thus, imagine his surprise, or consternation, when in 1909 his stockyards bosses assigned him a new task: bring in more hogs to the Fort Worth market.

Meatpackers such as Armour and Swift were accustomed to large hog receipts at their slaughtering plants in the Midwest and North. Farmers in those areas raised pork and ate it more often than beef. They then raised

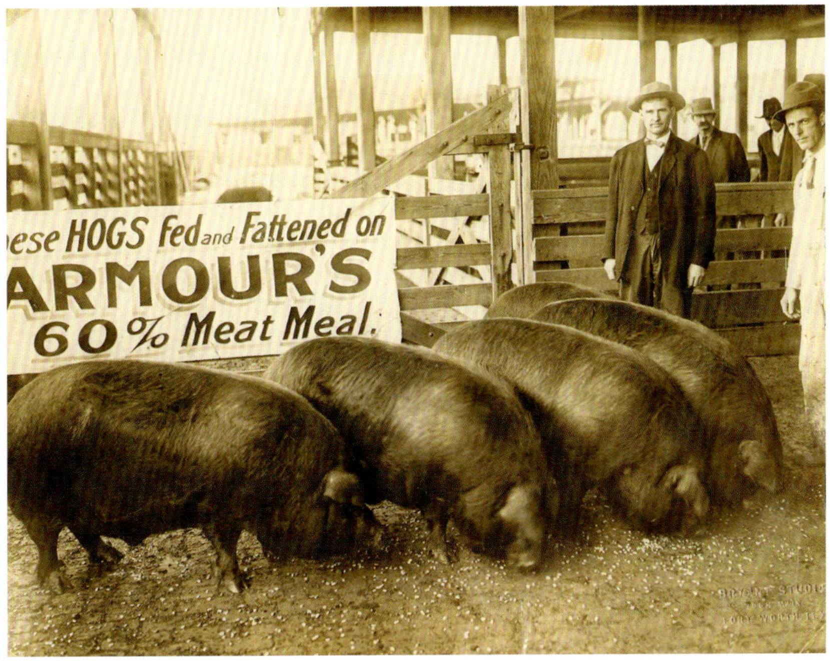

Note that even in the hog pens commission agents or buyers wore suits and ties. Courtesy of North Fort Worth Historical Society.

a few extra hogs to sell. Fort Worth, located in an area where huge cattle drives traditionally came through, witnessed cattlemen establishing large ranches to the west that ran cattle on their ranges extensively. Therefore, the Fort Worth Stock Yards officials saw their pens bursting with cattle but few swine being unloaded into the yards.

Thus, French, at age fifty-six, took on a daunting new task—recruit more hogs. It would take him on thousands of miles of travel to speak to tens of thousands of farmers and their youngsters in an attempt to persuade them to raise more hogs. East Texas farmers raised hogs for their own food, and cattlemen to the west of Fort Worth raised cattle for their money crop. French accepted quite a challenge.

A certain urgency at the Fort Worth market necessitated more hog receipts. Local businessmen wanted the Fort Worth yards to grow and surpass those of Chicago or Kansas City, or both. More hog receipts could induce additional meatpackers to build plants locally, giving

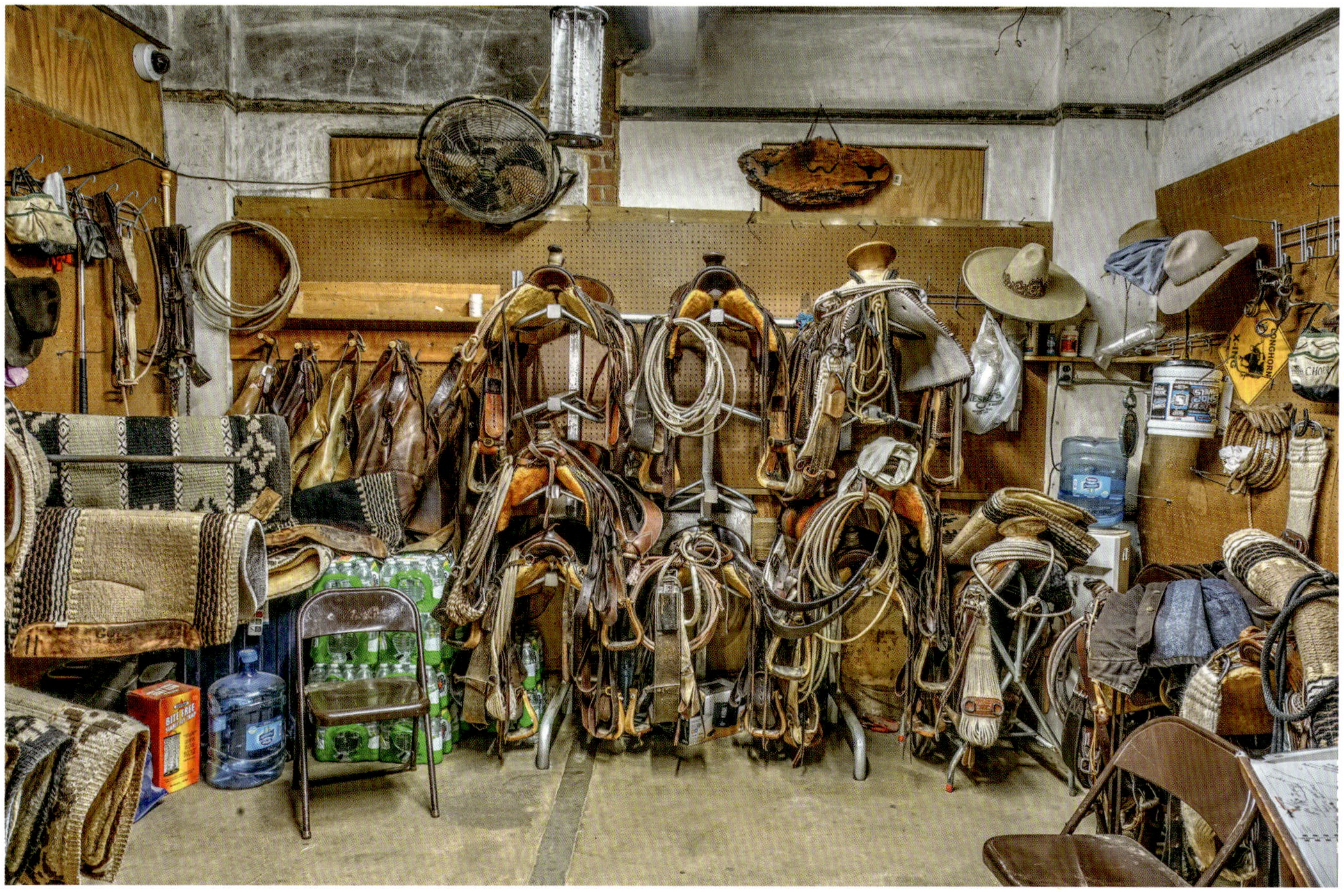

Saddles, saddle blankets, hats, bridles, mementos, and other riding equipment were kept in the tack room of the Horse and Mule Barns before the horses were relocated to make room for the Mule Alley redevelopment.

Many miles traveled are evident on this drover's dusty, well-worn boot, spur, and stirrup. Boots are to be only brown or black, with a coffin-shaped toe and a heel for safety, and there is no left or right—instead, they are put on wet to shape each foot.

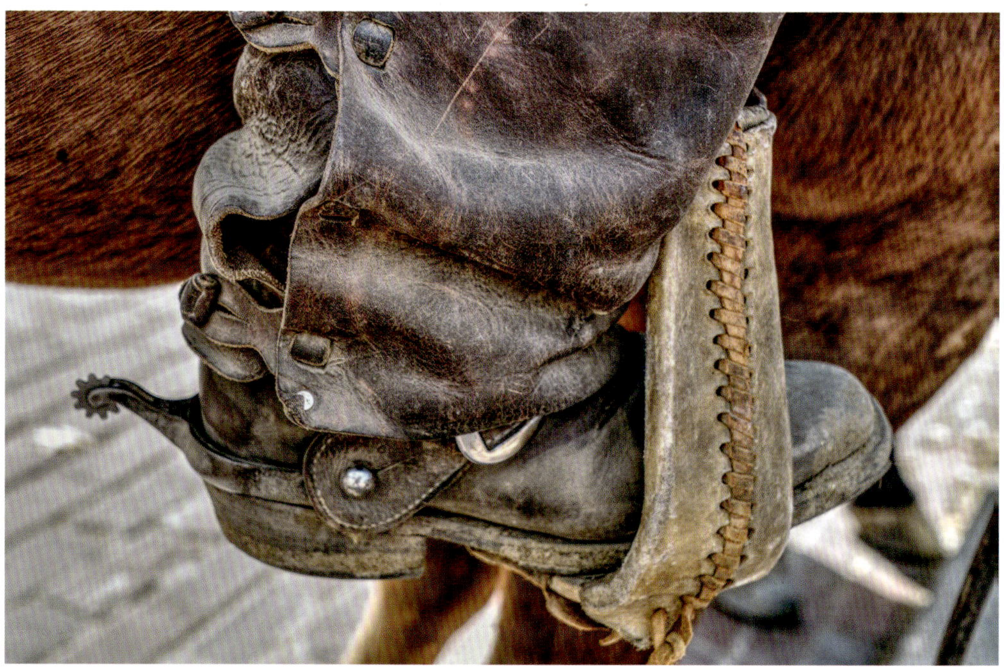

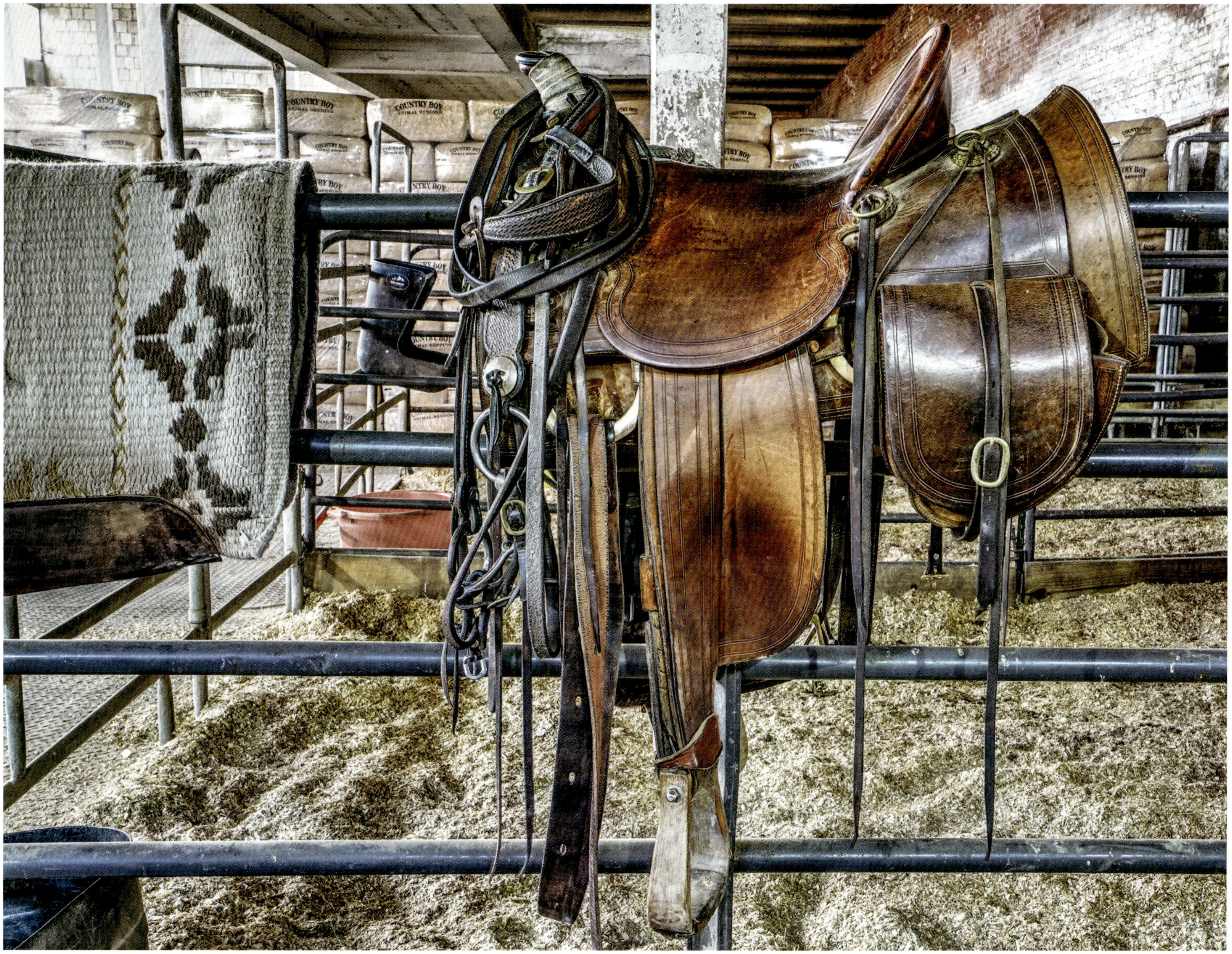

A seasoned saddle and blanket await their next riding adventure atop one of the magnificent horses that walk East Exchange Avenue at the stockyards.

the market needed growth. Of course, Armour and Swift officials should have realized that Texas constituted cattle country, especially Fort Worth's market to the west. The meatpackers acquired hogs in their midwestern cities. They should have planned their slaughtering activities around cattle at their Fort Worth plants, but they did not. They apparently failed to see the problem quickly enough to shift their expectations. Although the market acquired seventy-five thousand hogs per month, the meatpackers wanted at least twice that. They wanted three or four hogs for every head of cattle accepted. That just was not possible in the Texas market.

Nevertheless, the Fort Worth market tried all sorts of promotions and gave monthly prizes to shippers for the best wagonload of hogs. The Cattle Raisers Association even ran a special issue in its magazine, the *Cattleman*, on hog raising. The idea of a corn club among farm boys in 1908 began spreading throughout the country. French decided to try the idea of a pig club with the farm boys. Historians for years have debated just which type of youth club originated first and in what location. French began visiting towns along the railroad line of the Fort Worth and Denver City Railway and gave lectures to adults at every stop. He urged them to create pig clubs for their youngsters. Some folks called him a "pork evangelist."

The Smith-Lever Act of 1914 created the United States Extension Service. Its work included the establishment of pig, beef, corn, and other clubs for rural youth for which the name 4-H soon appeared. Clubs quickly spread throughout Texas, Louisiana, Alabama, Mississippi, Oklahoma, the Carolinas, and the Dakotas. Some credited the Fort Worth Stock Yards, and thus Charles French, with creating the idea, but the 4-H clubs multiplied so quickly and represented too great a movement to be able to associate any one man or any certain community with its establishment. However, towns throughout the Midwest claimed to have been the first; French, after all, copied the corn club idea.

French even quit the Fort Worth Stock Yards Company on October 1, 1915, to take a job as superintendent of livestock development in Texas with the US Department of Agriculture in its extension service at Texas A&M College (later University). French returned to the Fort Worth yards in 1920 as promotional agent again. In a single month that year he conducted fifty farmers' meetings in ten West Texas counties in conjunction with the West Texas Chamber of Commerce for a "poultry-dairy-livestock campaign." He showed a moving picture and slides to seven thousand people in that month.

The stockyards company continued working with 4-H boys as late as the 1950s. Although the original motive of the Fort Worth Stock Yards Company and the packers to attract more hogs for their market may have been only financial, their program nevertheless worked to the advantage of youngsters and their families. Many young men went at least partially into hog farming, gaining early business experience. Perhaps some even saved their money and financed a college education. In addition, the company, because of French's activities, considerably increased hog production in Texas. The Fort Worth yards continually added to its hog pens. Hog receipts reached a million animals in 1917 for the first time.

Unfortunately, the youngsters and other farmers even then did not raise enough hogs to keep the two existing packinghouses operating to capacity. That meant that no other big meatpackers moved to Fort Worth. The local plants wanted five thousand to ten thousand hogs per day, but often only one thousand to three thousand arrived. The plants thus operated at half capacity or less. In reality, the Fort Worth plants could easily slaughter fifteen thousand hogs per day, but they received only eight thousand per week. Sadly, the Fort Worth yards never grew to surpass those in Chicago and become number one, as many had hoped. The son of Louville V. Niles once wrote, "In spite of the best efforts of Mr. French and everybody in general it appears to be more difficult for the farmers of

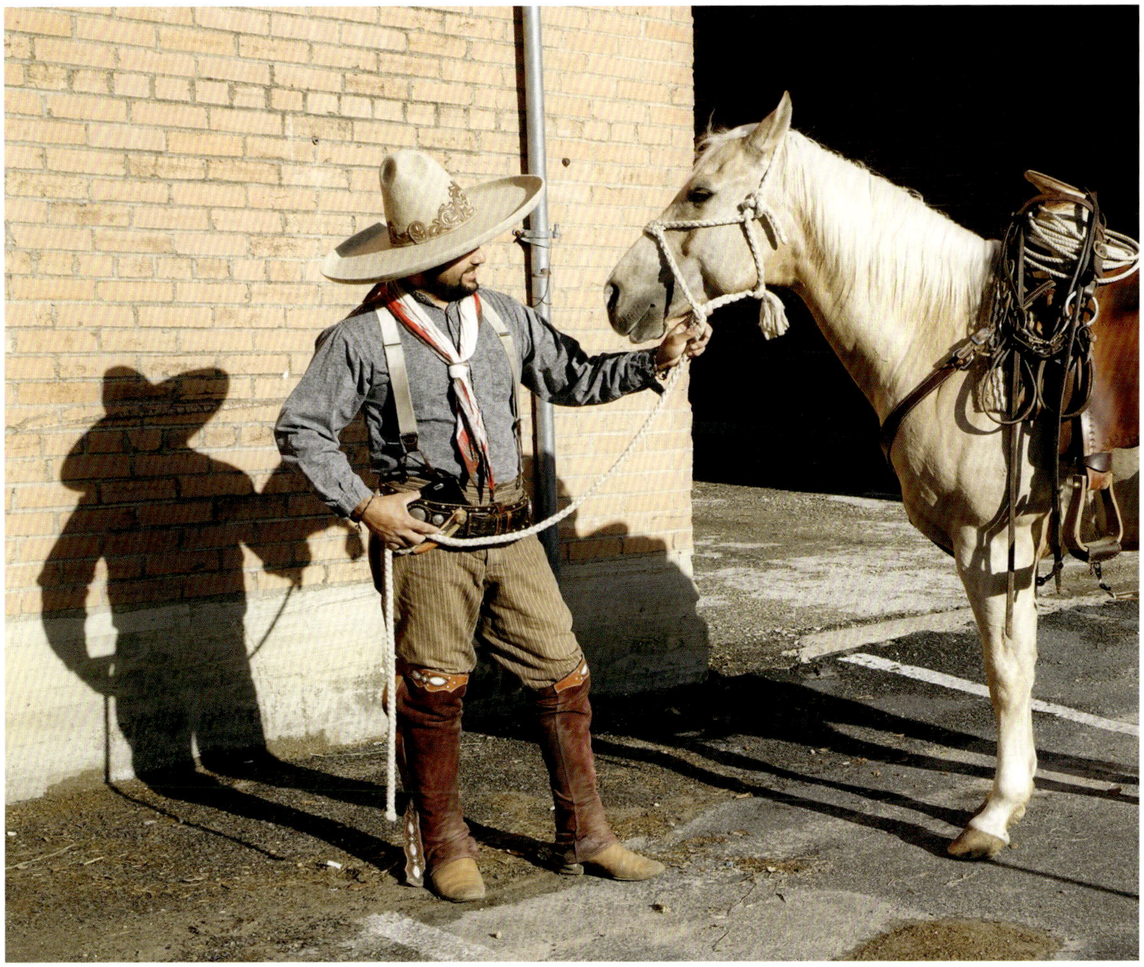

Drover José Hernandez and his horse, Charlie, pose along Mule Alley. José looks gallant in his typically vaquero-style hat and boots. Charlie's Spanish-style saddle has a large saddle horn.

Texas to raise any considerable number of hogs." What no one seemed to consider at the time was that Fort Worth was "Cowtown." Texans saw themselves as Westerners, and in the West one rode a horse and raised cattle.

Even East Texans did not raise enough hogs on their farms to sell to the Fort Worth market. Southern habits so influenced their heritage that they raised mostly cotton as their primary crop. Prices for cotton remained good, and owners of tenant farms usually pressured their tenants to raise cotton instead of hogs. Another factor was that hogs needed care every day, but cotton, once planted, grew on its own. Even a farmer/rancher who raised cattle enjoyed not being tied down, because the cattle grazed most of the time.

When President Franklin D. Roosevelt's New Deal government in the 1930s attempted to raise prices by creating scarcity, the stockyards officials wrote, "We discontinued our efforts to increase the production of hogs in this state which were inconsistent with the government program." Fort Worth thus had to settle for being the largest market south of Kansas City and largest market in the Southwest. Its grandiose dreams suffered defeat, not caused by a lack of cattle or absence of ingenuity and hard work but by too few carloads of hogs arriving at its market.

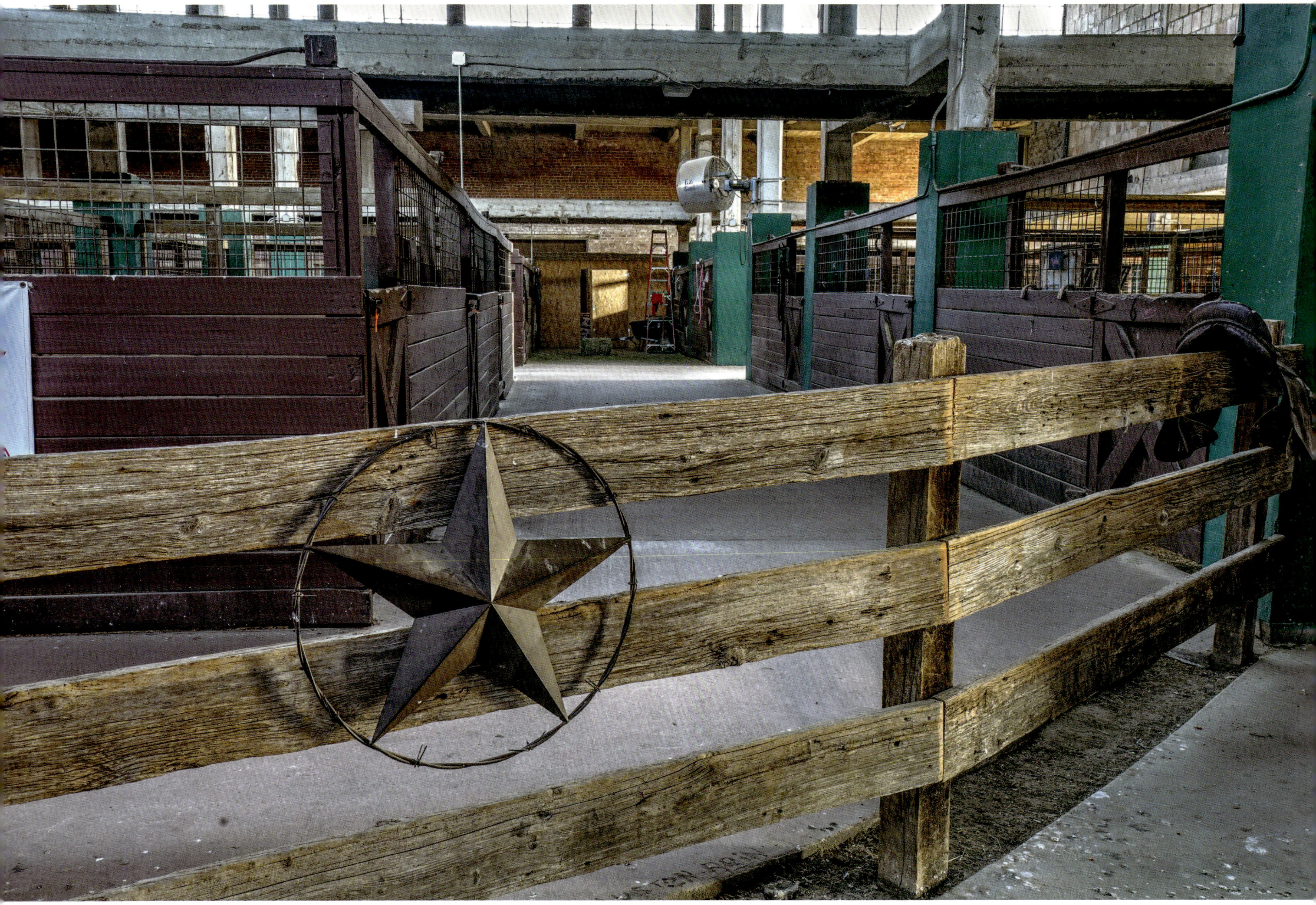

The interior of the historic Horse and Mule Barn included a wooden fence with a big star loosely hanging on it. The horse and mule pens are behind the fence.

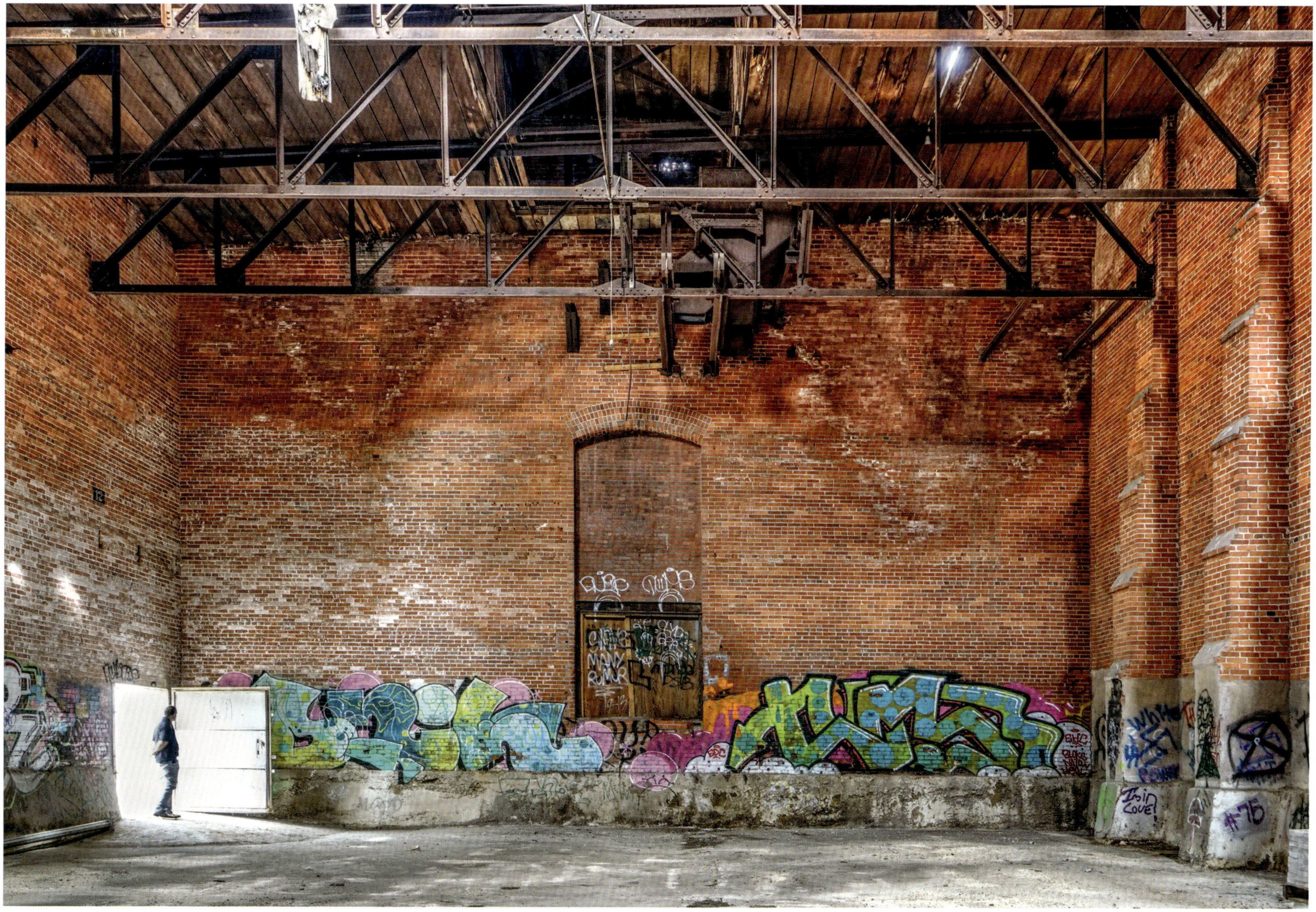

Superintendent David Berry, with Majestic Realty, enters through a light-filled door to the vast ground floor of the Swift Fertilizer Mill House. It is one of two buildings structurally sound enough to save for redevelopment at the Swift meatpacking site.

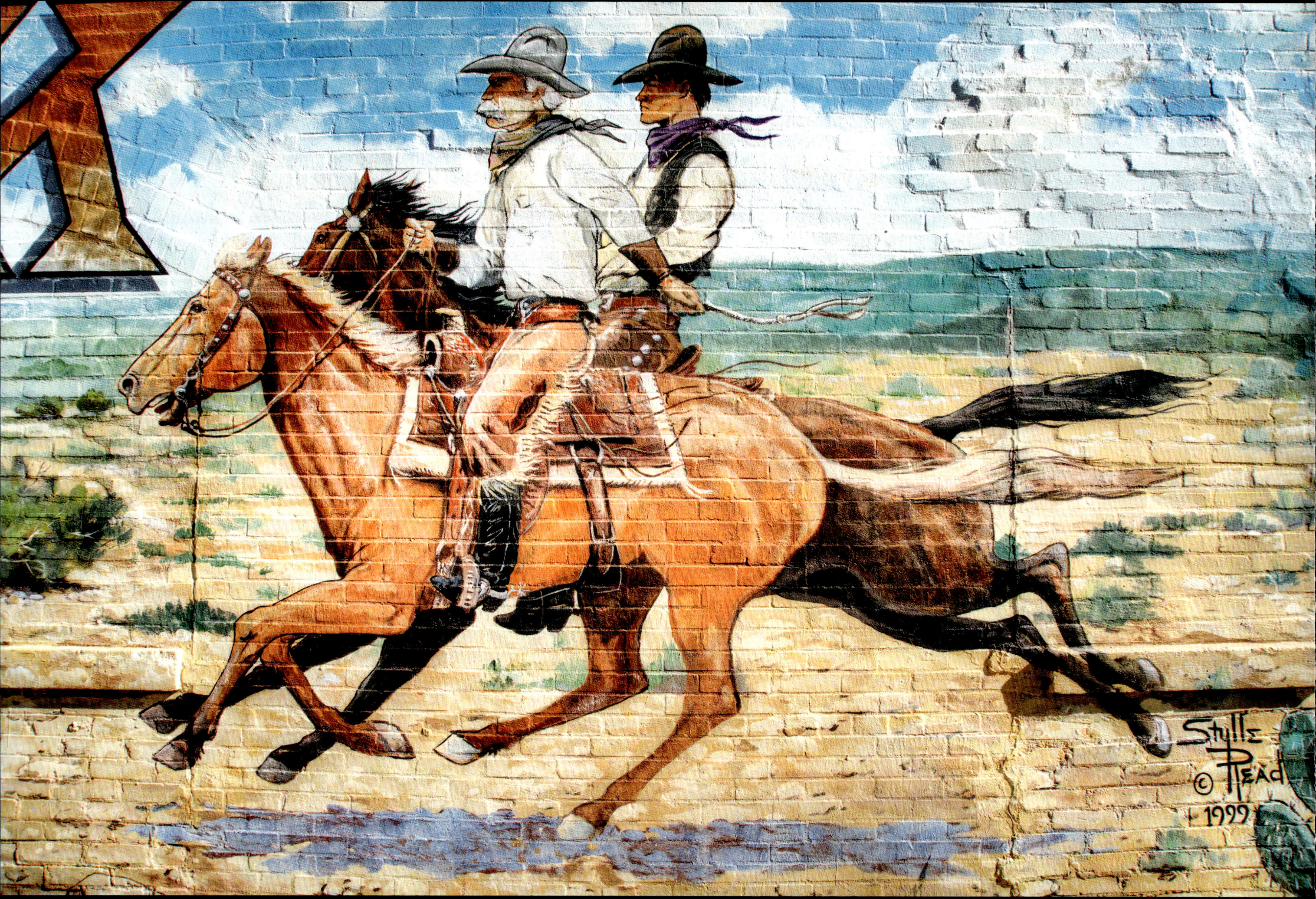
Stylle Read
© 1999

CHAPTER 3

Community Concerns

Although the city of Fort Worth benefited greatly from the livestock market that called itself by the city's name, in the beginning the yards existed outside its boundaries. Owners of the market quickly incorporated as a separate municipality to avoid paying taxes to the city of Fort Worth, which was located south of the Trinity River. Because original founder Louville V. Niles became well known and spent a lot of time at the yards, promoters incorporated the stockyards area as Niles City. The two communities got along well enough until certain officials in the city of Fort Worth realized that they could gain substantial tax revenues if they extended the boundaries of Fort Worth to include the stockyards district. The area north of the Trinity River, which ran just north of the bluff on which the courthouse sat, had remained outside the boundaries of Fort Worth mainly because it existed as open prairie for many years.

When city leaders created the Union Stock Yards in 1889–90, the area was known as Marine because of Marine Creek running through it. Only about five hundred people lived in the Northside when Armour and Swift arrived in 1902. A vote that same year created a town called North Fort Worth, which absorbed Marine. Numerous officials of the stockyards or meatpacking plants held positions on the new town council. The state legislature at this time could merge incorporated cities whenever it chose. The Fort Worth mayor and city commissioners urged their own state representative to get the legislature to annex North Fort Worth, which it did on March 11, 1909, catching North Fort Worth by surprise.

The actual stockyards were not located in North Fort Worth at that time but feared that Fort Worth might soon annex them. Fort Worth originally left the stockyards outside its city limits to attract factories, which would be exempt from the bigger city's taxes. Too few new busi-

Two stylish cowboys gallop like the wind across the land in a wall mural painted by Stylle Read in 1999. The background brick texture adds to the composition.

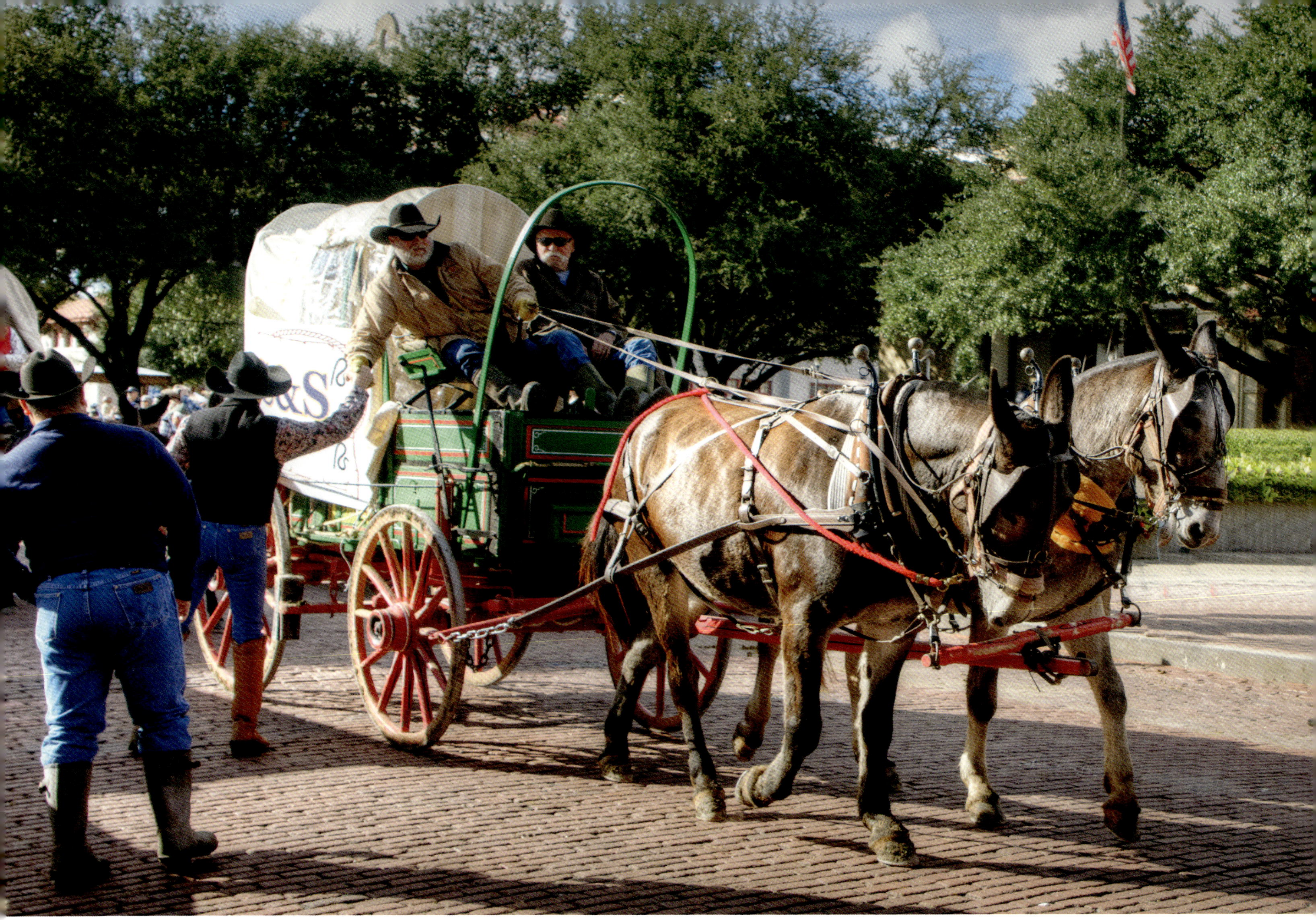

Wagon teams come from throughout the state to help celebrate Western heritage with cowboy/poet/musician/performer Red Steagall every October. The wagon train leaves Jacksboro, Texas, arriving days later at the Fort Worth Stockyards, where they set up in front of the Livestock Exchange Building.

nesses arrived in the area to compensate for the loss of the tax revenues, so in 1911 Fort Worth decided to annex the stockyards area as well.

In an attempt to stop the impending annexation, the stockyards interests decided to create their own city. The stockyards earlier spent thirty thousand dollars to construct rent houses. Only a few private homes existed because stockyards and private interests or other corporations owned most of the land. Thirty-three men met in T. E. "Dad" Carson's grocery store at 126 Decatur Avenue on February 21, 1911, and voted unanimously to incorporate a new city. Some wanted to call it Carson City, but Carson suggested that they name it after the man they deemed most responsible for bringing Armour and Swift to Fort Worth, Louville V. Niles. Near the turn of the century Niles had spent six months of each year for two or three years in Fort Worth operating an old meatpacking plant. The men of the area became acquainted with him and appreciated his efforts. Niles tried never to miss the annual stock show through the years. When he was back in Boston, he wrote letters inquiring about every aspect of the operation: painting the rent houses, roofing buildings, mowing lawns, or whatever interested him. His investment in the stockyards meant that he wanted to keep closely in touch.

When officially incorporated four days after the 1911 meeting, the new community of Niles City claimed only slightly more than five hundred residents, all working-class families. The new city was a one-half-square-mile area that also included the packing plants, the stockyards, a police and fire department, artesian wells for water, electric lights, telephone and gas service, five schools (four white, one black), two grain elevators, a pottery works, a roundhouse for the Belt Railroad, three grocery stores, and one drugstore.

When citing the estimated value of all property in the new town, the sum came to between twenty-five and thirty million dollars because of the value of the meat-

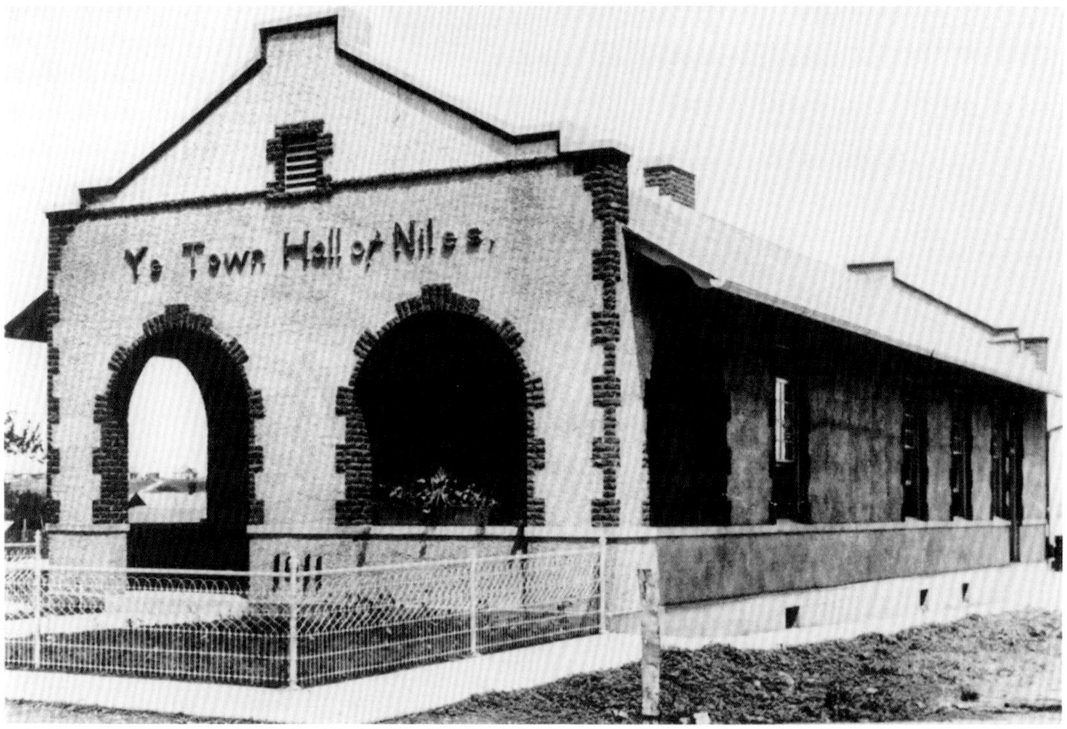

Before 1920 the address of the stockyards was in Niles City, but the small suburb was later incorporated into the city of Fort Worth. Courtesy of North Fort Worth Historical Society.

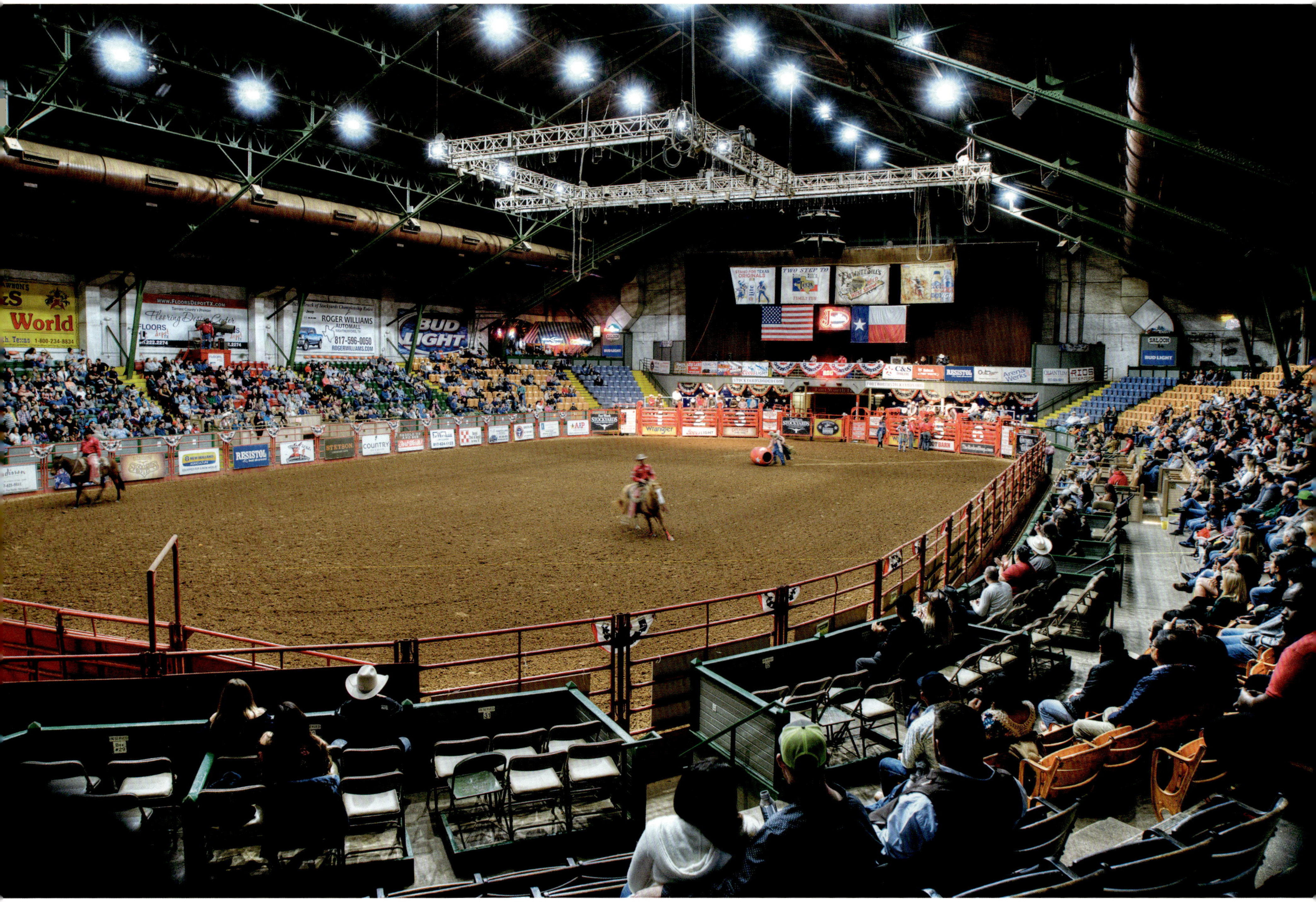

The stockyards rodeo is held at the Cowtown Coliseum. The first indoor rodeo took place in the coliseum in 1917.

packing plants and the stockyards facilities. The town claimed to be the "richest little city per capita in the United States" because of the proportion of wealth in relation to its small size and population. By March 1912, the city had constructed a brick and stucco city hall that cost $4,511 to build.

The most famous event ever to occur in Niles City (other than the visit of former president Roosevelt two weeks after the city's incorporation) was the visit of famous tenor Enrico Caruso, who sang to a standing-room-only crowd of eight thousand on October 19, 1920, in the coliseum that the stockyards company constructed in 1908 for its stock show. Caruso, forty-six years old, enjoyed an enthusiastic foot-stomping welcome and commented, "This is the first time I have ever been stampeded." He added, "Wonderful audience. Wonderful audience." He apparently did not mind the wild, Western reaction of whistling and throwing hats in the air either. All nine policemen from Niles City and their chief, Frank Averitt, served on duty to handle the crowd.

One reason that the city of Fort Worth decided to annex Niles City was a series of strikes that the small police force of Niles City had trouble handling. Mainly, though, it wanted the tax money from the lucrative enterprise at the stockyards. Fort Worth officials took the first steps to annex Niles City and other suburbs in 1919. The bill failed because of organized opposition. Fort Worth tried again in March 1921, and the legislature approved. With state approval, citizens of Fort Worth then voted on July 22, 1922, to annex Niles City. The mayor of Niles City protested the annexation but lost the fight in court.

Former officials of Niles City sold the former town hall to private interests, and it served as a residence for several years. Later, after being vacant for a while, a syrup factory used the building. It was a Works Progress

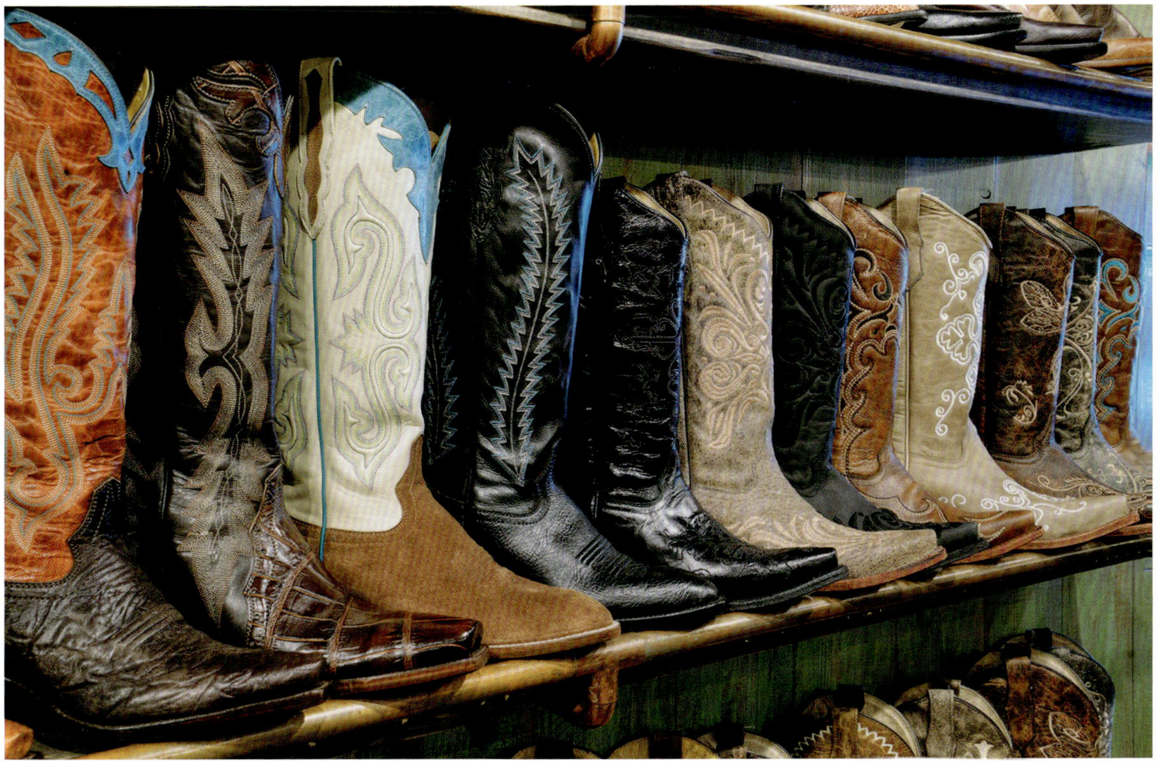

Various boot styles are available for purchase at Fincher's White Front Western Wear, originally opened as White Front Western Store in 1902.

Administration canning plant in the 1930s. Then after being vacant for a few years, it was demolished in 1975 to make room for a parking lot. That later action so upset local citizens that they were inspired to form the North Fort Worth Historical Society to prevent demolition of any other historic buildings in the North Side.

Cattle interests influenced newspaperman Amon Carter such that in 1922, when he invested in radio, he chose a cowbell as the sound symbol. He named the station WBAP, which stood for We Bring a Program. By 1923 his newspaper, the *Fort Worth Star-Telegram*, boasted a circulation of 115,000, which at that time made it the largest newspaper in the South.

Because of flooding at the stockyards during heavy rains, the Tarrant County Water Control District was created in October 1924. Supporters called it the first combination flood control and water supply plan in America. Engineers constructed two lakes on the West Fork of the Trinity: Lake Bridgeport, fifty miles upriver to the west; and Eagle Mountain Lake, closer to Lake Worth, which the city developed ten years earlier.

In the 1920s stockyards interests throughout the country became concerned about their connection to the meatpacking trust of the Big Five and made charges that the Big Five set prices and acted in collusion to limit competition. The Big Five included Armour, Swift, Morris, Cudahy, and the partners Schwarzschild and Sulzberger. The Cattle Raisers Association of Texas claimed that in 1916 the Big Five's control of interstate slaughter at the twelve largest packing centers accounted for 94.4 percent of cattle, 89.1 percent of calves, 94.3 percent of sheep and lambs, and 81 percent of all swine brought to these markets. The public became incensed at the profits the meatpackers earned, especially when they learned

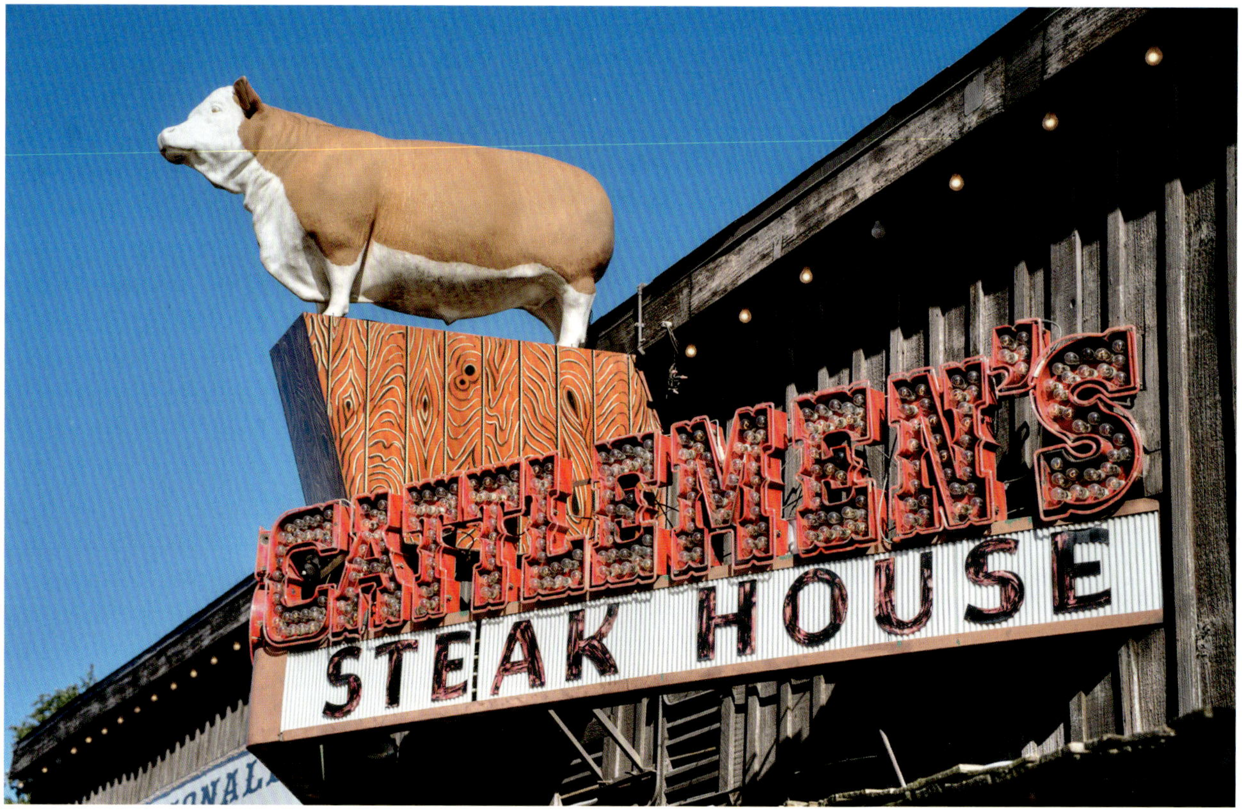

Famous for steak, the Fort Worth Cattlemen's Steak House opened at the stockyards in 1973. It has experienced a robust business since.

that the packers also owned the stockyards where most livestock were sold as well as railroad cars that carried much of the nation's processed meat and even perishable fruit and vegetables. Many people feared that the "meat trust" would control the food supply of the nation. Some even called for the "meat monopoly" to be operated as a public utility, leaving only small, independent companies to continue as free enterprise.

In his book *The Packers, the Private Car Lines and the People*, J. Ogden Armour defended his industry by explaining that packers built and operated their own railroad cars so that they would be available when needed, for the railroads could not be depended on to supply them in a timely manner. Once they had the rail cars, the packers found it more profitable to ship fruits and vegetables on them at least a part of the time than to move empty cars. They bought and operated stockyards for basically the same reason, he said, to see that a market existed to provide sufficient animals for their packing plants to operate efficiently. The Fort Worth Stock Yards Company formed an integral part of this meatpacking trust, since Armour and Swift, the two largest of the Big Five, each owned one-third of the shares of the company.

In testimony before the Senate Agricultural Commission on January 25, 1919, Armour admitted that he had induced Swift to build in Fort Worth and had promised him half the business to keep him from building across the river in Dallas. However, published accounts of

The bronze statue of African American cowboy and rodeo film star Bill Pickett by artist Lisa Perry was installed in front of the 1908 coliseum in the Stockyards National Historic District. This statue was commissioned by the North Fort Worth Historical Society, and the bronze was given to the city of Fort Worth as a gift in May 1987.

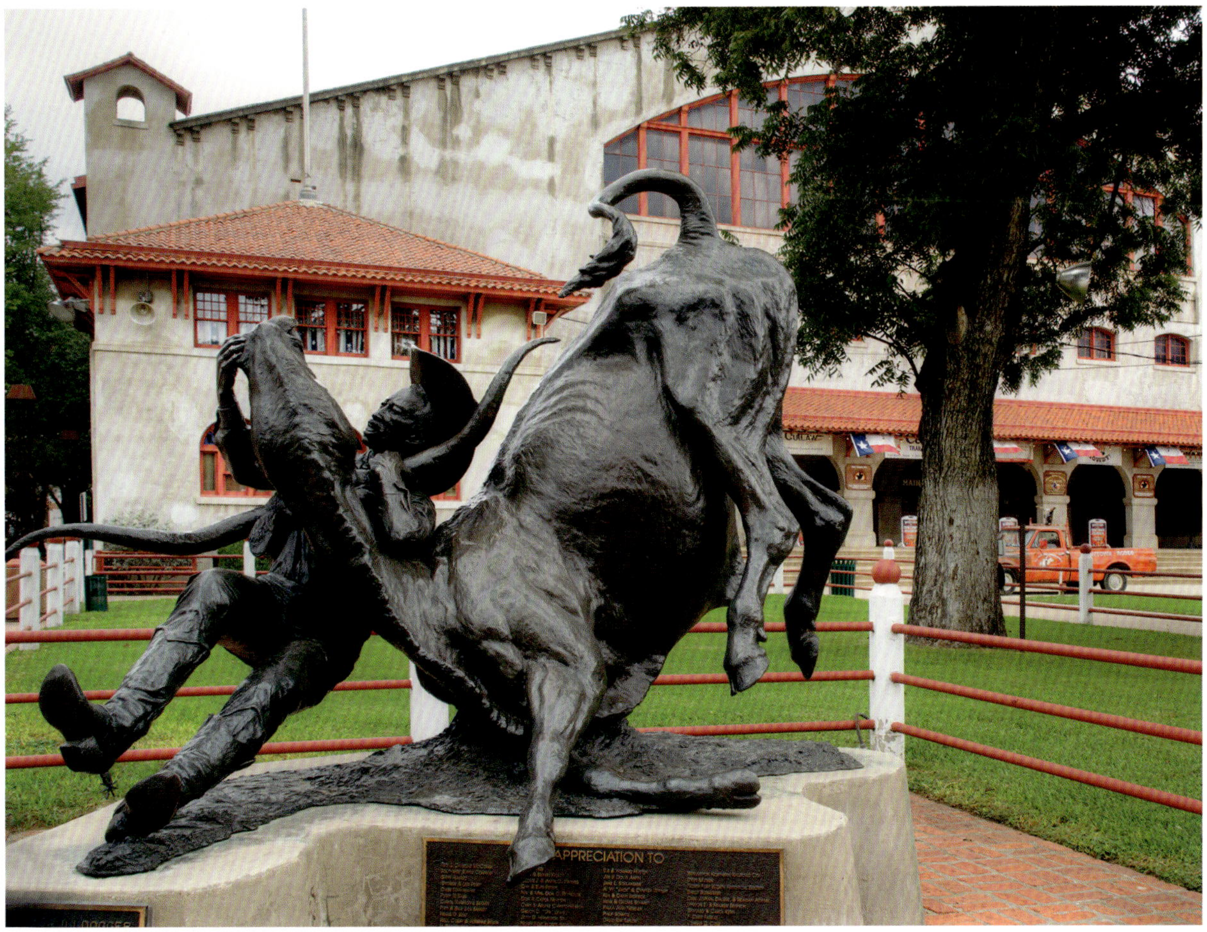

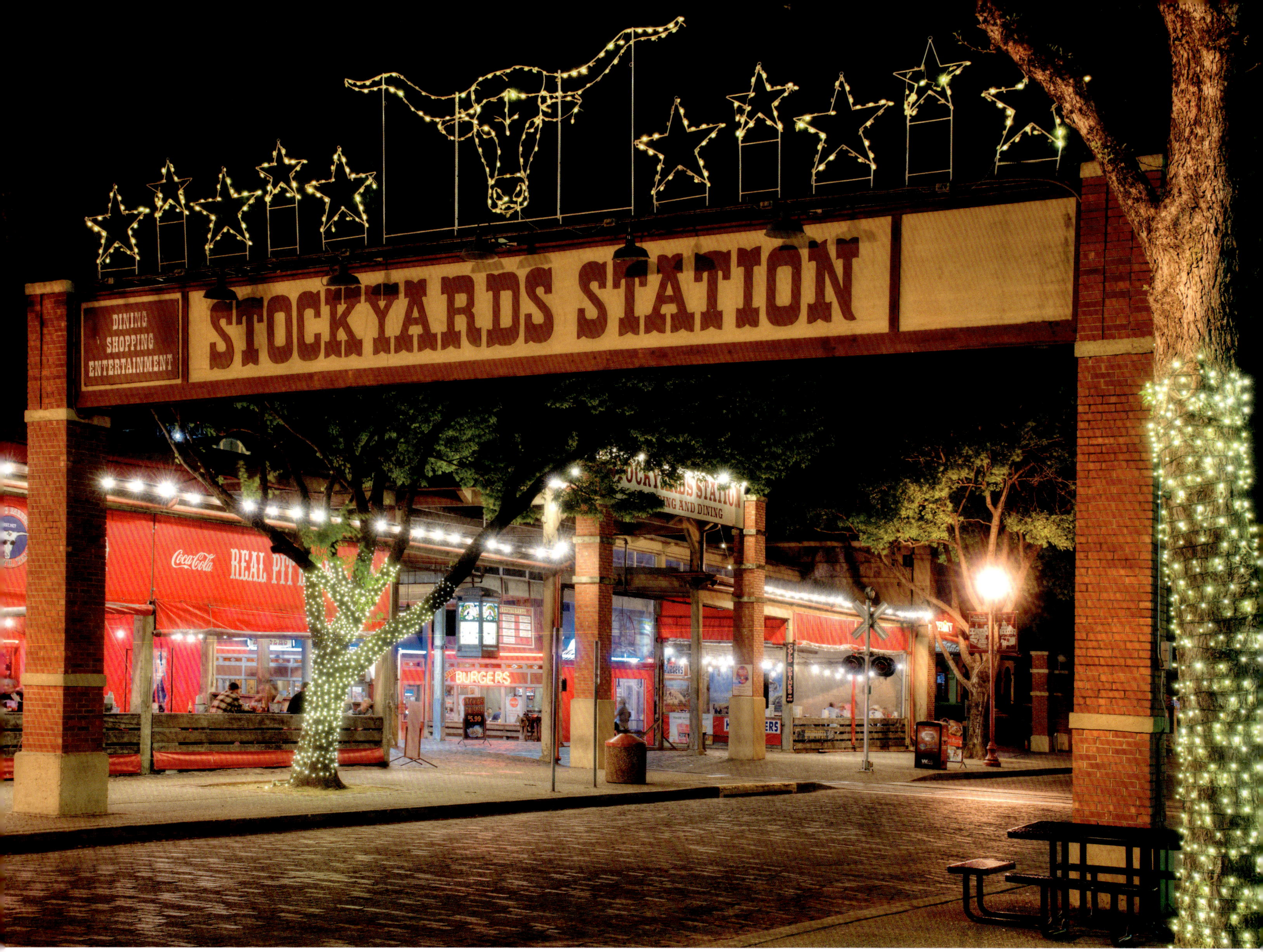

Glowing lights adorn the departure gate and thriving businesses at night in the stockyards.

livestock purchases of the two packers at the Fort Worth Stock Yards indicate that their buyers often contracted for almost identical amounts, particularly of cattle, each day over the years.

Roy Weeman, who worked as a cattle buyer for Swift most of his forty-nine years on the Fort Worth yards, from 1913 to 1962, denied that Armour and Swift got together to agree on what to buy. He said that the commission men could sell to anybody, and a lot of buyers always existed: Cudahy, Wilson, Bluebonnet, and others. He said the packers could not pay just what they wanted to pay because a commission man was fighting for the last nickel for his producers all the way. One of Weeman's jobs when he was a youngster working for Swift in 1913 was sending the daily telegrams. He says that the company did not "wire ahead" to other markets the prices quoted to people on the Fort Worth yards who were shipping on to Kansas City or places north.

Harry Butz, who served as head sheep buyer for Swift for more than forty years, said that no one at the Swift plant ever told him how many sheep to buy or to limit his purchases. They respected that he knew his job and the value of the sheep, so his supervisors just left him alone. He said that a lot of competition existed with Armour and insisted that the rivalry "couldn't have been any stronger."

Others on the Fort Worth yards, such as order buyers and commission men, expressed the same opinion that no collusion existed. Perhaps livestock producers living many miles from Fort Worth, who became unhappy at prices they received, joined with other cattlemen or stock owners in protesting against the Big Five, but local people defended their market. One speculator explained philosophically the difference between producers and the Big Five: "It depends on which side of the fence you are on. There never was a cattle producer who sold at a high enough price to satisfy him or a packer who got it cheap enough to make enough profit."

One thing that probably most Fort Worth citizens did not know was that the Fort Worth Stock Yards Company owned many other businesses, including a real estate corporation to sell lots and houses; cattle loan corporations; major control of the Stockyards National Bank; the Belt Railway Company; the *Fort Worth Daily Live Stock Reporter*, which became a weekly in the 1920s; and a utility company. Stockyards owners "always denied connections between interests," one official admitted to another in a telegram.

Reformers began to urge that the federal government curb such activities of the meat trust nationwide and wanted federal regulation of the industry. In 1921 Senator George Norris of Nebraska argued for such legislation. He contrasted the sixty cents his wife had paid recently for a pound of bacon with the ten to twelve cents per pound farmers received.

Cries for help originated as early as 1888 when the Senate investigated the dressed-beef plants. Ten years later a Supreme Court ruling favored the beef industry. However, in 1903 a court ruling called the Big Five meatpackers "a meat monopoly." Because the meat industry made large profits during World War I, many disgruntled people called for reform, even though the government regulated the packers under the wartime Lever Act. High prices and excessive profits, which were published, caused complaints and accusations of unfair competition. The American Federation of Labor became irate at the Big Five's resistance to collective bargaining and decided to challenge. President Woodrow Wilson called for stricter antitrust legislation.

Farmers and ranchers from the western states made probably the most effective calls for reform as they complained of the low and fluctuating price of meat animals. They also feared that the commission men, who rented office space in livestock exchange buildings owned by packers, might favor the packers to keep on good terms with their landlords. As early as 1914, the American

Each year the annual Red Steagall Cowboy Gathering features an exciting chuckwagon camp and competition, ranch rodeo auction, trappings show, cowboy poetry and music, Ranch Cutting Horse Association rodeo finals, youth poetry contest, youth fiddle contest, youth chuckwagon cook-off, Texas Trail of Fame, cowboy church, cowboy gospel concert, Western swing dances, and Texas Lone Star open live bid-calling contest.

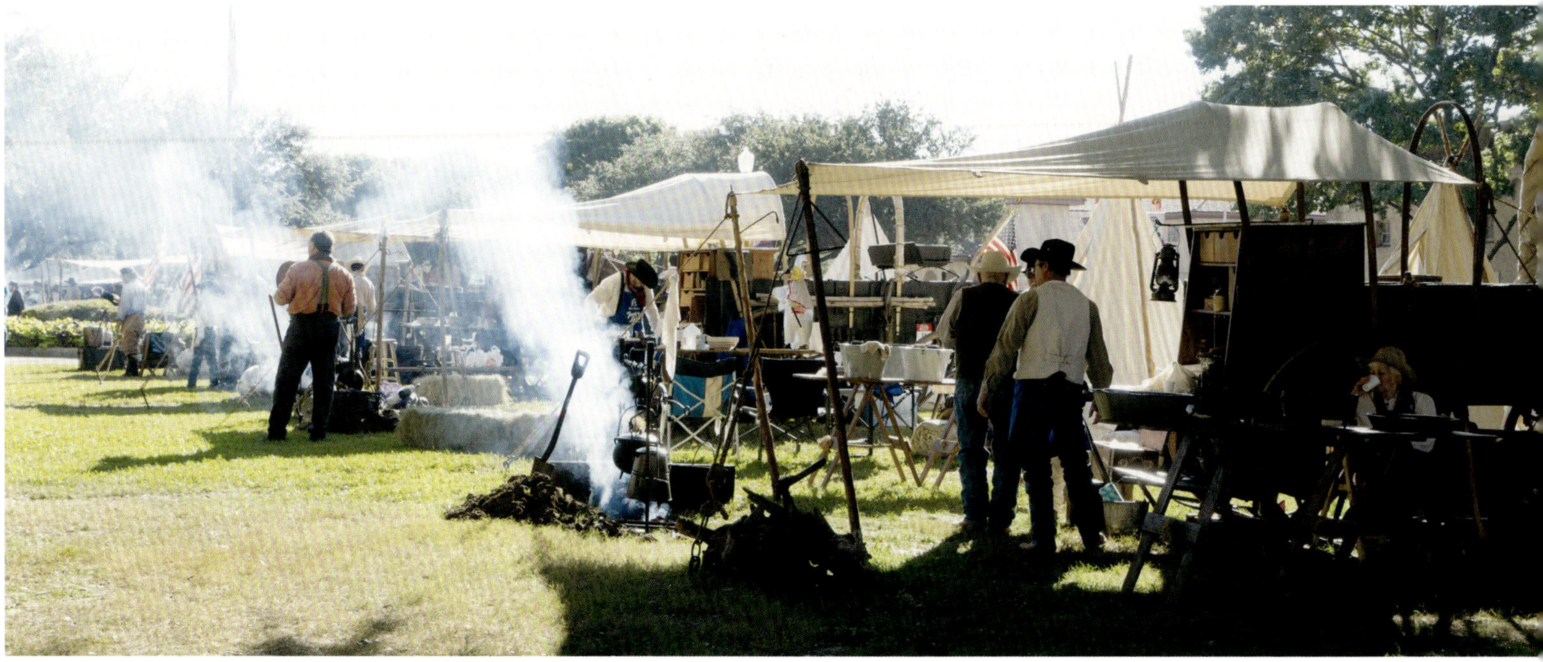

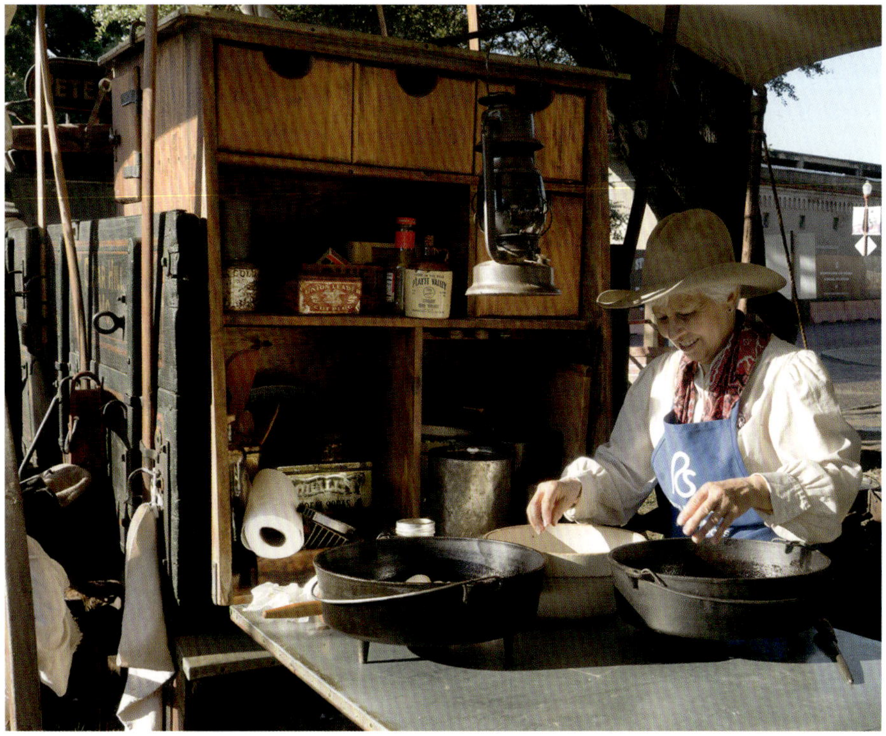

Pioneer cook Annette Wilson of Stamford, Texas, mixes ingredients using cookware of copper, brass, graniteware, and cast iron and flatware of old German nickel silver, steel, or steel with wood or bone handles. Camp competitors are scored on the authenticity of their presentation.

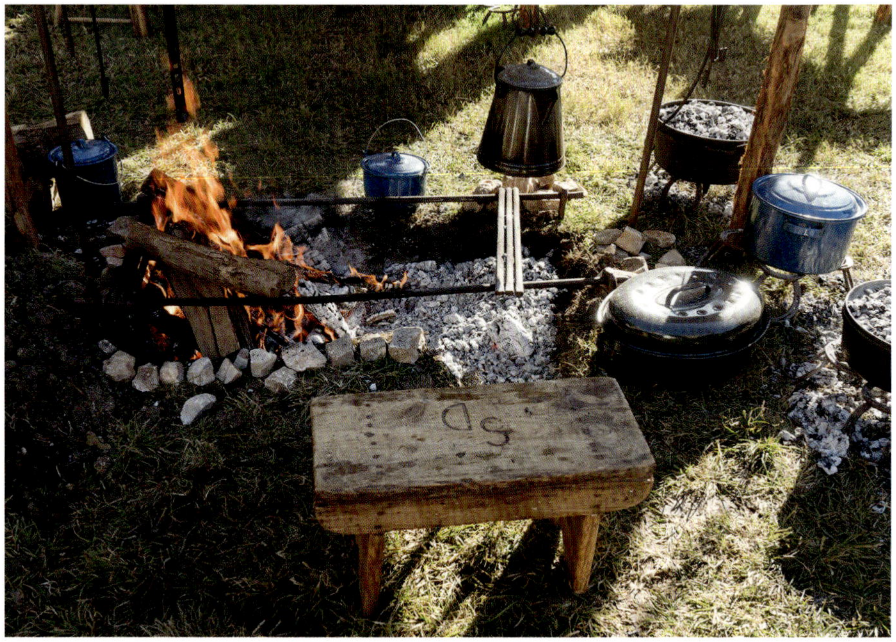

Pioneer chefs build fires and mix ingredients in camp style, all by hand, cooking over campfires, using authentic ingredients and cooking tools at the fall Red Steagall Cowboy Gathering.

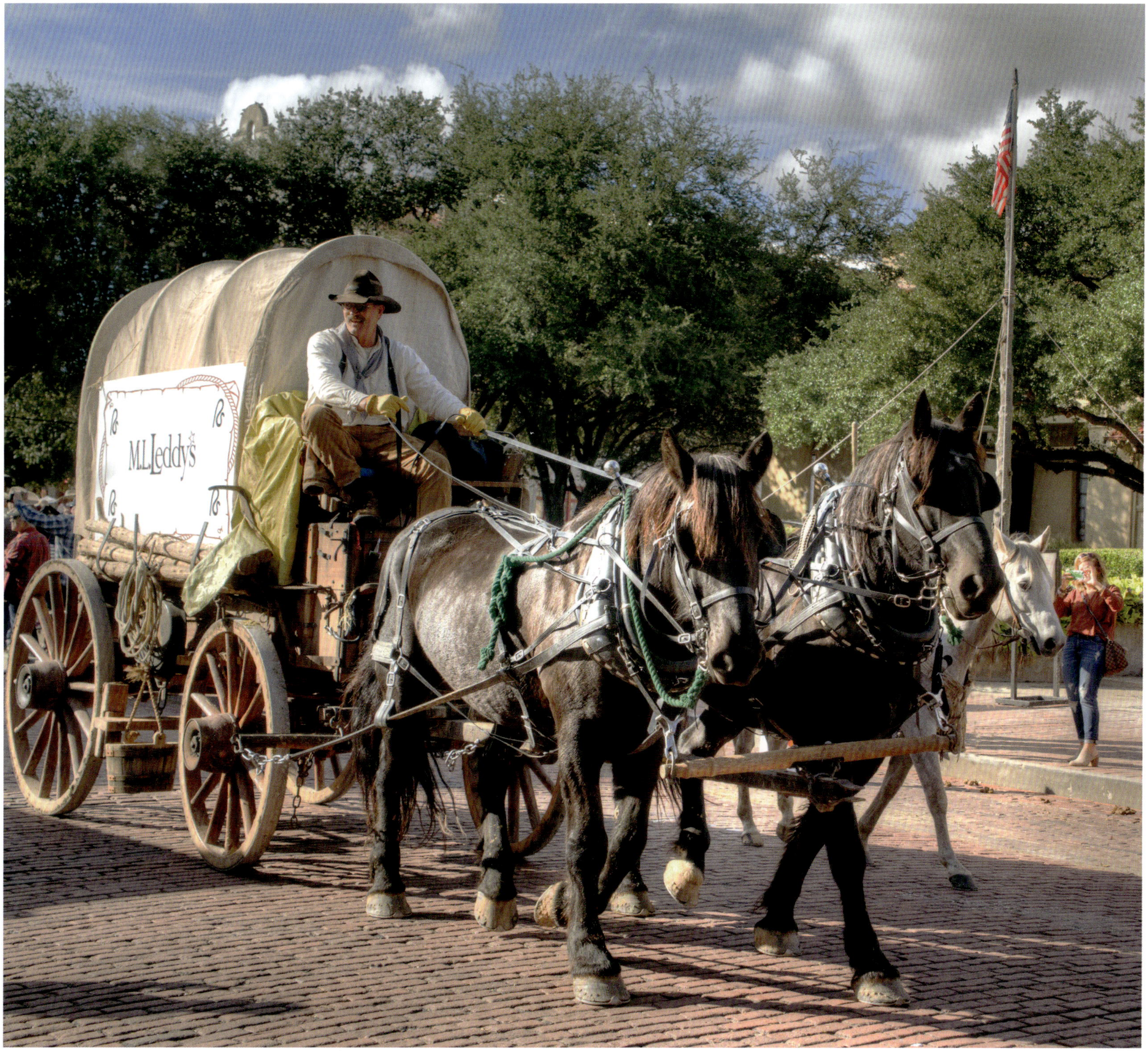

The chuckwagon parade includes historically authentic cowboys and cowgirls, wagons, and horse or mule teams as they parade down East Exchange Avenue on Red Steagall Day.

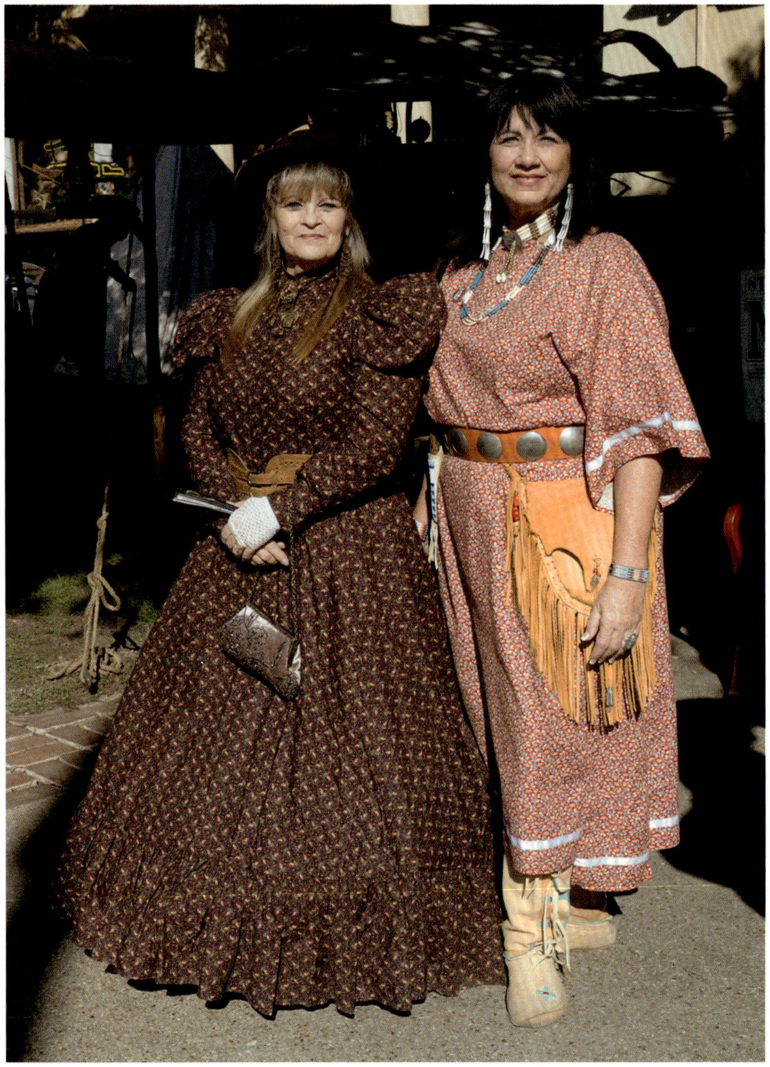

Two women celebrate in authentic historic costumes, including properly dressed and fashionable Jeannie Haliday of Grandview, Texas, wearing a long dress, hat, and purse; and Kim Gilbreath of Joshua, Texas, wearing Native American beads, gingham, and leather.

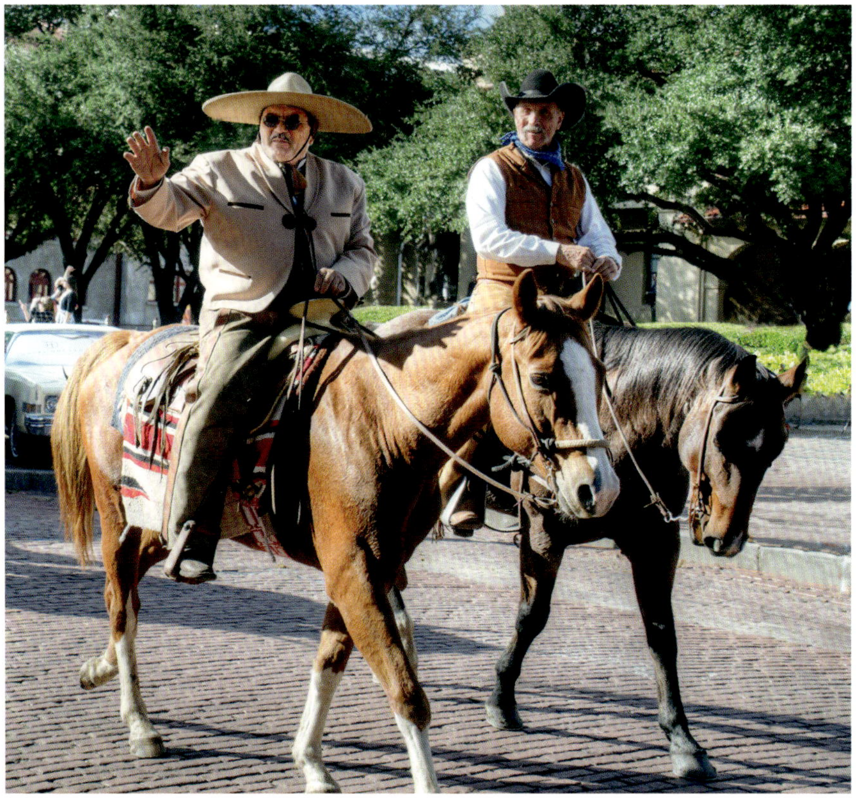

A Mexican vaquero and a Texas cowboy ride down East Exchange Avenue. The vaquero, sometimes considered the first working cowboy, is a horse-mounted livestock herder in a tradition that originated in Iberia.

National Cattlemen's Association formed a committee to investigate the growth and control of the large packers. They concluded that in the marketing of livestock, supply and demand "has ceased to have very much to do with the matter of price making."

A pro-packer and an anti-packer faction existed within several of the livestock organizations, some of whom asked Congress to enact legislation to correct the abuses of the packers. Congressman William P. Borland introduced a resolution directing the Federal Trade Commission (FTC) to investigate any violations of the antitrust laws by the big packers. He said, "Indications are . . . that the Standard Oil Company in its palmiest days never had as complete a system of controlling the supply and demand price of a great necessity of life as has now been developed by the packers' trust."

Packers tried to forestall such investigations by meeting with livestock associations. Officials of four of the

Big Five came to Fort Worth in May 1916 to meet with a committee of members of the Cattle Raisers Association of Texas. Their efforts failed, however, and the committee still recommended that the American National Cattlemen's Association continue its investigation.

As a result of these calls for government action, President Wilson on February 7, 1917, requested that the FTC investigate the meatpacking industry to determine if agreements in restraint of trade or other monopolistic practices existed. After several months of hearings and other investigations that included five volumes of collected material, the commission concluded: "It appears that five great packing concerns of the country—Swift, Armour, Morris, Cudahy, and Wilson [the latter replacing S & S in the Big Five]—have attained such a dominant position that they control at will the market in which they sell their products and hold the fortunes of the competitors in their hands." Some estimates placed as high as five hundred the number of subsidiary companies in which they held joint stock, agreements, communities of interest, or family relationships.

In a chart that the FTC later revealed, its report listed thirty-one major stockyards (including Fort Worth's) showing percentages of ownership by the Big Five meat giants. The dominant companies controlled over 50 percent of all but two of the yards cited, and the percentage of ownership for most stood at over 80 or even 90 percent. The two packers at Fort Worth owned 66.67 percent of the Fort Worth Stock Yards. The FTC also charged the Big Five with making agreements to buy cattle in specified percentages. The report cited the Fort Worth and Denver stockyards, markets where only two of the Big

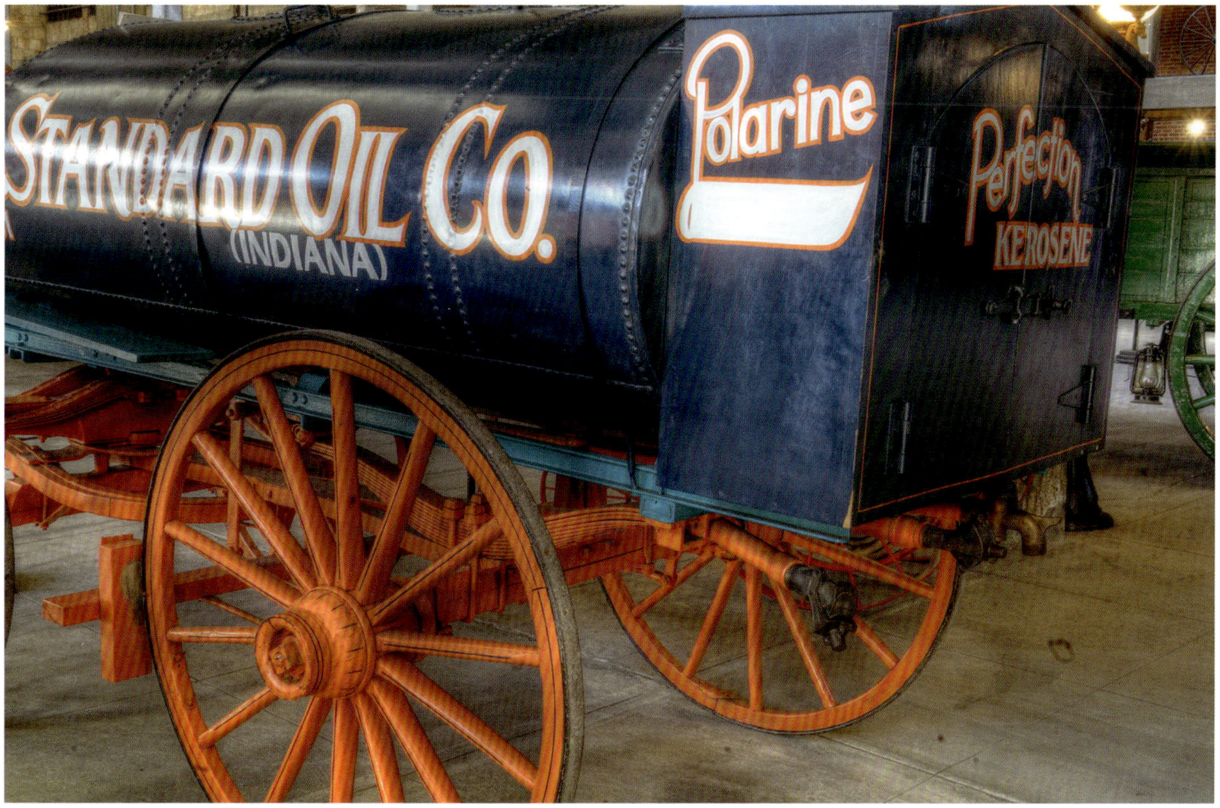

The Standard Oil Company wagon is among the antique Sterquell Wagon Collection at the Texas Cowboy Hall of Fame.

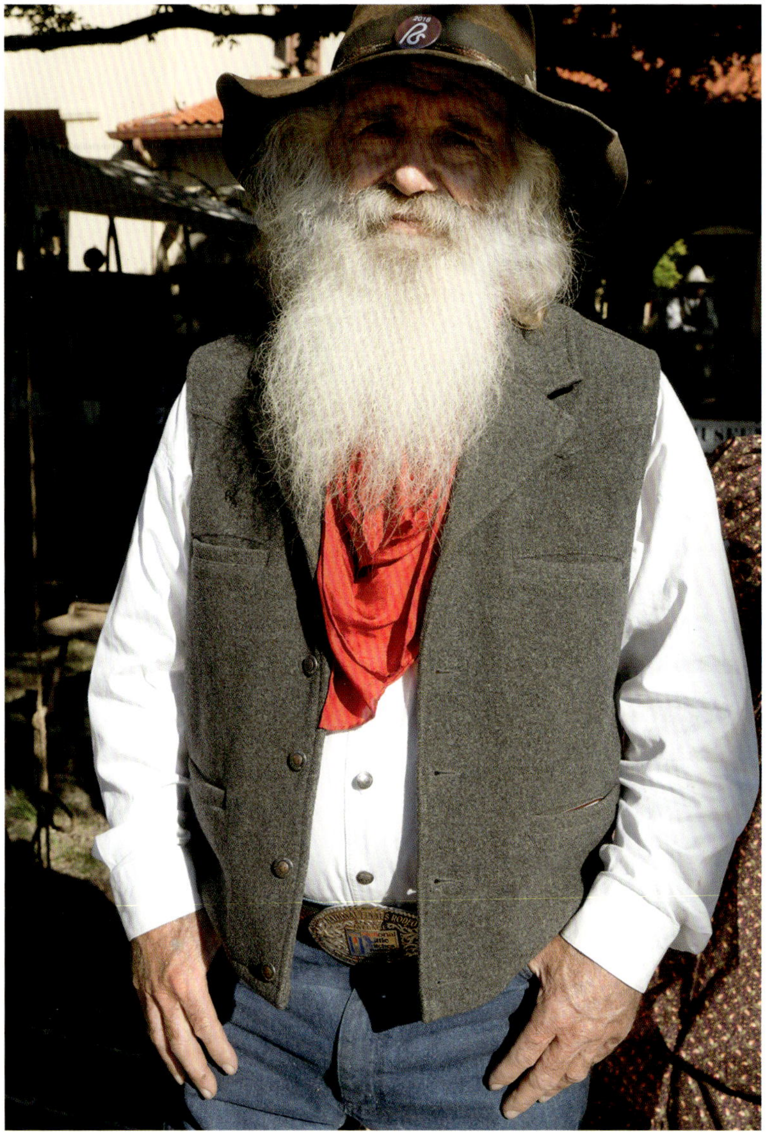

A well-dressed, heavily bearded cowboy stops to be photographed. His bushy white beard nearly covers his traditional red bandana.

Five operated, and claimed that they divided everything fifty-fifty. They allowed independent packers, local butchers, and speculators to purchase up to, but not more than, 5 percent of the livestock, which constituted too small a percentage to influence the market strongly, "much less fix the price." The report asserted that at Fort Worth the two packers that owned the stockyards "have refused, contrary to the wishes of the citizens of Fort Worth, to allow other packers to come in on the ground that there is not enough stock in that market to support another plant." Unsaid or acknowledged in the report was that other packers did not move to Fort Worth because of the lack of hogs, resulting from farmers not raising enough hogs, not a discouragement by the two existing packers.

The livestock industry became divided concerning the guilt of the packers and the need for strict regulation. Robert J. Kleberg, owner of the huge King Ranch in South Texas, opposed government regulation of packers, claiming that such regulation would be ruinous to everyone: packers, meat producers, and consumers. Fort Worth cattleman Marion Sansom also opposed the requested regulations. He argued that one could not get a larger market for beef by breaking up the packers, for they represented the only ones large enough to expand into a world market. Despite the opposition, the forty-fourth annual convention of the Cattle Raisers Association of Texas in 1920 voted 299 to 127 to ask the government to regulate the packers.

The meat industry created the Institute of American Meat Packers, composed of at least two hundred small packers as well as the Big Five, to combat the anti-packers' publicity and the proposed confiscatory legislation. The organization later became the American Meat Institute.

To forestall drastic regulations, the packers requested a meeting with the US attorney general, A. Mitchell Palmer, in which they proposed to clean up the industry from within. They signed a consent decree in 1920, voluntarily agreeing to dispose of their interests in public stockyards, stockyards terminals and railroads, market newspapers, and cold-storage houses and to relinquish the business in unrelated lines and the use of the distribution system for other than meat products.

Litigation began over the decree almost immediately and continued for a decade, during which time the packers did not comply with all of its provisions. However,

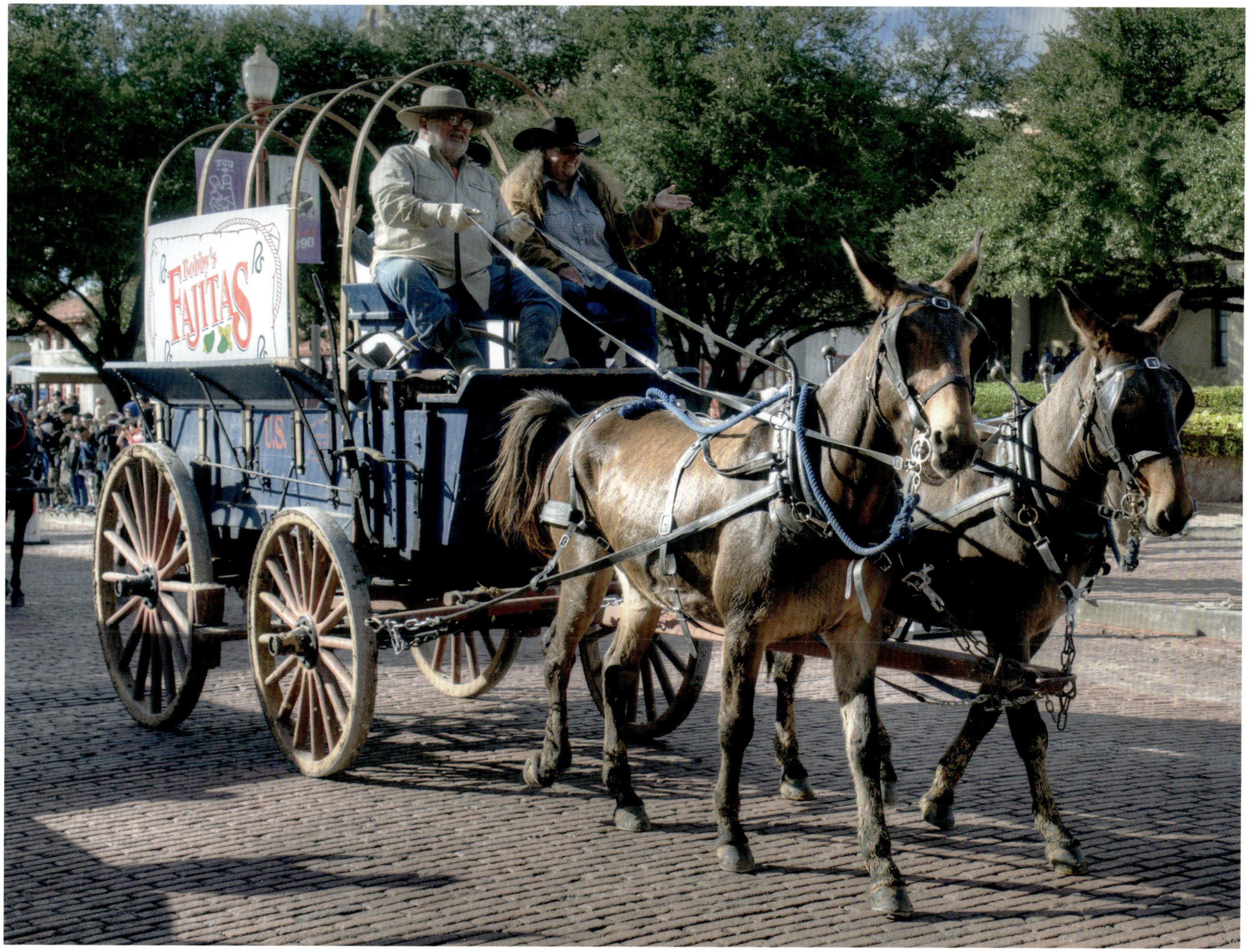

A team of mules pulls an antique wagon across East Exchange Avenue in the October parade at the stockyards.

the American Farm Bureau Federation and its Washington director, Gray Silver, got behind the legislation to regulate the meatpacking industry, and Congress passed Public Law 51, effective August 15, 1921, as "an Act to regulate interstate and foreign commerce in live stock, live-stock products, dairy products, poultry, poultry products and eggs and for other purposes." The act created the Packers and Stockyards Administration. A court case immediately tested its constitutionality, resulting in no drastic change happening to the Fort Worth Stock Yards and the other stockyards of the nation for several years.

A traditionally dressed cowboy wears a cowboy hat; boots; trophy buckle on his belt; jeans such as those manufactured by Wrangler; and a button-down, preferably long-sleeved cotton shirt. A riding cowboy wears leather chaps and brush cuffs on his wrists.

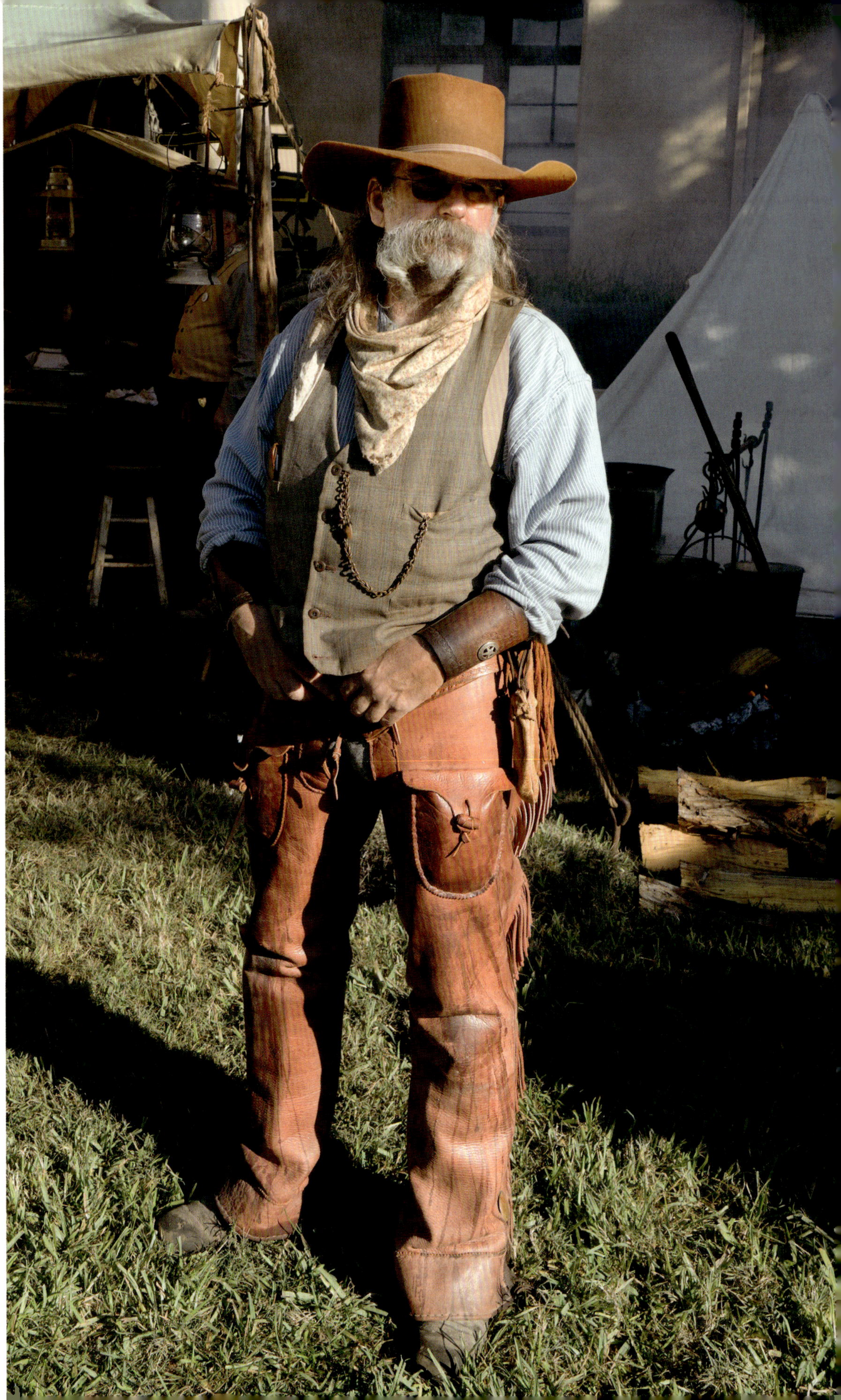

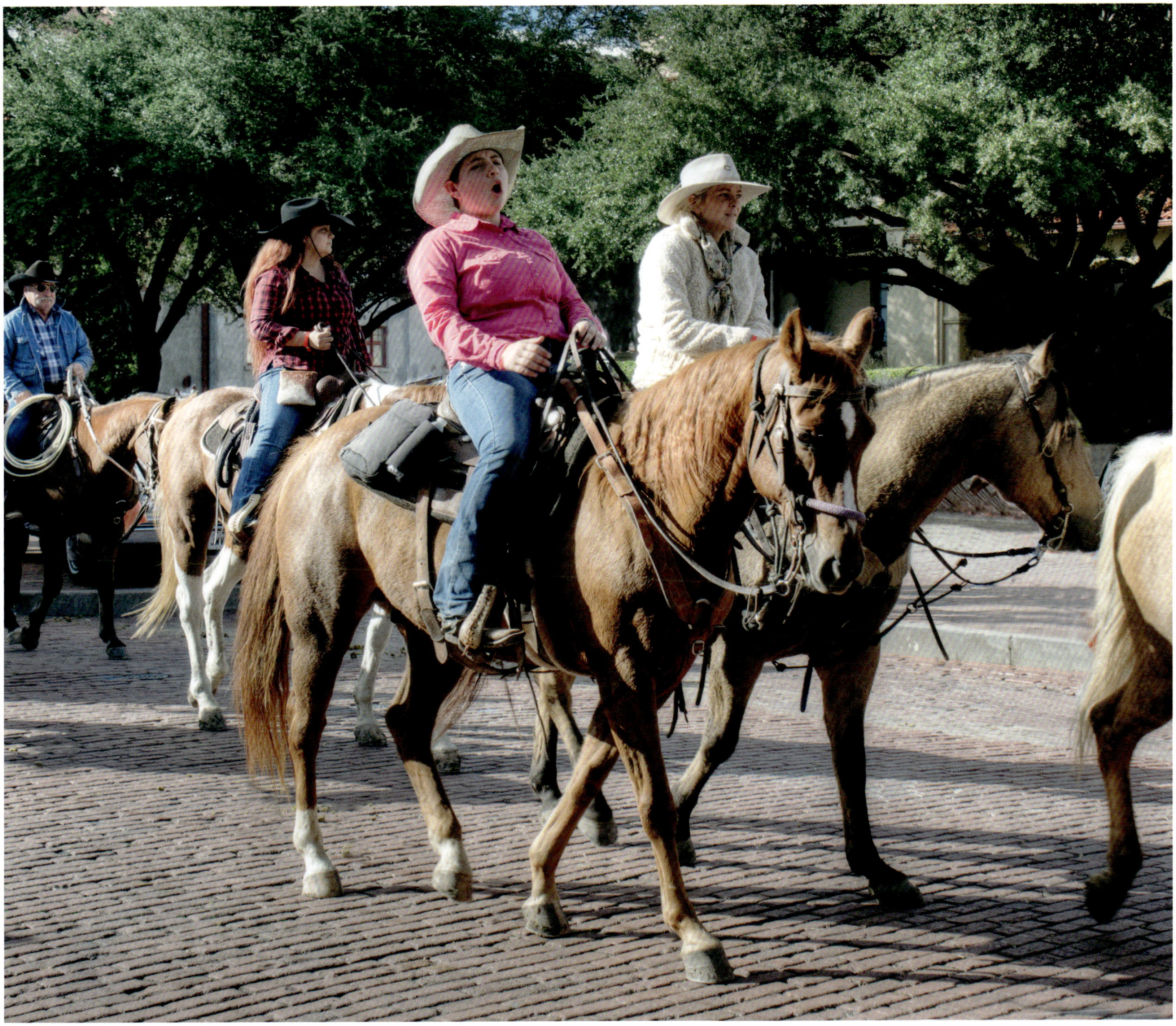

A young cowgirl dressed in a bright pink shirt "whoops" as she rides her horse down East Exchange Avenue. She is having a very good time.

However, the larger markets sent buyers to producers in the country to avoid regulations and did not wait until the livestock arrived at the stockyards. This resulted in the unintended consequences of cheaper prices for the animals for producers, and they became very unhappy. Farm groups then protested against the country auctions and asked for an amendment to the Packers and Stockyards Act to include provisions against "direct marketing." Some farmers liked it, though, because they did not have to pay yardage or commission fees or drive farther from home to the bigger markets. When the court finally ruled that the Packers and Stockyards Act was valid, it required the packers to dispose of their stockyards and other interests before December 31, 1931.

The Fort Worth yards, meanwhile, remained optimistic that its market would grow. Tom Wallace, head sheep buyer for Armour and Company at the time, suggested to C. C. French to build up the sheep market in Fort Worth. The Fort Worth Stock Yards Company continued to do well in the 1920s, and profits soared to 16 percent.

An innovation that helped the local market tremendously was the idea of General Manager A. G. Donovan to add radio coverage for the market report. The Bureau of Agricultural Economics provided a livestock market news service that Fort Worth market analysts bragged about, saying it represented one of the most complete news services in the country. Service began October 1, 1925, in cooperation with Amon Carter's WBAP radio station, with market reports twice a day at 10:00 a.m. and 2:00 p.m. The stockyards company provided a padded, well-equipped booth on the second floor of the Livestock Exchange Building for the broadcasts.

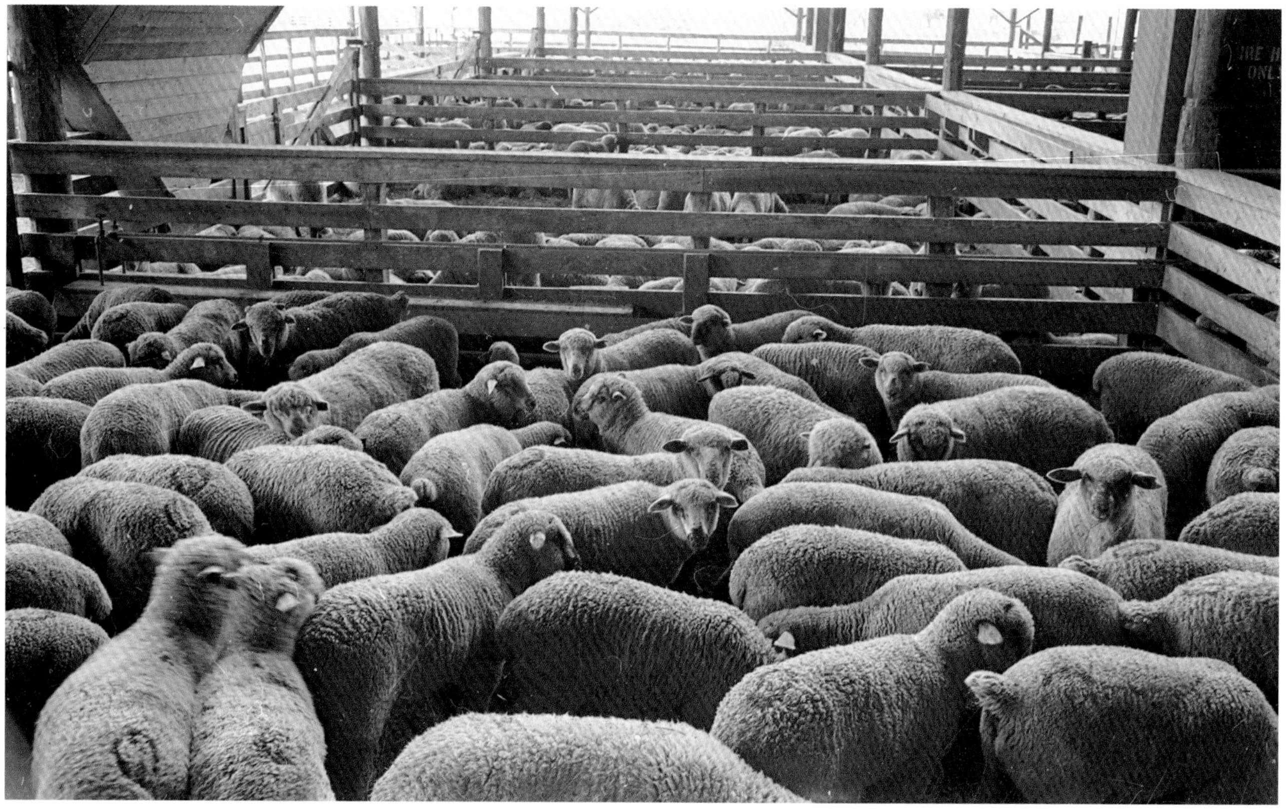

Sheep would become very popular by the 1940s, the yards receiving two million per year. Courtesy of North Fort Worth Historical Society.

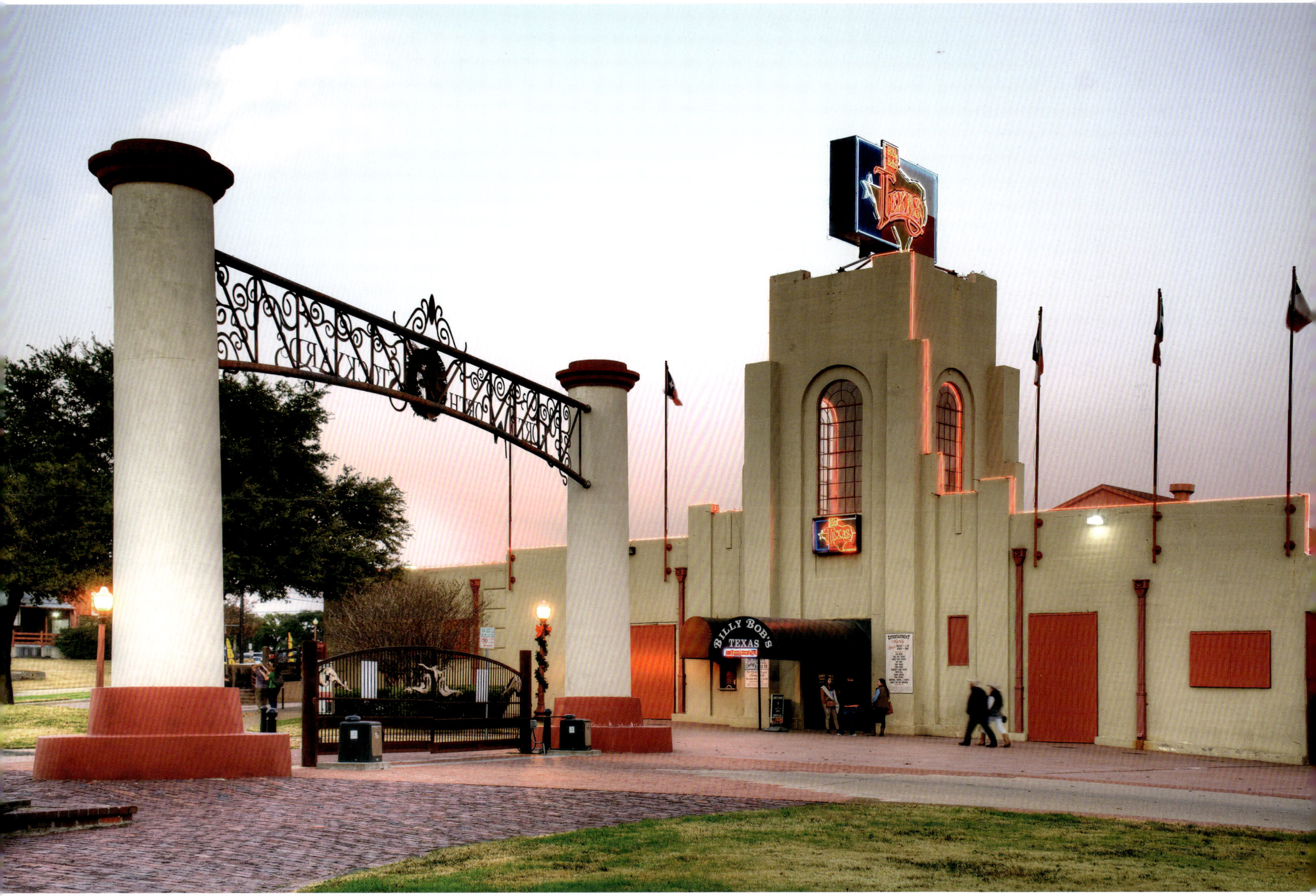

This building was originally constructed in 1910 as an open-air barn for housing cattle. In the 1950s and 1960s, it was used as a department store. Famous Billy Bob's Texas, which opened on April 1, 1981, became one of the premier entertainment clubs in the United States.

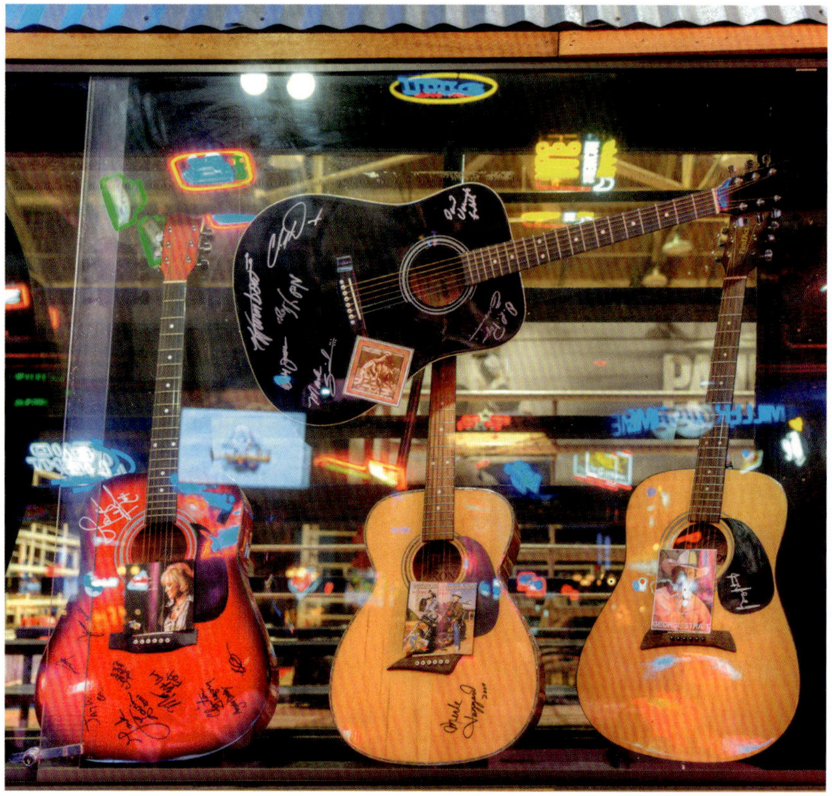

The Guitar Bar at Billy Bob's, the world's largest honky-tonk, has seventy-five guitars autographed by stars who have performed at the club, such as Tanya Tucker, George Strait, and Merle Haggard.

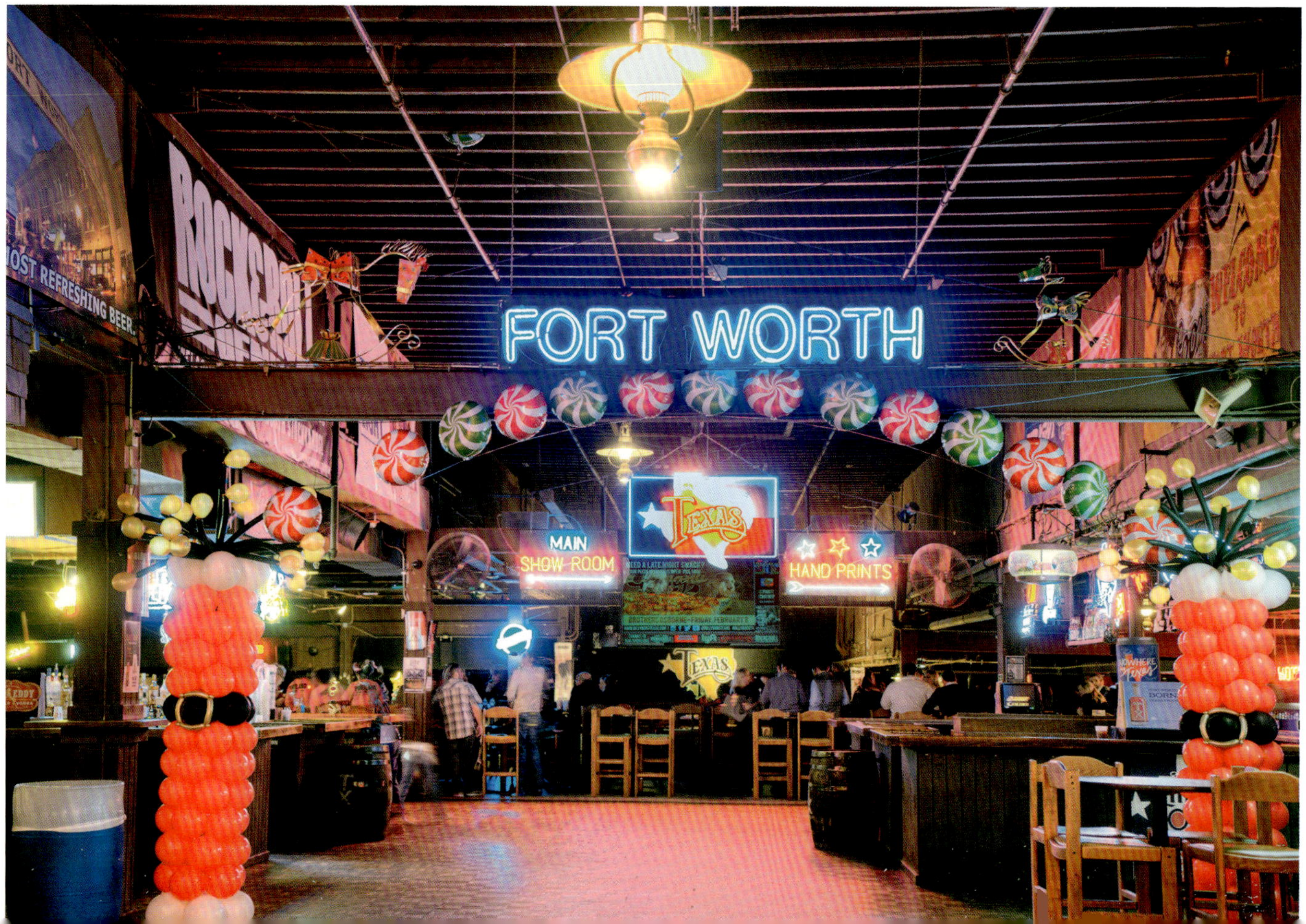

Everywhere one looks inside Billy Bob's is a feast for the senses.

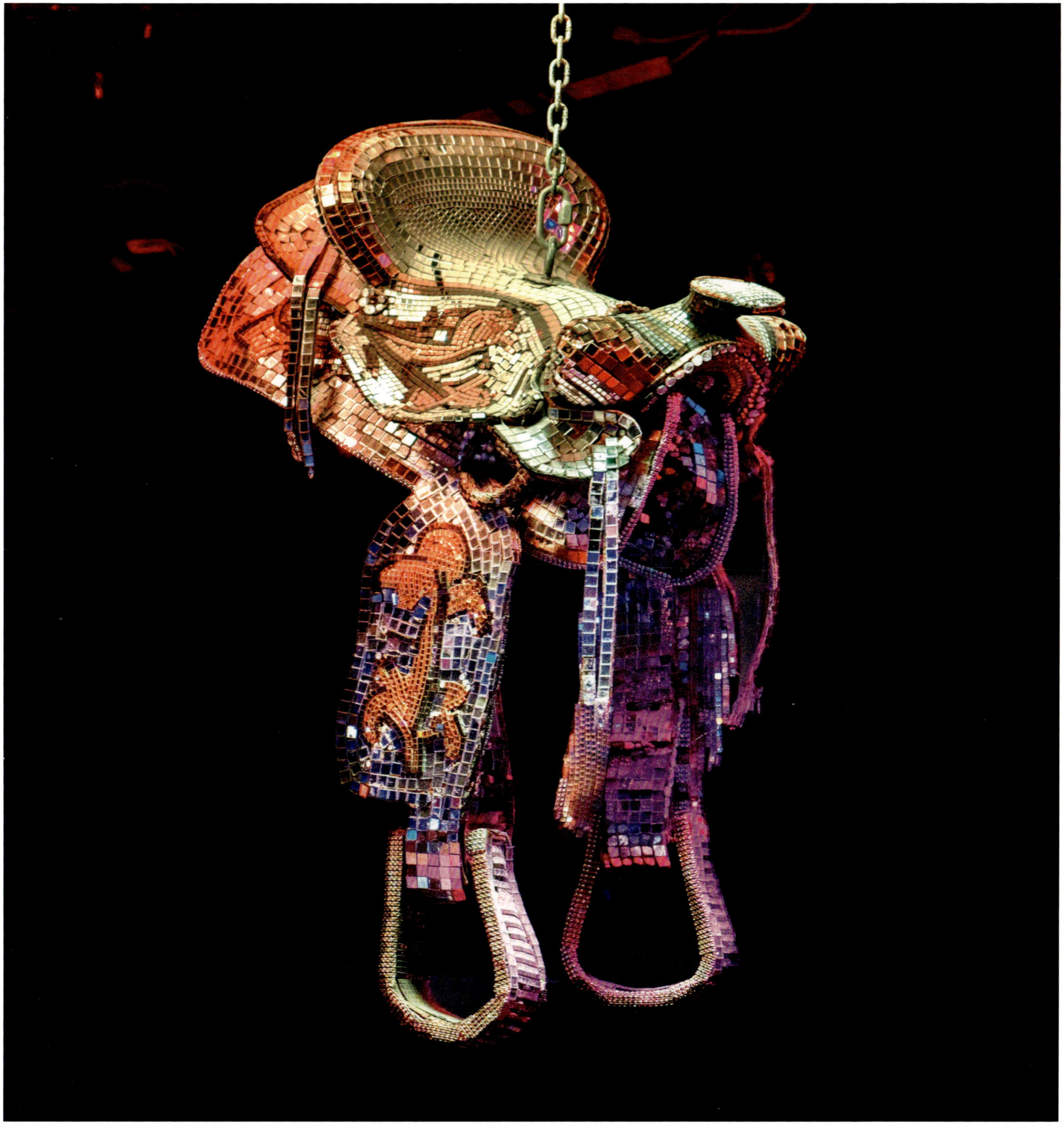

A glittering, colorful, mosaic-encrusted saddle rotates as a mirror ball above the active dance floor at Billy Bob's Texas.

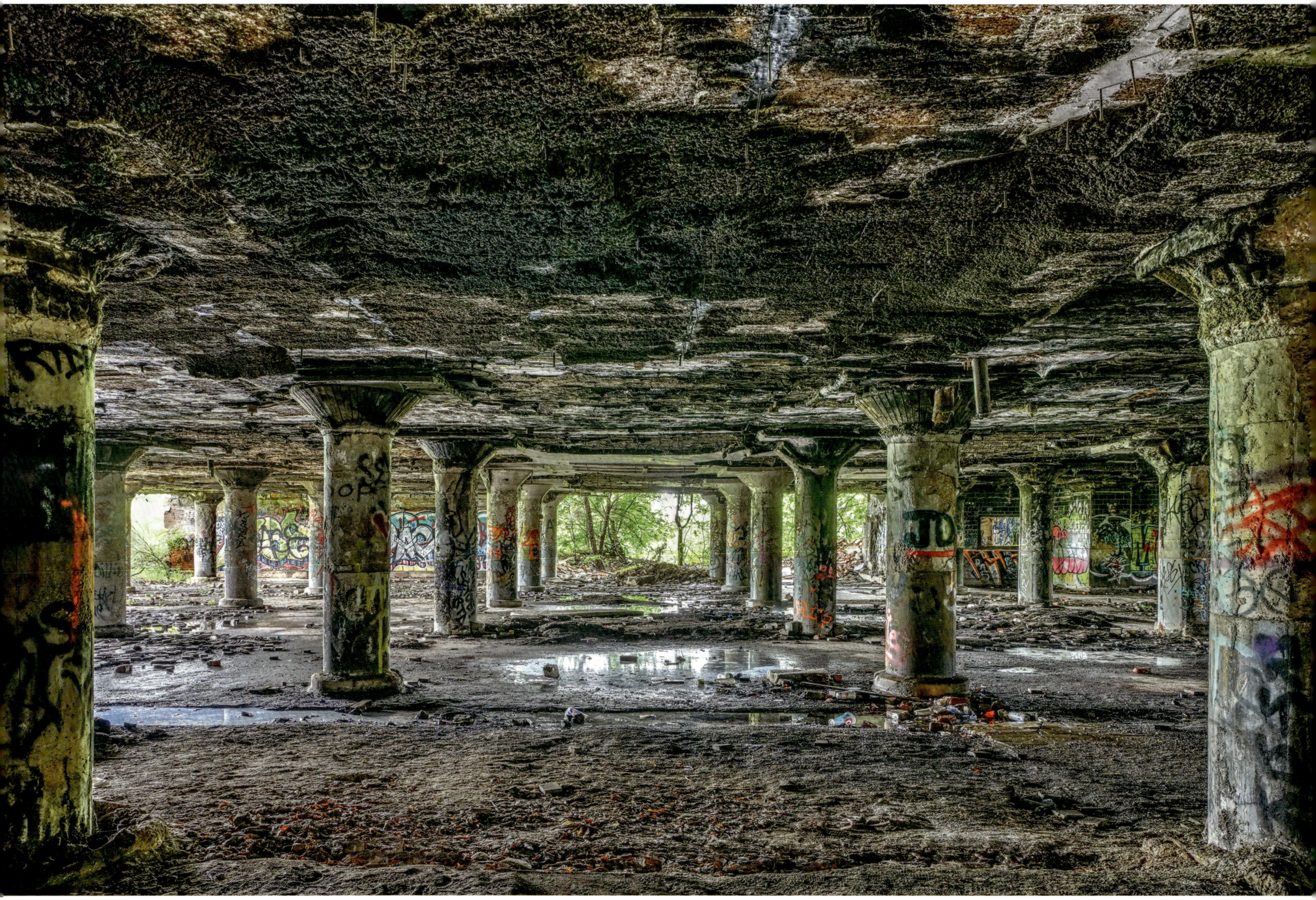

After fires and vandalism, the lower level of the Beef Cooler Building at the Swift meatpacking company in 2016 was returning to nature. Spring rains left pools of growing green algae. This building, among many others, was demolished later that year.

The 1920s ended before the actual implementation of the Packers and Stockyards Act took place, and even before the binding provisions of the packers' consent decree of 1920 changed much in Fort Worth, because the latter agreement remained tied up in court appeals for a decade. Armour and Swift each retained one-third interest in the stockyards company as late as May 1, 1928, although Armour had shifted its stock by that date to a new company created for the purpose, General Stockyards. Correspondence indicates that Swift still owned one-third of the local sewage disposal plant in 1929.

The Big Five became a Big Four again when the Morris company sold its meatpacking operations to Armour, but it did retain its stockyard interests. When the government finally insisted on enforcement of the requirements and the big packers divested themselves of many of their operations, things changed. Armour created General Stockyards and Swift created United Stockyards to hold their stock from several yards in which they held shares. The packers created these separate companies, but the stockholders of the original companies then held stock in the new ones as well. What changed for Fort Worth and the other big markets was a different relationship with their former mentors, the meatpackers Armour and Swift. The stockyards company existed, and struggled before the two big packers took control, and the company continued on after the packers relinquished direct ownership. However, for the stockyards of the country, the loss of a rich benefactor undeniably altered their circumstances.

Because of government regulations, the Fort Worth Stock Yards Company was forced to divest itself of the Fort Worth Belt Railway and the Stockyards National Bank, which merged with the Fort Worth National Bank on October 13, 1934. W. L. Pier, former president of the Stockyards National Bank, became a vice president of the Fort Worth National Bank and later became president of the Fort Worth Stock Yards Company, a position that he held for fifteen years. The Fort Worth Stock Yards and Armour and Company jointly owned a cattle ranch in Reagan County, Texas, that also had to be sold in 1938.

Strict government regulations changed the relationships between the nation's stockyards and the meatpacking companies that they had enjoyed for decades. The Fort Worth Stock Yards and the other major yards found themselves on their own. Both good times and bad would follow.

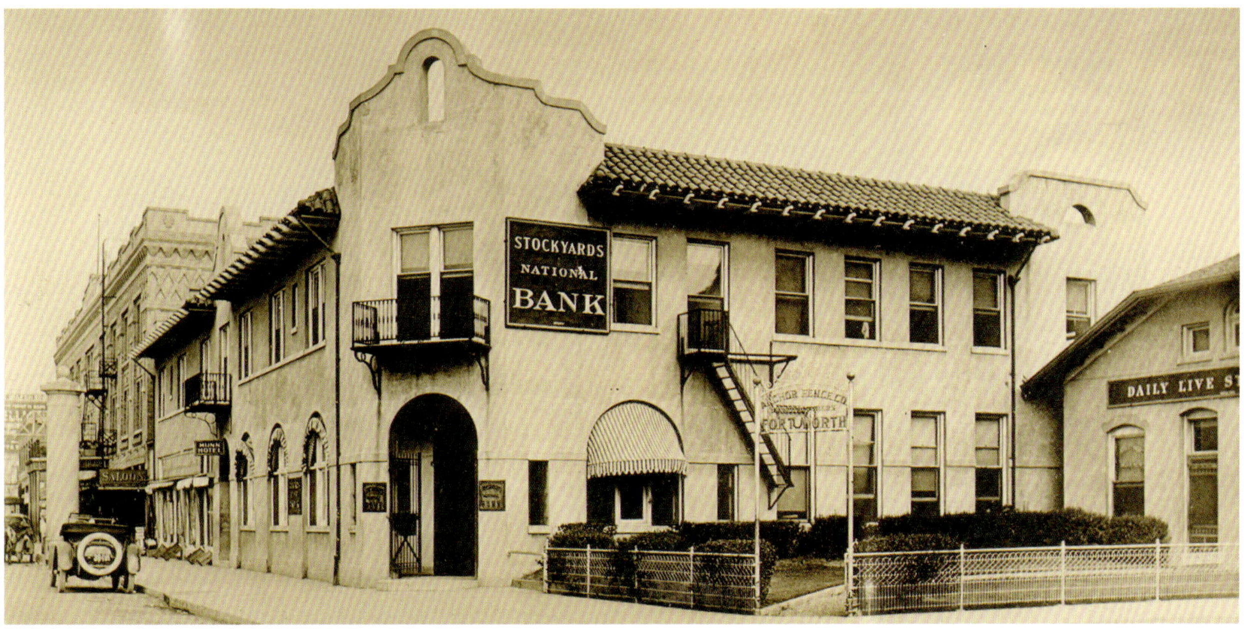

Just to the west of the Cowtown Coliseum on East Exchange Avenue sits the former Stockyards National Bank, which experienced an unusual robbery in 1930. Courtesy of North Fort Worth Historical Society.

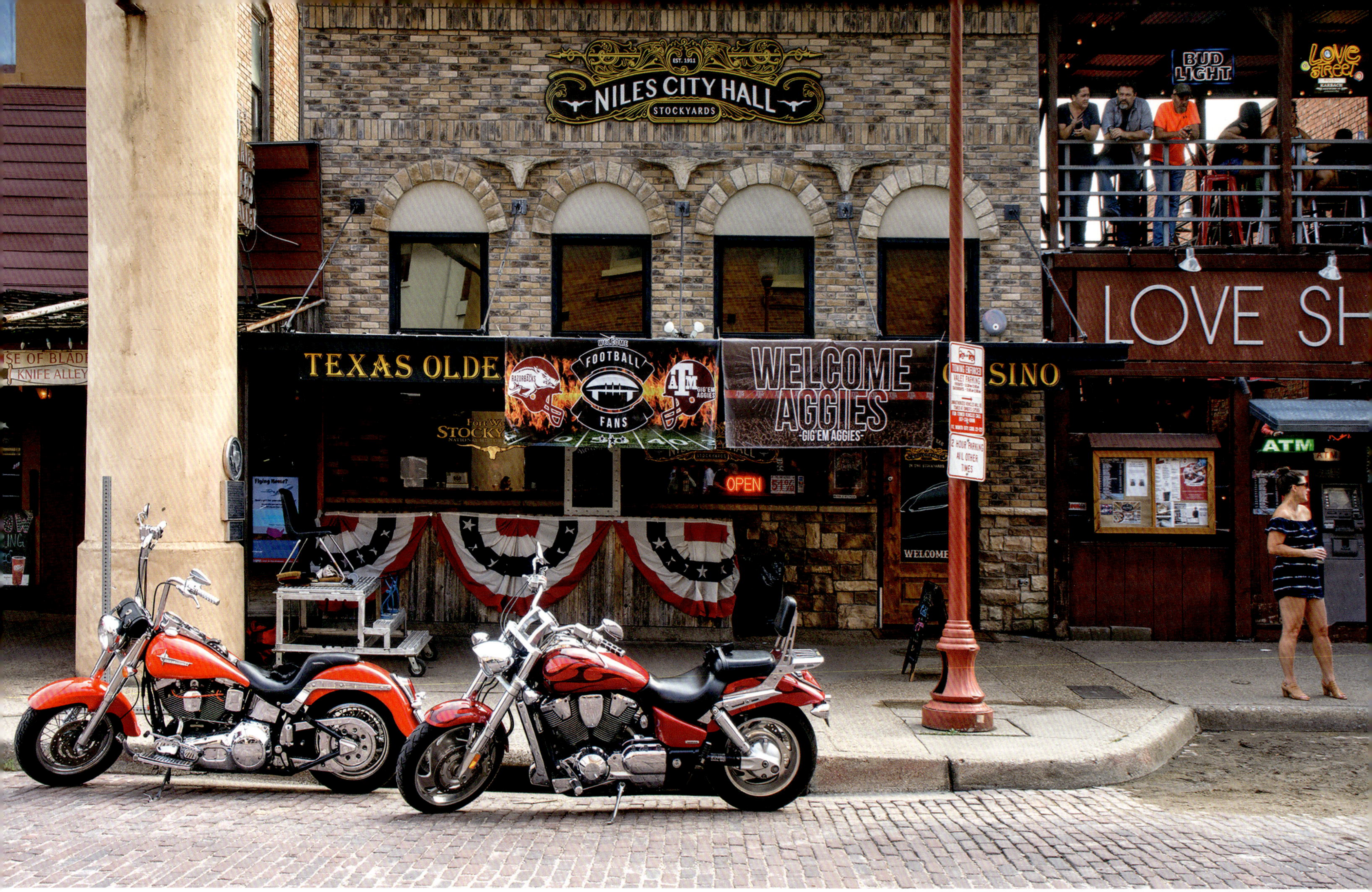

Niles City Hall Saloon, named after the famous Niles City—once considered the richest little town in the world—is now a stockyards speakeasy. A "Welcome Aggies" sign and two motorcycles decorate the facade.

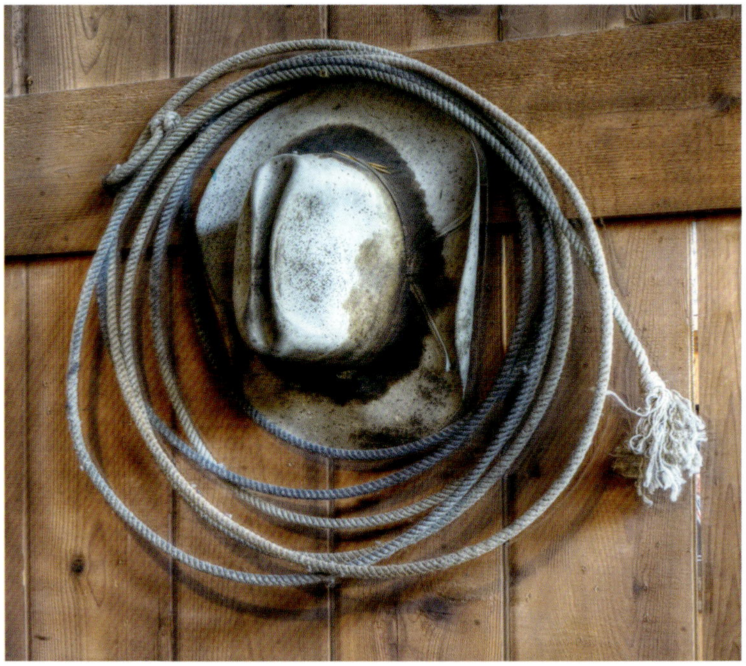

A sweat-stained, well-used hat and lasso display at the Texas Cowboy Hall of Fame captures the essence of a cowboy's hard work.

Longhorns enjoy their much-deserved lunch after their twice-daily walk on East Exchange Avenue. They can be observed by a walkway above these historic cattle pens.

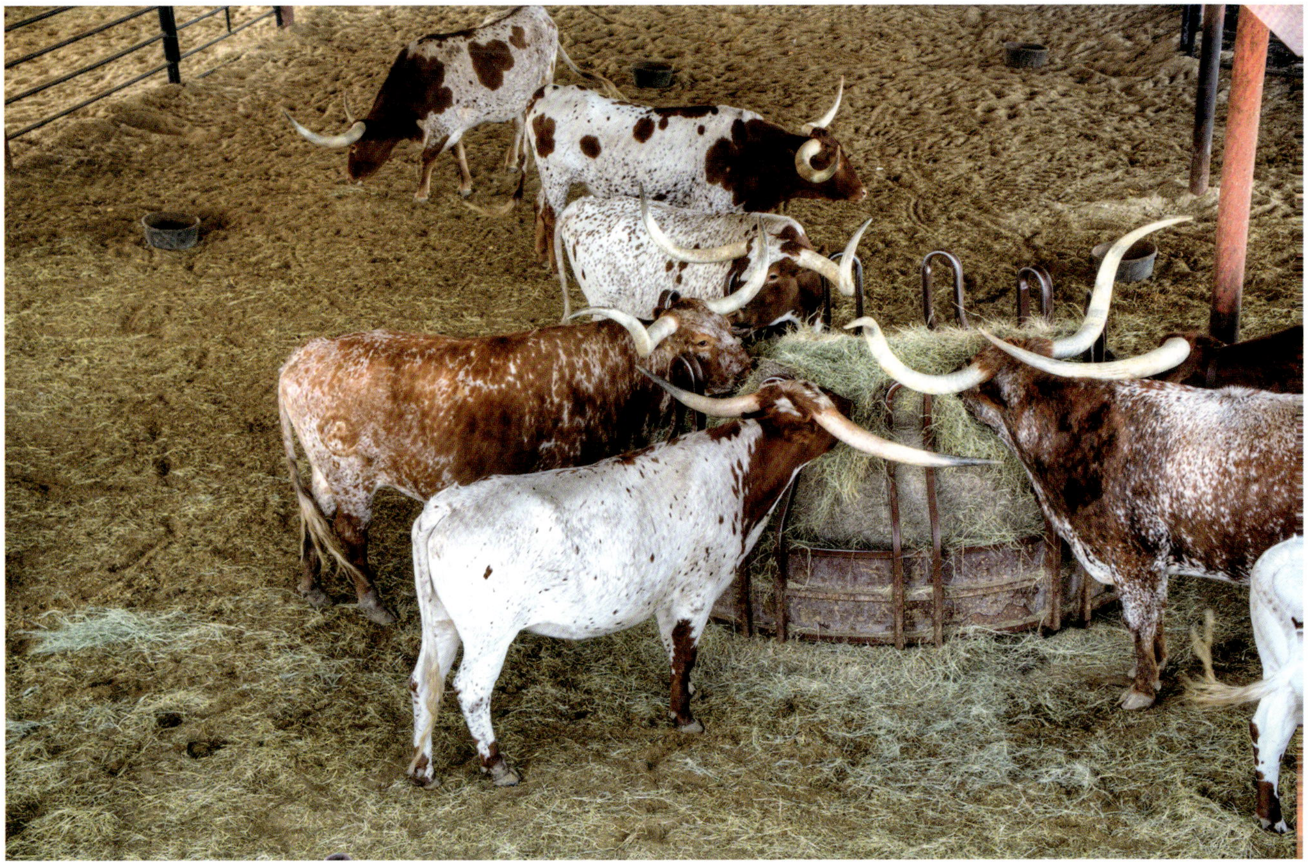

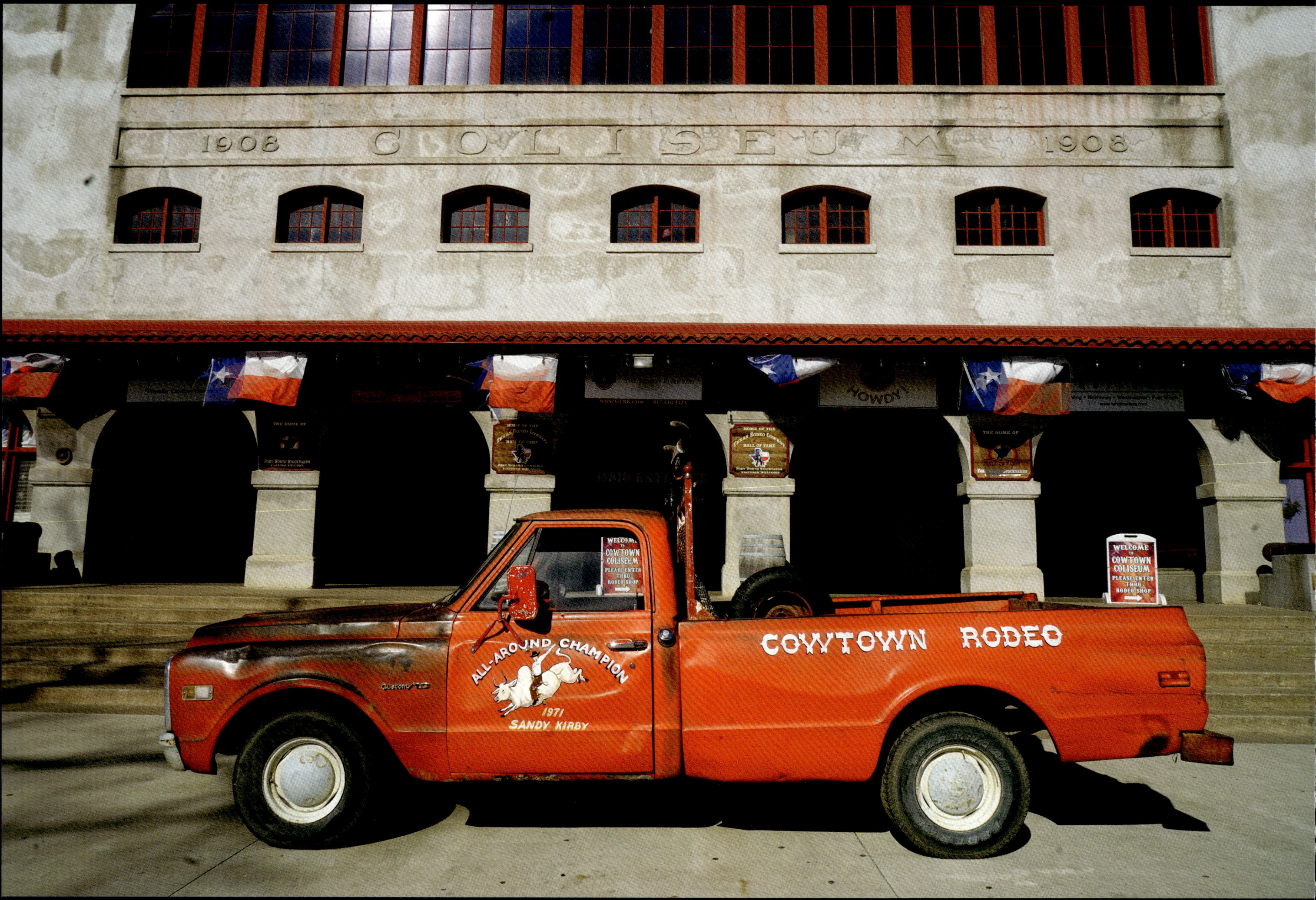

1908 COLISEUM 1908
HOWDY!
WELCOME TO COWTOWN COLISEUM PLEASE ENTER THRU RODEO SHOP
ALL-AROUND CHAMPION
1971
SANDY KIRBY
COWTOWN RODEO

CHAPTER 4

Depression and War

Excitement like an old-time Western bank robbery took place on August 9, 1930, at the bank that the local stockyards at that time still owned. However, the incident featured a modern twist, for instead of a gun, the robber carried a satchel as he approached the desk of the bank president, William L. Pier. The robber told Pier that he carried a bottle of nitroglycerin in his satchel that he could explode if his demand for ten thousand dollars in cash was not met immediately.

Vice President Fred L. Pelton came up to talk to the man as Pier went to the cage and told the tellers to count out the money. With Pelton distracting the robber, Pier look the chance of telephoning the police. He told them not to turn on a siren and to wait until the man left the bank to apprehend him. Unfortunately, the police either assumed that the man already would have left by the time they arrived or Pier's request was not repeated to them. Therefore, when the lawmen opened the door and walked inside, the bank robber, a thirty-year-old deranged man named Nathan Morrow Martin, dropped two ounces of nitroglycerin on the floor.

The explosion killed Martin and Pelton instantly. Debris was scattered throughout the room. Fortunately, only two other persons were injured, but people heard and felt the blast a half mile away. Trees near the building lost leaves, and a shower of glass and other flying objects struck people outside the bank, located just west of the coliseum on Exchange Avenue. The explosion caused three thousand dollars' worth of damage. Contractors worked around the clock over the weekend to replaster the building, replace window panes, and clean up the debris. The bank opened as usual at 9:00 a.m. on Monday morning.

The appearance of this hardworking pickup, sitting outside the coliseum, likely reflects the life of the rodeo cowboy commemorated on the driver's door.

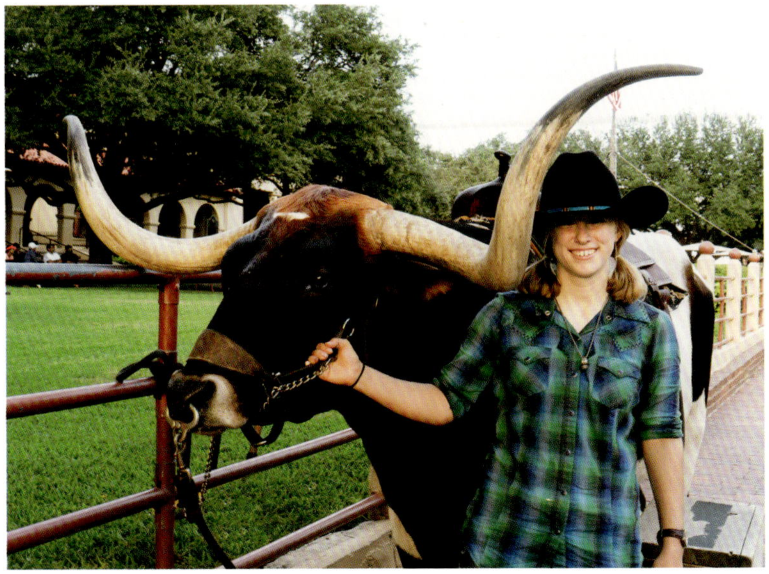

A young woman poses with a saddled Longhorn. Visitors can sit atop the Longhorn for a small fee. Young and old are thrilled as they straddle this up to twenty-two-hundred-pound steer for a photo opportunity.

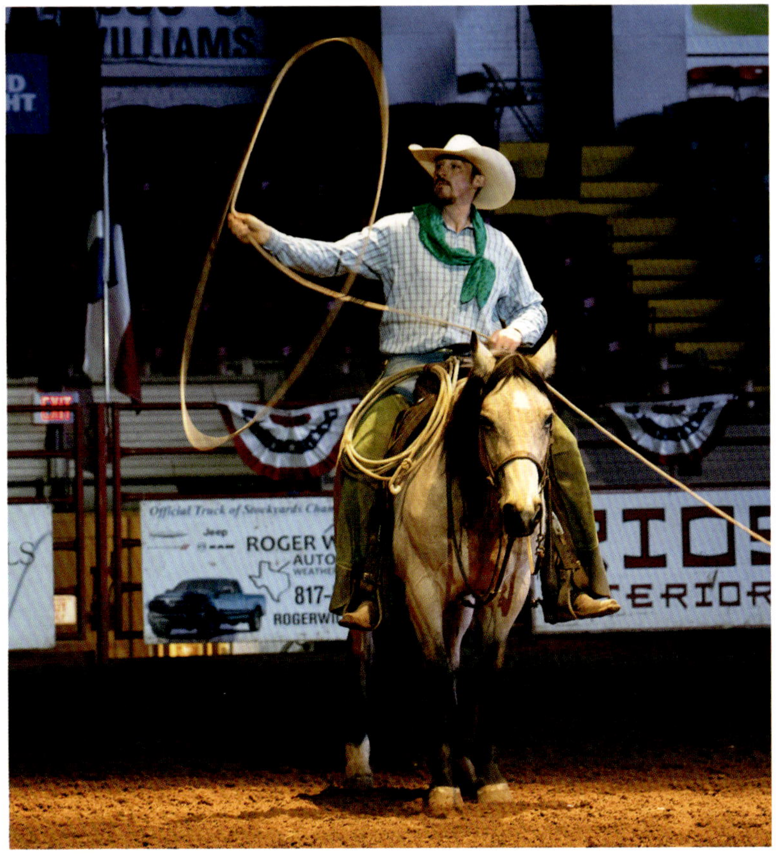

Pawnee Bill's Wild West Show at the famous Cowboy Coliseum features a lasso artist on his well-trained horse.

The Depression decade that followed the dramatic event experienced erratic market receipts, lower prices, and federal programs designed to stabilize the market. Stockyard owners saw profits drop, not just because of the business decline but also because of trucks bringing in more livestock and the expansion of feedlots that began to break the power of the meat trust. Also, packers finally finished their mandated task to sell their stockyards, railroads, banks, and other businesses. However, thanks to the livestock market in Fort Worth, employment citywide fared better than in many other places.

In 1930 the capacity of the yards reached thirty-seven thousand cattle, twenty thousand hogs, twenty thousand sheep, and five thousand horses and mules. Thirty-nine commission companies existed to handle the stock. Daily receipts fluctuated wildly, however, and totals began to decline. Farmers and ranchers started feeding and fattening their own livestock as a way to dispose of surplus grain. Some cattlemen who began losing money on their herds decided to raise sheep instead, which explains the much higher sheep receipts at Fort Worth a decade later.

Because of decreased cattle receipts and falling prices, the Fort Worth Stock Yards Company needed to institute certain economies. The market newspaper, the *Weekly Live Stock Reporter*, that the stockyard once owned and later subsidized, lost its support. The company reduced payroll expenses by 10 percent. Yard superintendent Harry "Cap" Henderson worked his men only on alternate days to keep more men on the payroll. He told them he wanted everyone to be able to eat.

The company maintained an intense advertising campaign during the Depression years to try to increase receipts at the yards. It joined with Armour and Swift

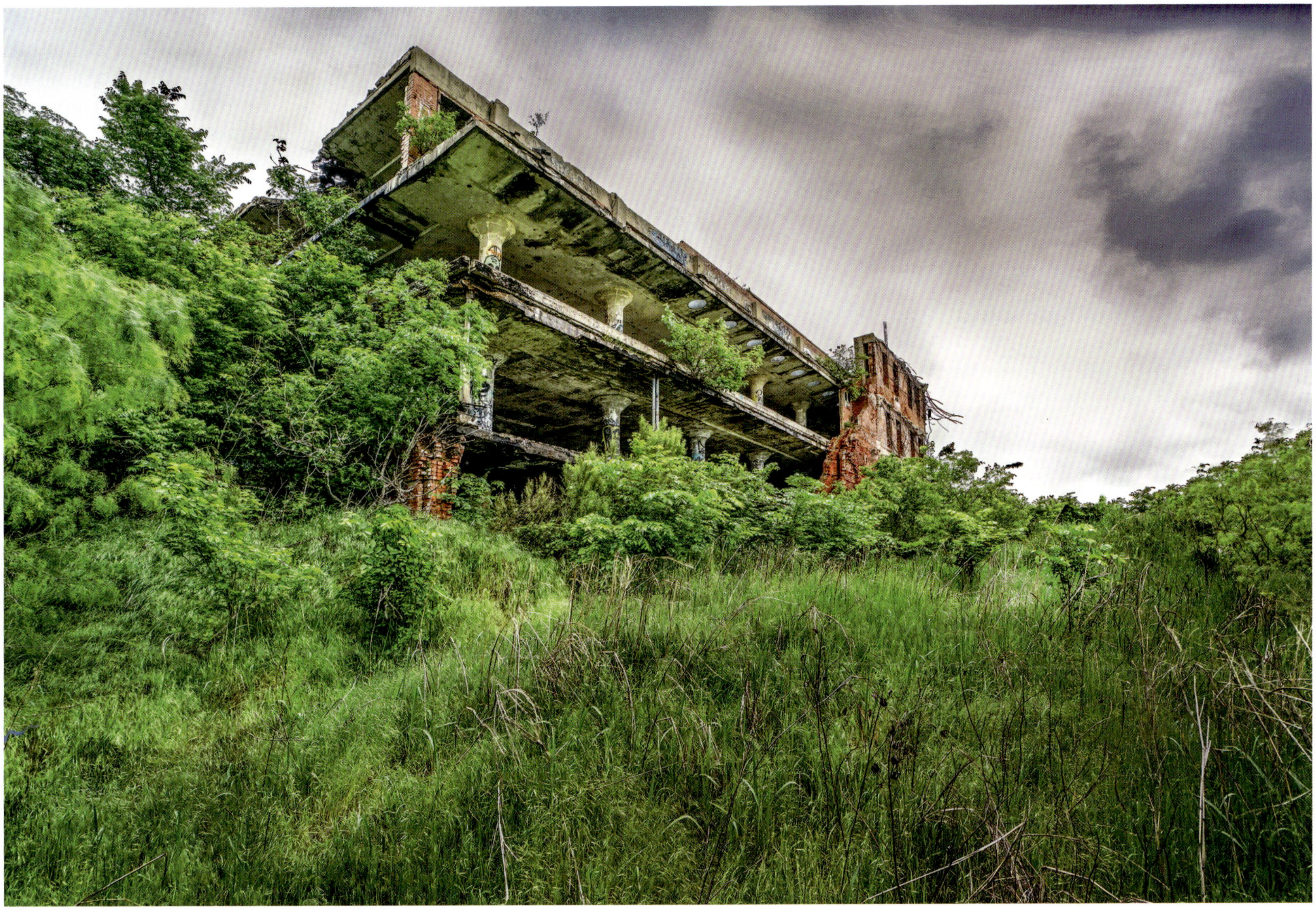

The five-story Swift Cooler Building, constructed in 1949 with some walls dating back to 1902, experienced many fires after 1971 when the plant was abandoned. This building was demolished in July 2016.

as each contributed five hundred dollars to the West Texas Chamber of Commerce for its promotion of the Fort Worth market in its member towns. To try to solve common problems, the nation's stockyards in 1933 created the American Stock Yards Association, and the Fort Worth yards became a member.

Federal action concerning the nation's agricultural problems arrived with President Franklin D. Roosevelt's New Deal, mainly the Agricultural Adjustment Act (AAA). A hog-reduction program and the drought-inspired cattle-purchase plan affected the local yards more than anything else. Texans at first expressed their aversion to federal assistance and even elected officials such as Senator Morris Sheppard and Governor Ross Sterling, who agreed that the New Deal would destroy initiative, states' rights, and the American way. However, when the

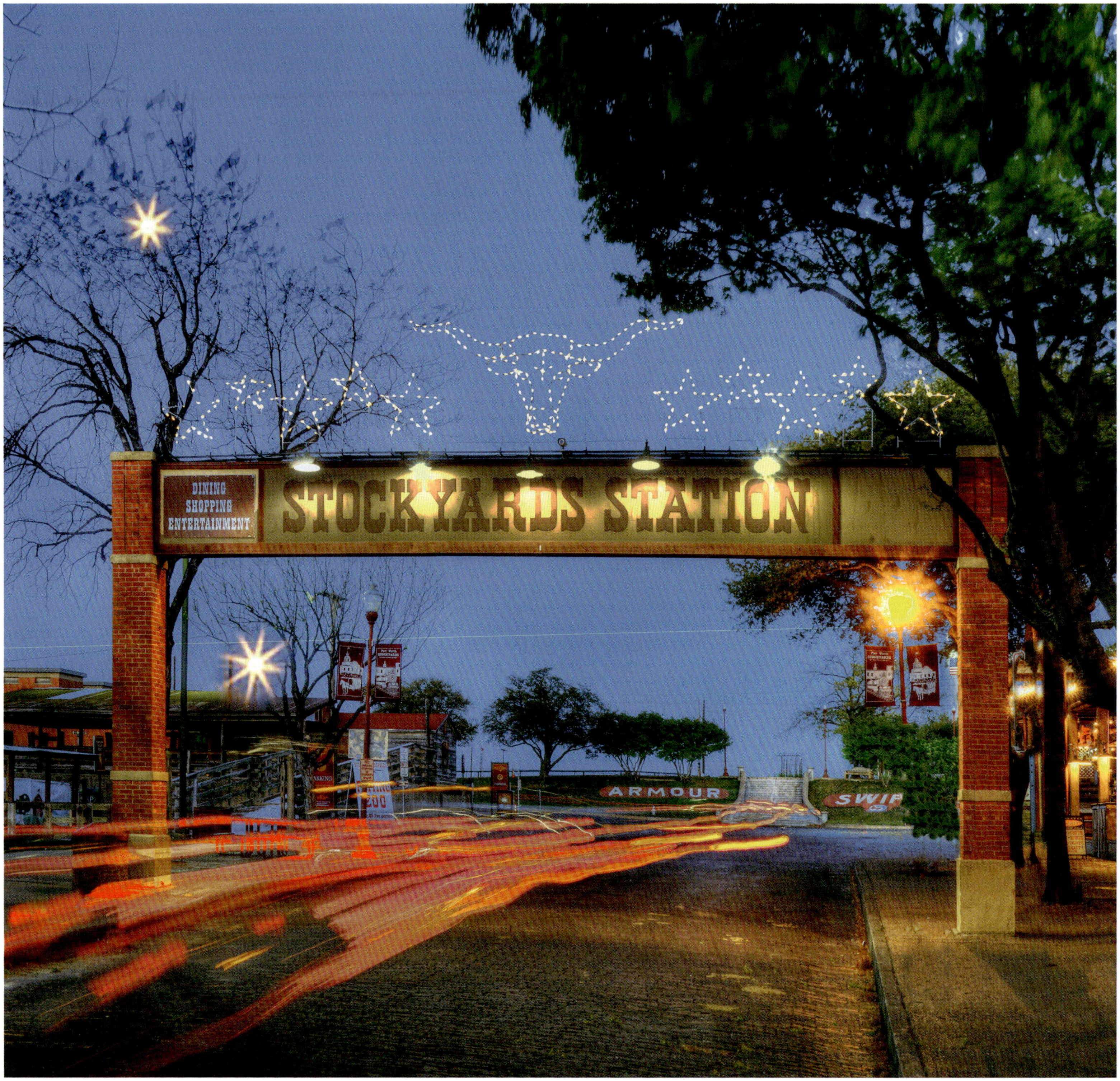

This beautifully lit arch, with an image of a Longhorn among Texas stars across the top, announces one's departure from the main stockyards complex. Car brake lights decorate the evening light in this time-exposure photograph.

situation reached serious proportions, many abandoned their philosophy "temporarily" and accepted assistance.

As the hog-reduction program began, the AAA planned to buy four million pigs and one million sows within six weeks beginning August 23, 1933. A processing tax on hogs and pork would be imposed on all meatpackers to pay for the program. The Agriculture Department withheld the meat from entering regular market channels to keep it from affecting prices. During the emergency six-week campaign, the government actually purchased nearly 6.5 million pigs and sows. The plan cost $33 million—$30.5 million for the animals and $2.5 million for processing. Nonetheless, the purchasing plan appeared to have little if any effect on hog prices during the last half of 1933. The government, however, continued purchases into 1935.

One story surfaced in the local market newspaper of a hog-reduction program gone awry. W. J. Calhoun of Sherman agreed to get rid of two of the three sows he owned, so he signed up in the government hog-reduction campaign in the spring of 1934. The third sow he kept, though, did the duty of three, for "she littered once, and thirteen piglets blessed the home pen. She littered twice and septuplets arrived. She littered thrice, and eighteen were added to the family." The reporter headed his story with the rhyme:

> This little pig went to market
> This little pig went too
> This little pig stayed at home in the pen and found
> she had plenty to do.

New canning plants opened on the North Side to take care of government-purchased meats. It provided jobs to destitute individuals as well as food to be given to the needy. A Texas Relief Commission canning plant opened December 18, 1933, and hired 572 workers. The plant operated four shifts of six hours each. Rules required that workers come from the city's relief rolls, and they earned forty cents an hour. During at least part of the time, the building on Decatur Avenue that originally served as the city hall for Niles City became a canning plant. While funds to purchase cattle were omitted from the government purchase program at first, an appropriation act in June 1934 provided the money. Government agents made the purchases in the field, not in stockyards. Only poorer cattle were to be slaughtered and the canned beef given to the needy, but some complaints surfaced that sometime better grades were being killed. The Texas Relief Commission, which headed the canning and distributing, gave six cans of beef consisting of one and one-fourth pounds of meat per can to a family of five each month. Nineteen canning plants, including those in Fort Worth, existed throughout Texas. The major intention was to provide work for the unemployed. Because of inexperienced workers, a poor quality of meat resulted, with bone and hide frequently in the can.

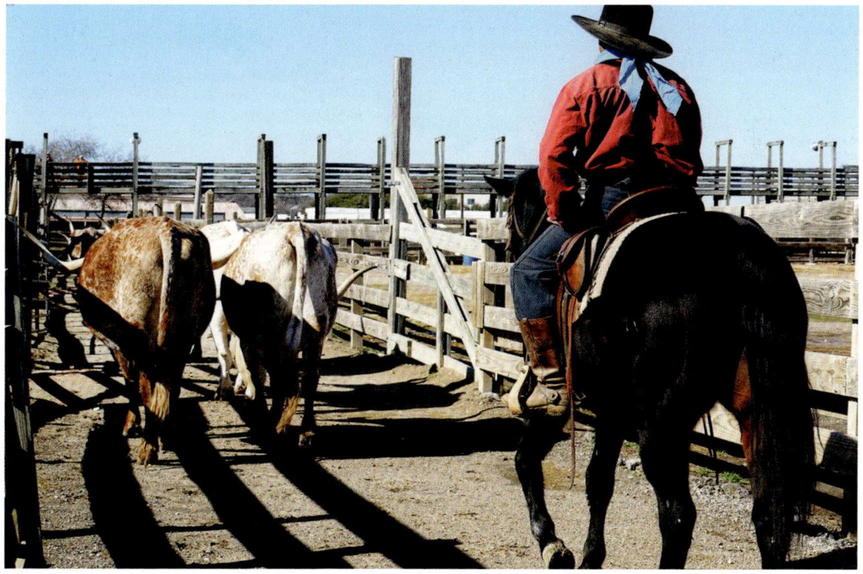

Drovers dress in period clothing, including colorful bandanas. This drover follows the herd as they head toward their dinner feeding for the day.

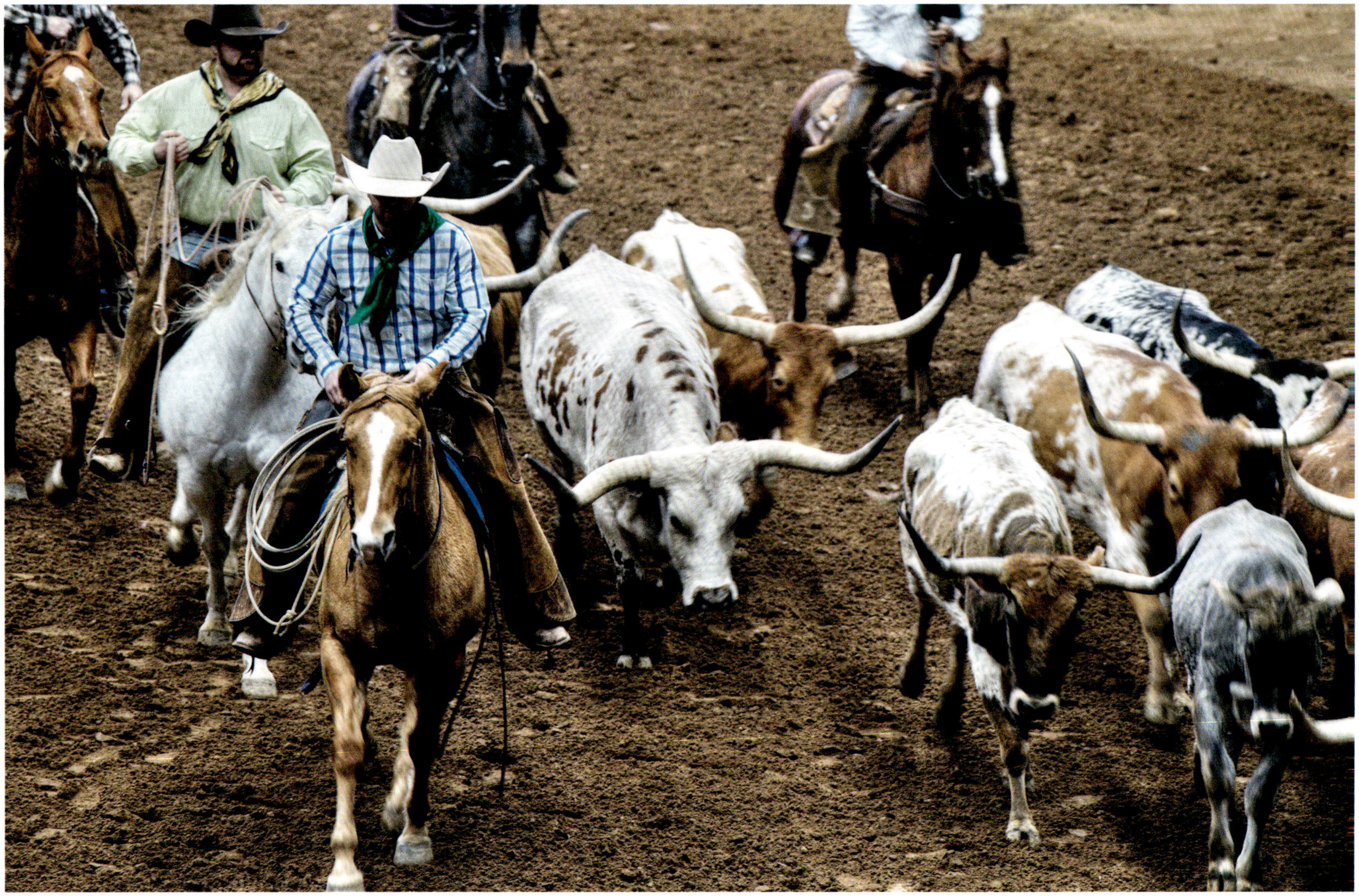

Herders urge a group of Longhorn cattle back to their pens after performing at the weekly Championship Rodeo.

The government purchased cattle in 233 of the 254 counties in Texas, including Tarrant, where the Fort Worth Stock Yards was located. Many Texas farmers refused to cooperate in the program and ridiculed their neighbors who did. One of them, the author's grandfather, protested, "I worked hard to take care of my animals and feed them, and I don't plan to give them over to Uncle Sam to kill." The Swenson brothers at Stamford also refused to let their cattle be killed. Instead, they rounded their surplus animals up and shipped them to market, presumably Fort Worth, selling them at six dollars per head, half the price being paid by the government. Stories are told of strong men weeping as they watched the cattle condemned under the program being shot. Other cattlemen cooperated, however, and seemed grateful to Uncle Sam.

Cattle indeed sold cheaply on the Fort Worth market. Reporter Ted Gouldy remembered when a load of cattle brought only enough money to pay for train freight, yardage fees, and the commission, with not even enough money left to pay for the hay they ate, much less to offer a profit to the owners. The stockyards company tried to collect money due for the hay, though. One story that made the rounds at terminal markets such as Fort Worth represented a recurring experience. There was a shipper whose animals did not bring enough to pay the freight or stockyards charges. When informed he owed more money—so the Fort Worth story goes—the West Texas goat raiser wrote back: "I don't have any money, but I can send you more goats."

Prices remained so low that if a cow intended for slaughter gave birth to a calf while in the stockyards, Armour or Swift could find no market for the calf, even after letting it nurse its mother for a couple of weeks at the yards. Someone could take the calf as a free gift, put feed in it until it weighed two or three hundred pounds, and still not be able to sell it for more than a dollar, not nearly enough to pay for all the feed it ate.

By mid-decade rising cattle prices brightened the economic scene for Texas cattle producers, leading most to refuse any more government assistance. Of the 8.3 million head purchased, the government bought nearly 25 percent in Texas and over 20 percent in the Dakotas. They condemned an overall 18 percent nationwide, but in Texas the proportion reached 34 percent. The program reduced the number of beef cattle by 17 percent, which not only improved the market but brought a better balance between feed and cattle. By 1935 herds began to improve. On a typical day cattle came from Arkansas, Louisiana, Oklahoma, and at least 42 percent of the 254 Texas counties. In May 1937, for the first time in history, total receipts in Fort Worth tallied the largest in the nation, exceeding even those of Chicago and Kansas City. The year 1937 produced the largest receipts since 1917, for over three million head of all types of livestock arrived, with more than 70 percent brought in by truck. By March 24, 1938,

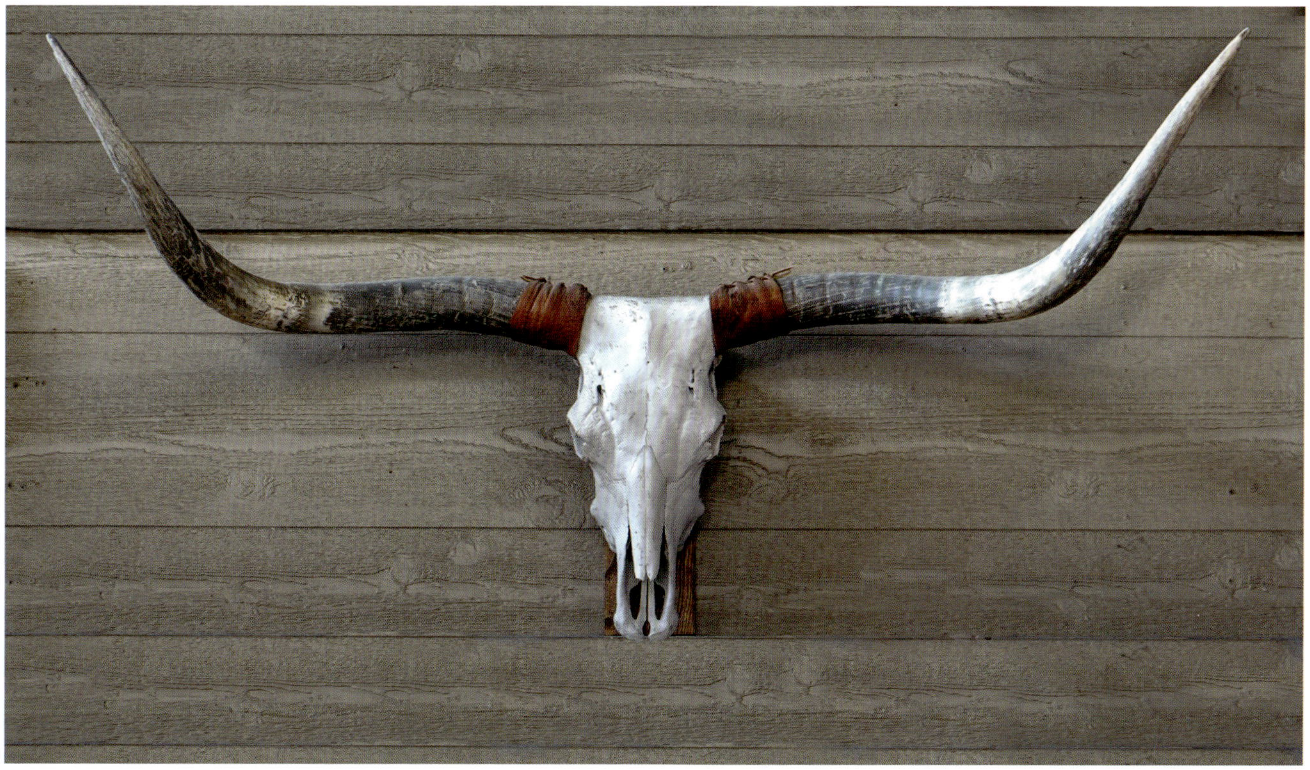

An iconic Longhorn skull decorates an exterior wall in the business district where visitors can purchase Western clothing and gifts and refuel at Western-style restaurants.

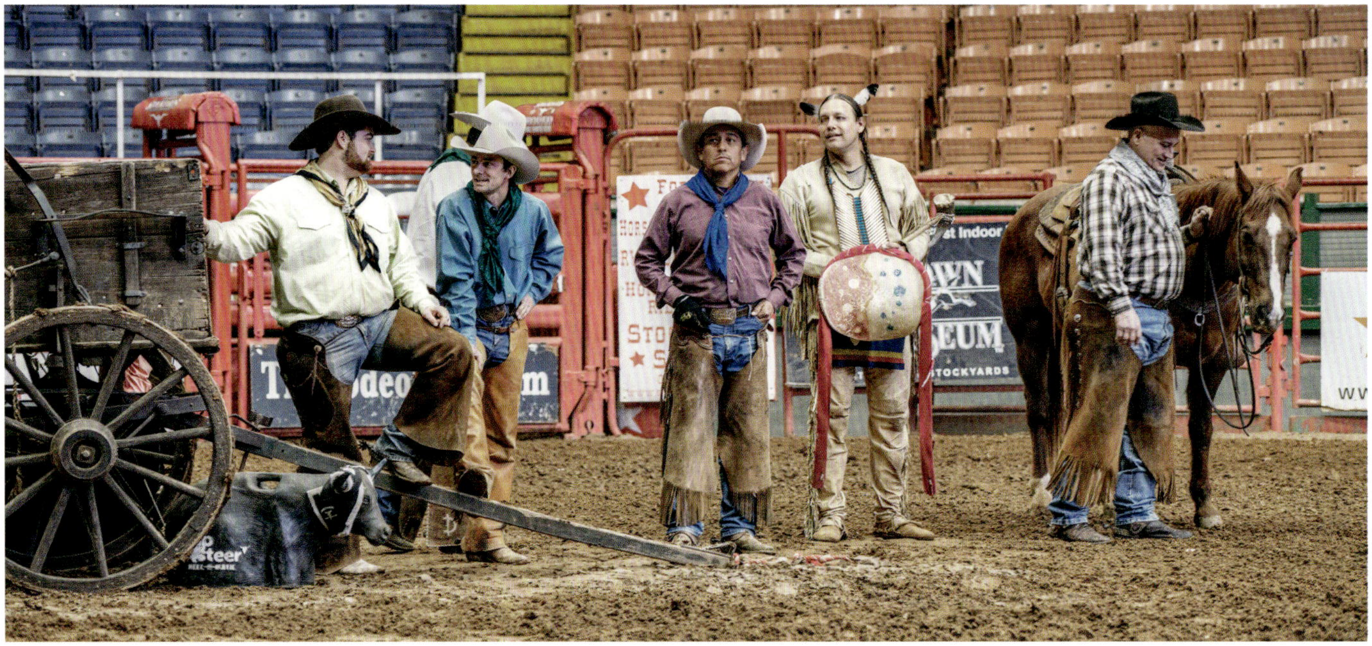

The revival of the original Pawnee Bill's Wild West Show features trick roping, trick shooting, trick riding, cowboy songs, live buffalo and Texas Longhorn cattle, and an entertaining reenactment. Historical figures such as Pawnee Bill come to life and transport the spectator back in time.

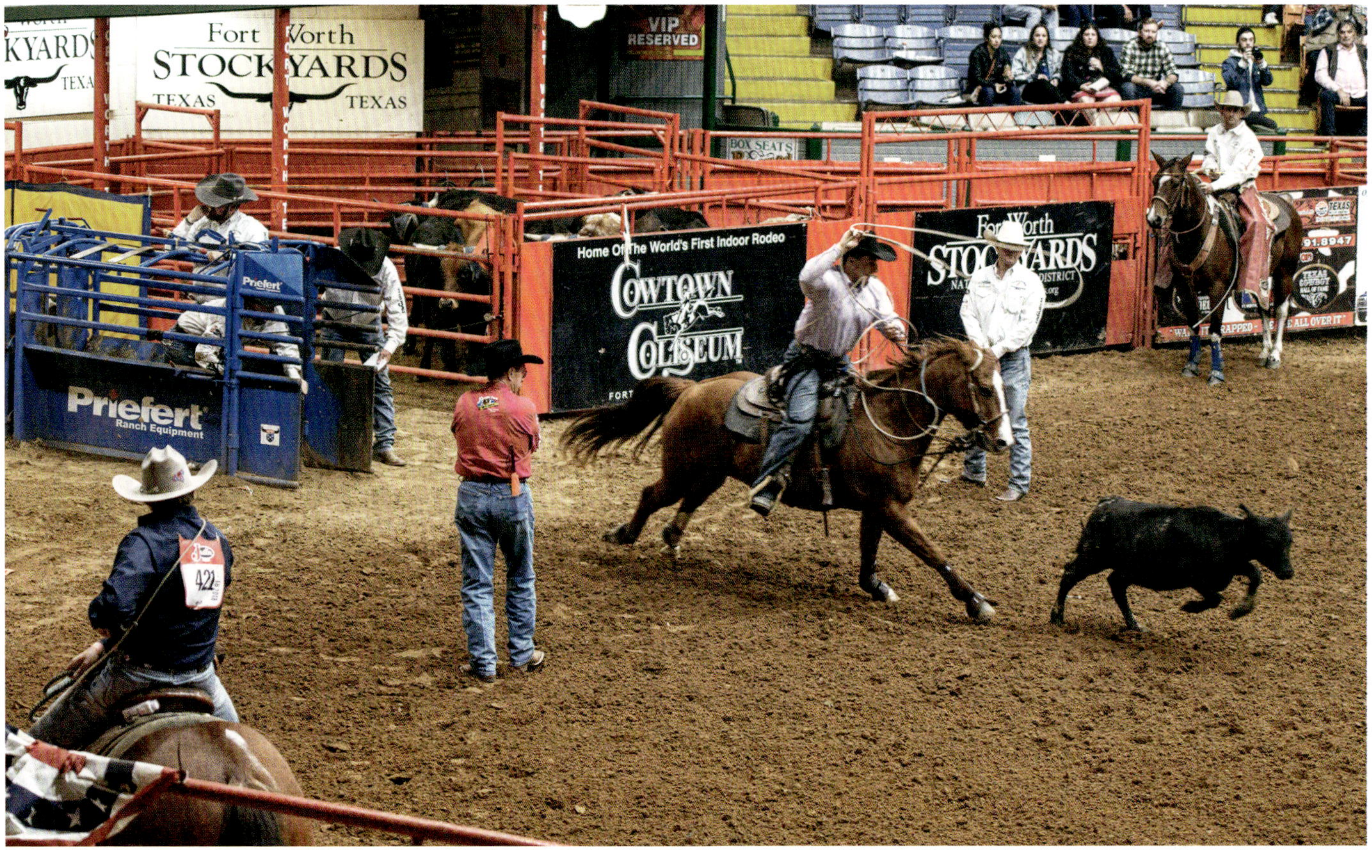

A mounted calf roper contestant throws his lasso toward a calf as they both burst out of chutes at the world's first indoor rodeo and only year-round rodeo in the world. The rodeo maintains a strong commitment to visitors looking for an authentic Western cowboy experience.

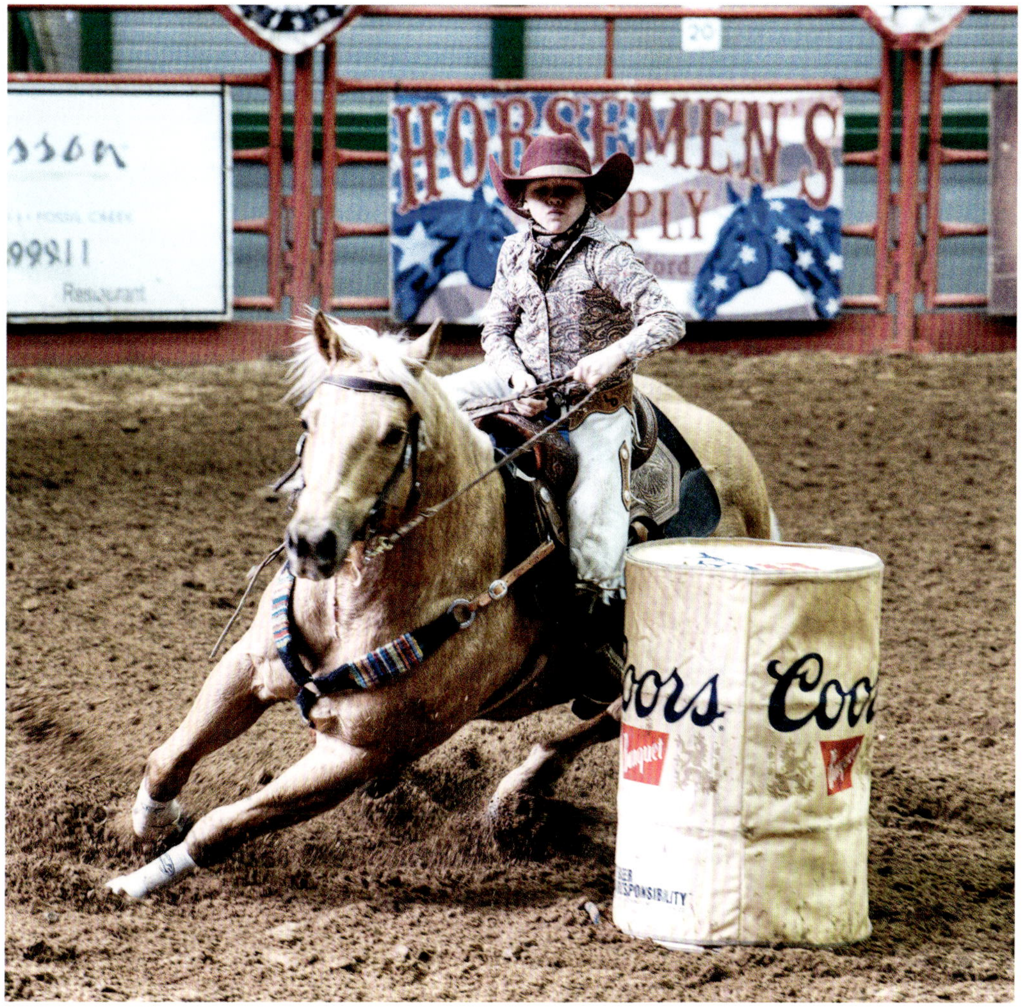

A young contestant guides her well-trained horse at the barrel-racing event at the Fort Worth Cowtown Coliseum.

forty-two commission companies operated in the Fort Worth market. Producers selling to the local market earned more than ninety million dollars for their animals.

Although many businesses declared bankruptcy during the Depression, the Fort Worth Stock Yards Company paid dividends during the entire decade. Sometimes they were small ones. During at least part of the Depression stockyard workers earned from thirty to thirty-six cents an hour. In August 1939 workers from the new Congress of Industrial Organizations staged a four-day strike and obtained vacations and as much as a ten-cent pay hike for the workers. During the last half of the 1930s the stockyards company employed two hundred employees to unload animals. Optimism gradually returned to Fort Worth by the close of the decade. Publicity about the city called the 253-acre stockyards north of town the third largest in the nation.

During the Depression decade the Southwestern Exposition and Fat Stock Show continued annually in the coliseum and exhibit building at the stockyards despite financial setbacks. In 1932 officials broadcast a performance of the rodeo in its entirety over Amon Carter's WBAP radio station. It became the first such broadcast anywhere in the country. In 1935 and for several years thereafter promoters held the World Championship Rodeo in Fort Worth in March as part of the annual stock show events. Cowboys competed for world titles.

During the Depression years, Fort Worth also began planning its official centennial celebration, honoring the one-hundredth anniversary of the state of Texas (1836–1936). It learned that cities could apply to the state for money, so it petitioned for funds to construct a "gigantic new plant" to house the annual stock show west of the city near Camp Bowie Boulevard. North Side residents opposed the idea because they did not want to lose the show from their stockyards area. Bonds had to be approved, so the city submitted its plans to the Public Works Administration in Washington. The story goes that Amon Carter twisted a few arms in the nation's capital, including that of President Franklin D. Roosevelt, for Fort Worth to get the money for the project. Some officials called it "Amon's Cowshed." However, Carter insisted that the complex, consisting of a coliseum and auditorium and tower, be named as a memorial for his good friend Will Rogers, who had died recently in a plane crash.

The Fort Worth Stock Yards Company gradually began to change the spelling of its name in the late 1930s or early 1940s, making "Stockyards" one word instead of two. For the sake of consistency, the one-word spelling will be used from this point on; however, the company itself, and especially the commission companies and others, never maintained such uniformity.

The decade of the 1940s came in with hopes for a busy future, which did occur, but only because of wartime-loaded pens, loss of many workers to the war effort

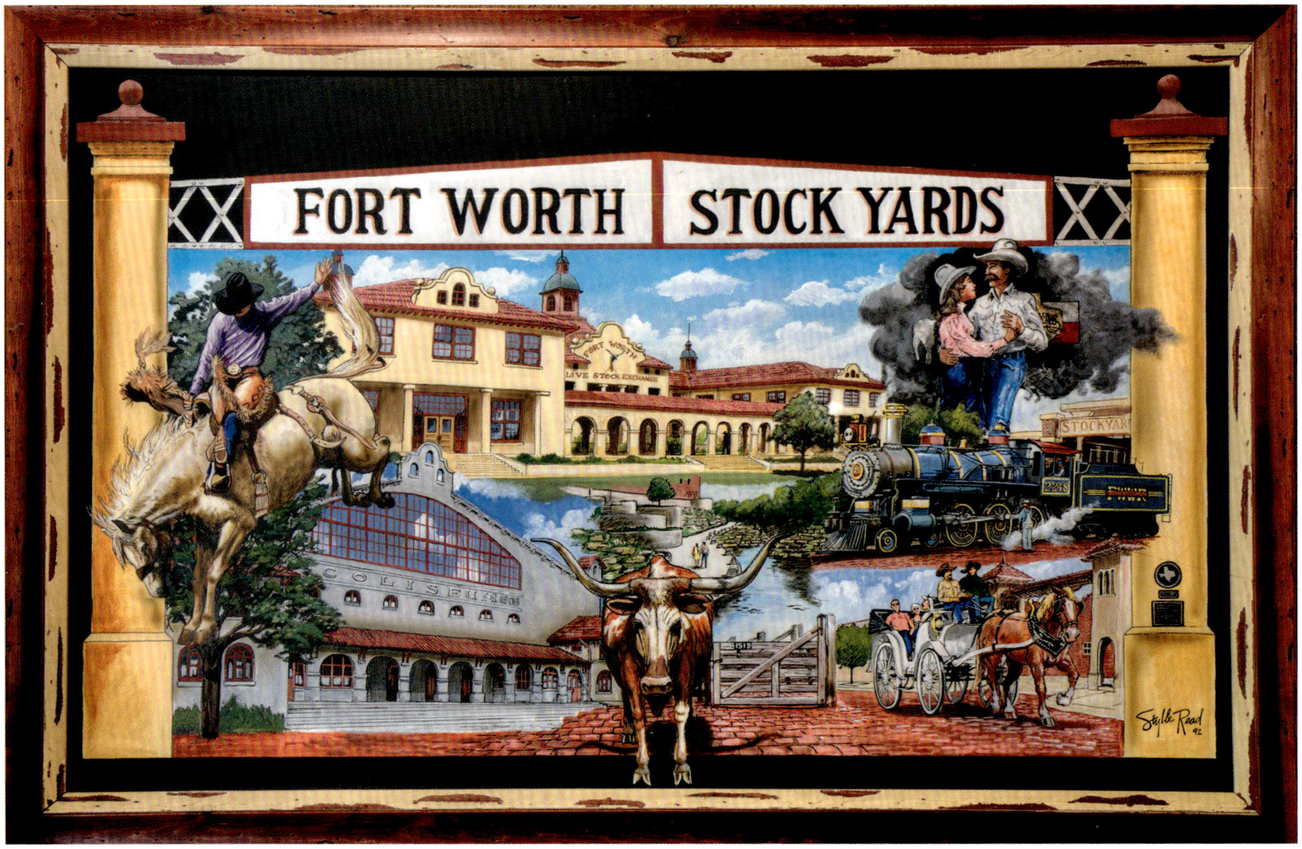

The vintage Stock Yards gate frames a painted collage of a bucking horse and cowboy, a Longhorn, a dancing couple, the coliseum and livestock buildings and more, in a marvelously detailed 1992 painting by Stylle Reed.

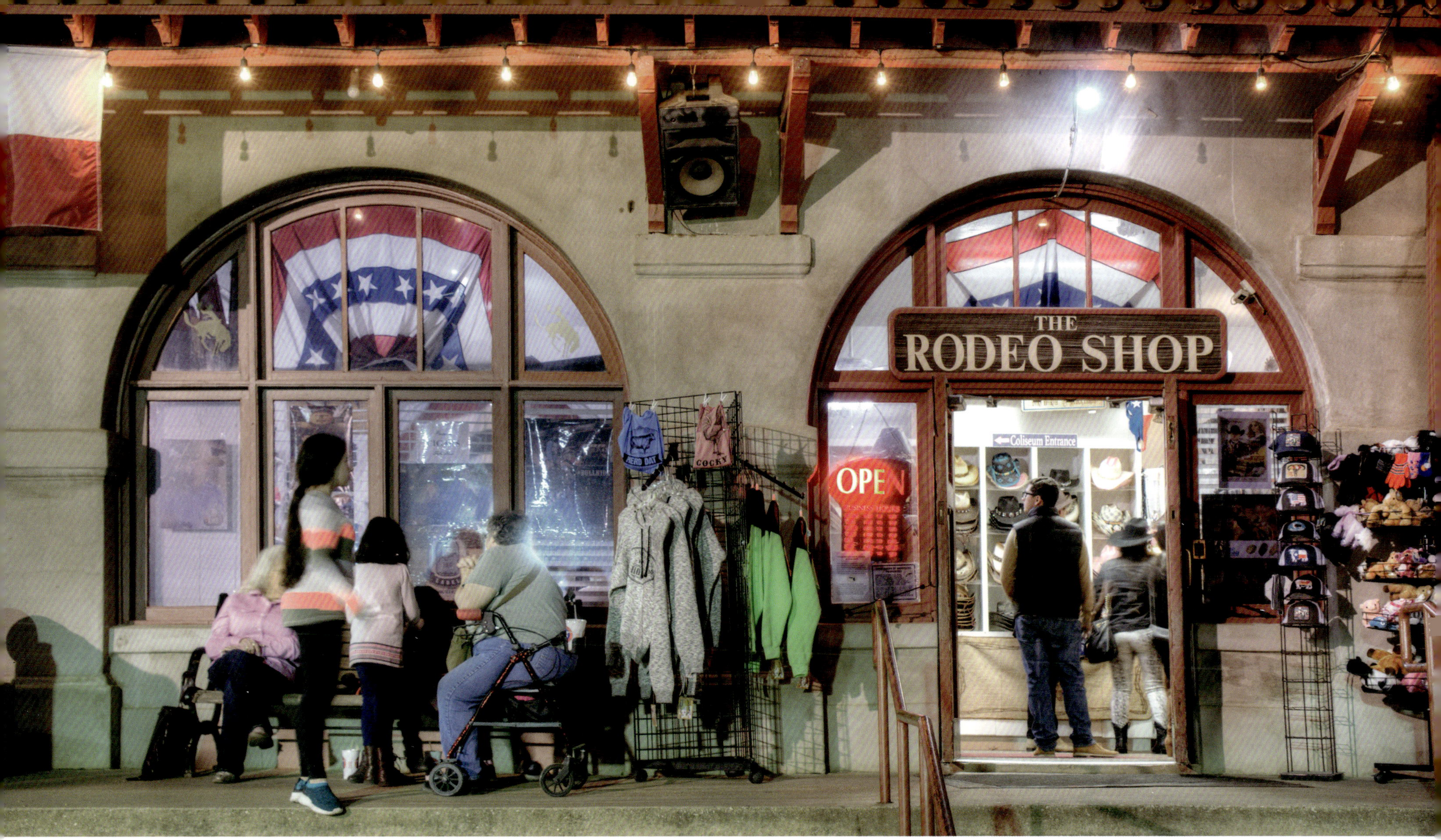

The official Rodeo Shop, located in the historic Cowtown Coliseum, handles exclusive stockyards Championship Rodeo merchandise.

in World War II, and increased government oversight. Because of the added activity, the total livestock industry at the local stockyards employed five thousand workers and furnished a $6.25 million portion of Fort Worth's payroll in 1941. Texas farmers and ranchers marketed their 1941 animals for more money than they had seen in several years.

In 1941 the sale of horses and mules boomed, and Fort Worth again became a leading market for those animals, having enjoyed huge sales during World War I. Foreign markets were buying the animals, not so much for cavalry mounts as in the previous war but as a cheap source of food for their armies. Once the United States entered the war in December 1941, however, the demand for meat and meat products multiplied. The nation needed to feed its own troops and help its allies. Cattle could not produce enough beef to meet the demand, and prices accelerated. The draft took many of the younger workers

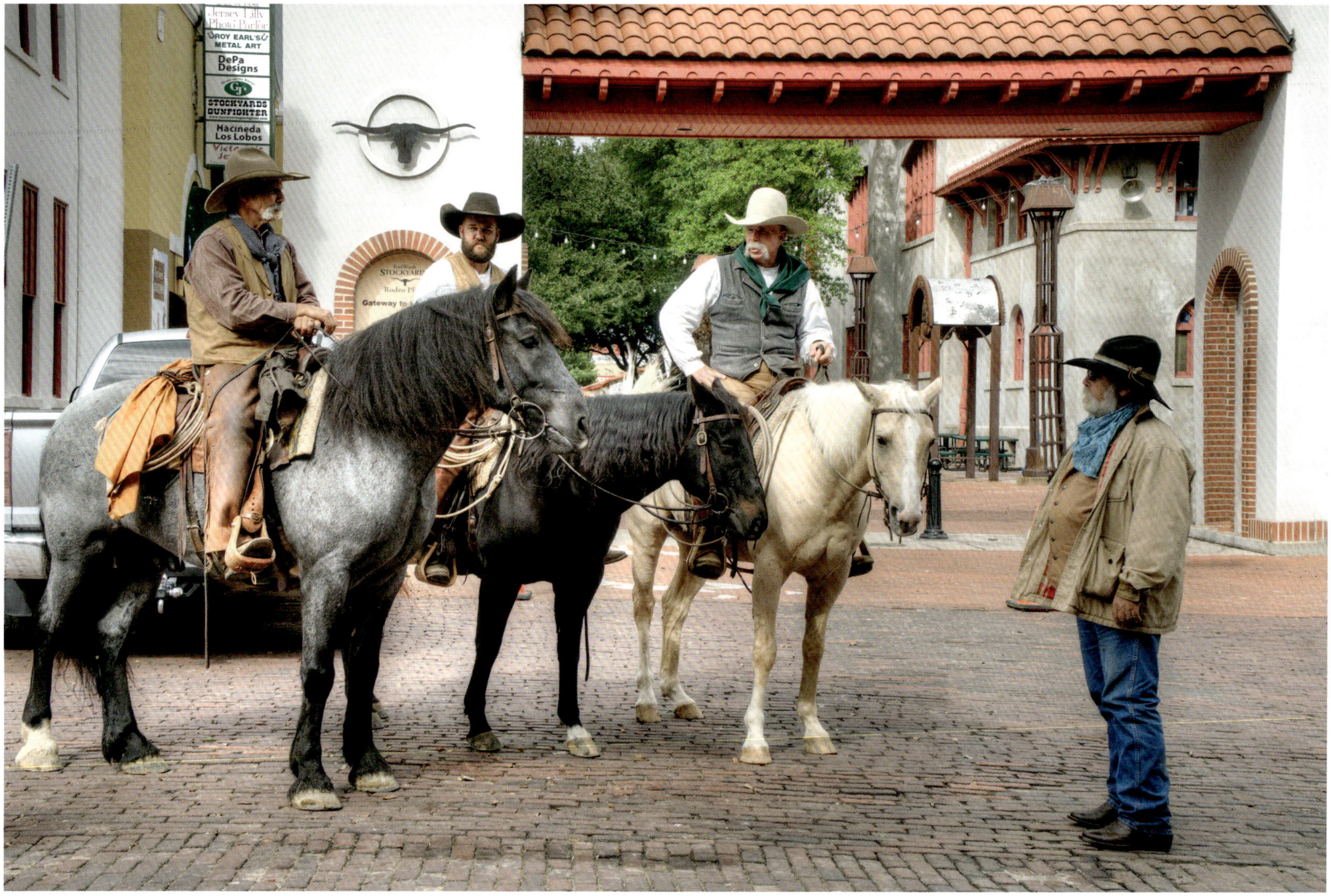

Dewayne Waldrup, operations supervisor and drover, chats with three drovers after the morning cattle drive on Exchange Avenue. Drover Ken Burrill rides Vaquero, the large horse on the left. He is part Percheron, a breed of draft horse from western France.

from the stockyards, and the company found it difficult to keep enough men at a time when receipts of animals at the yards became the highest in their history. They hired anyone they could.

Producers marketed a million more head of livestock at the Fort Worth Stockyards in 1943 than in 1942, setting a new record with nearly 4.5 million animals. The war years brought more than 2 million sheep each year into the yards. Sometimes stockyard employees would work thirty-three straight hours, unloading nothing but sheep. By the 1940s Fort Worth had developed into the largest sheep market in the country. On some days the yards received more sheep than the combined total of those animals in the eleven other major markets in the nation. In 1944 more than 2.5 million sheep passed through the Fort Worth market. Also, for only the third time in its history,

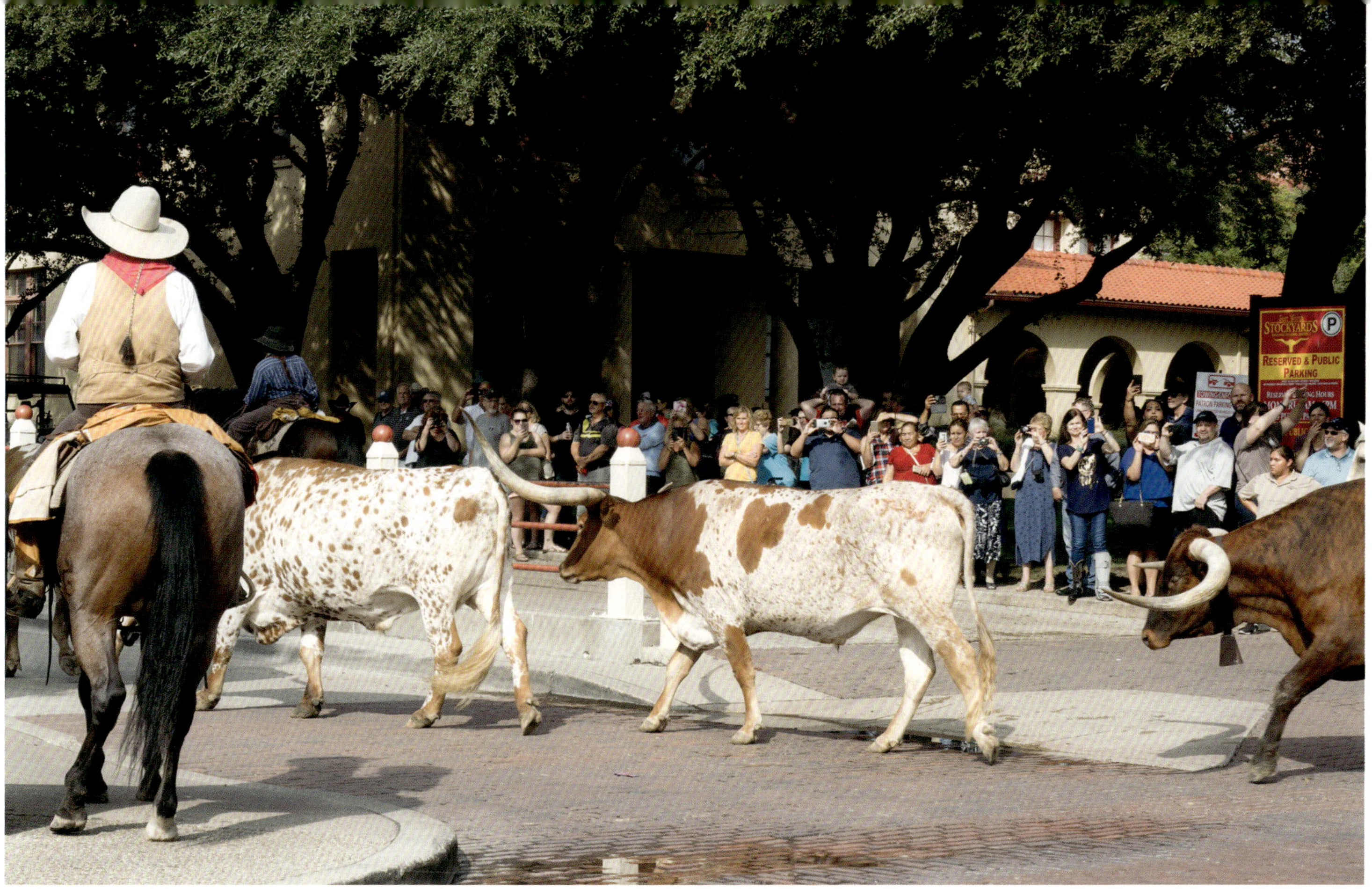

The Fort Worth Herd provides stockyard visitors with a glimpse into Fort Worth's rich Western heritage with the world's only twice-daily cattle drive of twenty Longhorns. In preserving its heritage as Cowtown, the city of Fort Worth has its own herd of more than twenty-three Texas Longhorns.

Drover Donald Lee stands with Whiskey Pete for a long drink of water after the afternoon cattle drive on East Exchange Avenue.

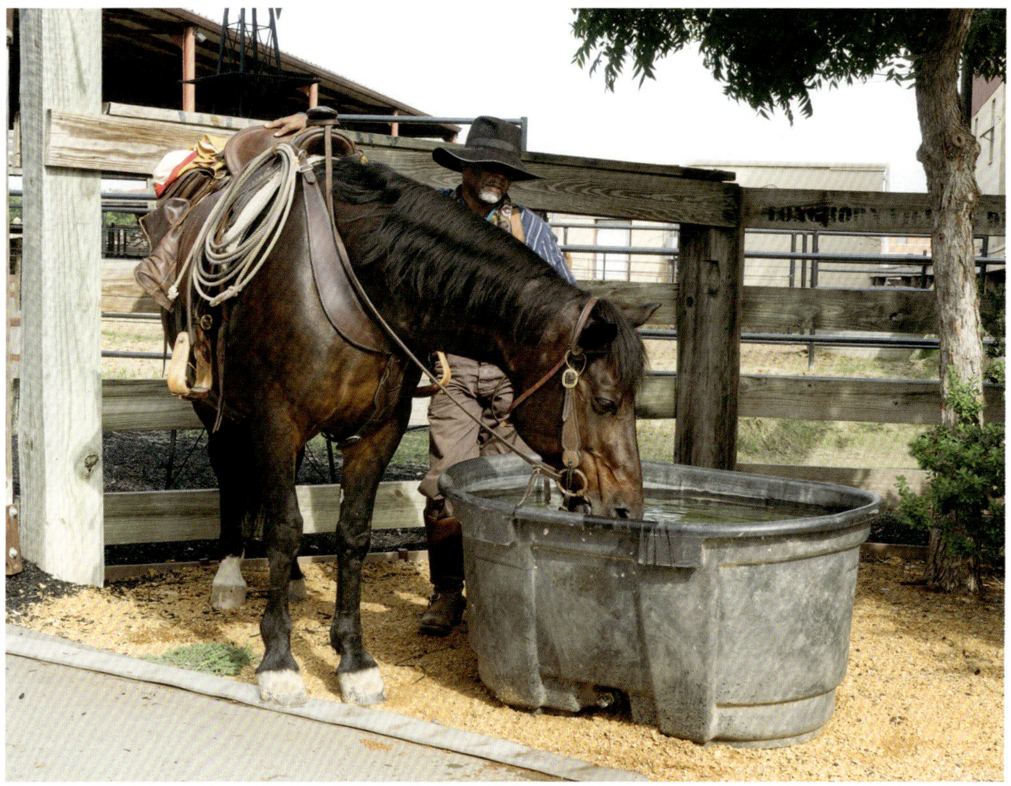

in 1944 more than a million hogs reached the market in one year. In that same year, for only the fourth time ever, a million cows arrived. The grand total of livestock for the year surpassed 5.25 million animals. The year 1944 remained the best ever in the history of the market.

In 1944 a new company called United Stockyards acquired all of the shares of stock of the Fort Worth Stockyards and became the sole owner. Local operations continued much as usual, but on Fort Worth Stockyards Company letterheads and advertising appeared the explanation, "a division of United Stockyards Corporation." United acquired all of the stock of several other stockyards as well in 1944. Perhaps because all attention of the nation was focused on the war effort, no antitrust concerns apparently emerged.

The war brought many changes to Fort Worth and its major industry in the stockyards. One of these became the transfer of the annual stock show to the west side of Fort Worth to facilities at Will Rogers Coliseum, which had been built in 1936. Officials canceled the show in the North Side in 1943 because of a flood in the coliseum the year before and other buildings being used for war work. In 1944 the show moved to the Will Rogers Coliseum, because the 1942 flood had not been cleaned up in the necessary buildings. The move would be "temporary" promised the promoters of the show. However, attendance at the 1944 stock show exceeded all previous records, so it again was held in 1945 at the Will Rogers complex. The 1945 show set a record high again, so directors decided to continue holding it there. In 2020 it was

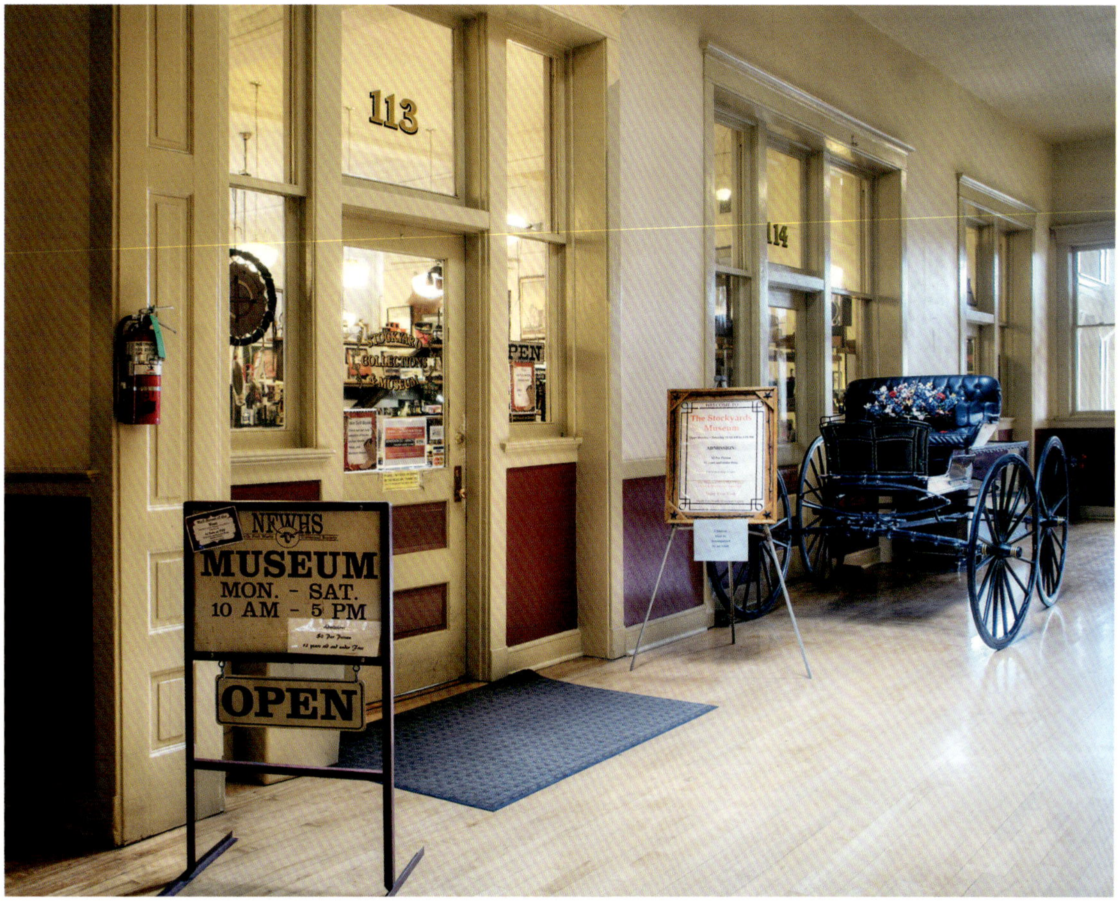

The Stockyards Museum is located inside the historic Livestock Exchange Building at 131 East Exchange Avenue. It showcases the rich history of the Fort Worth Stockyards and the North Side with a growing collection of artifacts, books, photos, and exhibits. The museum director is poet Teresa Burleson.

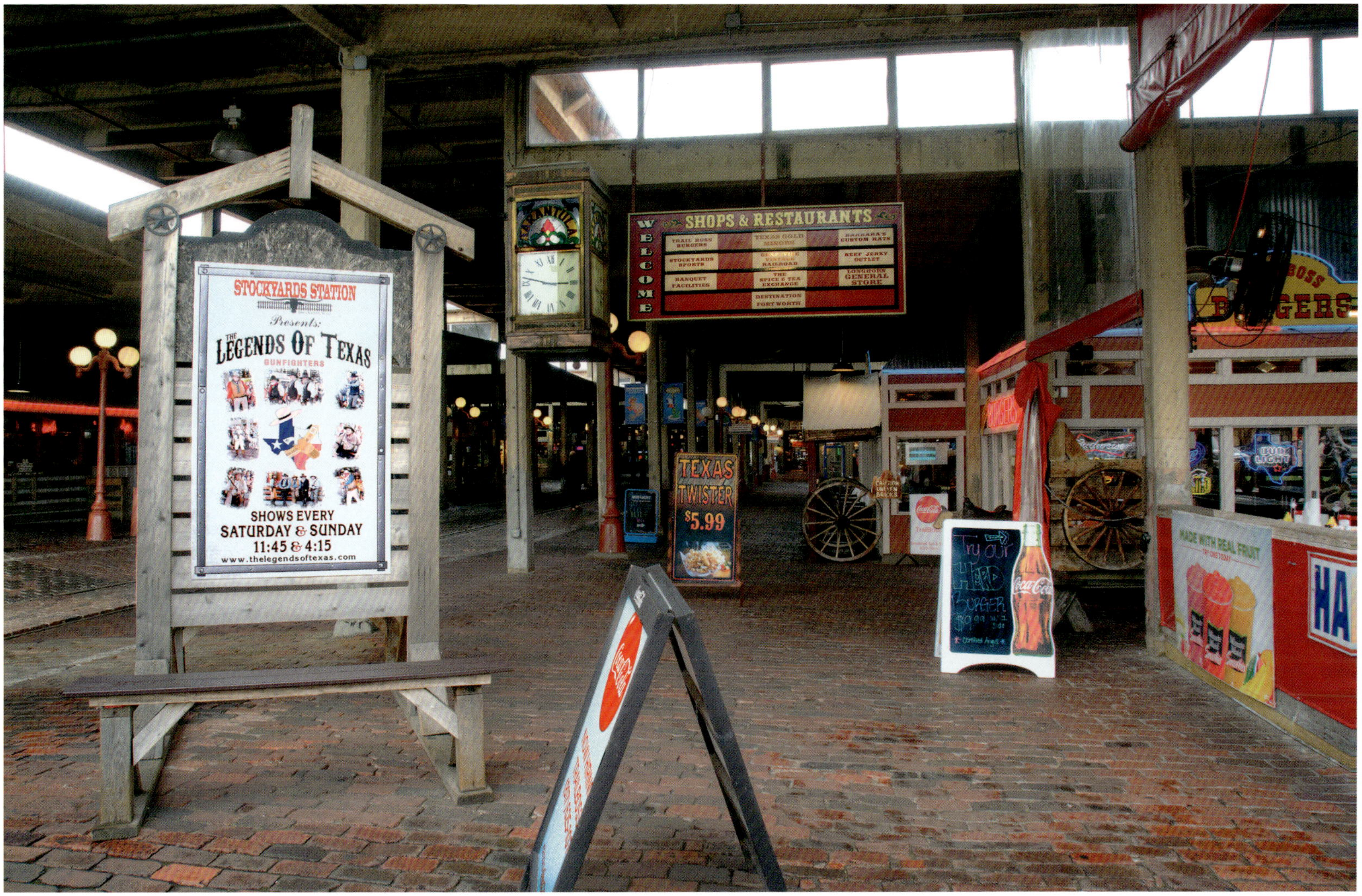

Stockyards Station was formerly an area to house hogs and sheep until they were delivered to the Armour and Swift meat-packing plants. It is now a collection of small retail shops mixed with local restaurants, many with outdoor dining.

to be held in the Dickies Arena but was canceled due to the pandemic.

North Side residents and others regretted that the show moved away, especially since they had nurtured it for nearly fifty years. They felt it belonged in the stockyards area. Thirty-five years after the show moved, one old-timer lamented, "It's not the same show now. People once came to the stock show from all over Texas to soak up the stockyards atmosphere. It's just a big show now. It was real then." For the 1946 show at the new site, when promoters celebrated fifty years, officials brought in singer and movie star Gene Autry as a special attraction. The practice of a known entertainer each year then became a new feature of the show.

As workers returned from war and a few of them came back to the stockyards, they witnessed busy activity. However, by then more animals arrived by truck than by train. Also, the Livestock Exchange Building had added more

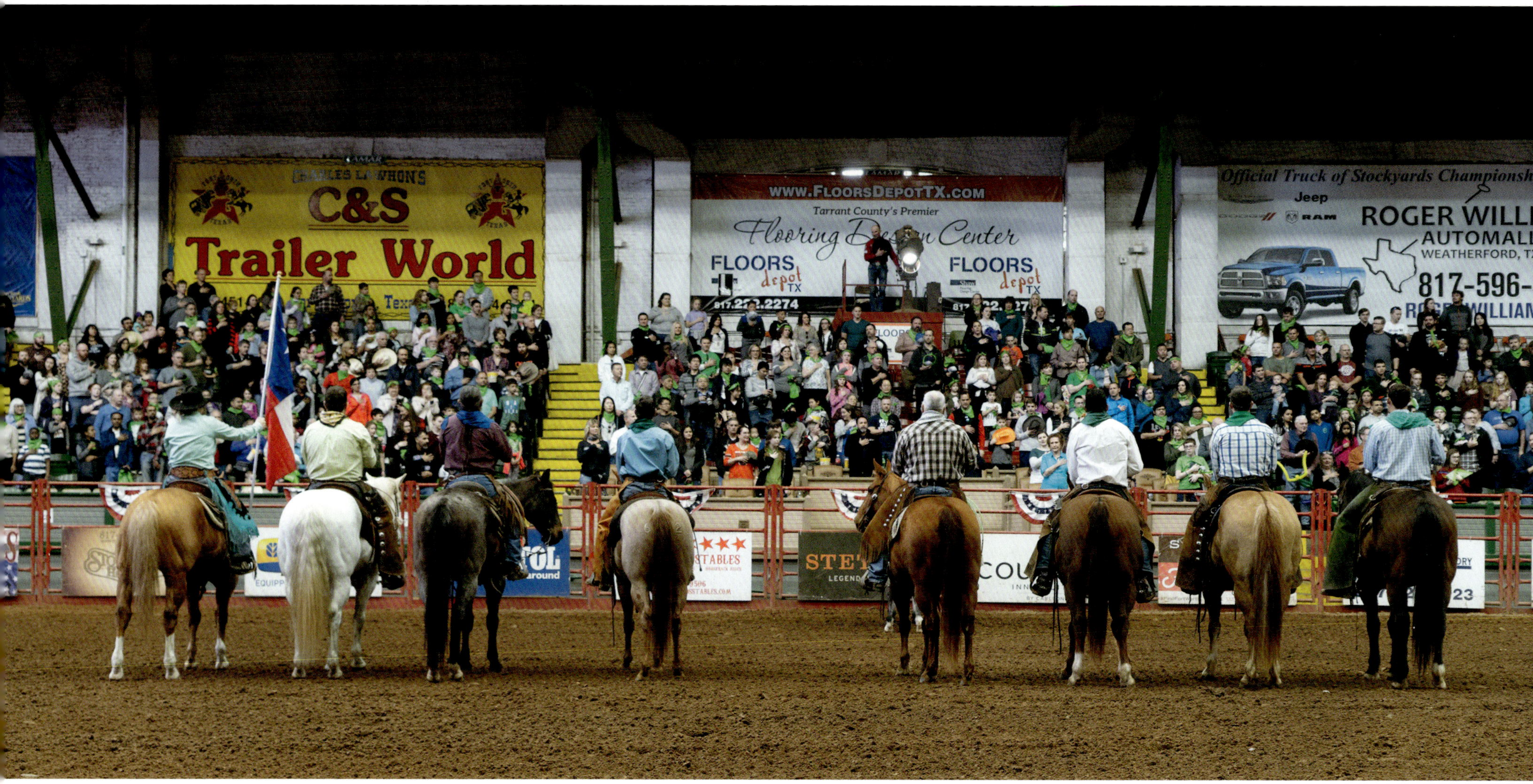

Pawnee Bill's Wild West performers face the audience during the Pledge of Allegiance prior to the opening act.

offices for as many as forty-eight commission companies, railroad agents, market reporters, feed stores, a telegraph office, Packers and Stockyards Administration officials, representatives of the Cattle Raisers Association, and even a barber shop.

Early in December 1946, the Fort Worth Stockyards Company publicized one of its many firsts. An airplane hauled a load of twenty commercially grown calves for the first time from a livestock market in the United States. A DC-4 transport airplane took off from Fort Worth's municipal airport, Meacham Field, located just north of the stockyards on Main Street, and headed for New York. Within seconds after becoming airborne, the plane crossed the old cattle trail, from which millions of head of stock had entered the Chisholm Trail in Indian Territory on the way to Kansas railheads. Bob Mason, vice pres-

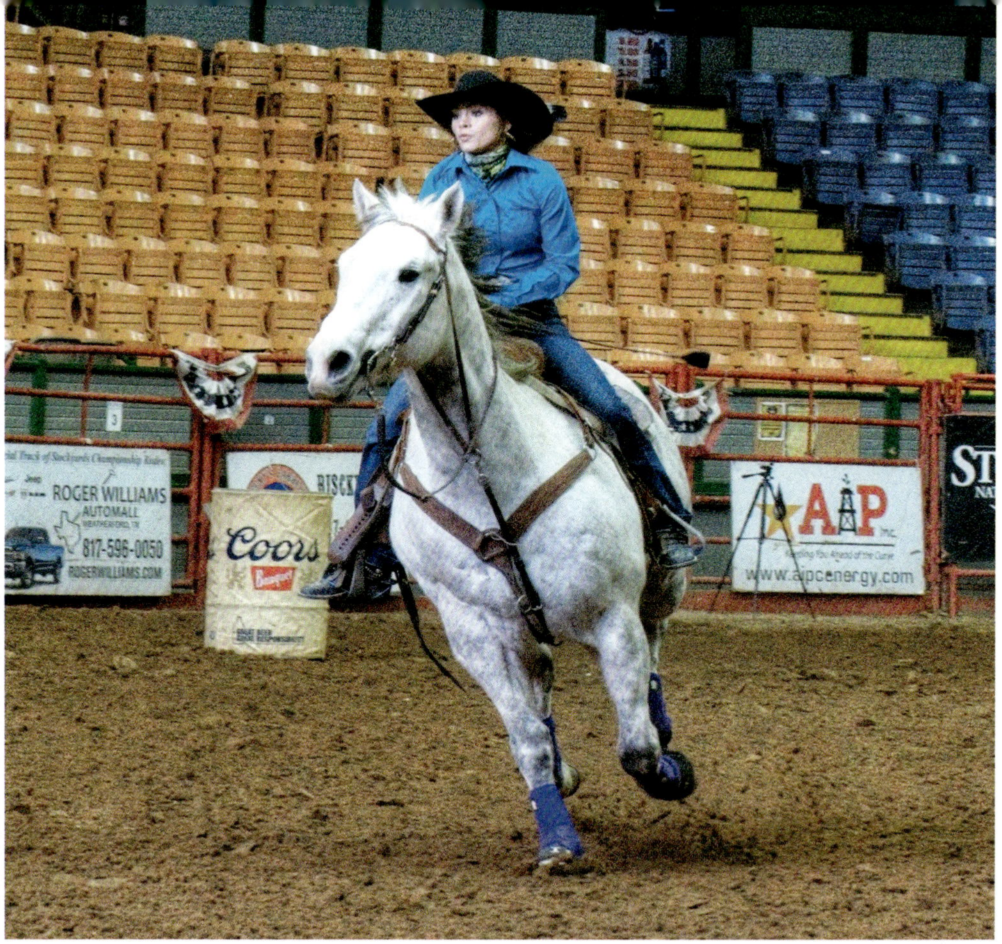

A young woman and her horse circle toward the next barrel in a barrel-racing competition at the Fort Worth Stockyards Championship Rodeo.

Rodeo contestant 797 mounts his bronco with help prior to release for a challenging and very bumpy ride. The bucking horse must be of a desired age, temperament, and athletic ability to qualify for competition.

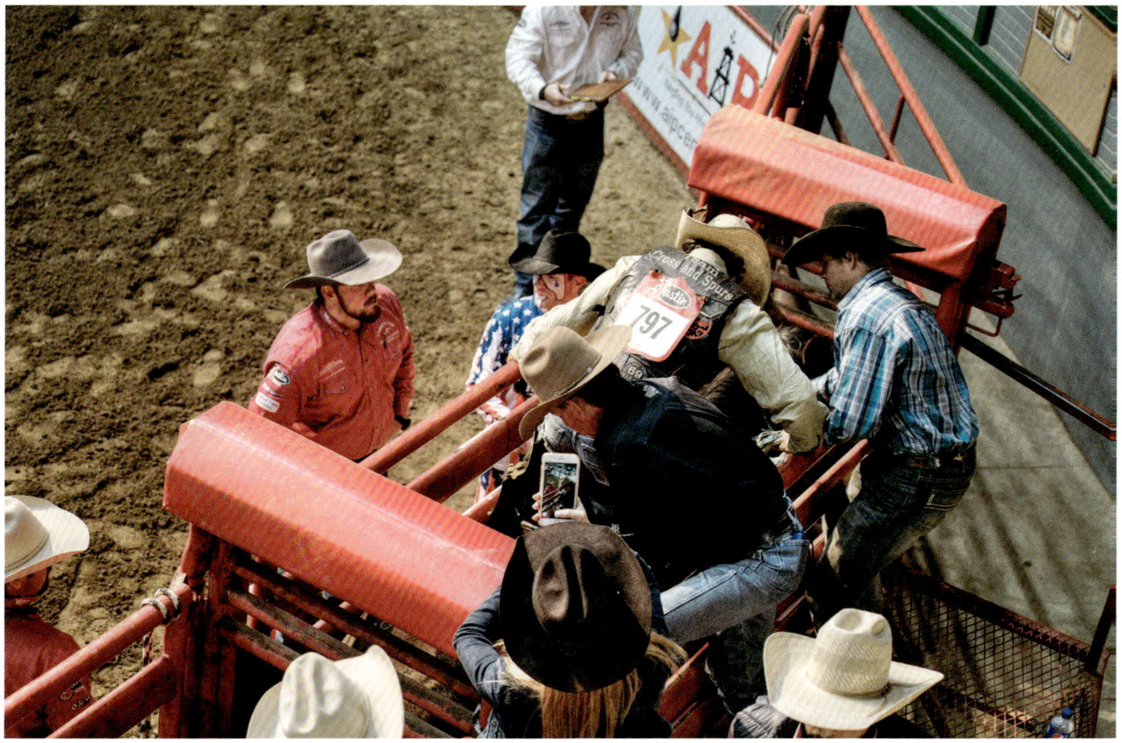

ident of World-Wide Trading Corporation, with headquarters in Fort Worth, bought the calves. They had been bred and fattened on the George A. McClung Ranch in Cleburne, Texas.

Someone in the Fort Worth Stockyards Company offices realized in 1947 that the company was nine years older than officials had been stating in brochures and other advertising. For forty-five years they had dated everything from the time that Armour and Swift had arrived in 1902. In that year the two packers bought two-thirds of the stock and reorganized things. Someone apparently found the original charter of the Fort Worth Stockyards dated March 23, 1893. Soon the company revised its advertisements and stationery to reflect the 1893 date and began bragging that the Fort Worth market was fifty-four years old and had operated twenty-four hours a day most of that time. It did not acknowledge the actual origin of the North Side market when it had operated under the name Fort Worth Union Stock Yards with its 1887 incorporation.

Although in 1948 Fort Worth's livestock market ranked first in the Southwest and remained the largest south of Kansas City, aircraft production during World War II surpassed livestock as the city's number-one industry. Cattle and meatpacking dropped to second place in the city's economy. The aircraft industry employed twelve thousand workers, while cattle and meatpacking hired seven thousand. Eleven meatpackers, small and large, operated in Fort Worth in 1949.

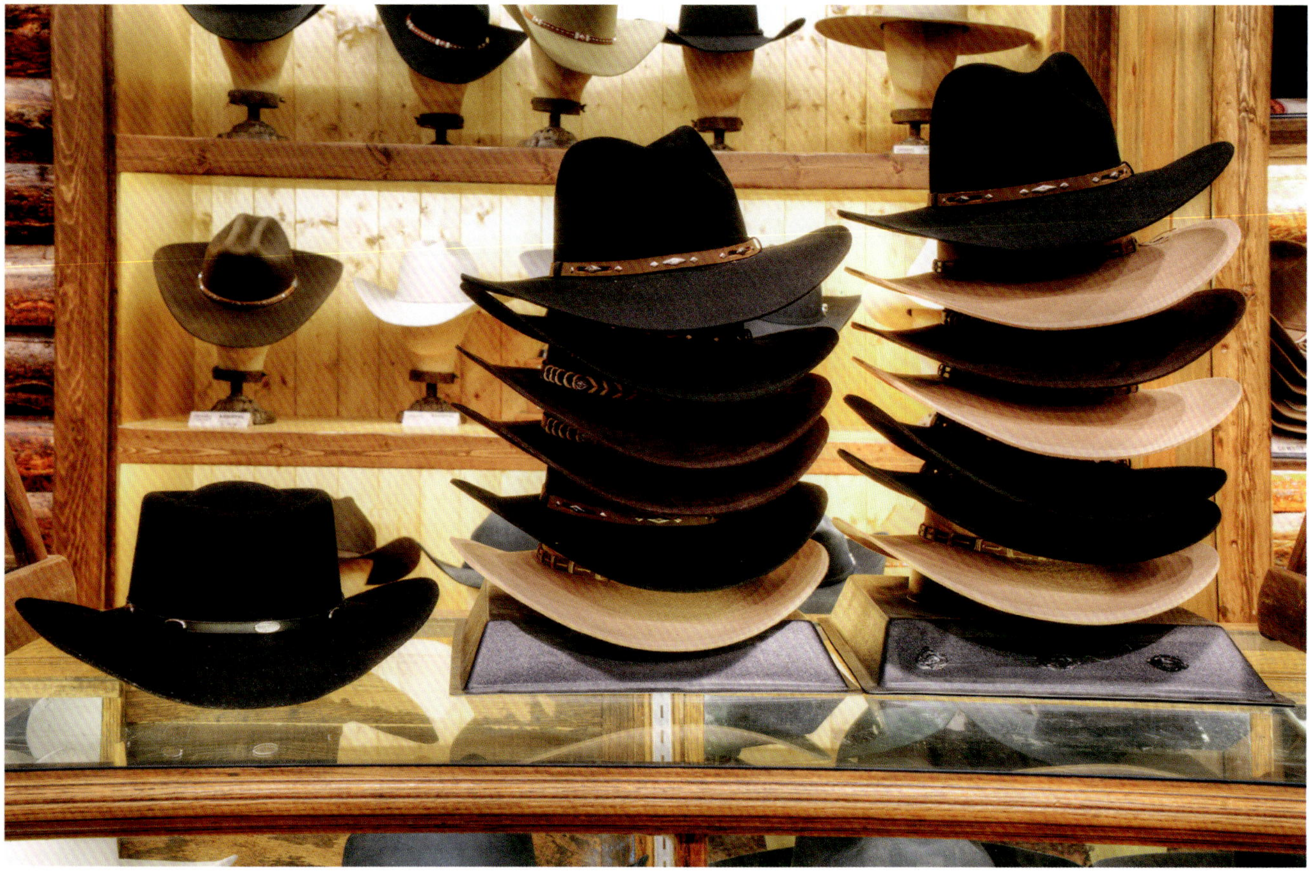

Stacks of cowboy hats are displayed at Cavender's Stock Yards Western apparel store on Main Street adjacent to the Fort Worth Stockyards.

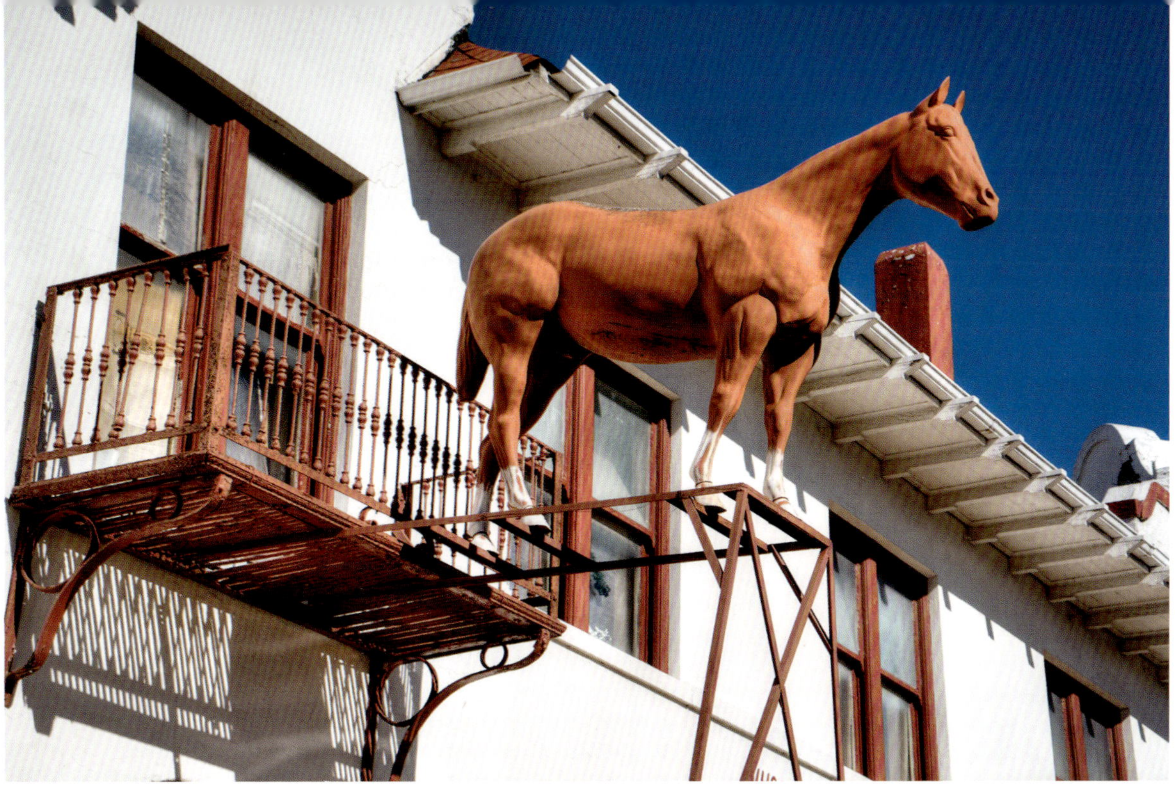

Fincher's White Front Western Wear is located in the heart of the historic Fort Worth Stockyards. The huge, white, two-story building with the rust-colored horse mannequin was originally the home of White Front Western Store, established in 1902.

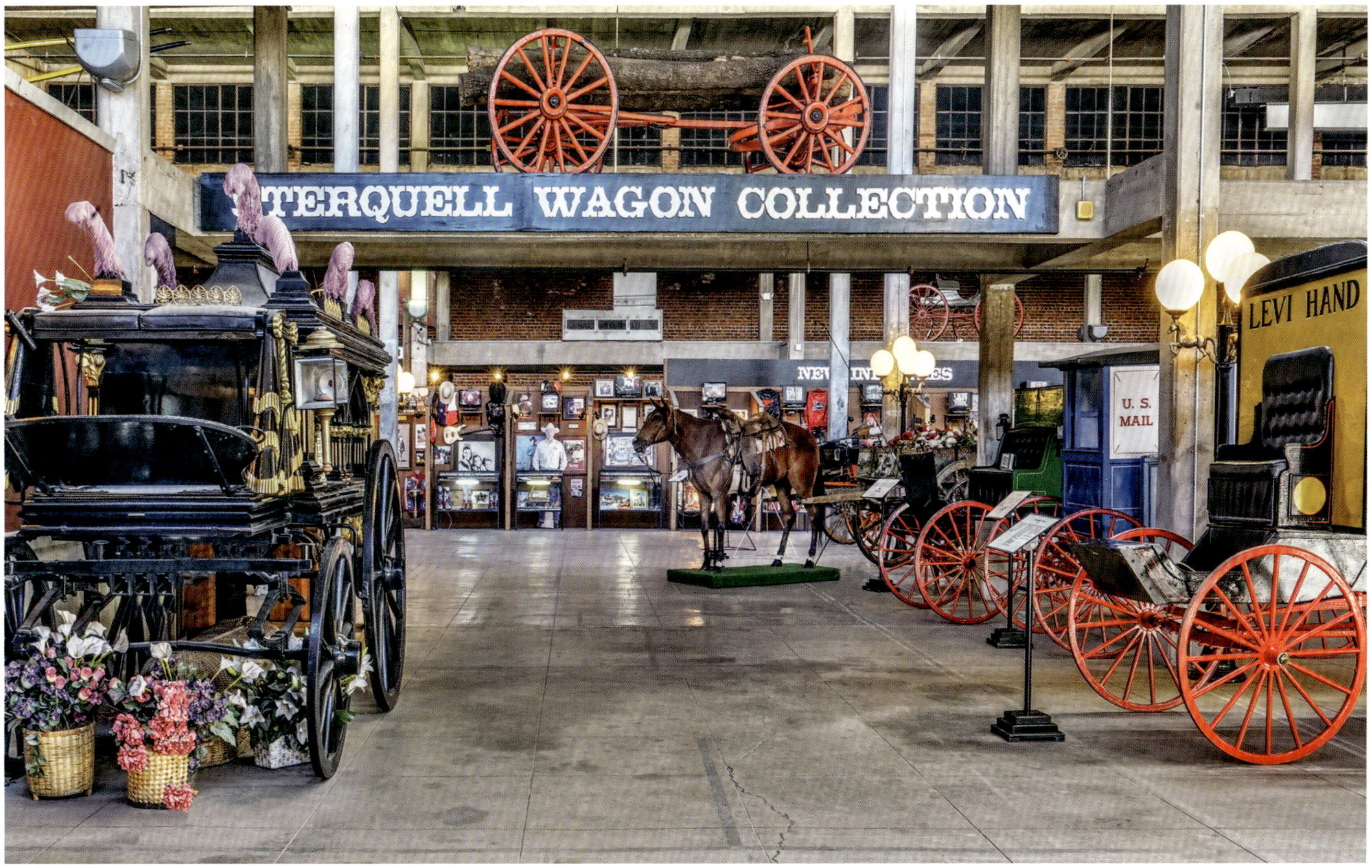

At the Texas Cowboy Hall of Fame, a highlight of the exhibition is the Sterquell Wagon Collection, featuring more than sixty Old West wagons, carts, and sleighs. The museum also features a collection of cowboy memorabilia.

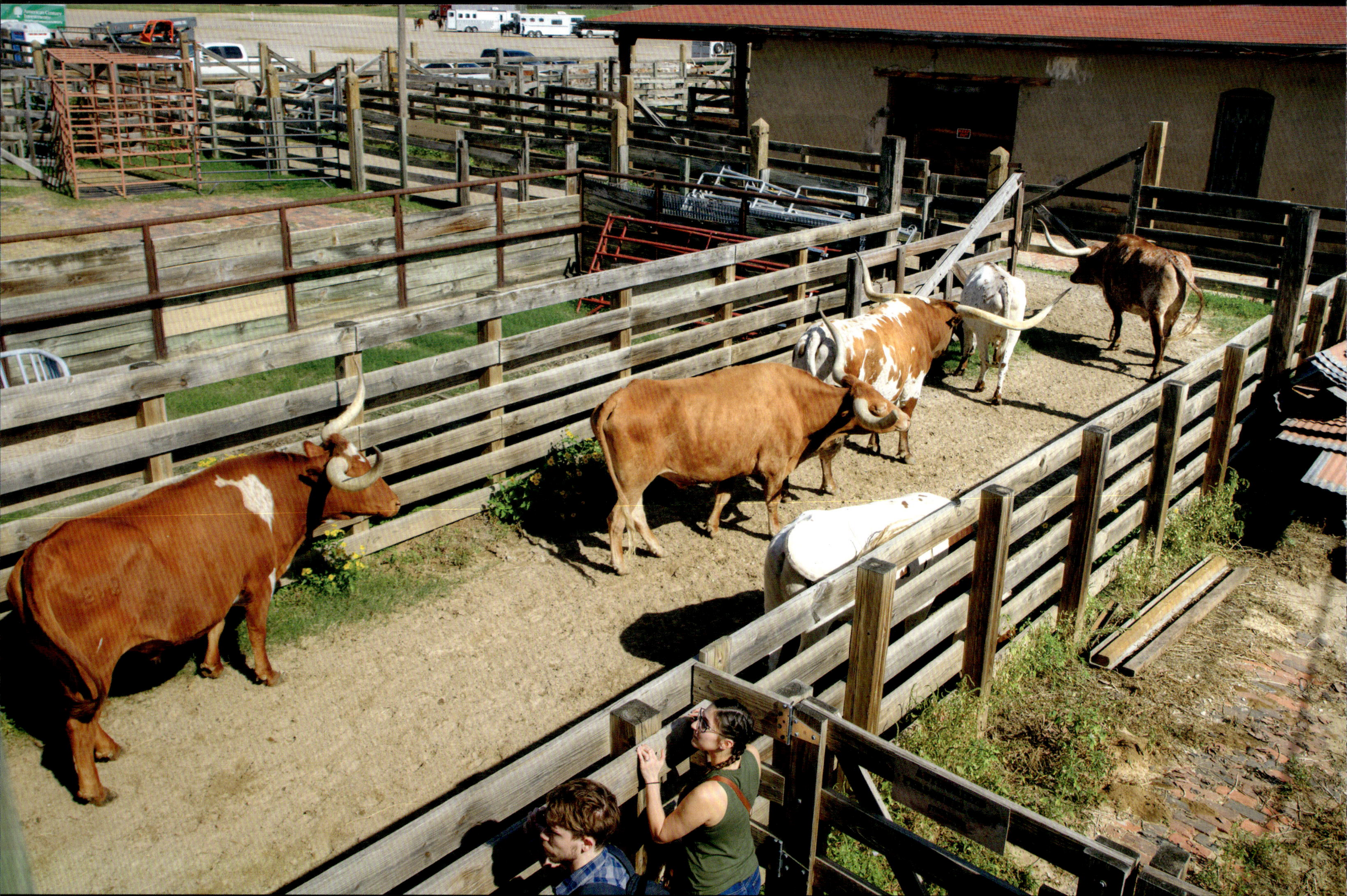

CHAPTER 5

Days at the Yards

Stockyard people in the first half of the twentieth century became a special breed who loved their work and did not seem to mind that it took up a great deal of their time. These were the commission men, buyers for the meatpackers, and office personnel in the Livestock Exchange Building. Everyday workers who unloaded the livestock from the trains or trucks and the ones who cleaned out the pens no doubt did not experience the same satisfaction. However, it was a way of life that many enjoyed. While accomplishing the necessary work of a large stockyard like the one in Fort Worth, the men sometimes had time to relax and have a little fun.

So what does a stockyard worker do during slow times between the arrival of rail cars or truckloads of animals being sent into pens for watering, feeding, and then selling? At the Fort Worth Stockyards, the men took their pocketknives out of their pockets and began whittling. General Manager Donovan once offered one of the commission company owners, Charlie Daggett, one hundred dollars if he would give up whittling. Charlie said, "No." Donovan tried to get Charlie to give up his habit because he had to hire carpenters to repair the wooden gates and fences that the workers' whittling damaged. Eventually, the stockyards company used tin to trim the edges of the benches, the upright posts, and any other exposed wooden edges they could find to deter the whittlers.

Independent commission men such as Charlie Daggett became the intermediary between seller and buyer of livestock on the yards. When five hundred railroad cars or more arrived daily, during the earlier days, and approximately a hundred buyers roamed the yards, a lot of transactions occurred in a day. Even so, participants in the process still took the time to dicker. The seller, for

Children joyfully watch the handsome Longhorn cattle as they return to their corral. A walkway above the pens allows viewers to see the cattle as they trek toward the corral.

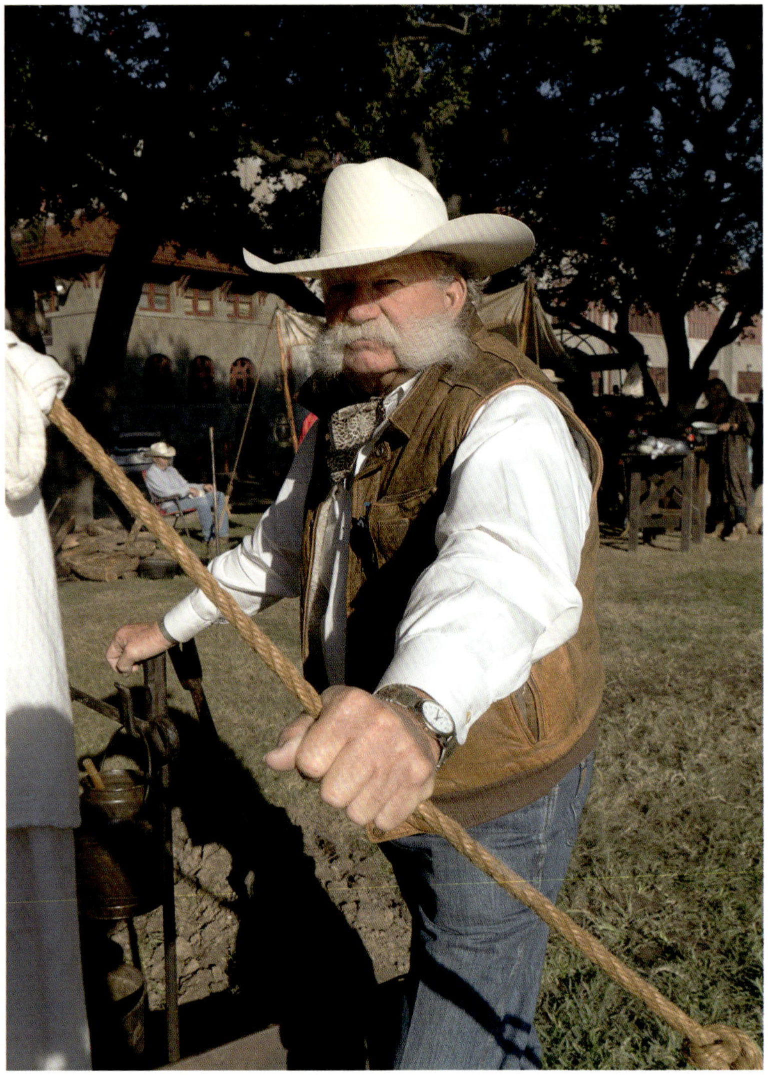

Cowboys nurture big mustaches, dress in their best Western apparel, and take on their most masculine attitude when bringing the West alive at the stockyards. Photographer Bob Moorhouse comes from a well-known ranching family and worked as the manager of the Pitchfork Ranch for twenty years.

whom the commission men worked, wanted the highest price possible for the animals belonging to him. The buyer wanted to purchase at the lowest price that he could, given the going market rates. The commission agent mentioned a high price that he hoped he could get, and the buyer cited a low price that he wanted to pay. They both knew that if they really wanted to deal, they would meet somewhere in the middle.

Meanwhile, in between the haggling, the two men pulled out their ever-present pocketknives and hacked on whatever wood they could find. They probably had a leg propped up on the lowest rung of the fence or were leaning against a gate with one arm resting on top, but one hand always remained free to give a whack at the fence. It gave the men something to do to fill the silence while waiting for the other person either to raise or lower his offer. Donovan knew the popularity of the whittling, so when he gave instructions to his carpenter to replace boards that had been carved to pieces, making them useless as gates or fences, he also instructed him to chip the leftover wood into convenient sizes for picking up and holding in one's hand. He hoped that the men would whittle on it instead. And somehow, during their busy days, the workers at the Fort Worth Stockyards Company and those of Armour and Swift fielded a baseball team. Pictures of the teams still exist.

Even though the stockyards could be muddy and smelly, Donovan always dressed in a suit and tie. He wanted to look the part of a businessman running the biggest business in town, which certainly he was before World War II. The stockyards combined with the meat-packing plants hired more people than any other Fort Worth industry and generated more dollars.

Cattle, hogs, sheep, horses, and mules arrived by rail twenty-four hours a day, seven days a week in the early days, so stockyard hands constantly needed to be on hand to unload. One of the six Beltway switch engines, owned by the stockyards, who had the monopoly on handling the cars, picked up the various cars of the other railroad lines that brought the animals into Fort Worth. Then it brought them to the proper dock at the yards. Each of the three docks—north, middle, and south—could accommodate eighteen cars. All three docks stretched from Twenty-Third to Twenty-Eighth Streets.

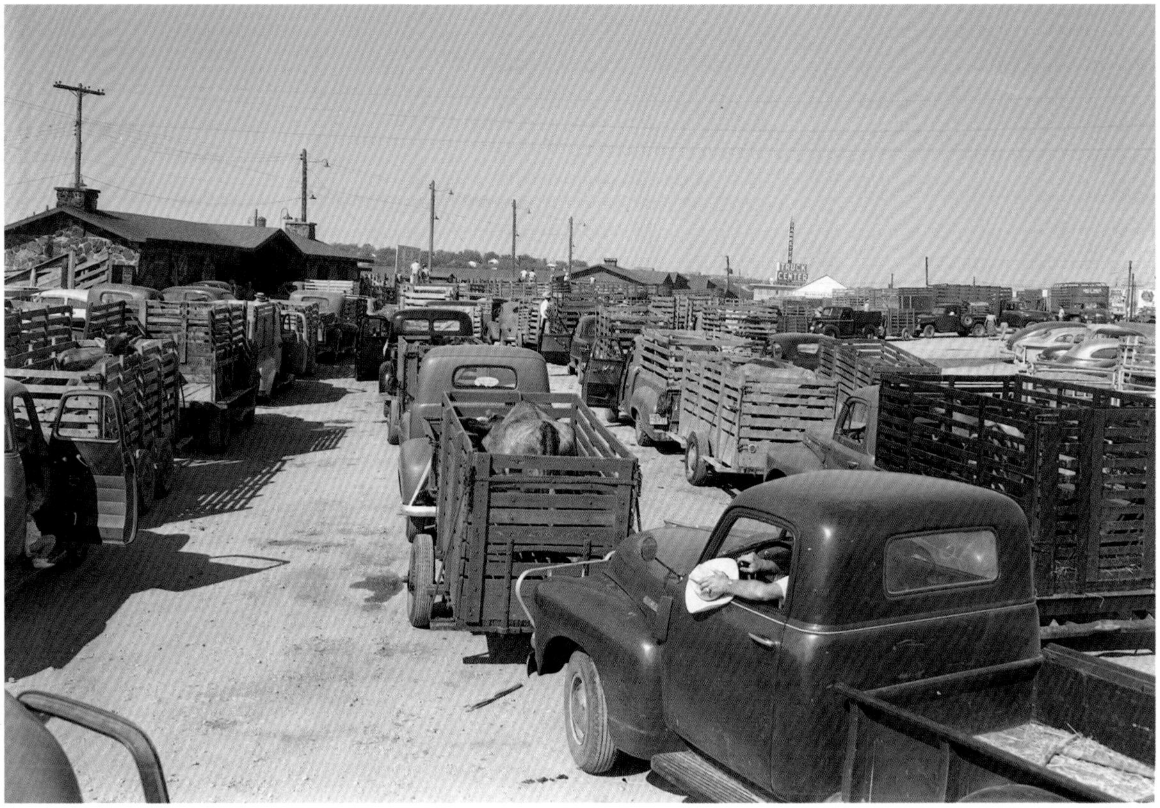

Pickups and trailers line up to unload cattle at the stockyards in 1951. Courtesy of Fort Worth Stockyards Collection, University of Texas at Arlington Libraries.

With so many animals being unloaded at peak times, the bawling of cattle frightened by their unfamiliar surroundings became the common background for every conversation—unless one worked in the covered hog and sheep pens with their own particular squeals and bleats. It was said that one adjusted to the noise and smell after a time and hardly noticed it. For a newcomer, however, the aroma and sounds could be overwhelming. Surprisingly, sheep remained relatively quiet. After being sold, they followed rather meekly behind a trained goat wearing a bell as he led them over the ramp to the packing plant to be slaughtered. For obvious reasons, the one or two trained goats used over the years for this purpose were called "Judas" goats. One had the additional name of "Popeye."

In the early days before government regulations, trading began at 6:00 a.m. each day except Sunday. One old-timer explained, "You started when you could and quit when you couldn't," meaning they started bidding when they could see the animals at daylight and ended their day when they could not see to trade anymore.

Mondays always represented the biggest day of the week for receipts. Things stayed very busy as a team of buyers for each of the two large packinghouses and out-of-state buyers, as well as small independents, scurried around to all seven divisions. The packer buyers for each company immediately sent the animals they purchased over the ramps that crossed the railroad tracks to one of the two 6-story, slaughtering houses at the east end of the yards that belonged either to Armour or Swift. Independent buyers directed their purchases appropriately.

The two major packers purchased enough to ship out seventy-five to eighty railroad cars of processed meat each day. Anywhere from ten thousand to twenty-five

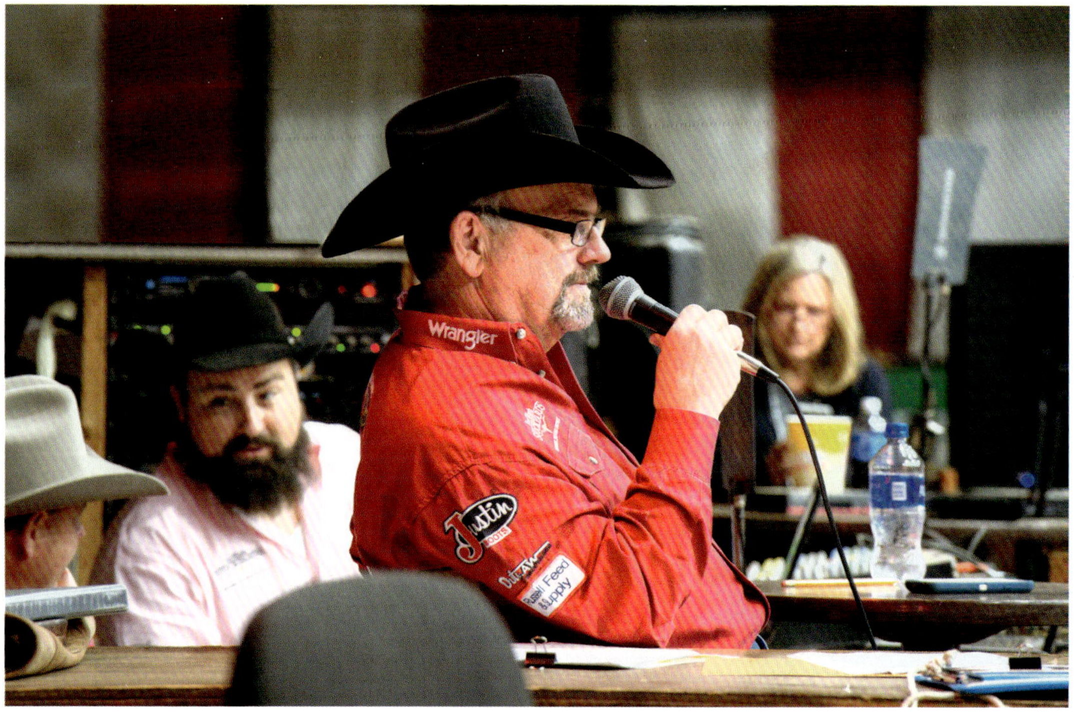

The longtime familiar voice of announcer Billy Huckaby at the rodeo fills the arena with information and excitement. Clay Barlow is seated behind Billy, assisting with the announcing.

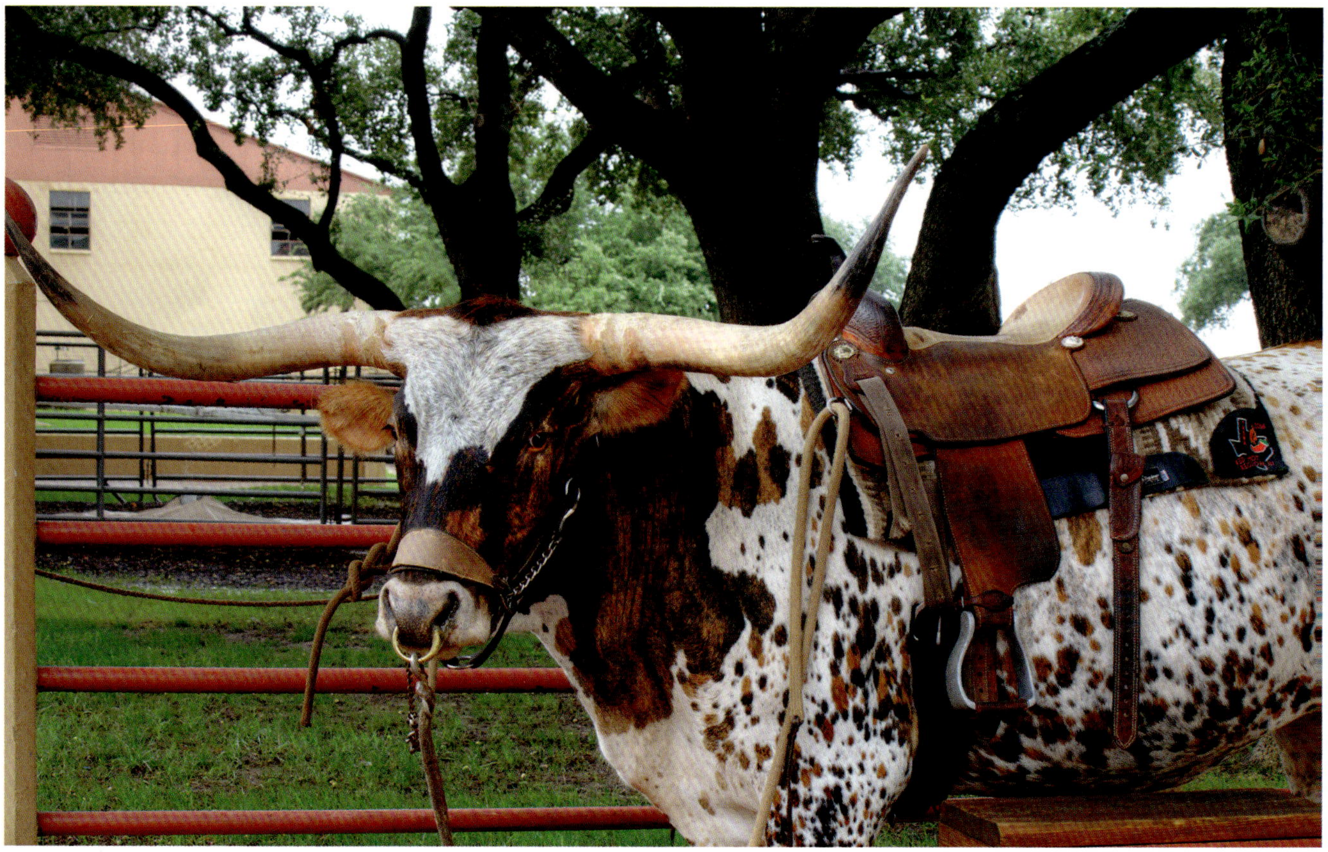

A gentle, saddled Longhorn patiently awaits someone who wants a photo taken.

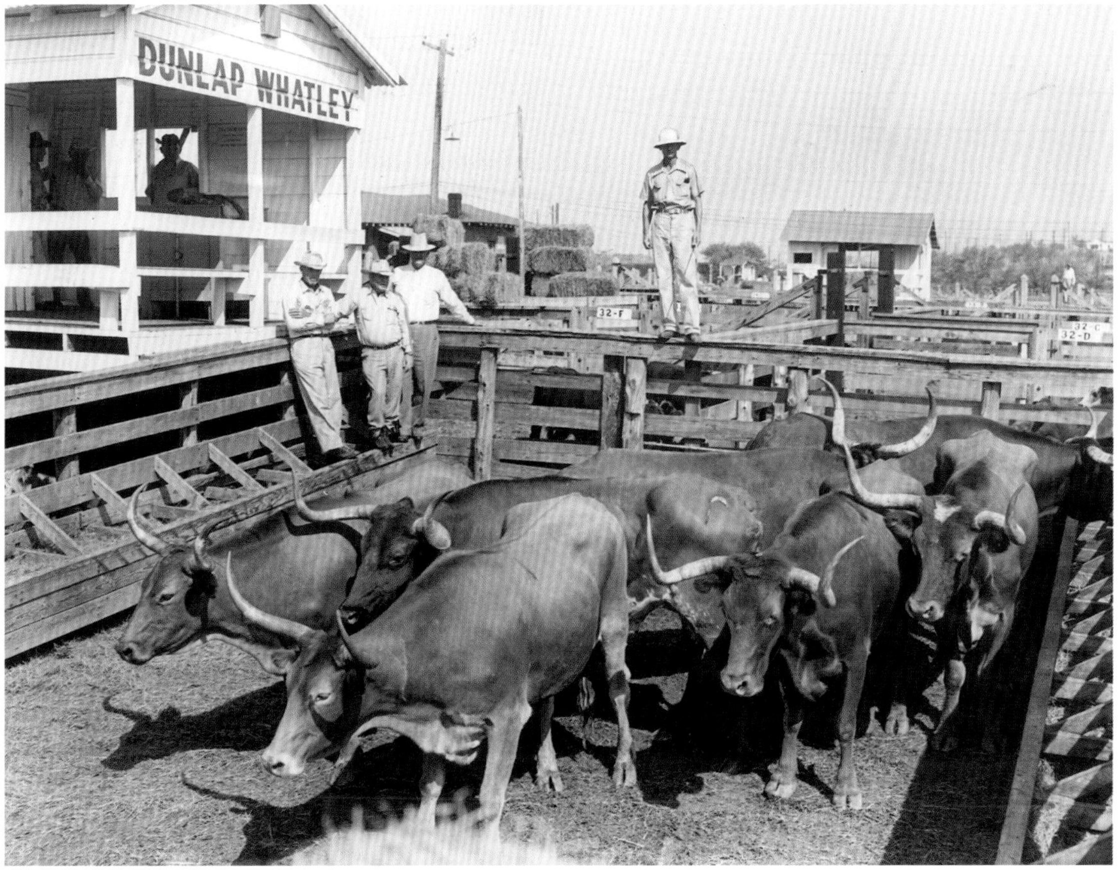

Longhorn steers sold by Cap Yates from Marfa ranch are herded into pens in the Fort Worth Stockyards: (*left to right*) Joe Whatley and R. K. Dunlap, salesmen, and Cap Yates, 1952. Courtesy of Fort Worth Stockyards Collection, University of Texas at Arlington Libraries.

thousand cattle and calves arrived each day during the summer and fall when big runs were common. There were fewer hogs and sheep. Sometimes stockyard workers did not stop unloading until 1:00 or 2:00 a.m. What made the stockyard work even busier was the added aspect of "feed and rest" cattle. A federal thirty-six-hour release law required railroads to unload animals from a cattle car before they had been on it longer than thirty-six hours and to feed and water them at a stockyard. Fort Worth accepted many "feed and rest" cattle on their way to northern pastures or markets. Sometimes stockyard workers would unload nothing but "feed and rest" cattle practically all day. Then their task would reverse itself, and they would begin reloading the first ones, for by then they had rested the legally required length of time. Scheduling of arriving railroads worked well, for agents called ahead to report how many carloads to expect.

When Bill Addieway first went to work for the stockyards company as a young man in 1926, he worked three days and two nights without stopping long enough to go home. His parents got worried about him, and his father came out to the stockyards to see what had happened. Obviously, he had been busy with a big run of animals.

Not all cattle arriving at the yards were for either slaughter or "feed and rest." Stocker and feeder calves arrived frequently in the 1920s, as indeed they did throughout the years. Stocker and feeder animals were calves that people bought to feed, fatten up, and then resell. Receipts were seasonal. Various types of livestock were brought in more heavily at different times. Fall or early spring saw the heaviest runs of hogs. Most sheep arrived in April, May, or June. Cattle arrived in larger numbers in the fall. Pens were just the right size to hold a railroad carload.

By the 1940s more than forty covered and enclosed wooden booths about twelve feet by twelve feet had been built above the livestock pens as a place for commission men to sit, store a little hay, hang up a saddle, and watch over what happened in their division. The booths provided the only shade available and gave protection from inclement weather. Men gathered in the booths to dicker, whittle, or listen to bids for the animals commissioned to them.

Stockyard employees kept water troughs in each pen full and maintained bins of fresh hay for the animals. As workers drove animals down lanes between the pens, others followed to shovel and clean up after them. The stockyards company once published a pamphlet calling their pens for servicing the animals a "livestock hotel." Most of the stockyards used this term, and it is difficult to know who originated it, but it was in common usage by the 1930s. After all, the animals "checked in," often spent a night in the pens, or at least several hours. They had to be fed and watered. Only after taken out of the pens, weighed, and sold, did they become the responsibility of the new owner, usually packer buyers who sent them over a ramp to the slaughtering plant.

Farmers and other cattle producers complained that services did not come cheap. However, the stockyards company needed to earn enough money to pay all its workers and maintain the upkeep of the yards. The stockyards company itself had no involvement in sales; it simply provided the facilities for the trading to occur. It charged rent to commission companies and traders and fees for feeding and watering each animal.

Packer buyers and commission men usually kept horses, which they rode when they went out on the yards. Perhaps they rode them partly to keep from stepping where a stockyard worker with his shovel had not yet cleaned. Sometimes the smoke from the nearby packinghouses would hang low over the yard and cause a bad odor. Swift cattle buyer Roy Weeman remembers complaining loudly on those days about that "horrible smell from Armour." Of course, "it came from Swift too," he admitted with a grin.

Farmers or ranchers who came with their animals to the yards could later pick up their checks in the Livestock Exchange Building at the office of the commission company to which they had consigned the sale. If they stayed home and shipped by rail, they waited anxiously for a telegram to learn the sale price. Then they waited for their check to come in the mail.

Three telegraph services allowed people to see prices at other markets. About twelve large stockyards handled most of the livestock of the country. Fort Worth ranked with them, but with a different number of livestock sales in each category—cattle, calves, hogs, sheep, horses, and mules. The local market generally ranked higher in cattle receipts than anything else. Other major markets included Chicago, Omaha, Kansas City, St. Louis, St. Joseph, St. Paul, Sioux City, Sioux Falls, Denver, South San Francisco, and Portland.

Longtime manager Donovan made sure that the Livestock Exchange Building and grounds looked good when people came to the stockyards. Shrubbery, palm trees, and a beautiful green lawn surrounded the building. For many years he hired a hardworking German named Albert Whiff to do the work. However, Whiff did not speak English very well. He used a donkey and a wide mower in his work. One day he asked Donovan for "voots" for his donkey. When Donovan finally figured out what he wanted, he contracted for inlaid leather boots to be made especially for the little animal. Whiff, a short, heavyset man, would roll up his overalls nearly to his knees and trot along barefoot behind his little donkey as he mowed. Records do not show whether Donovan ever had "voots" made for Whiff.

Someone on the yards one day convinced Whiff that he ought to ask Donovan for more money because he worked so hard. Soon the one who suggested it watched the little man go to the Exchange Building to ask for a raise. In a few minutes he came out, and the instigator asked how he had fared. "Did you get more money?" "Naw," he grinned, "no more money, but I can take all the grass I cut as donkey feed." That seemed to satisfy Whiff, for he worked many more years for the stockyards.

Al Donovan managed the stockyards longer than anyone else, from 1916 to 1946. He was general manager, then president. His superintendent, Harry "Cap" Henderson, handled the two hundred or so stockyard workers. The going rate for employees in 1928 was thirty cents an hour. Henderson let them work overtime to earn more money. No smoking was allowed on the yards because of all the hay lying around. Gambling was against the rules too, but younger employees liked to find a quiet spot for some fun after they got paid on Saturday mornings. Stockyard policemen seemed to have an uncanny way of finding out where the game was being held each week, even though it moved around. The fine for gambling at the yards was $14.95, which was more than a normal week's wages.

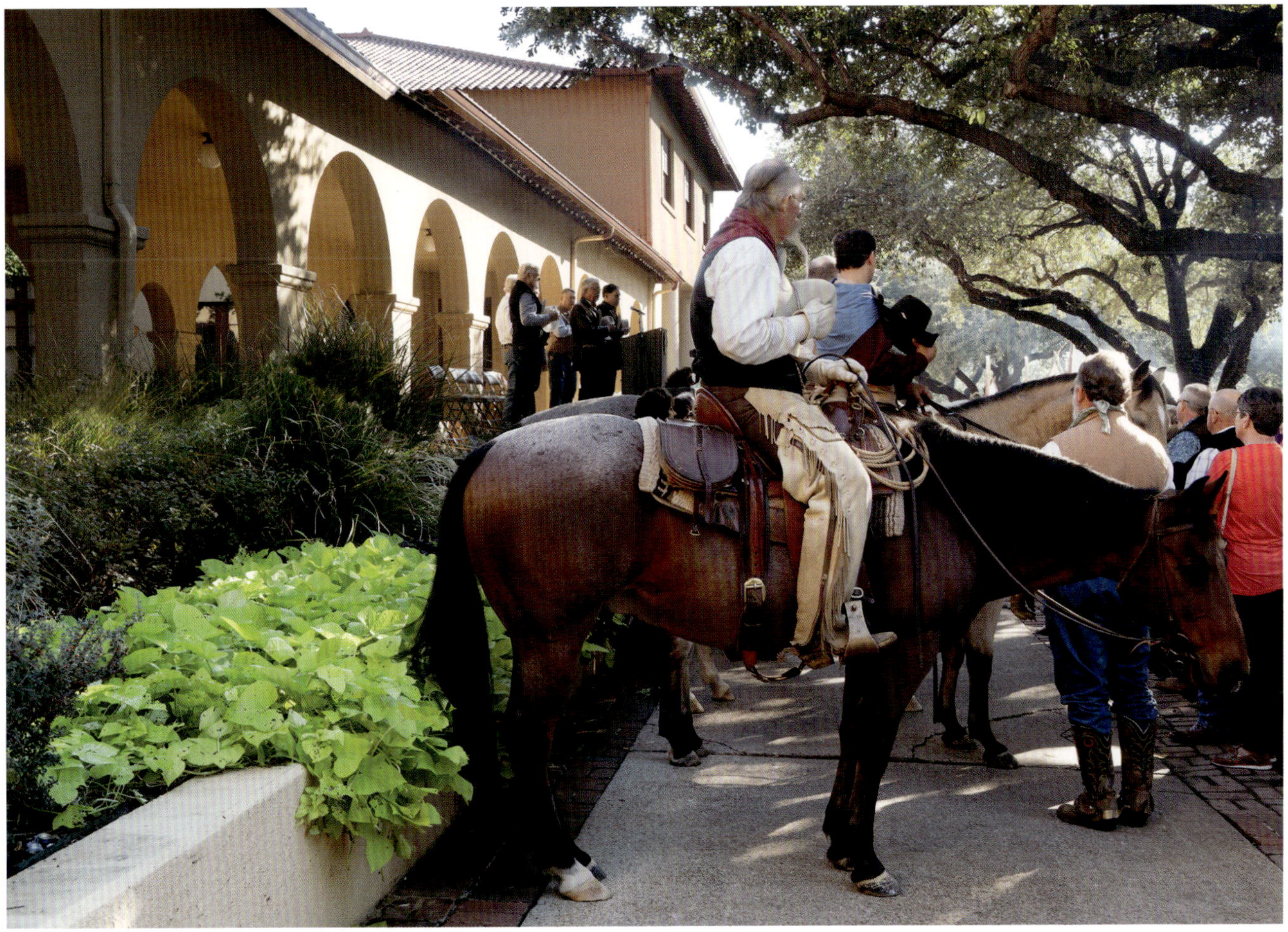

Along with a large audience of visitors and stockyard admirers, drovers pause for a prayer prior to hearing notable speakers in celebration of Red Steagall Day.

Assorted vintage chuckwagons, pulled by horses or mules, trek from Jacksboro, Texas, to the Fort Worth Stockyards for the annual Red Steagall celebration. They set up shop in front of the Livestock Exchange Building, where they participate in a grand and authentic chuckwagon feast competition.

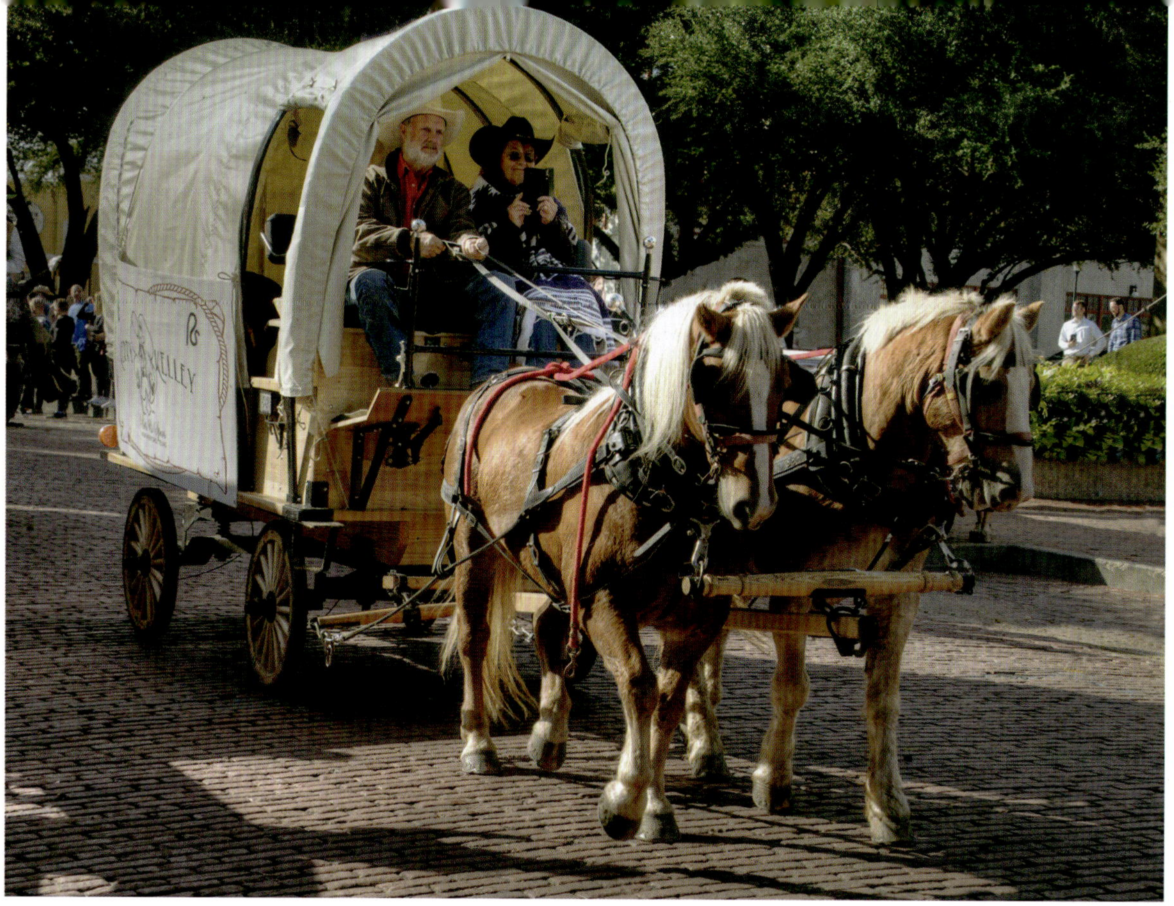

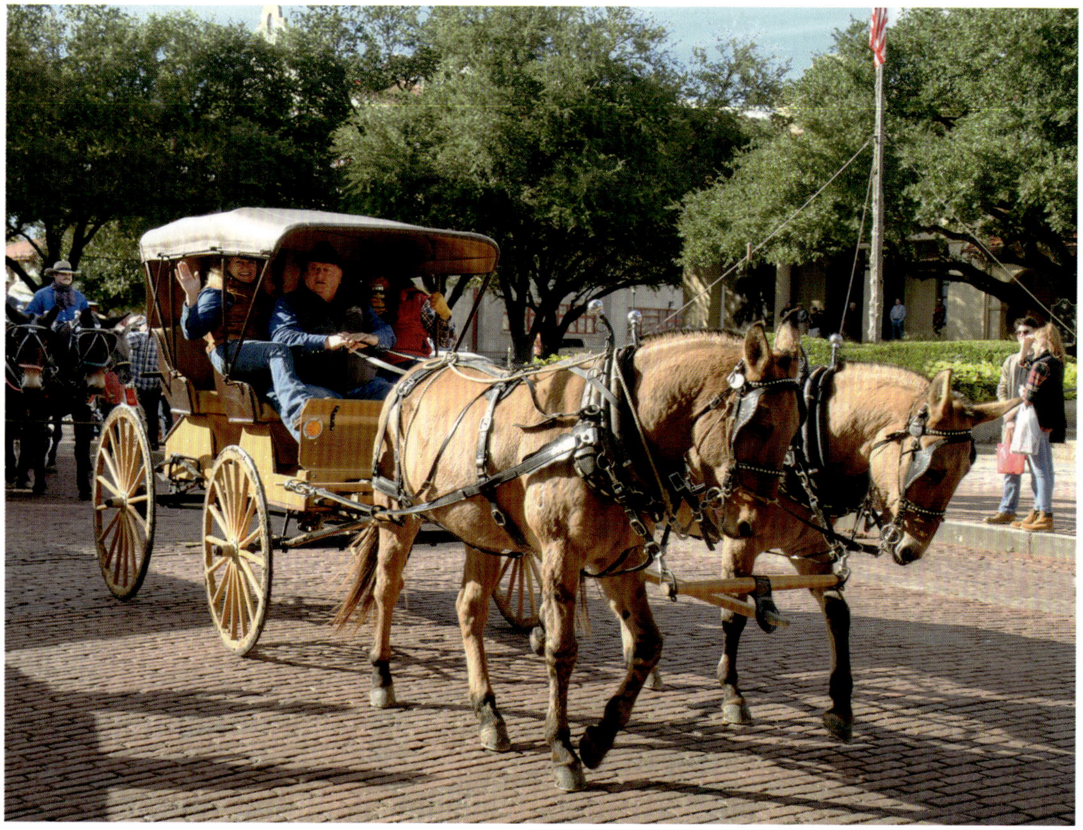

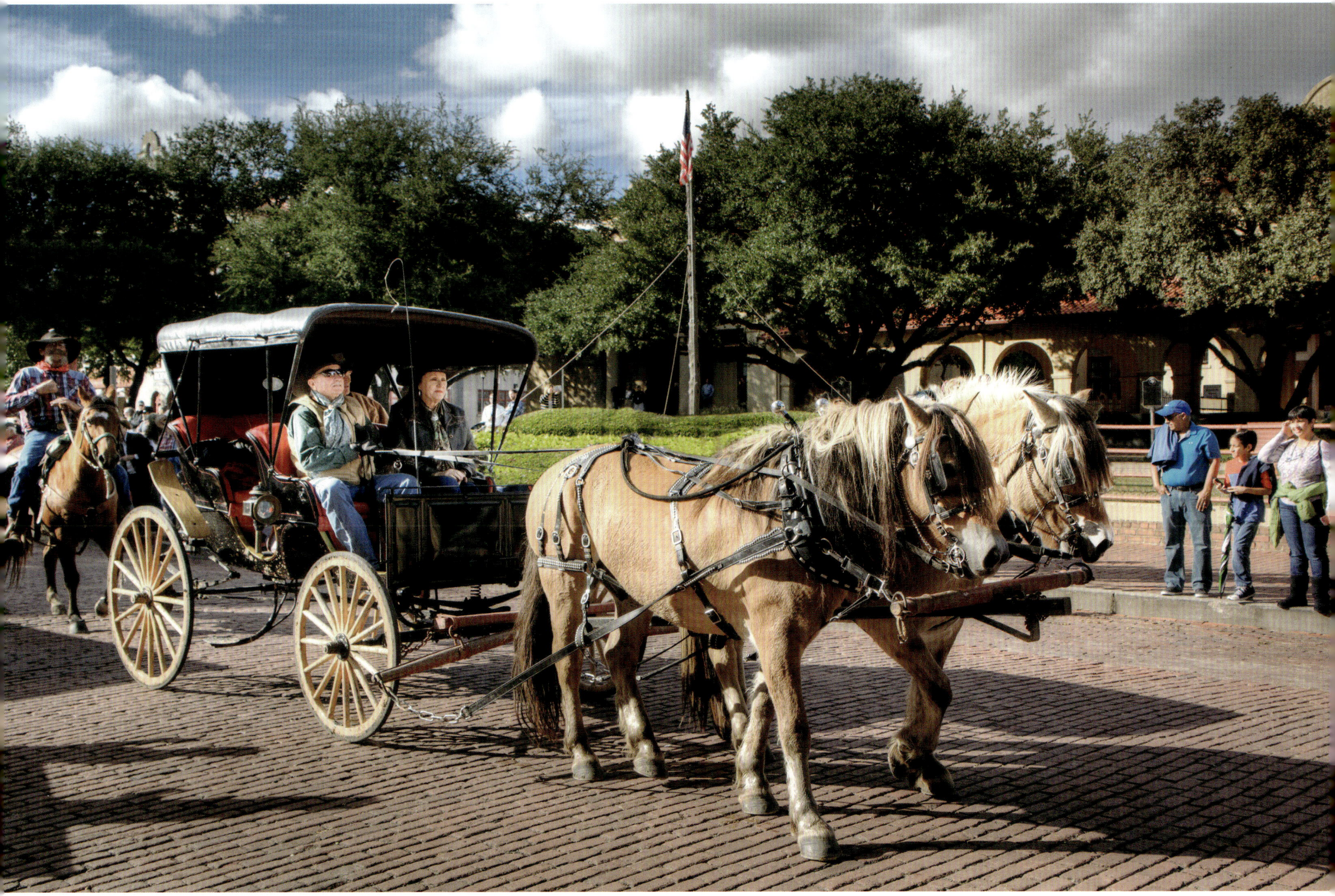

Gambling, drinking, and visiting the prostitutes who lived in the hotels on West Exchange Avenue occupied the after-hours' time of some of the workers. Many of the stockyard employees, however, were family men who went straight home when their long days finally ended. The wife of one commission man remembered that her husband always worked in his rose garden every day after he got home. She once told him he was watering the flowers too much. "Listen, men have to do something," he told her. "Many stay at the yards and play poker, shoot craps, drink, and flirt with the hookers. Hadn't you rather I'd come home and work in the garden?" His wife thought a minute and said, "I guess those roses do need more watering than I thought they did."

As a youngster and later as a teenager, Bill Jary worked for his father's commission business on the yards each summer. The elder Jary, who formerly had worked for his father-in-law, George W. Saunders, by 1928 owned his own firm. He assigned his young son Bill to "chase tickets" on the yards. The pens were divided into seven sections, with commission companies and order buyers each assigned a portion of a section in which to put their livestock. The scale houses were spread among these divisions. Young Jary would carry tickets from the scale back to his father in his assigned booth above the pens after the animals had been weighed. His father would then put the price on the ticket. A lot of young men got their start doing this kind of work for their fathers. They would also spread out hay, water the stock, drive the cattle, and perform similar chores. It was the way a second and then a third generation could almost literally grow up at the Fort Worth Stockyards.

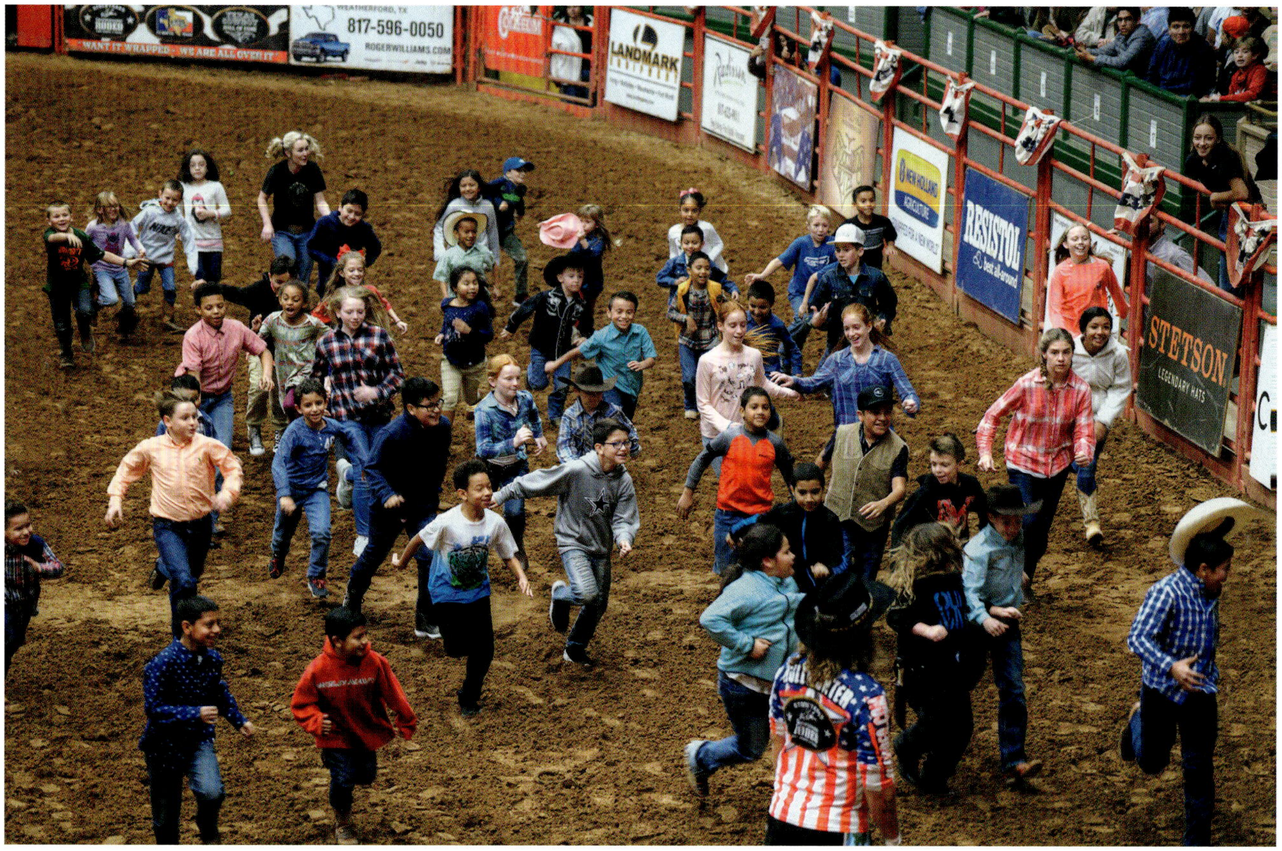

Children race in the calf scramble in hopes of grabbing a ribbon off a calf at the rodeo.

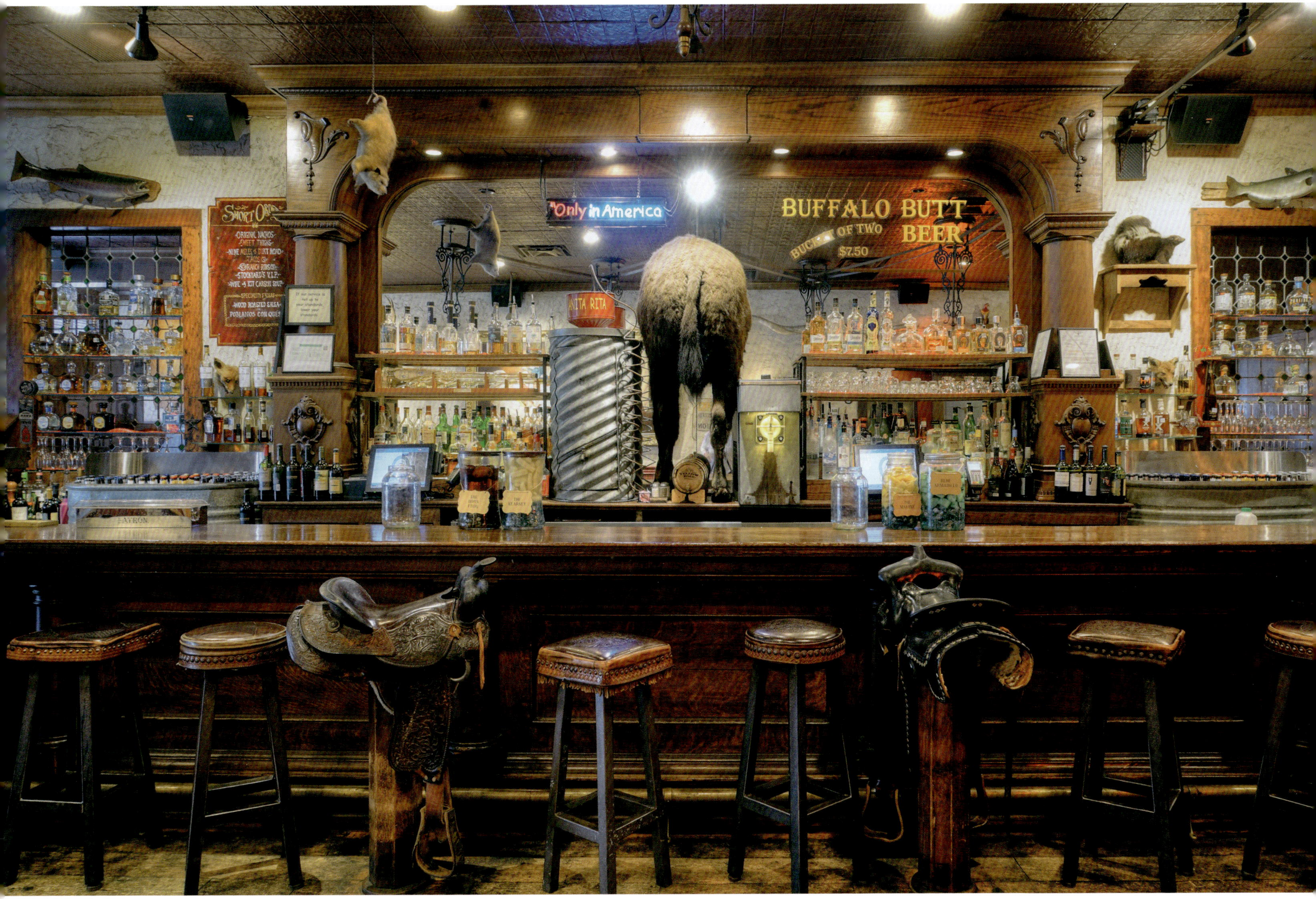

In 1904, Colonel Thomas M. Thannisch built a wood-frame, two-story hotel on this site called the Stock Yards Club. Over the years the hotel has operated under several names and in 1949 became the Stockyards Hotel. Customers can sit in saddles at the bar.

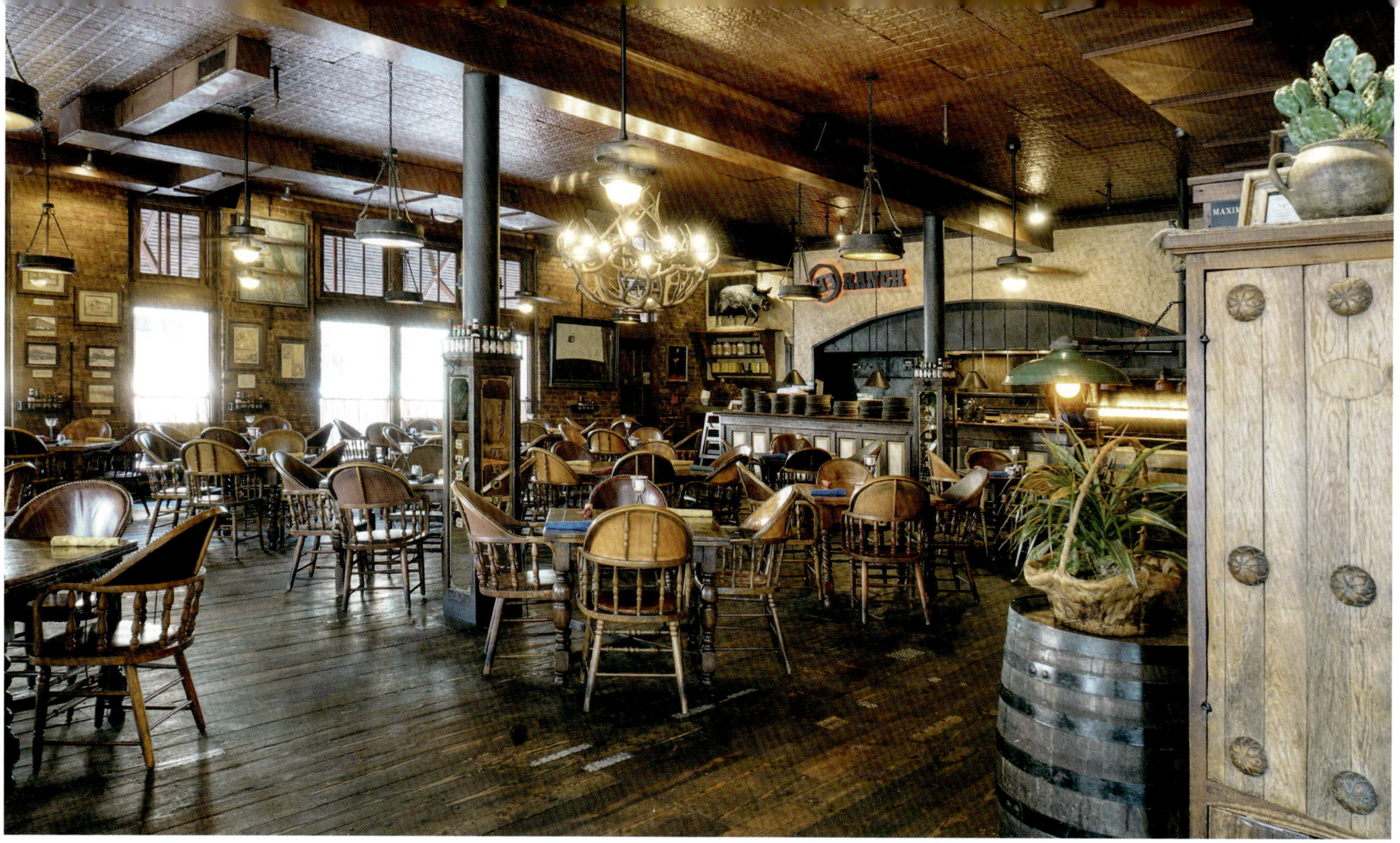

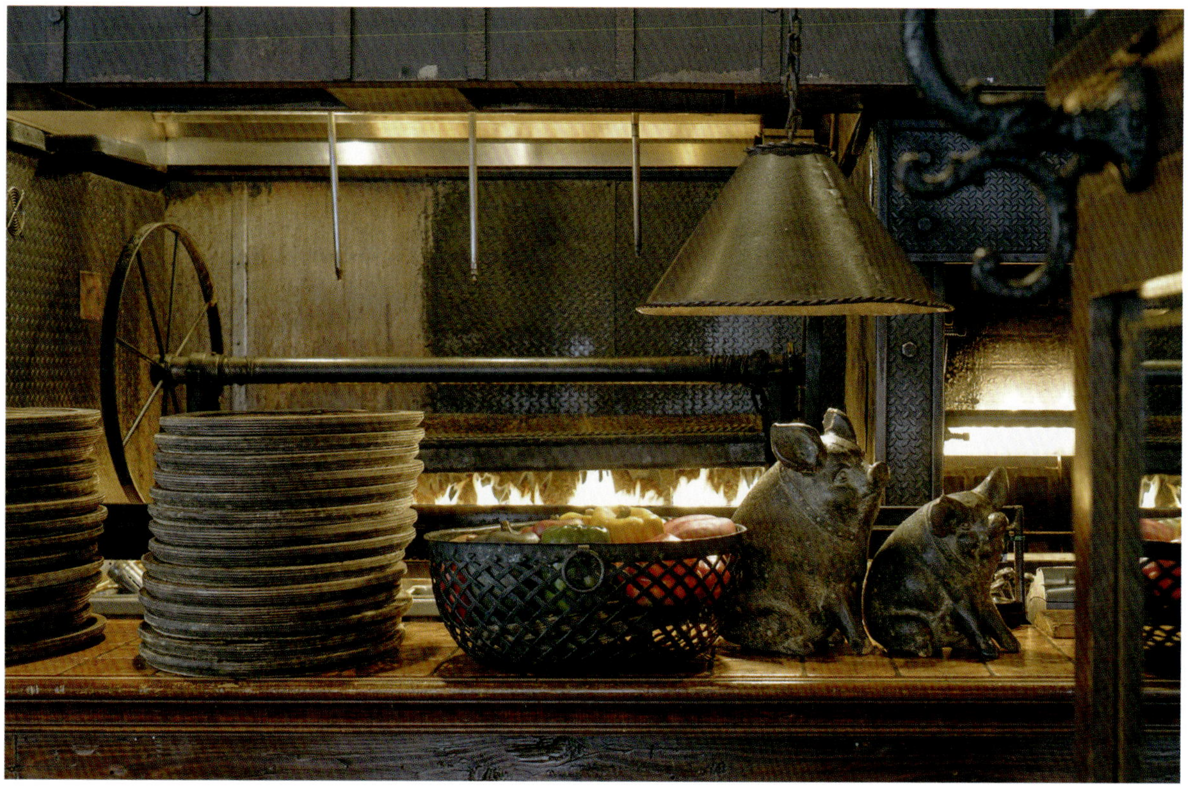

The bar and restaurant at the Stockyards Hotel, Booger Red's Saloon and H3 Ranch, enjoy a five-star reputation for excellent service, food, and drink in a wonderful Western atmosphere.

The tickets the young men carried back and forth included the total number of head sold in a group, the gross pounds, and the price. They showed the ranch from which the animals came, the name of the commission company, and the buyer. The sale was complete when the animals stepped off the weighing scale.

When he was in high school, Bill Jary worked in his father's office in the Exchange Building helping mail out the five thousand letters each week to customers of their company. He worked on the address-o-graph every Thursday during the summers. With each of the thirty to forty commission companies sending out a market letter to its customers every Thursday, the North Fort Worth branch of the US Post Office received more than one hundred thousand pieces of mail that day. These newsletters informed customers of the current market price for their animals. This information kept the sellers coming back to the yards and was one of the reasons that each of the companies could do between twenty thousand and thirty thousand dollars in business each day during peak periods.

On weekends, agents from commission companies went out into the country to visit the customers who shipped to them and to meet others who might be wooed. They called their customers from Fort Worth to tell them when prices had jumped and when they should ship. People accused Charlie Daggett of not even needing a telephone to be heard clear out in West Texas when he talked long distance from the instrument in his office. He yelled so loudly that people heard him all over that wing of the Exchange Building.

Employees and owners of commission companies did not go home at night until the day's work was completed. This included tallying the paperwork for all the transactions that day, often without benefit of an adding machine, and writing checks, many accompanied by a personal note, to producers who had shipped in the livestock. Someone from the office mailed these letters each night on the way home. If it was too late for the mail to go out at the North Side Post Office, the carrier mailed the checks at the downtown branch. Houston Hutchens's wife said her husband, who worked for fifty years on the Fort Worth market, most of the time in his own commission company, often came home at 11:00 p.m., midnight, or even 2:00 a.m. "He was ready to go back the next morning," she said. "He loved it."

The ability of each commission man to judge cattle and please his customers and the service and satisfaction he gave built loyalty among the producers who sent livestock to the market. This kept them coming back to the same commission company or order buyer. The men on the yards could look at an animal and tell within a few pounds what it weighed and what it would weigh when "dressed out" by the packing company. In fact, through the slaughtering process, packing companies kept separate records of the lots of livestock purchased by each buyer and determined how close actual yield came to the earlier projection of dressed-out weight. Anyone who often missed it very far did not long remain a buyer for the company. Buyers also could look in an animal's eyes and tell if it had been wheat-fed or grain-fed in a feedlot. Wheat would produce a yellow fat on the animal that consumers did not like.

Typical clothing worn on the yards consisted of medium-sized Stetsons or large straw hats in the summer, blue cotton shirts, and khaki pants. Men could purchase this kind of outfit at the White Front Clothing Store on Exchange Avenue (still in existence) for fifty cents for the shirts and a dollar for the pants. "But you didn't necessarily pay what was marked," claimed William Barse, a long-time commission man. "You bid a little lower." Although a brief fad for overalls developed at the yards in the early 1920s, it soon died down, and only farmers wore overalls. While some of the men claimed that good heavy shoes felt more comfortable on the uneven bricks of the pens than boots, most men at the yards wore Western boots.

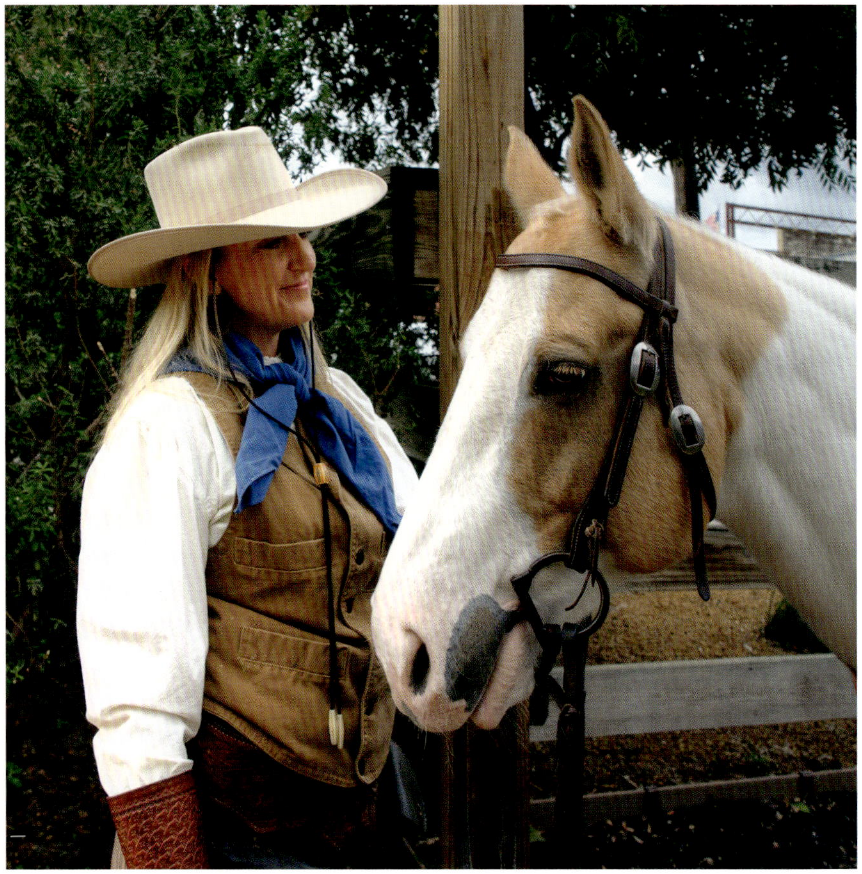

Since 2002 Kristin Jaworski has served as Fort Worth Herd trail boss, responsible for the day-to-day management of the city of Fort Worth's twice-daily cattle drive. She is shown with her gorgeous horse, McCoy. The herd enjoyed a twenty-year celebration in 2019.

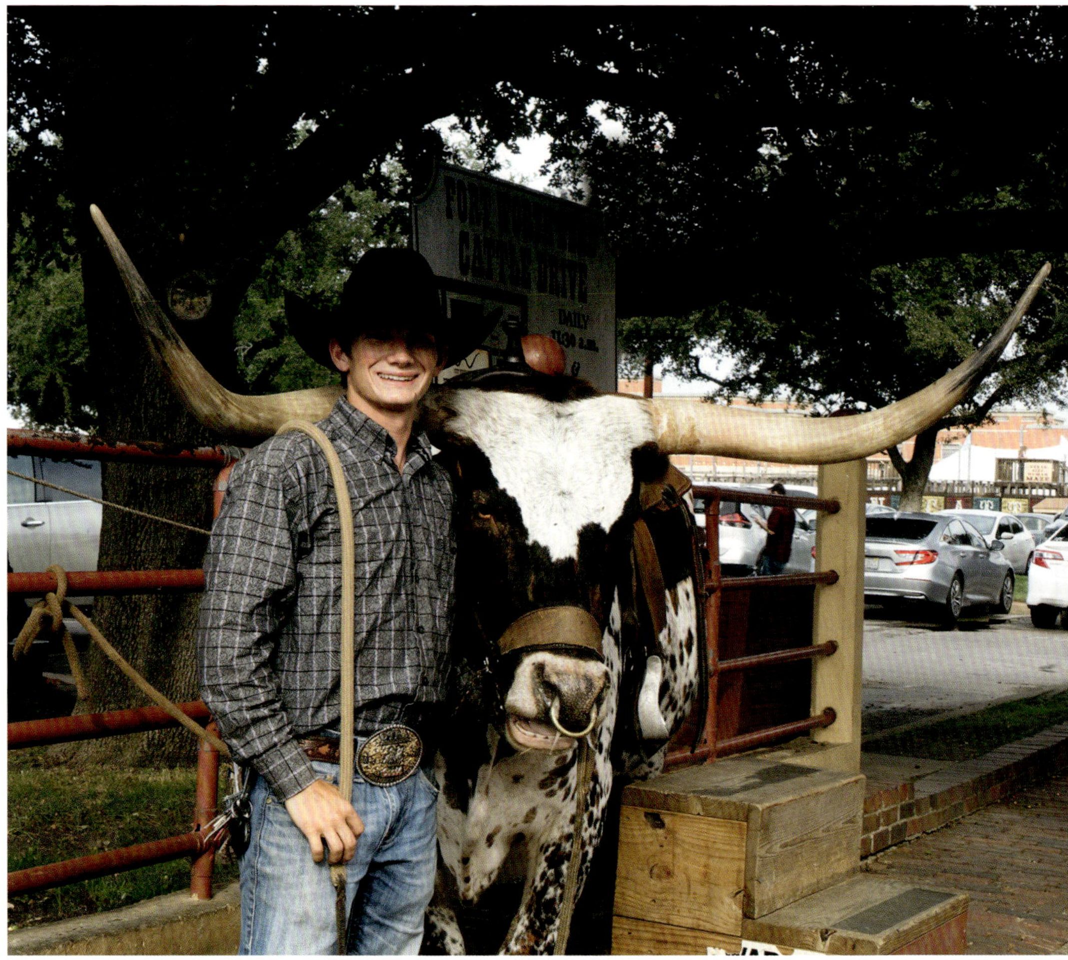

A smiling youth oversees the saddled Longhorn and those wishing to sit on his back for a photo to remember.

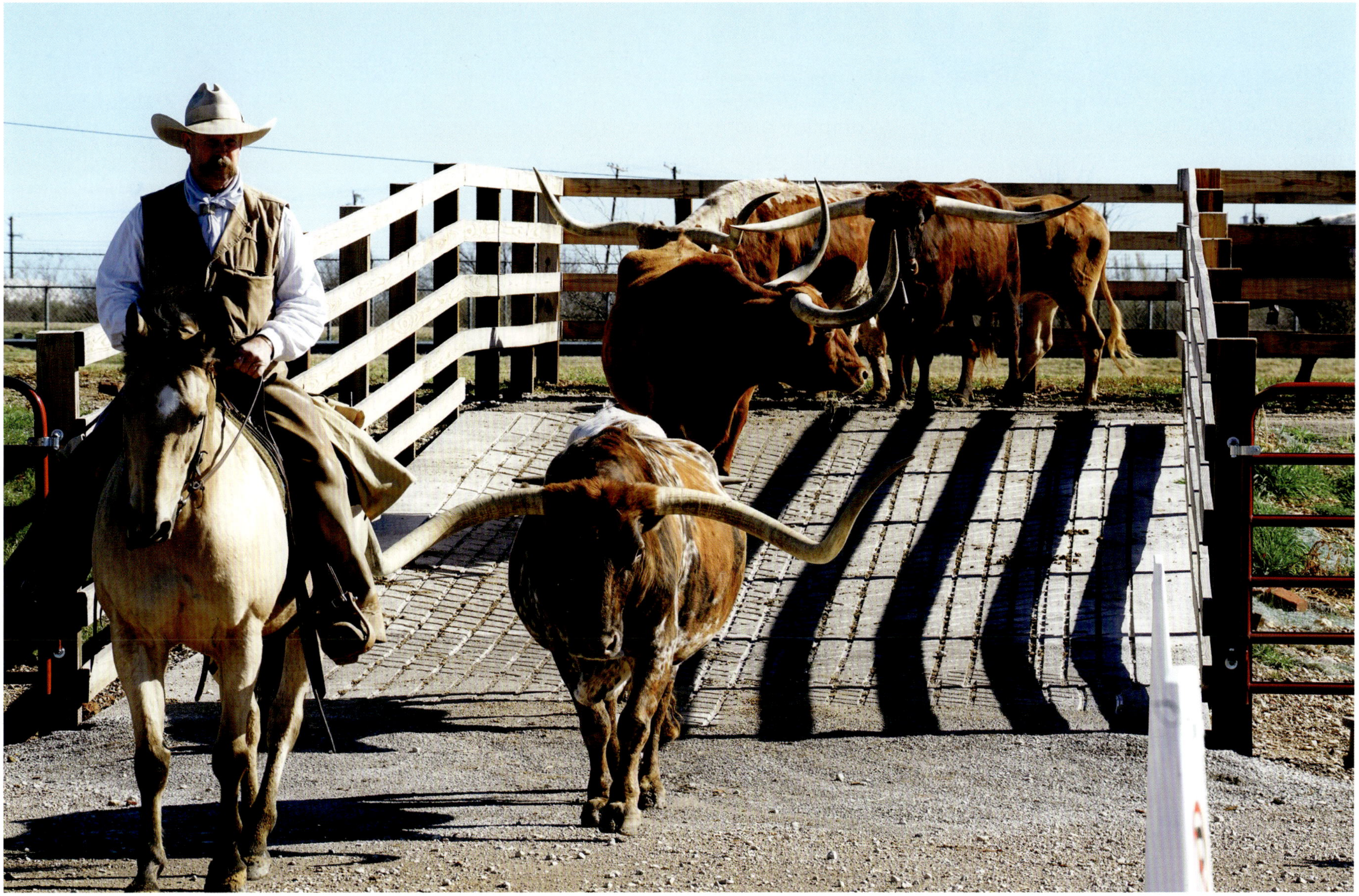

A lone drover on his horse accompanies the herd as they trek toward their pens, where hay is served as a reward for a day's hard work.

In the early days, every morning that dealing occurred, representatives of each trader or speculator gathered in the large lobby of the Livestock Exchange Building before daylight. They squatted down in a big circle and tossed a coin for a position to begin the trading for the day. While some stockyards allowed traders to run for position to see who could reach the biggest and busiest commission agents first, the Fort Worth market for many years followed the practice of tossing coins for the first three chances to begin dickering at the pens of specific companies. After all the traders had tossed for their positions and looked at the animals of the particular company for which they had won the toss, then anyone could bid if the cattle had not been sold.

Later the Packers and Stockyards Administration required that buyers be bonded and referred to all of them as "dealers," so that term came into more common usage than "traders" or "speculators." As each trader headed for the particular commission company to which his toss entitled him, he saw heavily loaded hay wagons being

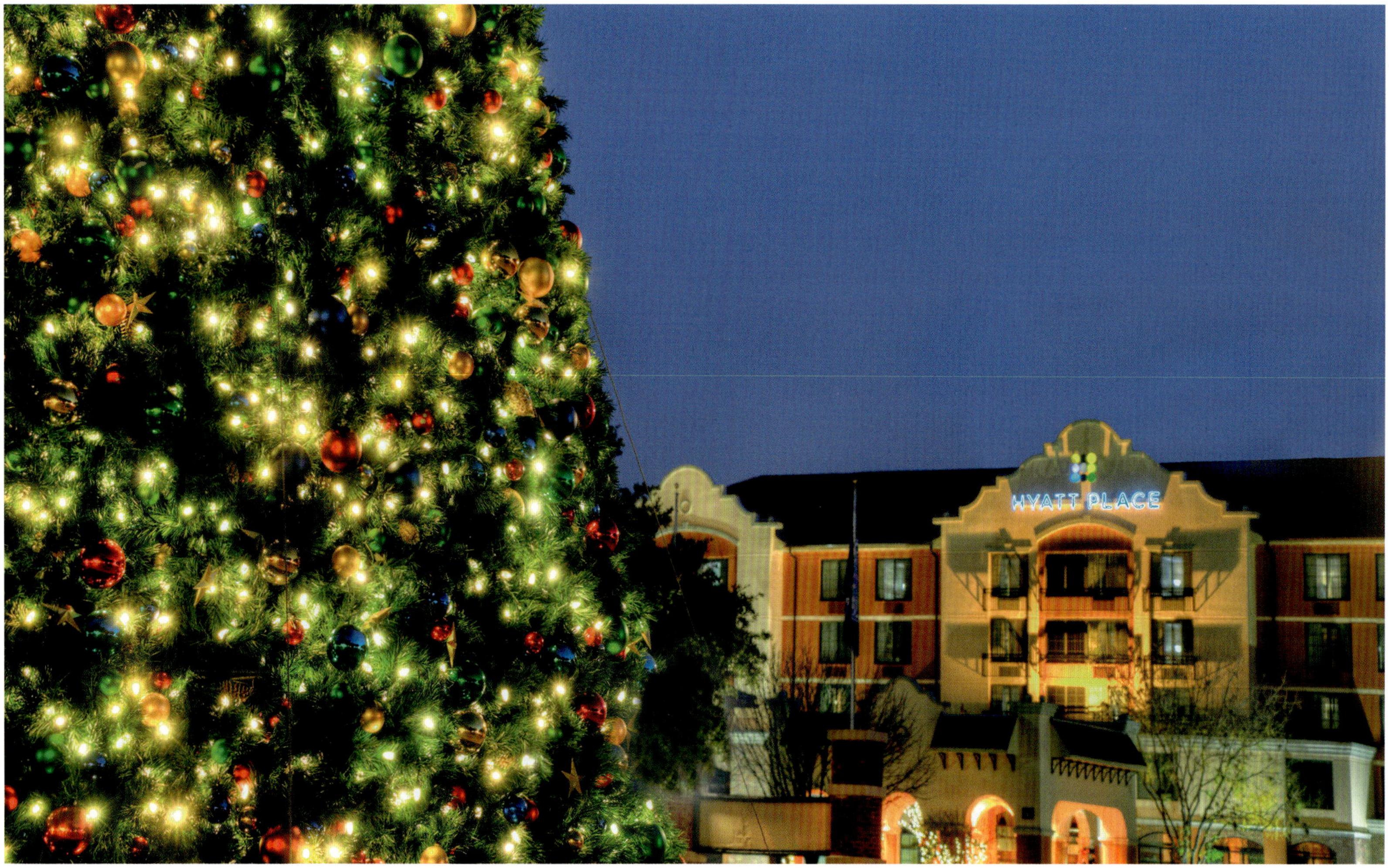

Christmas is a marvelous celebration at the stockyards. An extravagantly decorated tree with brilliant lights, glass stars, and sparkling balls near the famous Hyatt Place, a comfortable hotel where visitors can stay in the center of the stockyards.

pulled slowly down the main alley, which ran from Exchange Avenue to Twenty-Eighth Street. They would see some of the approximately 200 to 250 stockyard workers filling the pens on each side with fresh hay or delivering extra hay to the booths of the commission firms. Head packer buyers from Armour and Swift sent their assistants down each alley to the several divisions to look over the fat cattle ready for slaughter.

Roy Weeman, who became head buyer for Swift in 1940, remembered instructions from Swift manager John Holmes not to be too friendly with the Armour buyers, not to drink a lot of coffee with them or do anything that would cause suspicion that collusion in buying might be taking place. They did not want the agents from the Packers and Stockyards Administration after them.

Stockyard workers could be a frivolous bunch if the situation called for it. Folks who worked in the Livestock Exchange Building found the excuse on Christmas Eve to drop fireworks down to the lower front lobby from the banisters of the second story. Also, young women working in the various offices could not leave their desks for fear someone would throw a "chaser" firecracker at them.

In fact, the stockyards area renewed its reputation as a rough part of town, and women did not walk unaccompanied down Exchange Avenue or even into the lobby when the traders gathered for their early-morning tossing for place. However, on New Year's Day stockyard folks welcomed women at the annual dance in the lobby as different bands and callers performed in each wing of the building. The men maintained a sense of humor out on the yards. A prankster might unsaddle someone's horse that had been left unattended, put the saddle on a mule, tie the mule in the same spot, and go hide the horse.

Al Donovan, after he had worked for the Fort Worth Stockyards Company for thirty years, retired in 1946, having been the president from 1931 to 1944, then later division manager under United Stockyards. W. L. Pier, who replaced Donovan, calculated that some seventy-five million animals passed through the yards during Donovan's tenure. Pier began his career at the stockyards as president of the Stockyards National Bank.

A new rule that the Packers and Stockyards Administration passed and enforced concerned "Rules and Regulations of the Market." On June 21, 1946, the new regulations allowed the nation's stockyards, including those in Fort Worth, to operate only during the hours of 8:00 a.m. to 3:00 p.m. A whistle would blow to start and end trading. No longer would the traders gather before daylight in the Exchange Building to begin an early day. They quickly tossed for position in the alleys just before the 8:00 a.m. whistle. Old-timers figured a real era had ended when trading became limited to the specified hours. One can assume that a few of them expressed

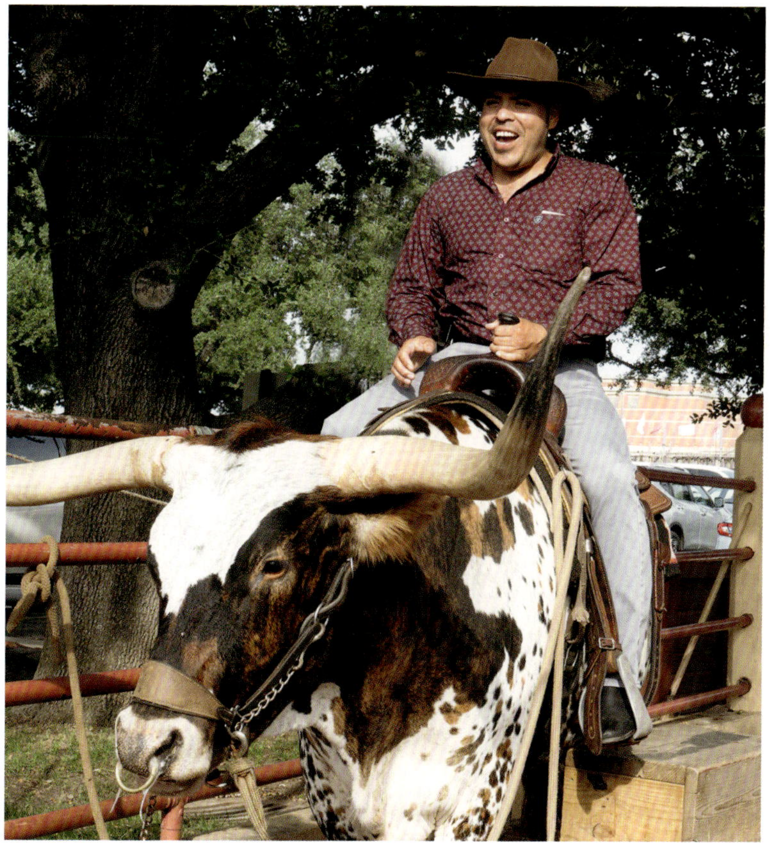

A stockyards visitor saddles up for a one-of-a-kind experience.

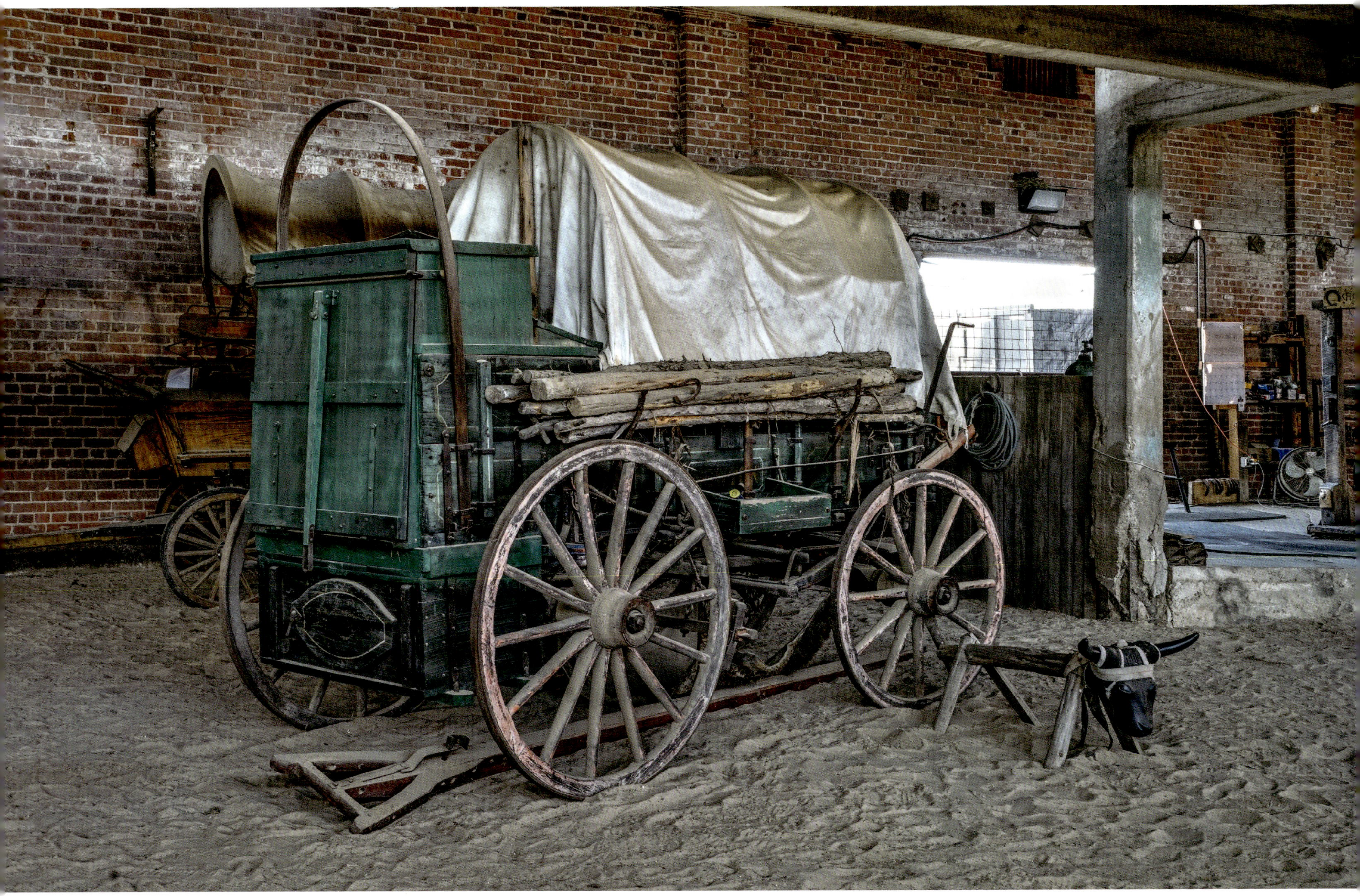

This antique chuckwagon is a perfect example of an invention attributed to Charles Goodnight, a Texas rancher who introduced the concept in 1866. Some cattlemen needed to eat on the road for months at a time. The "chuck box" at the back of the wagon held drawers and shelves for storage.

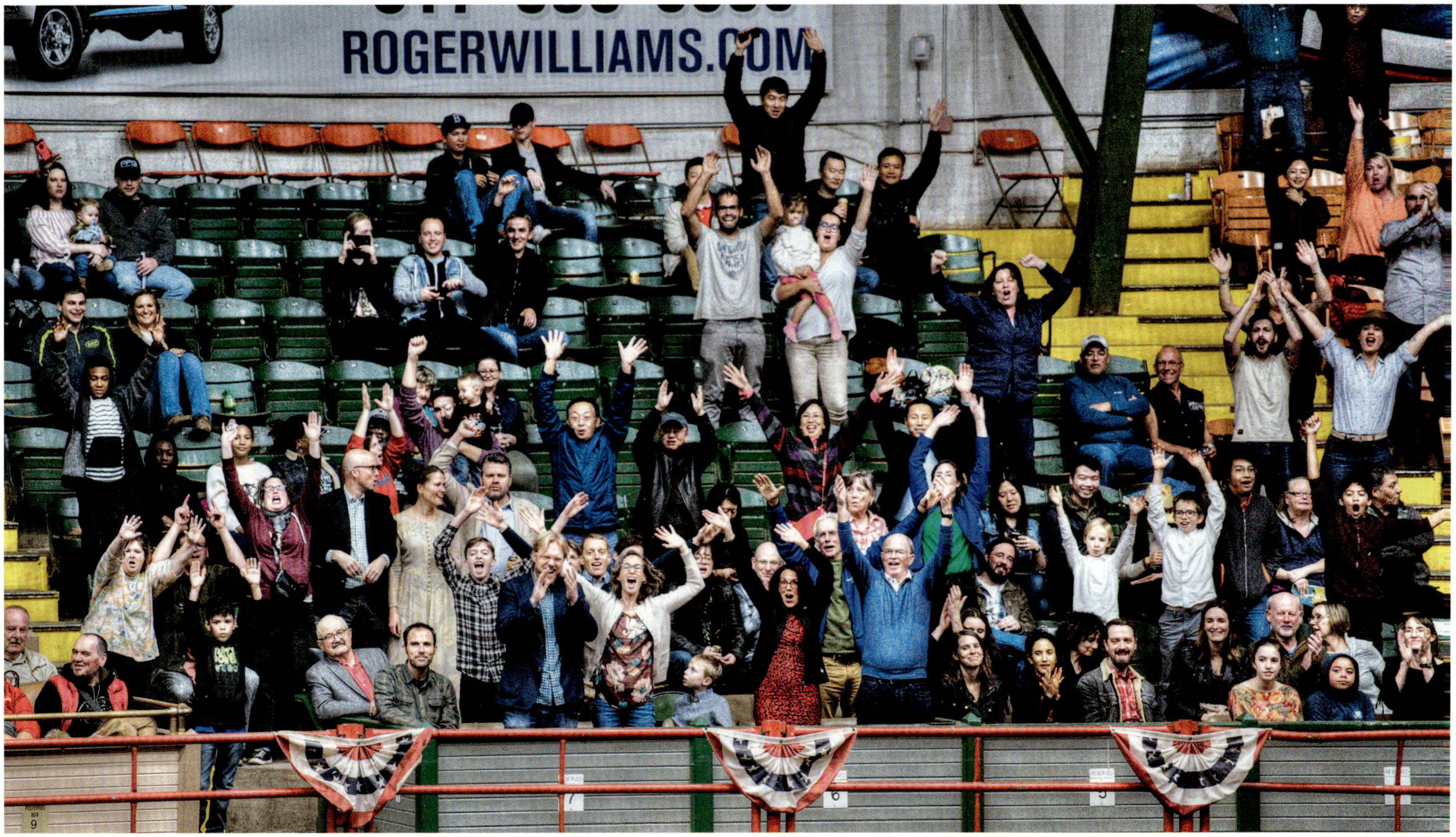

Rodeo fans stand and wave their arms, hoping to attract the attention of performers shooting souvenirs out of an air cannon.

their feelings about Uncle Sam in strong language not appropriate for gentle ears.

A special feeling existed at the Fort Worth Stockyards, and perhaps at the other large terminal markets during their boom years. The private-treaty market system involving commission companies and the huge shipments of livestock by rail, which occurred during this special era in history, is unlikely ever to be duplicated. Just as railroads replaced covered wagons in an earlier day, motor trucks eventually replaced the railroad as the major method of transporting the nation's goods, including livestock. When livestock did not have to move by rail, they could be carried anywhere, so the large, terminal market centers designed mainly to receive rail shipments began to decline. Packers and others began to buy livestock directly from the producer or in small-town auctions nearer the producing areas. By the 1930s this unique period of American livestock history, the terminal-market heyday, in which Fort Worth played a major role, began its slow but inevitable change. However, the romantic spirit, Western character, and close camaraderie of stockyard people, that buoyantly alive feeling of being someone special, seemed as distinctive as the livestock markets themselves.

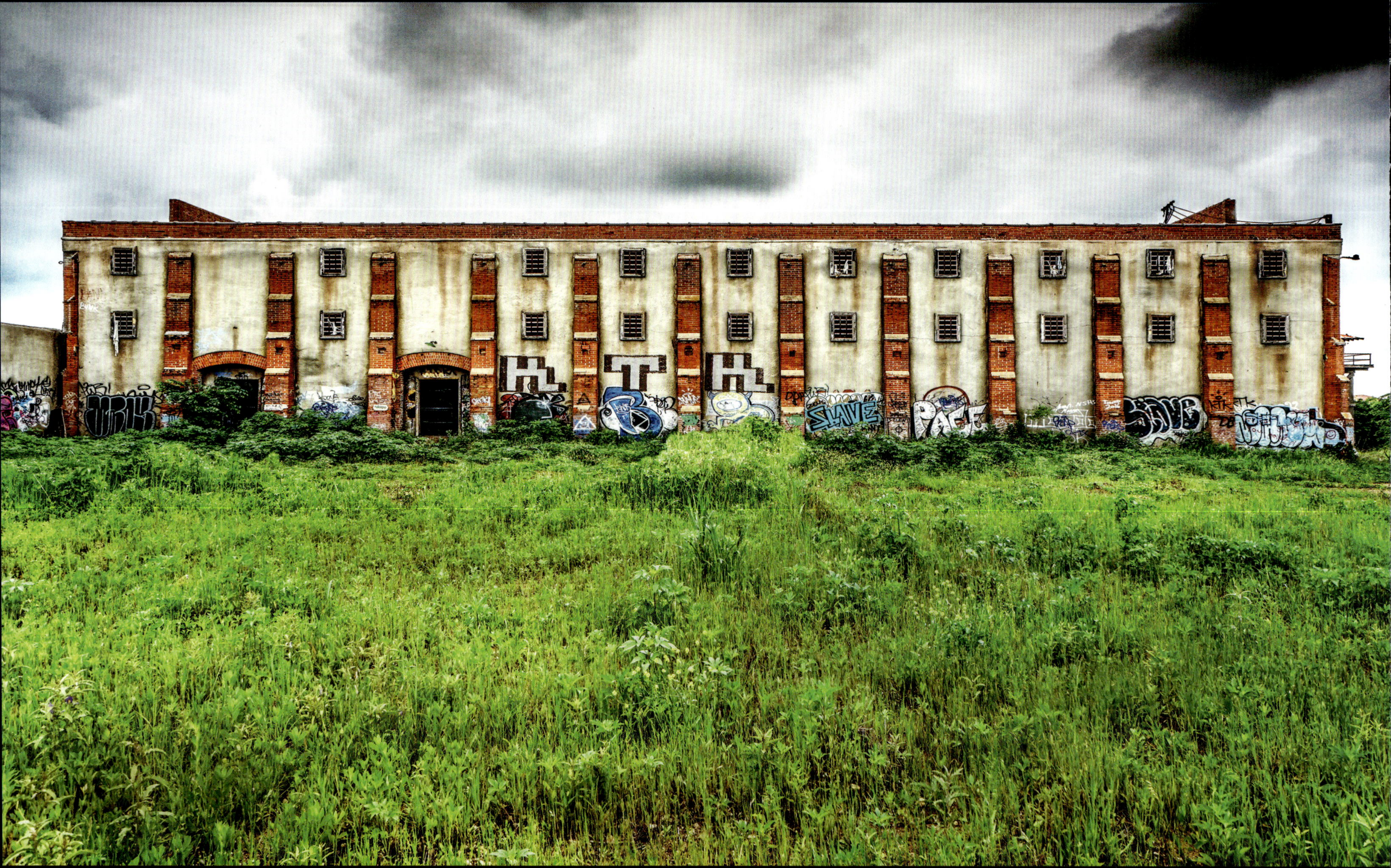

CHAPTER 6

A Slow Decline

Following the end of World War II with its huge livestock receipts and high prices, it became inevitable that things would slow down at the livestock markets of the nation, including the large one in Fort Worth. The massive effort to feed America's troops, who were fighting the war and giving additional aid to the Allies, kept livestock production booming and the pens in the stockyards crowded. However, changes in marketing livestock affected the big stockyards like the one at Fort Worth as well.

A major issue that surfaced in the late 1940s was the problem of decentralized markets. In small towns closer to the farms and ranches, auctions developed, even during the war, that allowed farmers and the larger livestock producers to sell their stock closer to home without having to utilize the larger public stockyards such as the one in Fort Worth. During World War II, while the big packers sold the processed meat in great volume to the government, openings developed for small independent packers to operate. Ordinary consumers bought from these independents if they got any meat at all. The scattered country auction barns in various Texas communities accommodated this new demand. An advantage to the smaller auctions was that, because of their size, they did not have to follow federal price controls. Thus, farmers could obtain higher prices in the new auction barns than in the large stockyards.

In the 1930s and earlier, the bulk of the livestock slaughter and meatpacking occurred in some twenty of the nation's larger cities, with Fort Worth ranking high on that list. As of 1946, thirty-five hundred meatpacking plants in all sections of the country and twenty-six

The Fertilizer House was one of two buildings saved from the Swift meatpacking company when others, abandoned since 1972, were demolished in 2016. This building sits on the southern edge of the vast site. It is three stories tall with impressive buttresses on the exterior.

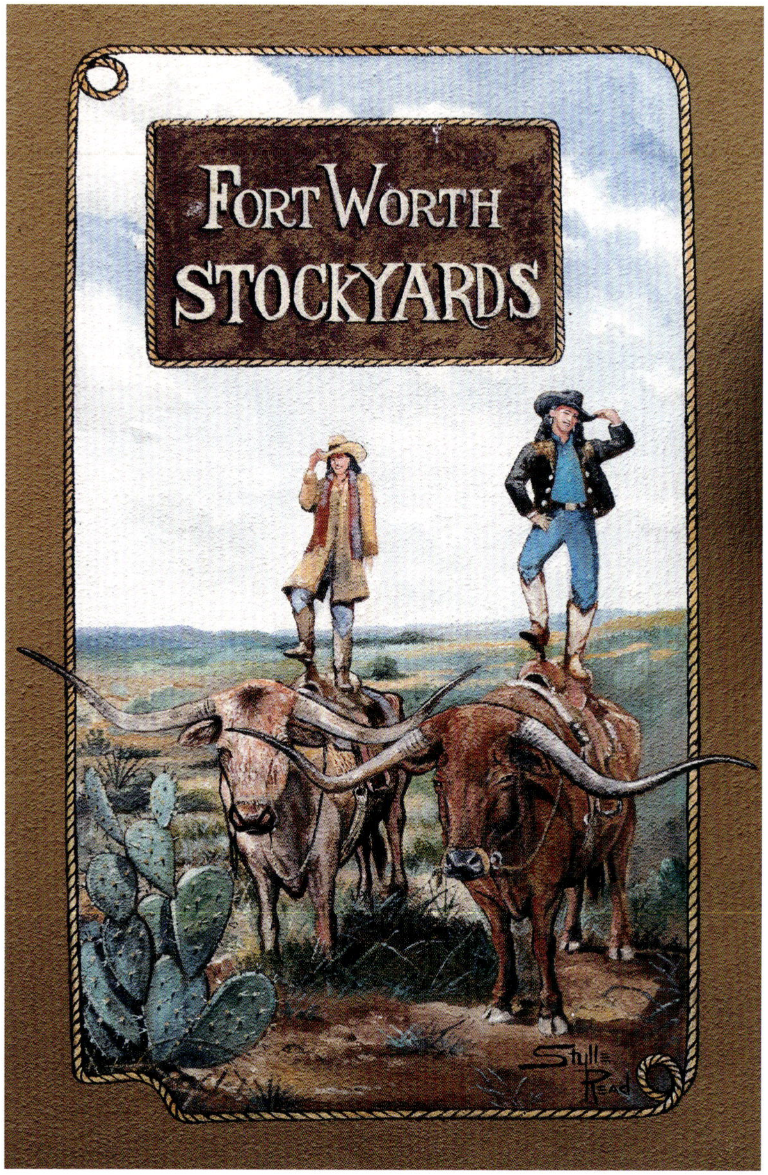

Playful cowgirls stand atop their saddled Longhorn cattle and tip their hats to visitors in a 2012 painting by Stylle Read. This unusual painting is surrounded by a rope pattern around the image.

The 1902 Laboratory Building is one of two still-standing brick buildings from the Swift meatpacking area. A large bird guards the building in spring 2016. Because of this bird family, the surrounding tall grasses were free of snakes and rats.

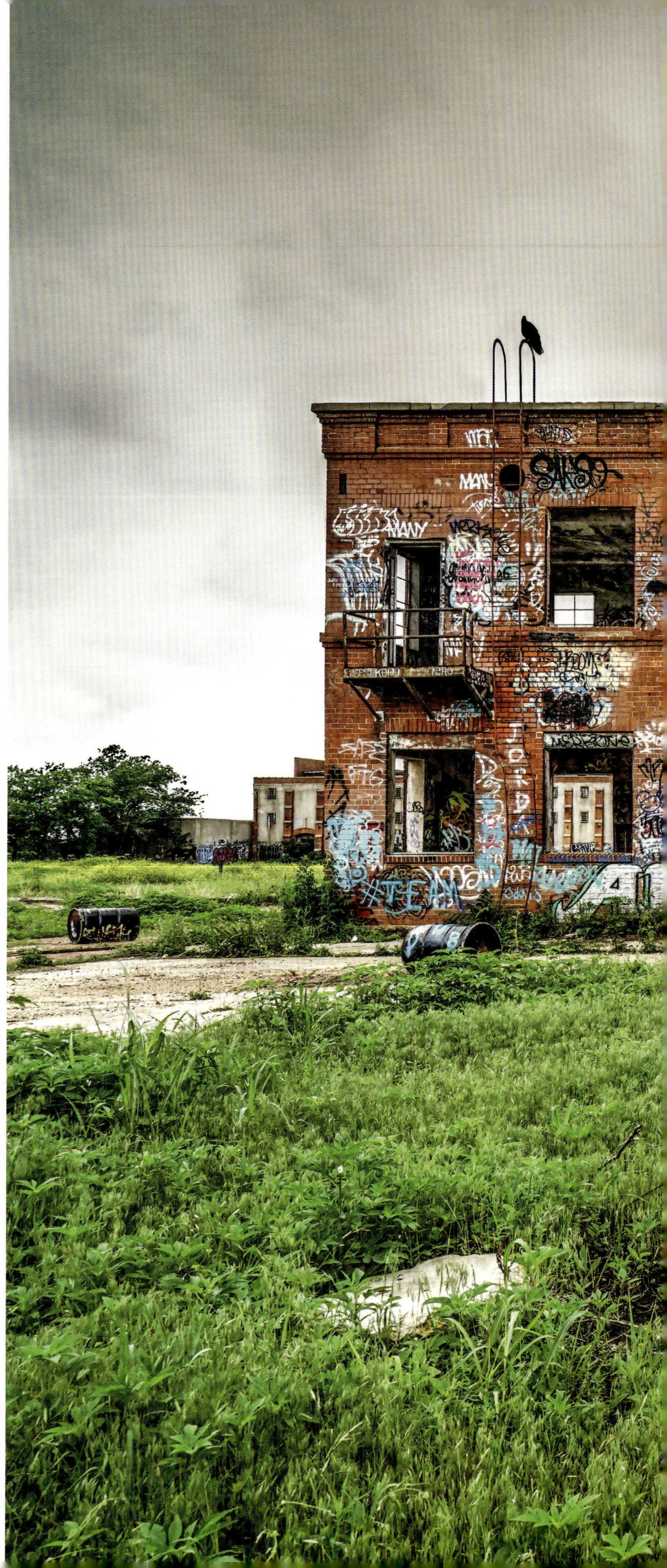

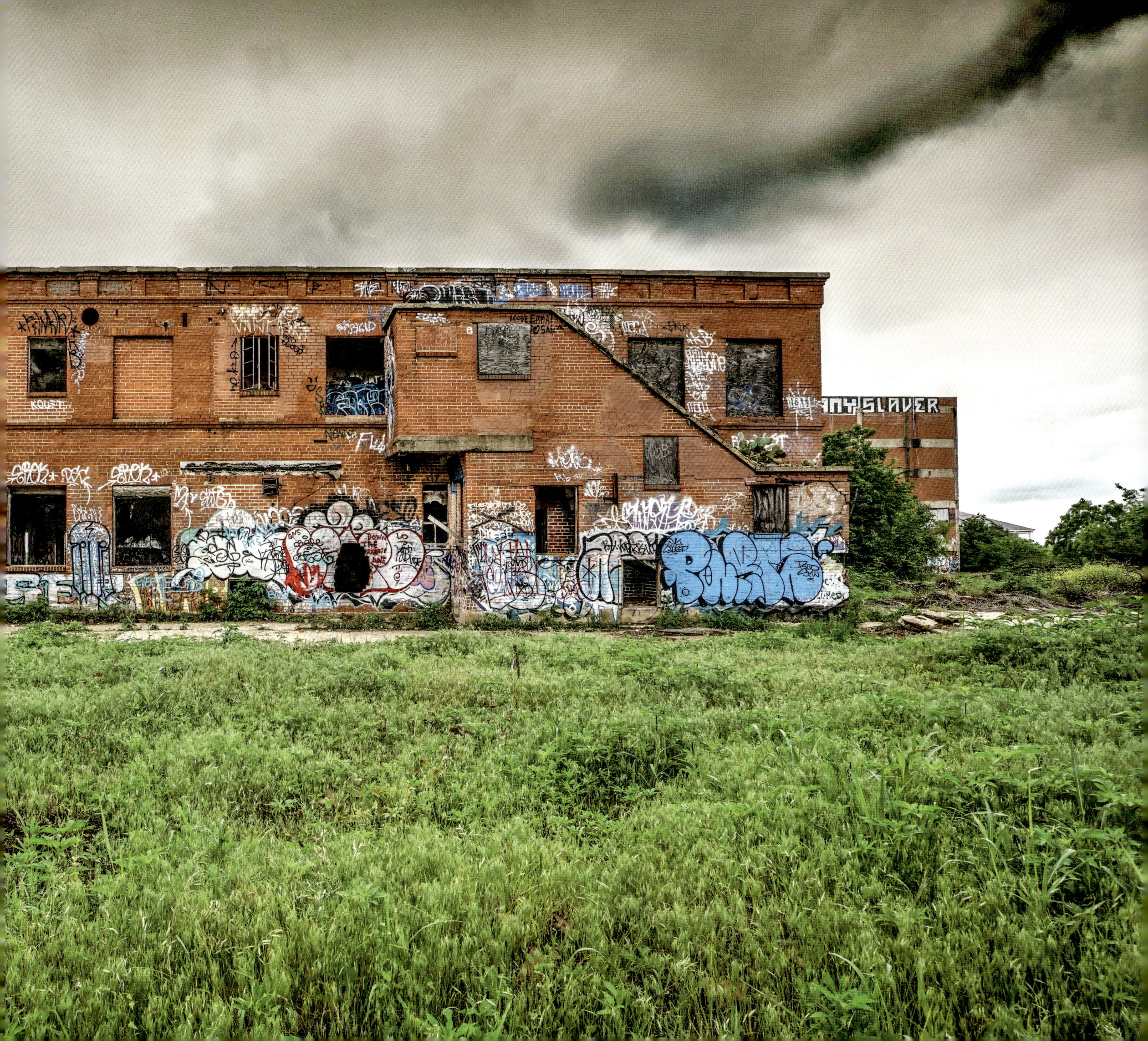

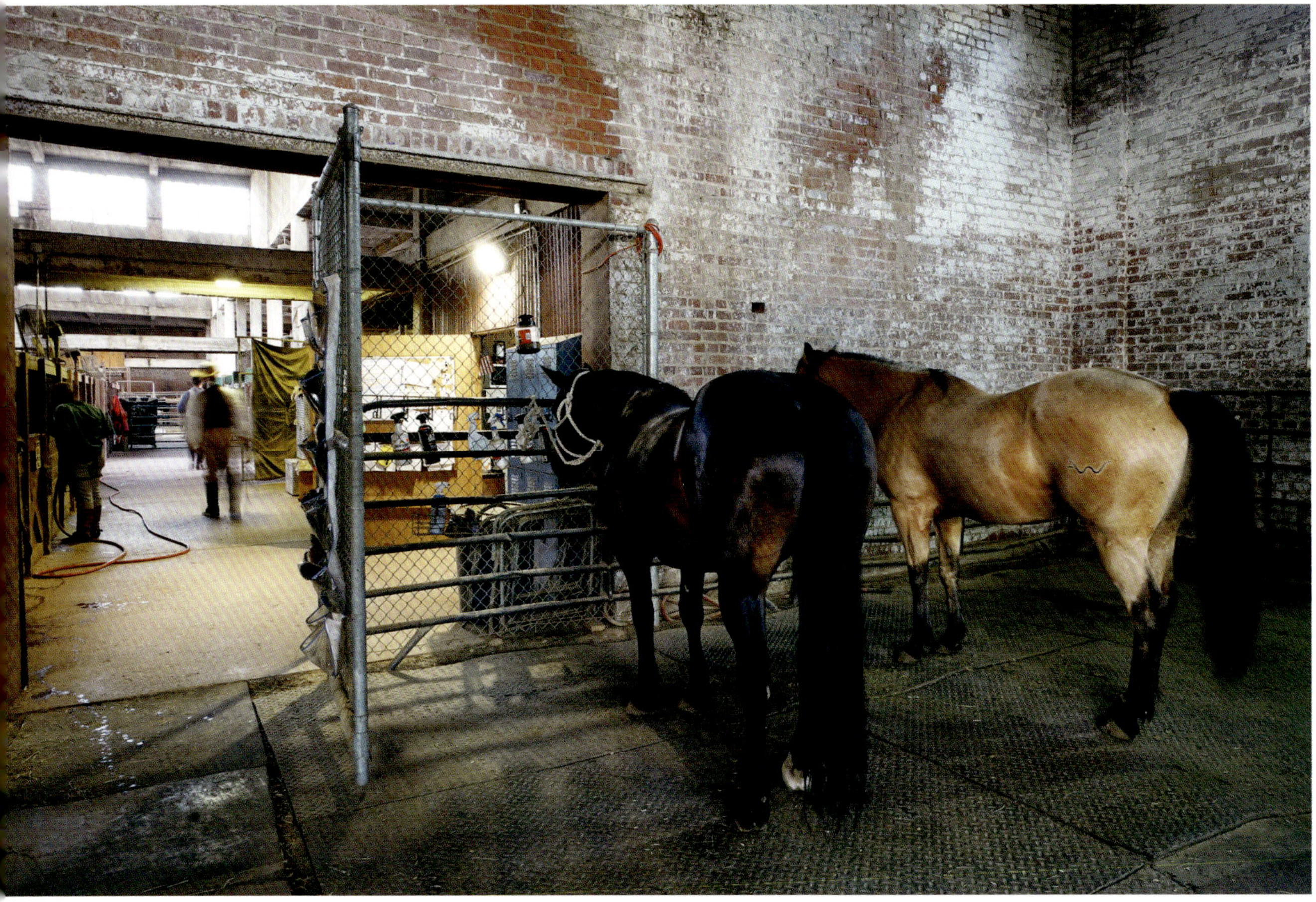

Two horses await grooming at the historic Mule Barn in the center of the stockyards complex. In 2019, the building was vacated, the horses and mules relocated, and the Mule Barn and Mule Alley area restored, ready for new businesses in 2020.

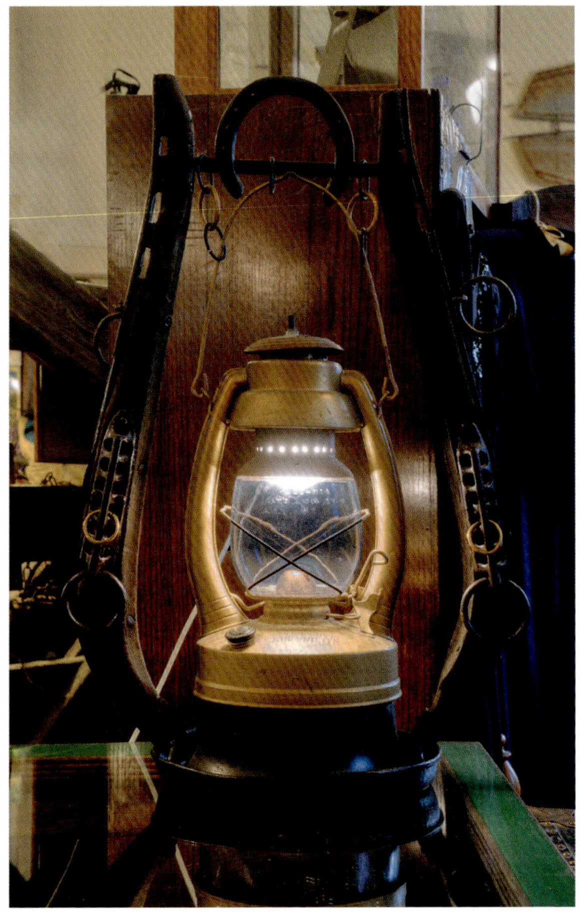

A whimsical version of an old lantern is displayed at the North Fort Worth Historical Society Museum inside the Livestock Exchange Building. The lantern has antique hames that attach to a horse collar and hook to a wagon.

yards utilized forty-eight commission companies during the World War II years, but that number began dropping.

W. L. Pier of the Fort Worth Stockyards sent out pamphlets to producers warning of the "danger" of direct marketing in the smaller towns. The American Stockyards Association published a pamphlet titled *Dollars and Sense in Livestock Marketing* and distributed it in bulk. Terminal-market officials wrote editorials, advertisements, and pamphlets to argue that the central markets were the only place where volume could be large enough to attract all kinds of buyers, and thus it remained the only fair place for prices to be set. With these activities the nation's large terminal markets such as the one in Fort Worth began fighting for their very existence.

One situation that no doubt aided the country auctions and hurt the Fort Worth market occurred when the Fort Worth Stockyards began closing the Saturday sales. The commission firms requested the new procedure so that they did not work six-day weeks. Also, the stockyards would not have to pay overtime to its employees. The small country markets, on the other hand, usually operated on Saturday. The large terminal markets, when facing the new competition, thus inadvertently made changes that aided the small markets and hurt themselves. Even the noon-hour, livestock radio program at Fort Worth ended in February 1949 when the station reclaimed the broadcast time.

In the summer of 1949, Pier began sending weekly reports of losses, not profits, to the owner of the local market, United Stockyards. However, of 211 posted public stockyards in the nation in late 1949, the US Department of Agriculture classified only 12 as major markets, and Fort Worth remained one of these. It received the second-largest number of sheep and lambs in the nation that year and still ranked as the principal livestock market in the Southwest.

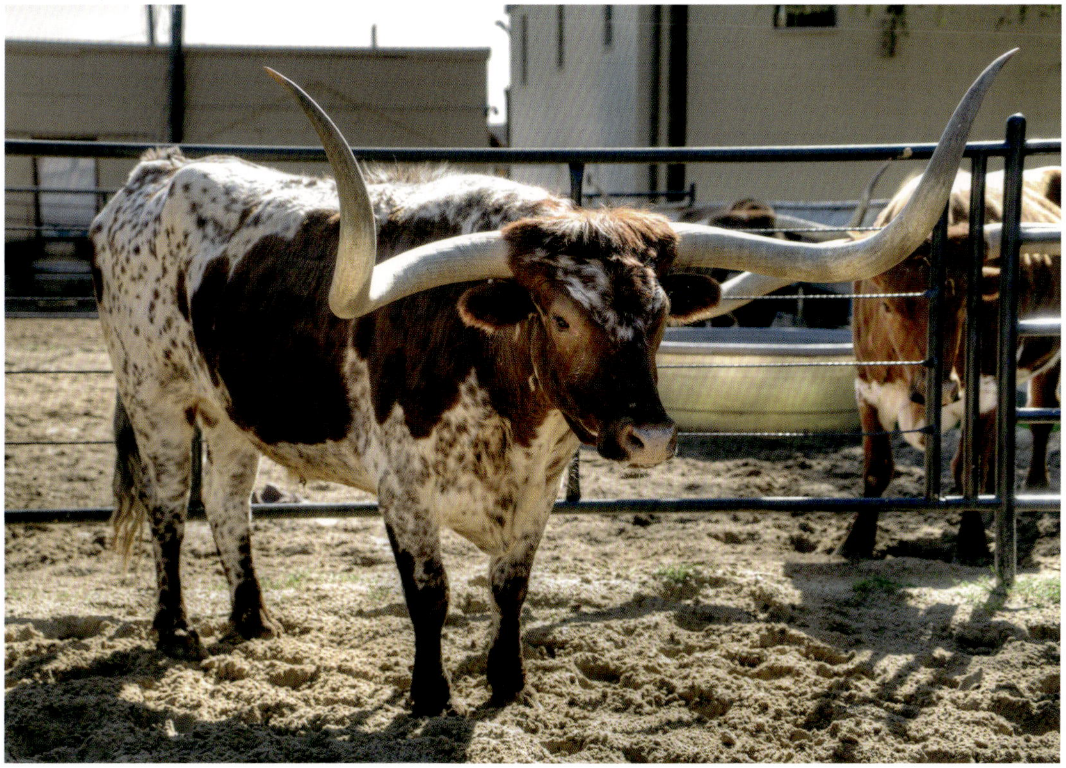

Visitors can get close and view Longhorn cattle when they visit the Educational Program the herd provides. Support from the community allows the Fort Worth Herd to keep the legacy of the Texas Longhorn alive. The Friends of the Fort Worth Herd, a 501(c)(3) nonprofit organization, directed by a volunteer board, is committed to providing monetary and in-kind support to the herd.

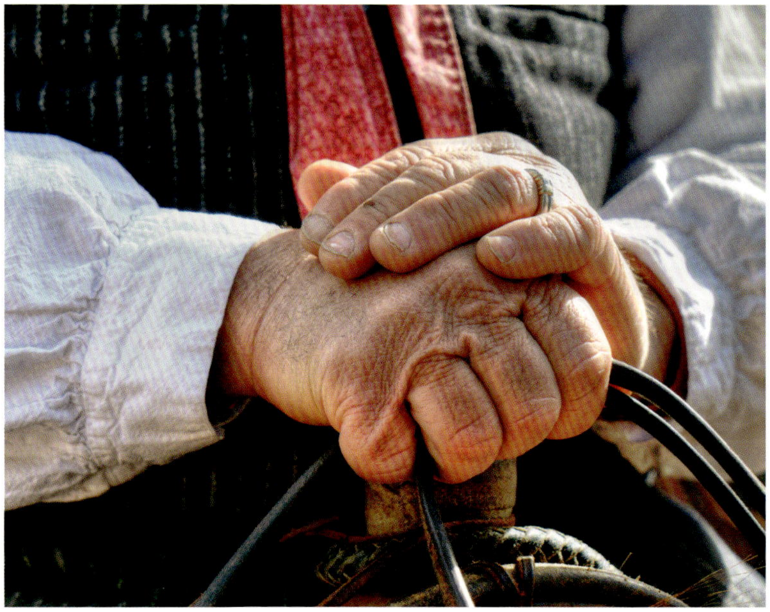

Hardworking hands of drover Jeff Hoffman hold the reins as they rest on the saddle horn.

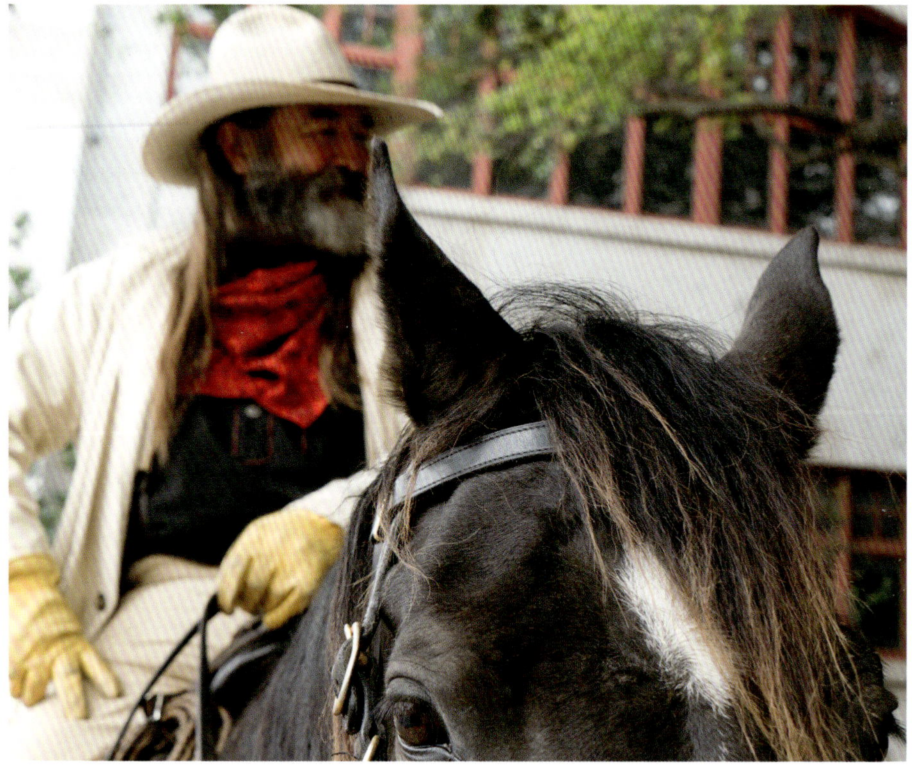

A well-dressed, happy Texas cowboy, who portrays a gunfighter, and his handsome horse join the celebration of the twenty-year, twice-daily cattle drive on East Exchange Avenue at the Fort Worth Stockyards. The bearded gunfighter wears a traditional cowboy hat, bandana, shirt, and gloves.

Livestock interests at the Fort Worth yards created a new organization in April 1950, the Fort Worth Livestock Market Institute. Its major task became to create goodwill and increase market receipts by promotional activity. Similar groups existed in other large markets such as those in St. Paul and Sioux City. Those who organized the local institute and became its leaders were Ted Gouldy, who published a livestock newspaper; W. L. Pier, division manager and president of the Fort Worth Stockyards; and J. C. "Buck" Weaver of Cassidy Commission Company. Members of the various commission companies became directors. The stockyards company agreed to pay half the cost, and commission firms contributed the other half. Virtually all livestock commission firms, dealers, and order buyers participated. Obviously, all had a stake in increasing receipts to the declining market. The institute spent $5,079 in its first year but by the end of the decade was paying as much as $2,000 to $3,000 per month for advertising in newspapers and magazines, printed matter, radio coverage, dinners, equipment, management and secretarial costs, office supplies, postage, premiums, judging expenses, and wages. The institute sent weekly news releases to country newspapers throughout the territory adjacent to the Fort Worth market and to radio and television farm directors in the region. The institute freely distributed to eighty newspapers the columns Ted Gouldy wrote about the market, and sixty newspapers used them. Later Gouldy even supplied at no cost a market summary called "Let's Talk Livestock" to more than three hundred Texas newspapers.

In May 1950 the Agriculture and Livestock Department of the Fort Worth Chamber of Commerce created a Fort Worth Farm and Ranch Club to foster interest in the local

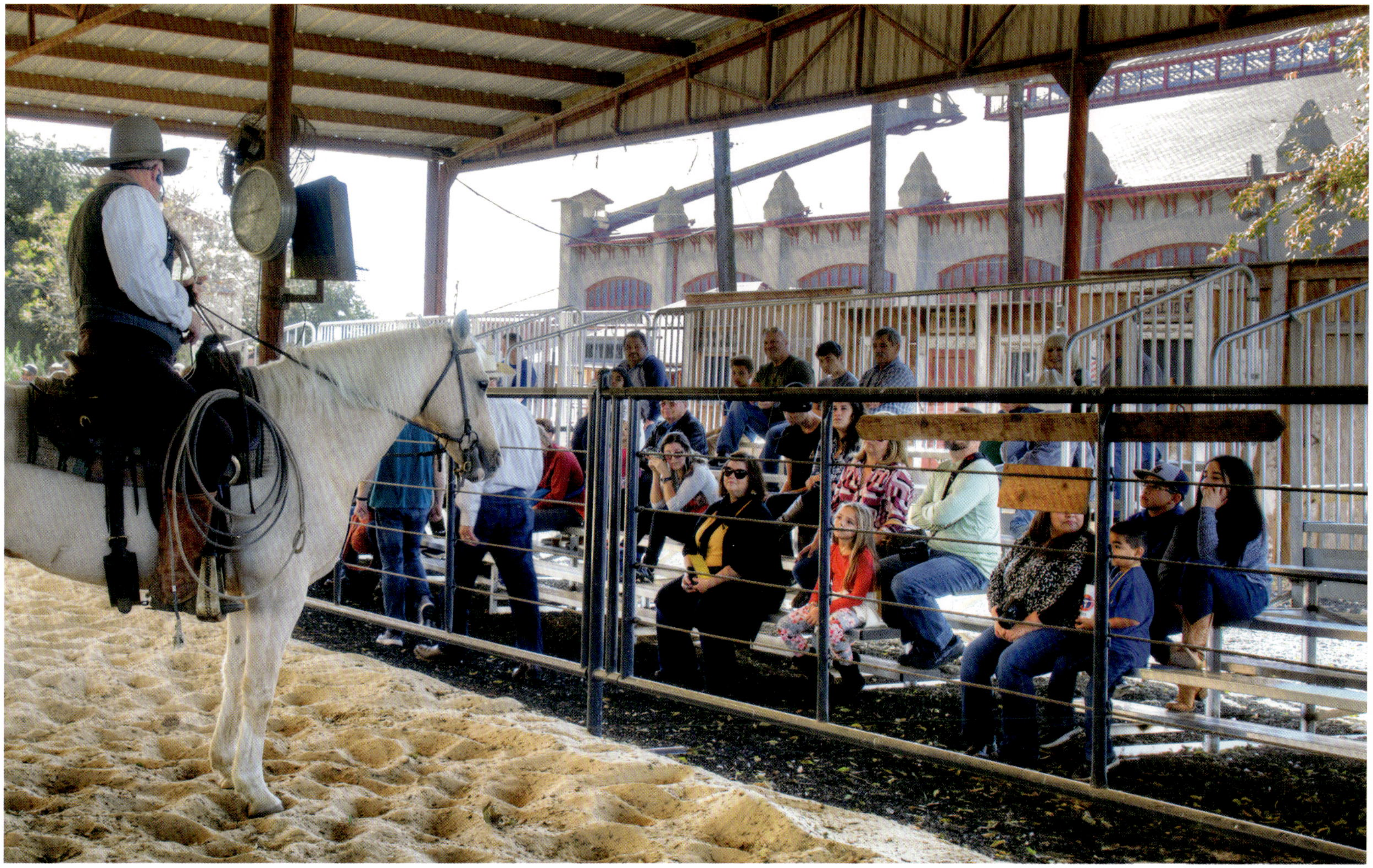

Drover David Mangold, with his horse, Oliver, tells stories about the Wild West. David also shows the audience how his horse obeys commands. The programs are represented by cowboys and cowgirls as a fun and educational demonstration about the tools, equipment, and techniques used during the cattle-drive era of the late 1800s.

livestock industry. Members met for lunch once a month to hear a speaker or see a film on some phase of agriculture. Pier became vice president of the organization.

Among the public relations tactics of the stockyards remained their usual tours for boys in 4-H or Future Farmers of America. When the youngsters brought in their cattle, the commission firm involved and the Fort Worth Stockyards Company paid for their hotel rooms at the Westbrook Hotel in downtown Fort Worth, and Armour and Swift invited them to a luncheon and tour of the packing plants. Files from the 1950s show requests for the tours from as far away as Kansas. Twenty-eight groups visited in one year. Also, promotional field agent Walter Rice judged shows for the youngsters, and the stockyards helped furnish the ribbons. Ted Gouldy's fifteen-minute noontime radio program "Roundup Time" gave market news throughout the state from a studio in the Livestock Exchange Building.

Strikes and livestock disease caused problems for the local yards in the 1950s. Lower profits meant cutbacks in advertising and even support to the West Texas Chamber of Commerce, which the stockyard interests had induced the Fort Worth Chamber of Commerce to create. The company also canceled its usual full-page ad in the Southwestern Exposition and Fat Stock Show premium list.

The business problems of the Fort Worth Stockyards and packing interests did not prevent Armour and Swift from celebrating their fiftieth anniversaries in Fort Worth in 1952. A public relations agency planned the event. Their budget was seventy-one hundred dollars for doing all the publicity and airing radio promotions. They also suggested that merchants in the North Side area organize merchandise drawings and that everyone wear Western clothes. They sponsored a beard-growing contest and also played old Western tunes on loudspeakers on Exchange Avenue. The two packers sponsored tours of their plants.

Officials of the Armour plant bragged that its Fort Worth location remained the fourth largest among thirty-four meatpacking plants in the nation and employed twenty-five hundred workers in 1952. Although livestock receipts had dropped at the Fort Worth yards, apparently it remained a busy place. However, a drought and government price controls caused erratic receipts in the early part of the 1950s. Predictably, trading at the smaller country markets not regulated by the Packers and Stockyards Administration expanded while cattle and calf receipts at the nation's regulated public markets dropped. The large packers increased their buying in country markets to get the meat that they needed.

Everett L. Dobbs, manager of the local Armour plant in 1951, laid off workers because of the dwindling availability of cattle at the Fort Worth Stockyards. He said the

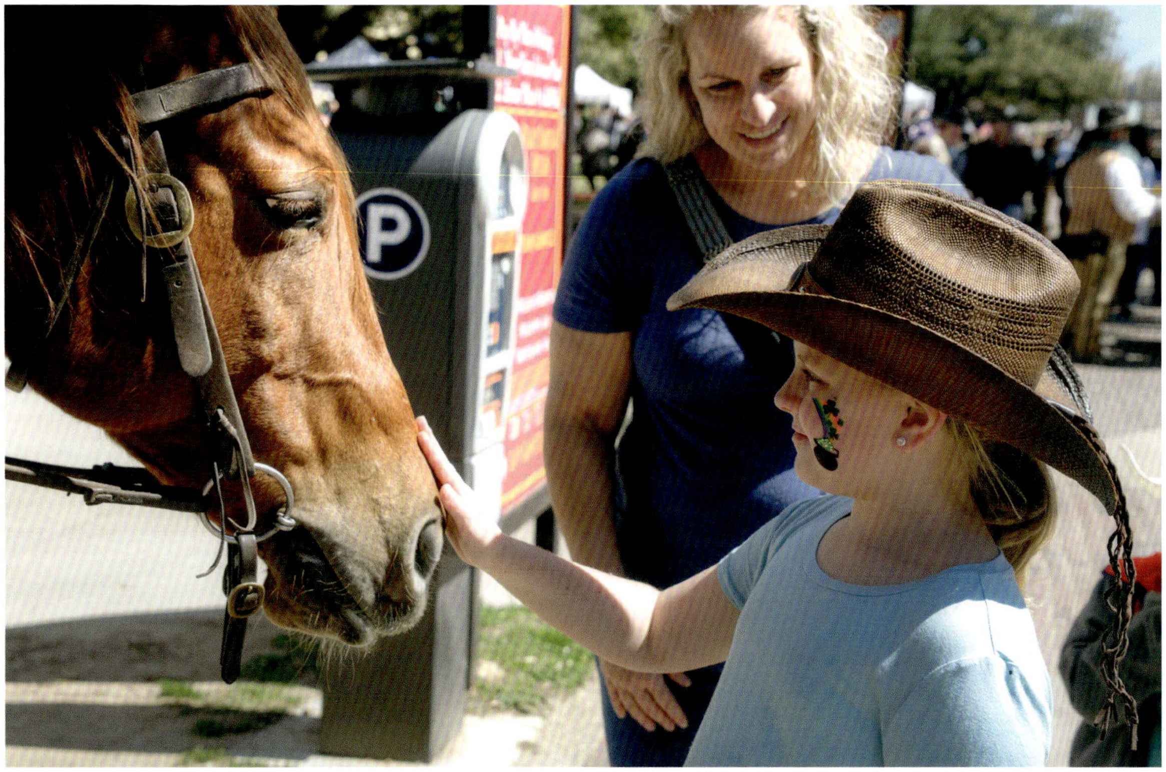

Visitors can also see and sometimes touch the horses between the cattle drives. Chances are good that a child will forever remember this moment.

average kill per hour before the government regulations became effective reached sixty head. In the first week of regulations the kill dropped to eighteen head per hour. Swift faced the same slowdown.

The Texas and Southwestern Cattle Raisers Association, the American National Cattlemen's Association, and most major organizations of beef stockmen launched an "eat more beef" campaign to try to double consumption. The well-organized campaign sent literature to banks and utility companies to include in their monthly statements and mailed advertising material to at least 522 Texas newspapers. In the first two years of the campaign consumption of beef in Texas rose 33 percent.

In fighting government subsidies, quotas, and controls, Bryant Edwards, president of the Texas and Southwestern Cattle Raisers Association, complained to Congress: "We can imagine the graphic language that would have been used by one of our trail driving ancestors to a proposal of a subsidy by the government, and we can imagine what would have happened to some economists who would have had the temerity to tell an old cowman that the government or in particular the Secretary of Agriculture would tell him how many cattle he could raise or how many he could sell, or where and when he had to sell them—and the character of the cowman has not changed."

So many cattle producers lost money during the drought that numerous small operators went out of business. Representatives for feedlots also began buying more cattle. By 1955 the country outlets had gained a slight edge over terminal markets in number of sales, twenty-three million to twenty-one million head. Still, the country auctions remained unregulated by the government because they were less than twenty thousand square feet. By 1957 fourteen hundred to fifteen hundred exempt country livestock markets operated in interstate commerce. To bring the Packers and Stockyards Act in line with the current practices, Congress amended it in 1958 to place under regulations all stockyards, regardless of size, engaged in interstate commerce.

The stockyards' publicity measures perhaps stirred other businesses in the North Side area to make their own attempts to turn things around. In September 1955 a small group of businessmen headed by Russell McElyea and DeWitt McKinley met at the Cattlemen's Steak House and created the North Fort Worth Business Association. Headquarters would be in the North Side Coliseum, which at that time McElyea leased from the city for Monday-night wrestling. Businessmen wanted better lighting for the area and street, among other issues, to attract more visitors and industry.

McElyea did his part to bring interesting programs to the North Side; for example, in 1956 he arranged for a popular new performer named Elvis Presley to sing at the North Side Coliseum. The story goes that McElyea paid Elvis only five hundred dollars for his performance and got an agreement for him to come back for a show the next year at the same price. When Elvis's asking price soon after skyrocketed because of his quick success, McElyea held him to the low fee. Elvis refused to come and, in fact, could not be persuaded to perform in Fort Worth for the next sixteen years. When he finally returned, he appeared in the Convention Center in downtown Fort Worth, apparently at a much larger asking price.

North Side businessmen wanted to create a tourist attraction like a Western Village. A bond issue to do so failed, so the businessmen at their own expense made new architectural fronts of their buildings out of wood shingles and boardwalks to give the area a Western look. Ironically, other communities that had played a part in the history of the cattle trade were voting "yes" in the 1950s, and Dodge City's Front Street, Abilene's Old Abilene, and Wichita's Cowtown soon began attracting tourists.

Beginning in 1956, the North Fort Worth Business Association sponsored a "Go Western Week" and then decided to do a celebration every year. The next spring it became "Pioneer Days" from May 30 to June 1, 1957. At the North Side Coliseum the association brought back a rodeo for the first time in fifteen years. Western bands, square dancers, free variety acts, a carnival, and a giant parade accompanied the show.

While area businessmen did their part to revitalize the stockyards district, the stockyards company continued its own efforts. It partnered with the Texas Hereford Association and the Fort Worth Livestock Market Institute to arrange a feeder calf show and a sale featuring Herefords on June 30, 1955. Judges selected outstanding animals in various classes and awarded ribbons and prizes. Then the Texas Aberdeen Angus Association and the stockyards also hosted a feeder calf show and sale on July 8, 1955, with about two thousand calves. Since the show netted nearly one hundred thousand dollars for producers, they hosted several events that season.

Similar shows continued, and the market institute advertised the special sales in seventy-three newspapers and magazines, placed paid announcements on sixty-three radio and television stations, and sent news releases to 350 newspapers and magazines. Fort Worth took some of its ideas from other stockyards that also wanted more action at its yards. In response to criticism of a lack of parking, in 1959 the stockyards company turned the front

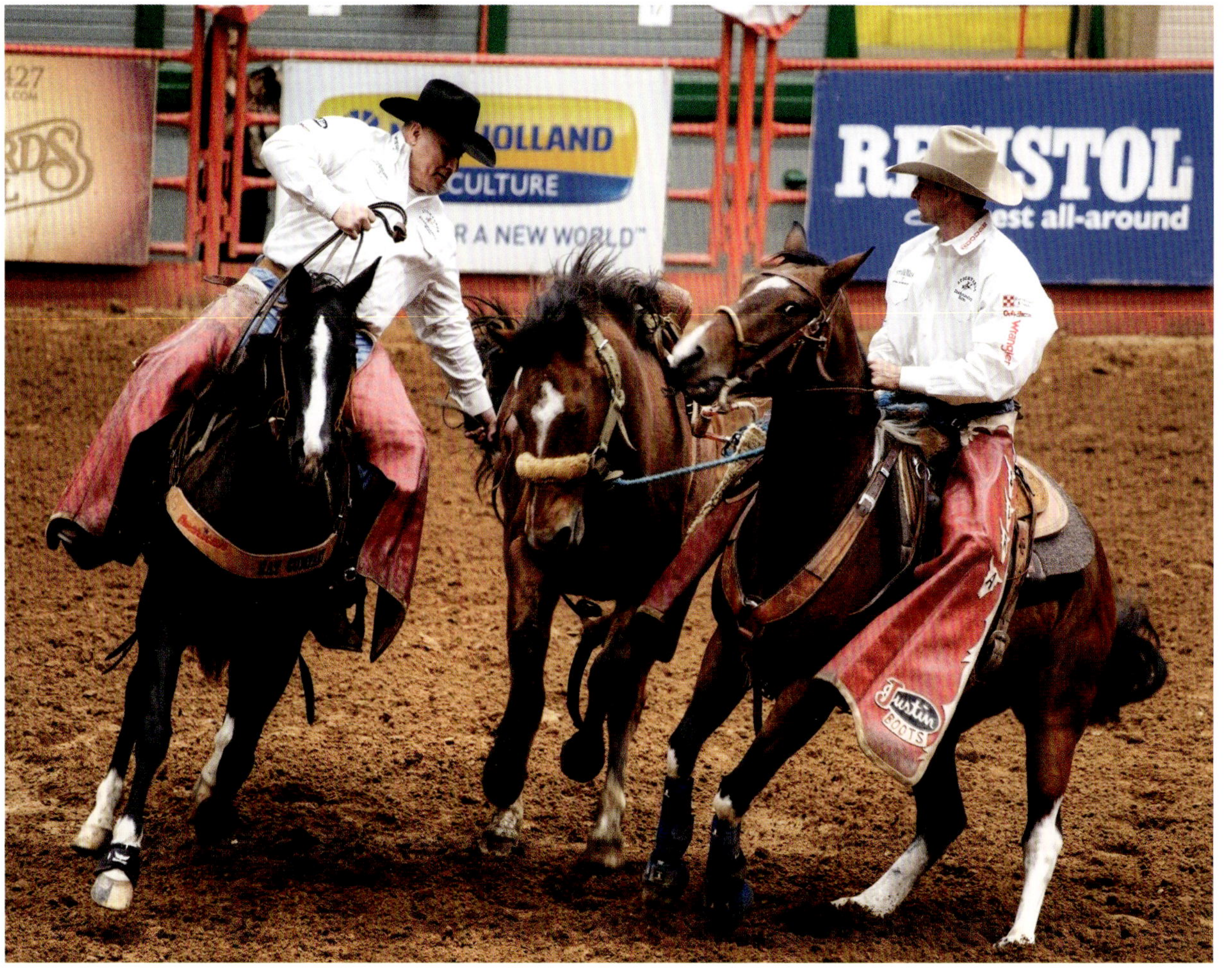

Cowboys rescue an excited bucking bronc who left his rider sprawled on the ground.

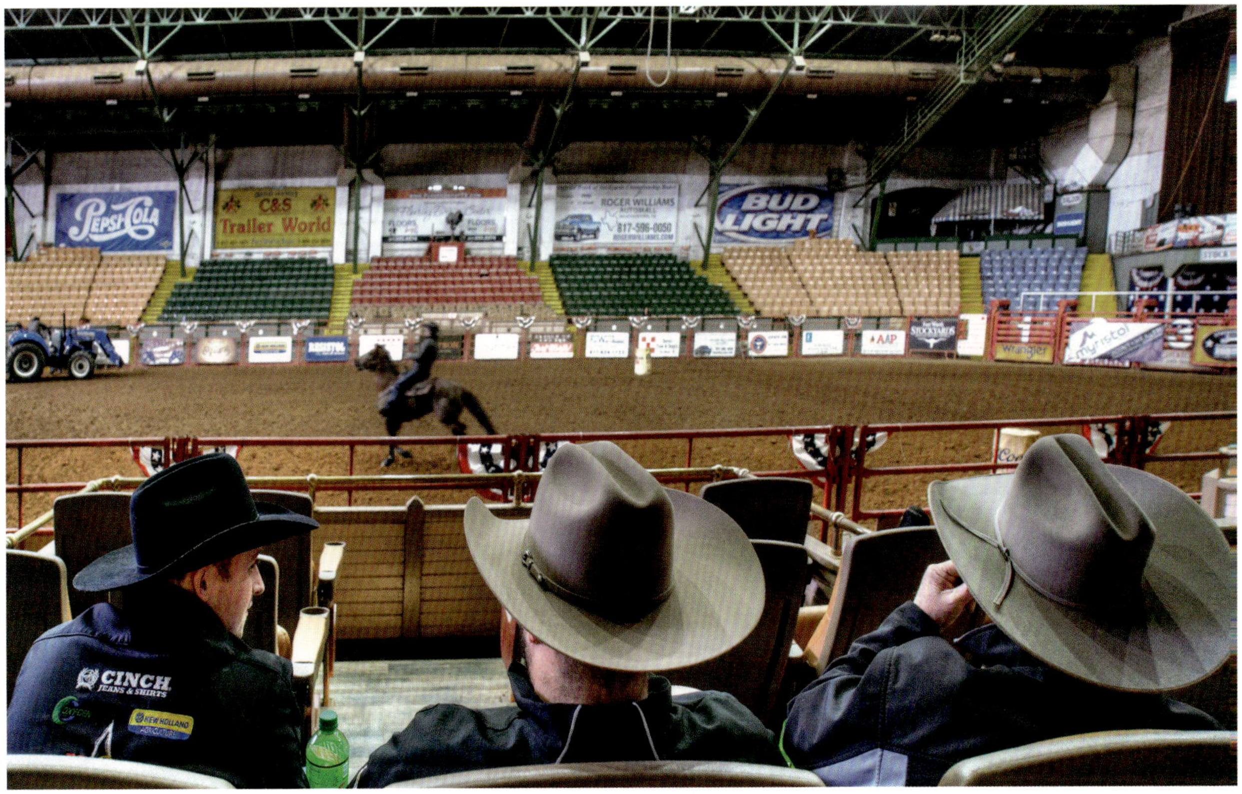

Cowboys watch the show. Their hats create a repeated pattern design in the foreground. Cowboy hats become a part of a cowboy or cowgirl's persona.

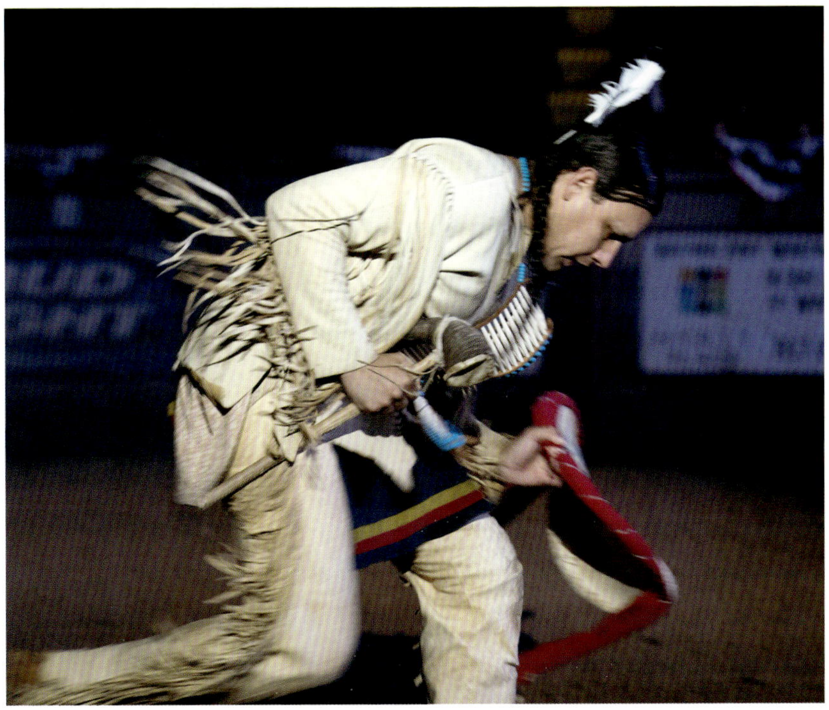

Pawnee Bill's Wild West Show features a Native American dancer dressed in traditional leather, feathers, and beads.

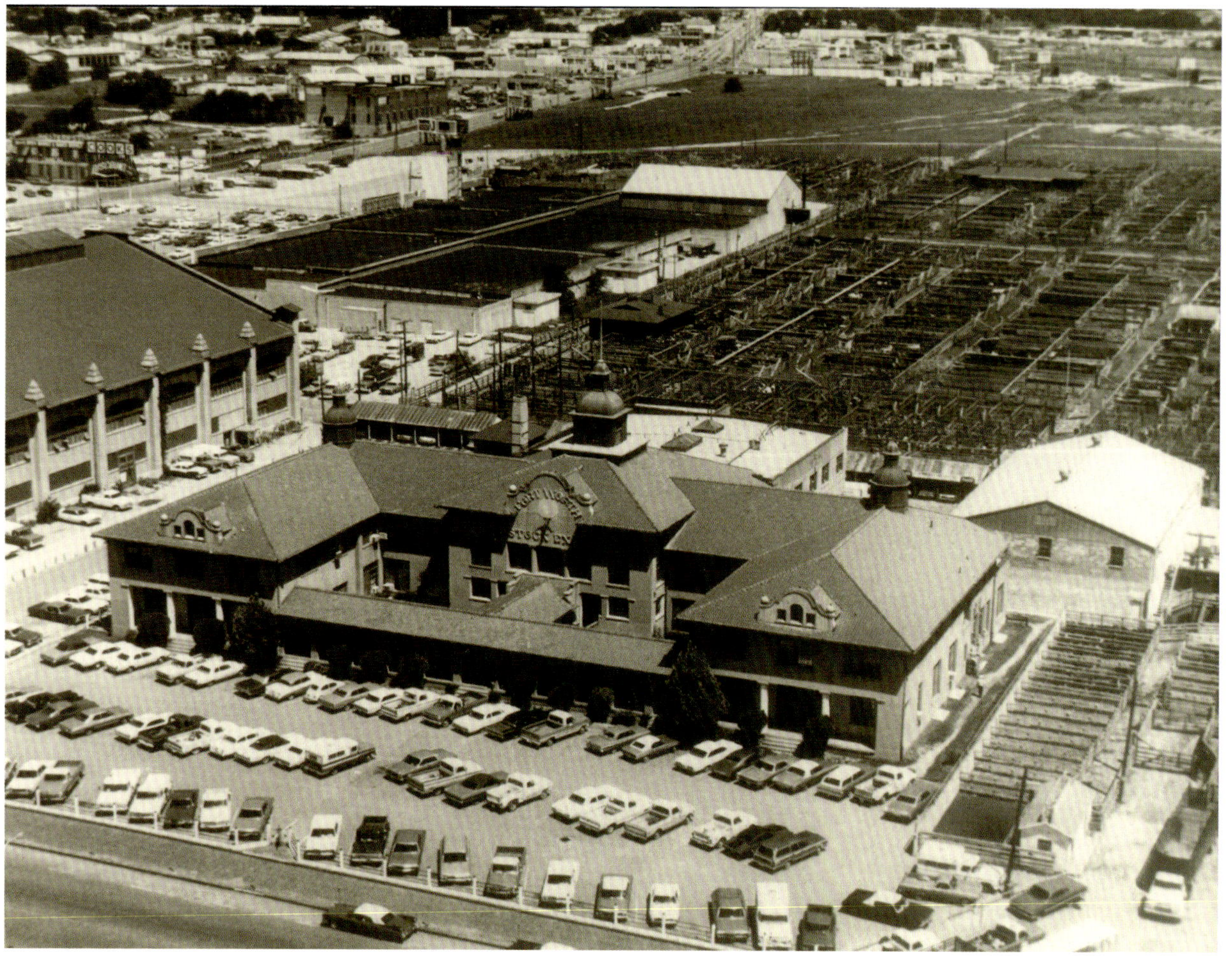

Needing parking space, the stockyards company replaced its lawn with cement in the 1950s. Grass has since been restored. Courtesy of North Fort Worth Historical Society.

lawn of the Exchange Building into a parking lot that accommodated eighty cars. Grass and landscaping have since been returned to the front lawn, however.

Toward the latter part of the 1950s some of the major terminal markets began to close, including the one in South San Francisco and the Los Angeles Union Stockyards. At Fort Worth, commission firms slowly decreased in number. While the high of forty-eight existed during World War II, the number dropped to twenty-seven by January 1958. One thing that helped the Fort Worth Stockyards during the decline was that both Armour and Swift paid direct yardage payments to it. The agreement made in 1902 between the stockyards and the two large meatpackers (for the land the stockyards gave them) specified that each meatpacker must pay customary yardage and other charges on each animal that passed through the stockyards.

Commission agents worked hard to obtain business because their only payment was the commission for animals sold. Gary Allen, who later became prominent on the yards, commented, "I hardly knew I had a daddy until I was twelve-years-old because he worked from daylight until dark at the yards every day and was gone all weekend to the country drumming up business." Besides visiting customers on their farms or ranches, commission company representatives also continued to mail out a market newsletter and wrote personal notes as they mailed their checks. Clint Shirley of Shirley Commission

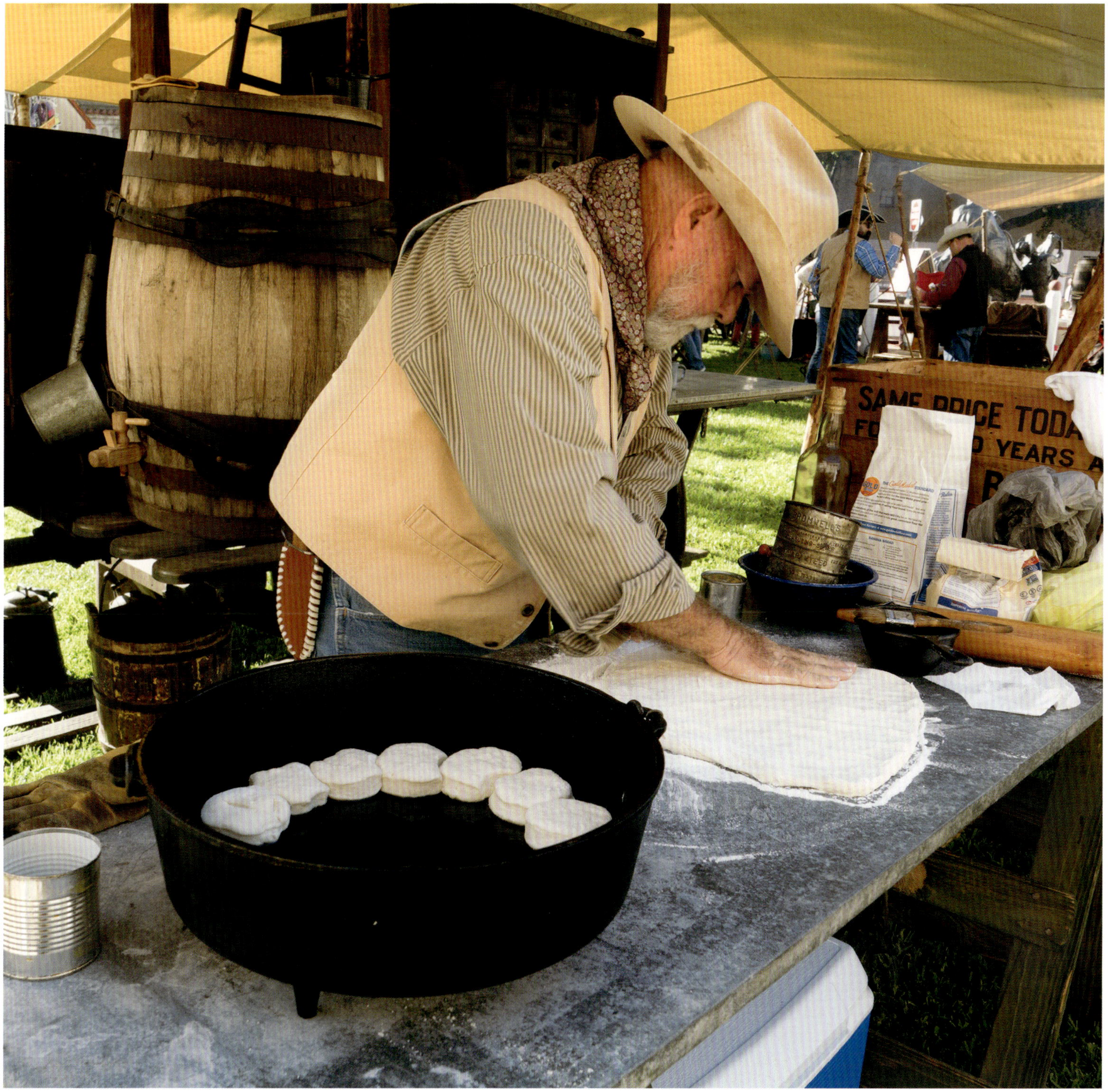

A pioneer-style chef prepares carefully made rolls to be baked in an iron kettle over his wood fire. His water barrel and tin cup are behind him.

Company sometimes flew an airplane trailing a banner that read, "Ship to Shirley." He also placed the same slogan on a sign in the rear window of his car, which he could illuminate at the push of a button.

One last change in methods came late during this promotion-filled decade in an effort to compete successfully with the country auctions. Private treaty buying and selling always had been the practice at terminal markets, but the Fort Worth Stockyards decided to provide an auction as well. It hired an experienced auctioneer named Don Muirhead, who worked in the Fort Worth market for twenty years. The stockyards held its first auction March 5, 1959, in an old livestock exhibit building behind the coliseum that had been left over from when the Southwestern Exposition and Fat Stock Show was in the stockyards. (It is the building that presently houses Billy Bob's Texas nightclub.) The stockyards eventually built its own auction barn just behind northeast corner of the Exchange Building. By the end of May 1959, the auctions became a once-a-week affair.

Despite labor problems, a drought, federal controls, and the growing threat of the decentralization of livestock marketing into smaller country auctions, the Fort Worth Stockyards fought a successful fight during the 1950s. Although erratic receipts existed at times, the market did not actually decline appreciably from the beginning to the end of the ten-year period. The market accepted somewhat more than two million animals the last year of the decade, just as it did at the beginning. The coming years would tell a different story.

No matter how hard the stockyards personnel and commission men worked to increase more livestock receipts in the 1960s, receipts declined. Also demoralizing, old-timers who had worked there for forty or fifty years began retiring. Frequent cakes and retirement parties meant that someone else would be missed.

The 1950s represented many changes for the Fort Worth market, and a huge one occurred on March 19, 1959, when the large real estate conglomerate Canal-Randolph acquired 73 percent of United Stockyards' stock through purchases. Thus, it gained authority to operate United's properties. The head of Canal-Randolph was Hanns Ditisheim of Chicago, who came to the United States in the 1930s after a successful banking career in Switzerland.

Stories in the local newspapers contributed to gloom in the stockyards, for reporters periodically snapped photos of empty pens. Leon Ralls, who started work at the yards in 1934 and was still there fifty years later, remembered that folks laughed at the idea that those first scattered auctions that sprang up in small towns would challenge the big terminal markets. During the 1960s no one laughed anymore, for country auctions began to threaten the very essence of the central markets, including the one at Fort Worth.

The large markets mistakenly thought they could revitalize things by publicity and promotional gimmicks. Decentralization of terminal markets into smaller country auctions nearer the producing areas was an inevitable change once trucks rather than trains moved livestock. Even meatpackers found it cheaper to buy at the country auctions, so they built new plants near livestock-producing areas. Obsolescence hit the older, city packinghouses such as Armour and Swift, and new one-story plants of ceramic-tile and stainless-steel construction emerged. Also, a farmer found it more convenient and cheaper to sell at a local auction; no shrinkage occurred as it did when traveling to the more distant, larger market. He avoided high feed charges and commissions and escaped crowded conditions, delays, and time lost in travel to the larger, distant market.

Nevertheless, promotional efforts continued on the Fort Worth market in the 1960s with special stocker and feeder sales and prizes; the Fort Worth Stockyards Company, the North Fort Worth Business Association, and the Fort Worth Chamber of Commerce, paid the costs. The new air-conditioned auction barn opened on June 3, 1960, and Fort Worth became one of the first terminal markets to create one. By 1961, the number of commission firms dwindled to twenty-two. By 1962, stockyards president John M. Lewis cut the number of yardmen down to eighty-four. However, the most devastating event of 1962 was the closing of the large Armour packing plant, although rumors of its demise had been circulating for four years. Only the year before Armour closed, its payroll reached ten million dollars, and it spent more than forty million dollars for livestock purchases locally. Armour reported that it could not compete with independent packers that had non-union plants that offered lower wages and fewer fringe benefits to their workers.

The Swift union voted on December 15, 1962, to take a wage cut of approximately twenty cents an hour and yielded some fringe benefits to permit Swift to compete better in the local market (and to keep their jobs). The fourteen hundred employees averted closing their slaughtering facilities for nine more years. Some local citizens believed that the Armour plant also could have remained open longer, but its union members refused to grant concessions.

Following the closing of the Armour plant, many of the businesses of Fort Worth, as well as local citizens, gave up on the stockyards district and turned their interests to oil, banking, and aircraft. They planned to make Fort Worth a business center like Dallas. Apparently, some Fort Worthians forgot their cattle roots, for in a *Guide to Historic Sites in Fort Worth and Tarrant County*, published by the Tarrant County Historical Society in 1963, no mention at all was made of the stockyards and meatpacking plants. The only cattle reference mentioned the Chisholm Trail, writing that a century earlier it had gone through the city. (Even that comment proved to be incorrect because local historians have since realized that the Chisholm Trail began

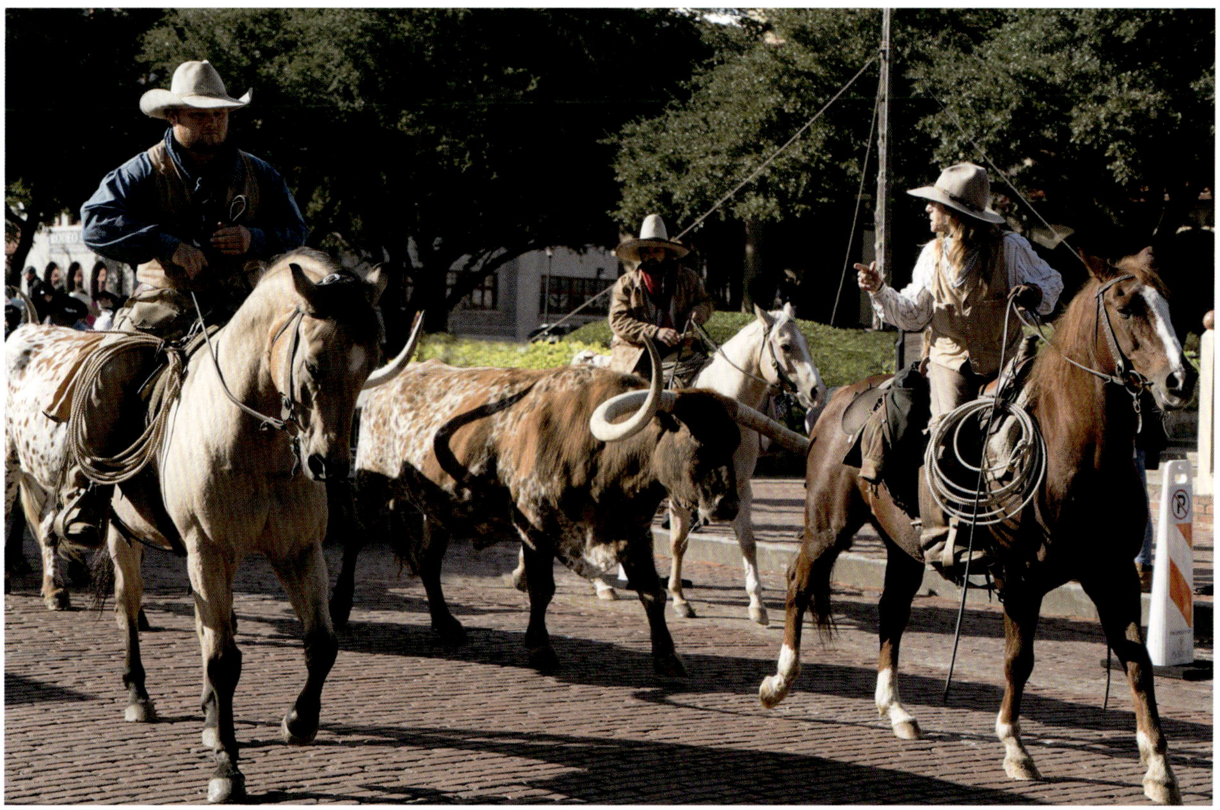

Drovers and their horses carefully guide the herd of Longhorns down East Exchange Avenue. It takes coordination and endurance to keep the Longhorns moving along the street while steering clear of the many visitors.

northward in Oklahoma; the Texas Trail passed through Fort Worth.)

Similarly, a Chamber of Commerce bulletin on Fort Worth's attractions published five years earlier made no mention of the stockyards whatsoever. Numerous persons in the livestock industry believed that the Chamber of Commerce leaders wanted to "write off" the North Side, which was becoming dilapidated and crime-ridden. Bumper stickers appeared in Fort Worth proclaiming "Now Town, not Cowtown."

The new livestock phenomenon of the 1960s became the expansion of feedlots, especially in the Texas Panhandle. They accelerated the decentralization process that already had made great gains. In 1956 about 63 feedlots with capacities of more than one thousand head existed in Texas. By 1964 this figure grew to 207 and increased to 280 by 1969. The *Texas Business Review* estimated that 160,000 head of cattle were fed in 1955 in Texas feedlots, but by January 1969 feedlots held approximately 1,452,000 cattle in the Texas Panhandle.

What really caused the decline of the Fort Worth market, and other large terminal markets like those owned by United, was the decentralization, first toward local country auctions in small towns and then to the large feedlot operations in the heart of the grain- and cattle-producing areas. Despite all the massive publicity effort, the stockyard officials at Fort Worth and the other terminal markets could not reverse the trend. Livestock marketing in the United States changed dramatically in the two decades following World War II.

Activities at the Fort Worth Stockyards rarely made news in Fort Worth in the late 1960s and 1970s with the result that most local citizens forgot that it still existed. "I thought it closed years ago when the packing plants shut down" became the common assumption. Just because North Side residents could not smell the distinct livestock "aroma" to which they had become accustomed, they thought that no more cattle, hogs, or sheep ever arrived. Three hundred thousand animals arriving over a period of a year just did not smell as strongly as had three million, or even two million.

Elmo A. "Mo" Klingenberg replaced John M. Lewis as division president of the Fort Worth Stockyards on July 30, 1971, when Lewis retired. Klingenberg grew up on an Illinois farm and studied livestock marketing and animal husbandry at the University of Illinois in the early 1940s. He became associated with United Stockyards in his home state after graduation. David Hunt of United Stockyards directed Klingenberg to Fort Worth in 1946 and told him to work there a couple of years. Because immediately after World War II, Klingenberg could not find a house in Fort Worth to rent, he asked if he could stay longer to make it worthwhile to buy. A quarter of a century later he remained in Fort Worth. He worked his way up as day yard master, superintendent, vice president, and on Lewis's retirement, division president. He inherited a job that saw even more declining receipts. The situation worsened just two months after he assumed the presidency, when on May 1, 1971, the Swift plant closed down. At least it had been anticipated since 1968, when Swift announced plans to close its all-purpose packing plants. Swift had already ceased operations in Chicago, St. Louis, Denver, St. Paul, and Omaha.

Numerous smaller meatpacking plants remained active at the Fort Worth Stockyards and slaughtered as many as two hundred thousand animals each year. However, many farmers and ranchers did not realize that they still existed and quit bringing their cattle to the Fort Worth market.

Unfortunately, several years after Armour and Swift closed their doors, fires destroyed their abandoned buildings. The old Armour plant caught fire at 11:00 p.m. on May 11, 1971. Soon more than one hundred firemen and between thirty and fifty pieces of fire equipment fought the blaze. The heavy wooden floors in the plant accumulated a great amount of grease through the years, and that caused dense smoke over the area. The building became a total loss.

Two fires struck the abandoned Swift building. The first was a brief fire on January 11, 1974, which lasted only three hours and involved the fourth and fifth floors of the plant. Apparently, a cutting torch used by workmen in demolishing the building started it. Thirty-one firemen and eight pieces of equipment answered the call. The more disastrous Swift fire started May 30, 1975, and burned all night. Fire officials again believed that a demolition team's cutting torch started it. The fire burned for two or three weeks because it extended into the basement and tunnel, and no way existed for firefighters to get down there to extinguish it. Also, oil and grease had saturated the thick floors. Again, nearly one hundred firemen and twenty pieces of equipment fought the blaze. A portion of this building remained standing for many years but has since been demolished.

The decline in receipts at the Fort Worth Stockyards continued during the 1970s, dropping by 10 to 15 percent each year. Doom and gloom set in because livestock receipts dwindled each year. From a high of 5 million animals annually at the yards in World War II, receipts in the 1950s dropped to 1,844,793. In 1964 receipts stood at 705,382, and a decade later only an average of 269,992 animals arrived each year.

By 1978 only six commission firms remained in business, and the stockyards reduced the pens, which once covered 110 acres, down to twelve. Part of the Livestock Exchange Building became leased office space. By the summer of 1981 only five commission companies remained to share the cost of any advertising, with the stockyards paying the other 50 percent. Each company obviously bore a larger share than when split with twenty-five or thirty others in the 1950s. Therefore, the stockyards company found it difficult to persuade the commission men to cooperate in advertising their market. Sales dropped considerably. The story became the same in the other large stockyards across the country. The mighty Chicago yards—largest in the nation for many years—shut its doors in 1971. Denver followed the next year, and Wichita closed in 1980.

Efforts continued to keep the Fort Worth market open. Canal-Randolph, owner of the yards by then, constructed the first auction barn in 1960, where it held special stocker and feeder sales. In addition it spent $750,000 to restore

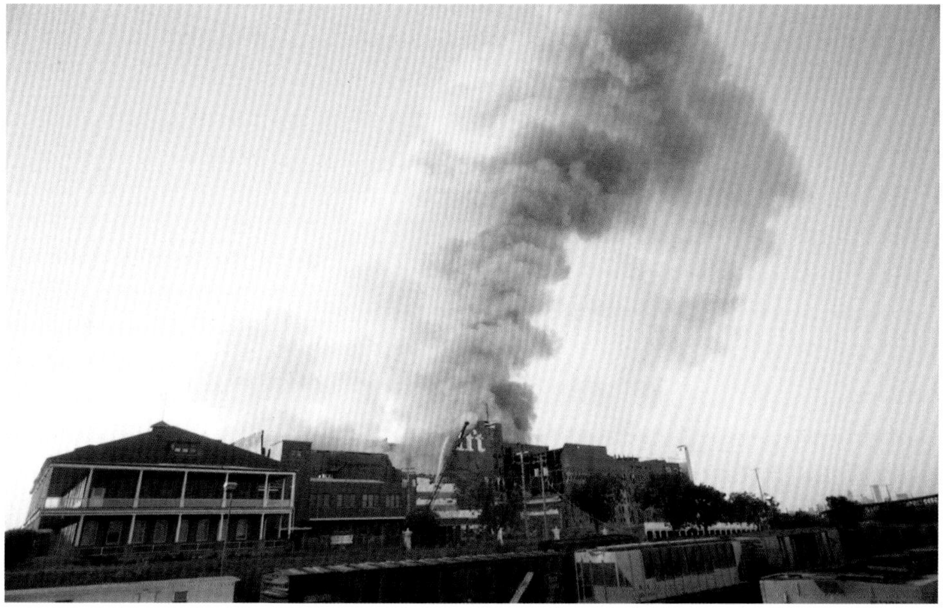

The Swift packing plant burned in 1975. Courtesy, *Fort Worth Star-Telegram* Collection, Special Collections, University of Texas at Arlington Libraries.

the aging Livestock Exchange Building and to modernize the pens. The city spent $2 million in federal funds to improve areas prone to flooding.

Because the Fort Worth Stockyards Company lost money in 1981, then-owner United Stockyards began looking at numerous options. With division president Elmo Klingenberg scheduled to retire in the spring of 1982, some change would be necessary anyway. Late in the summer of 1981, Klingenberg allowed Gary Allen of Foley-Allen Commission Company to announce the major change in operations that Allen and his associates had worked out with United Stockyards. The five commission companies remaining on the market agreed to dissolve and create one company. This new company officially registered itself as the Niles City Cattle Company, Inc., doing business as the Fort Worth Stockyards. The new company, operating under the old familiar name, leased the auction barn, pens, and other yard facilities from United Stockyards. Allen as president promised streamlined operations, more efficiency, lower rates, and more competitive sales. With no union involved, he could hire workers only on the days that he needed them. United agreed to install a new pneumatic tube system to speed sales tickets to the office and back to save customers time, to build a new trailer chute, and to enlarge the pens and watering facilities.

Allen called the new venture the "most positive thing that has happened in the last twenty-five years" and hoped to turn the trend toward decentralization around. He said that buyers within a 150-mile radius of Fort Worth often had to go to fifteen of the smaller auction areas in one day to obtain enough livestock to fill their quotas. Allen planned to induce more producers to ship to Fort Worth.

The five commission companies still in existence when they dissolved to aid Allen in the new venture consisted of Foley-Allen, Carson, John Clay, Farm and Ranch, and Leon Ralls. Of the owners, only Allen and Ralls joined in the new company, along with some of the employees of the previous firms. The other owners retired. Gary Allen had worked full-time at the stockyards since 1958 but had been on the yards off and on from age ten with his father and grandfather, who began Foley-Allen Commission Company in the 1940s. One of Allen's main problems would be the urban setting, for many old farmers preferred a rural atmosphere and disliked the freeways and traffic they encountered in selling in Fort Worth.

When the "new" Fort Worth Stockyards began operations November 1, 1981, several significant things occurred. After ninety-four years, no terminal market existed at Fort Worth, for according to a Packers and Stockyards Administration definition, a terminal market must have more than one commission company to which to assign cattle. Only one company remained. Also, for the second time in the history of the market, it would be managed by local livestock personnel, even though the market changed management on a lease basis rather than ownership. Since 1893 management always had been out of state. Perhaps just as important, the new owners made provisions for the market to continue under the name Fort Worth Stockyards. "As long as I'm making money, well, can squeeze out a little profit, I'll be here," Allen said. He and his coworkers admitted that they had financial interests other than stockyards and remained in business there because it always had been their way of life and they enjoyed it.

News stories that appeared of Billy Bob's group of investors planning a forty-five-million-dollar Western tourist attraction made local people assume that the active livestock market had closed. The project did not materialize, but Allen received thirty to forty telephone calls a day after the development stories appeared in the newspaper, asking if he was shutting down. Traffic from Billy Bob's nightclub already hurt the Sunday-night unloading of animals for a Monday sale.

Canal-Randolph Corporation, owner of United Stockyards and of the land and facilities of the Fort Worth yards, divested itself of its United stock in 1984, and United became independent again. United leased all of

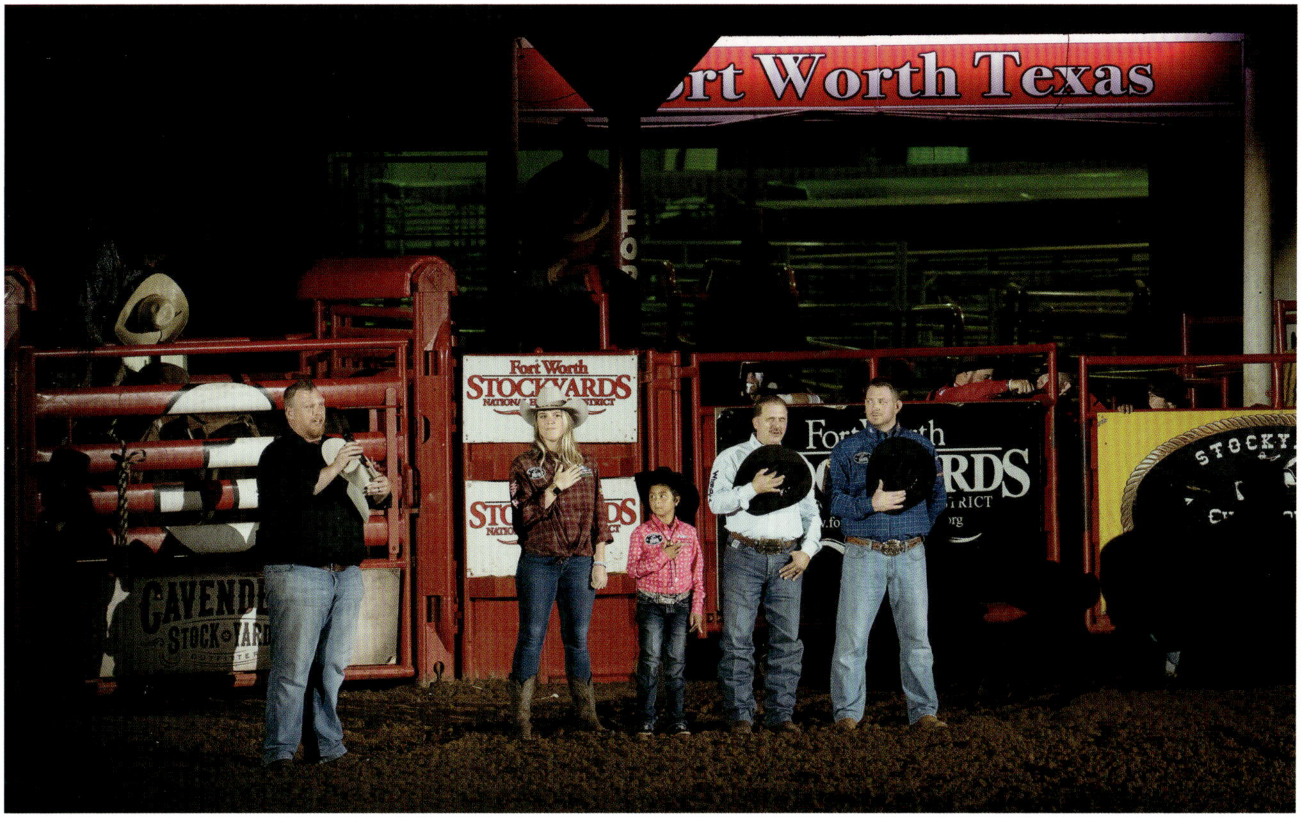

Everyone puts a hand on his or her heart when Nate Krieger sings the "Star-Spangled Banner" as the stockyards rodeo opens.

its Fort Worth real estate to Triad Corporation, the Billy Bob's investors, giving the lease held by Gary Allen and the Fort Worth Stockyards the status of a sublease under Triad. On December 31, 1984, United Stockyards closed its Fort Worth office, with the retired Elmo Klingenberg kept on retainer to see after its facilities in Fort Worth.

Then Gary Allen surprised nearly everyone and sold out his stock in the Niles City Cattle Company dba Fort Worth Stockyards as of December 31, 1985, to Hampton Butler, one of his employees since 1981. Butler had been a fixture on the yards since 1961, when he began working for Drive-In Commission Company. He assumed the management of John Clay Commission Company in 1973 and operated it until 1981.

To lower costs, Butler cut cattle sales back to Monday only, plus the last-Thursday-of-the-month sale, and condensed hog sales to three days instead of four. He employed twenty people, about half of them full-time. By 1985 only 88,156 animals, of all types, arrived at the Fort Worth Stockyards. January 1986, began with more cattle arrivals than usual, but sales proved extremely light in the late spring because of excessive rains. Nevertheless, Butler operated in the black and determined to continue the live market as long as he could do so profitably. He planned to sign one-year leases with stockyard investors and United.

Butler continued managing the dwindling market until December 21, 1992, when he held the last auction. Then he ended operations. The mighty Fort Worth Stockyards, the largest in the entire Southwest, ceased to exist as a livestock market. However, local citizens were already working to preserve the history of the area and to celebrate and share its story with the world as a unique Fort Worth tourist destination. Chapter 7 relates that successful effort.

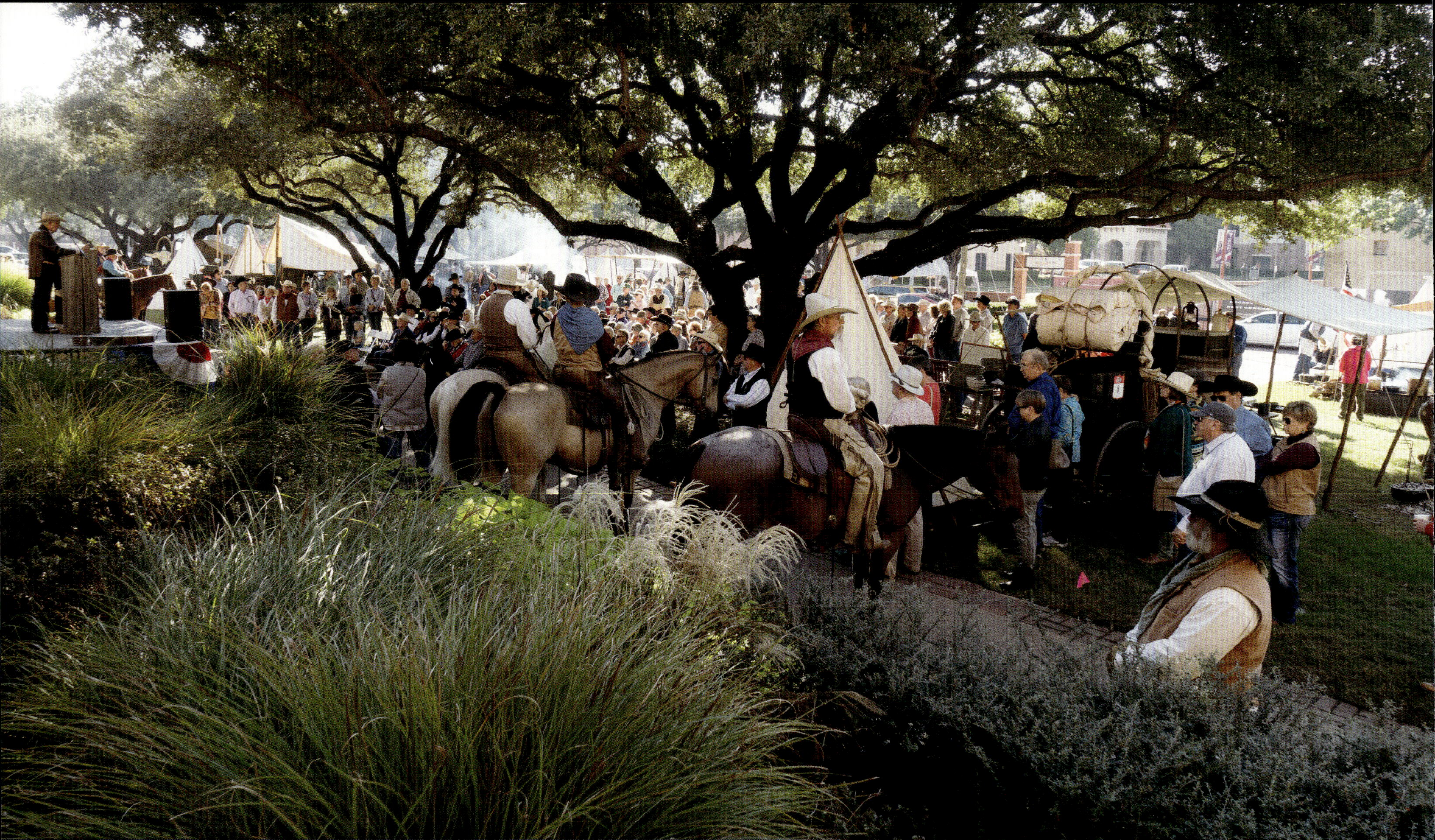

CHAPTER 7

Transforming the Stockyards

Two decades into the twenty-first century the Fort Worth Stockyards is booming, not with livestock but with tourists. Local folks proudly can proclaim the stockyards situation as vibrant and colorful; there are five and one-half million visitors a year, thriving businesses, full parking lots, and tourists coming from all over the world. The sixteenth-largest city in the United States, Fort Worth, claims to be the number-one tourist destination in Texas. A lot of things happened over several decades to create the popular and profitable Fort Worth Stockyards tourist district that presently exists.

One event that ignited early sparks of resolve and resistance was the unexpected demolition in the early 1970s of the old Niles City Town Hall on Decatur Avenue because its owners at the time believed that the location would serve them better as a parking lot. Longtime residents Charlie and Sue McCafferty responded to the Town Hall loss by organizing the North Fort Worth Historical Society in 1976 as a means of calling attention to a threat that other historic buildings in the area might meet the same fate. Perhaps they also became motivated at that time because of celebrations of the country's two-hundredth birthday. The US Bicentennial Committee urged citizens throughout the country to create organizations that would preserve their local history as a means of celebrating the nation's own festivities.

Charlie McCafferty called the North Side "the heart and the muscle" of Fort Worth because the larger city would not have reached its metropolitan status had it not

Cowboys and tourists alike come together for the opening of the Red Steagall Cowboy Gathering in October. This celebration of the nation's premier Western heritage event has been voted "best gathering and best family event" by readers of *American Cowboy Magazine*.

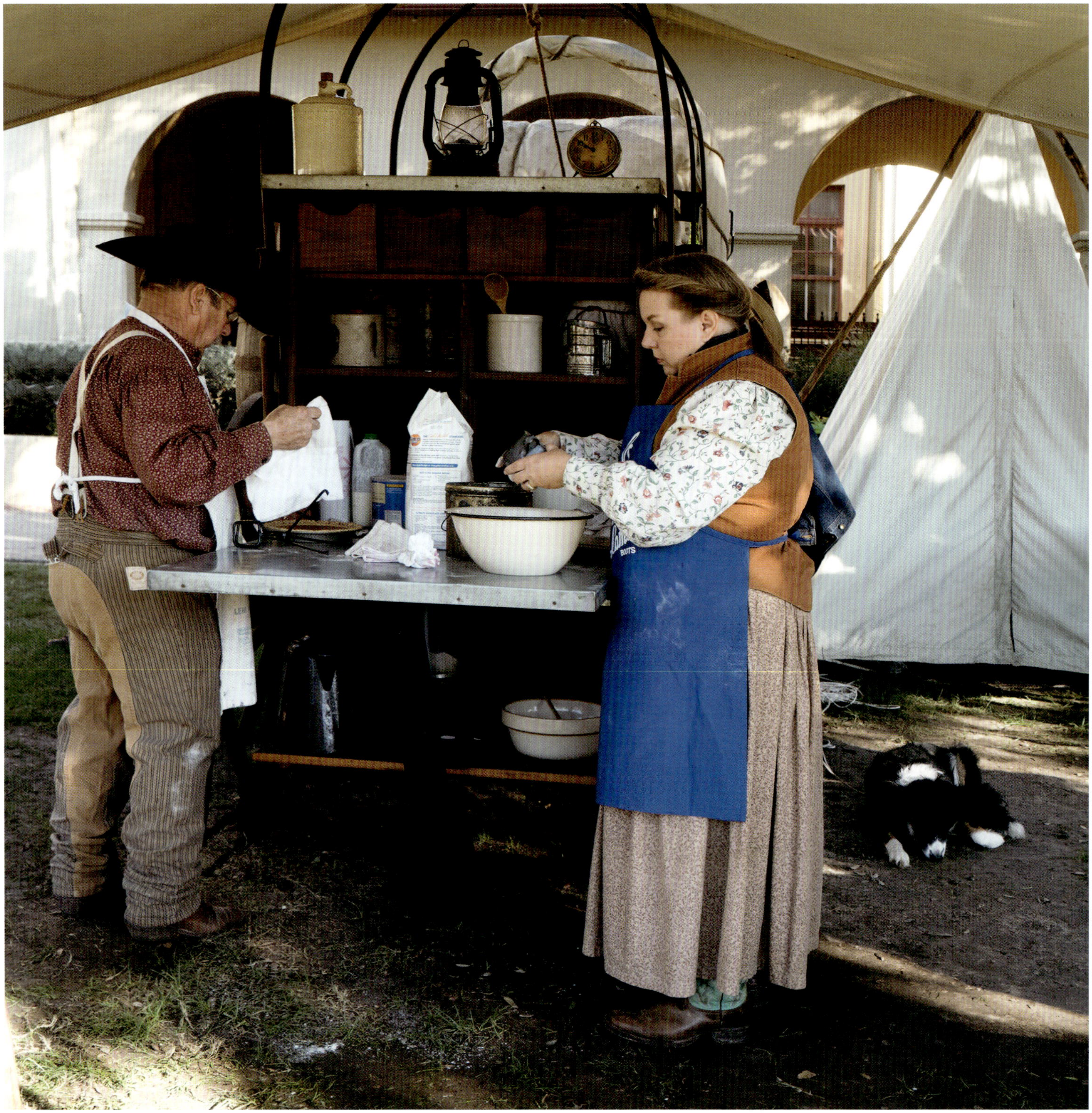

Cooks Bobby Burleson and Jennifer Crites of Weatherford, Texas, prepare food for the fall chuckwagon competition. Meg, their Border collie, waits close by—probably hoping for a treat or two.

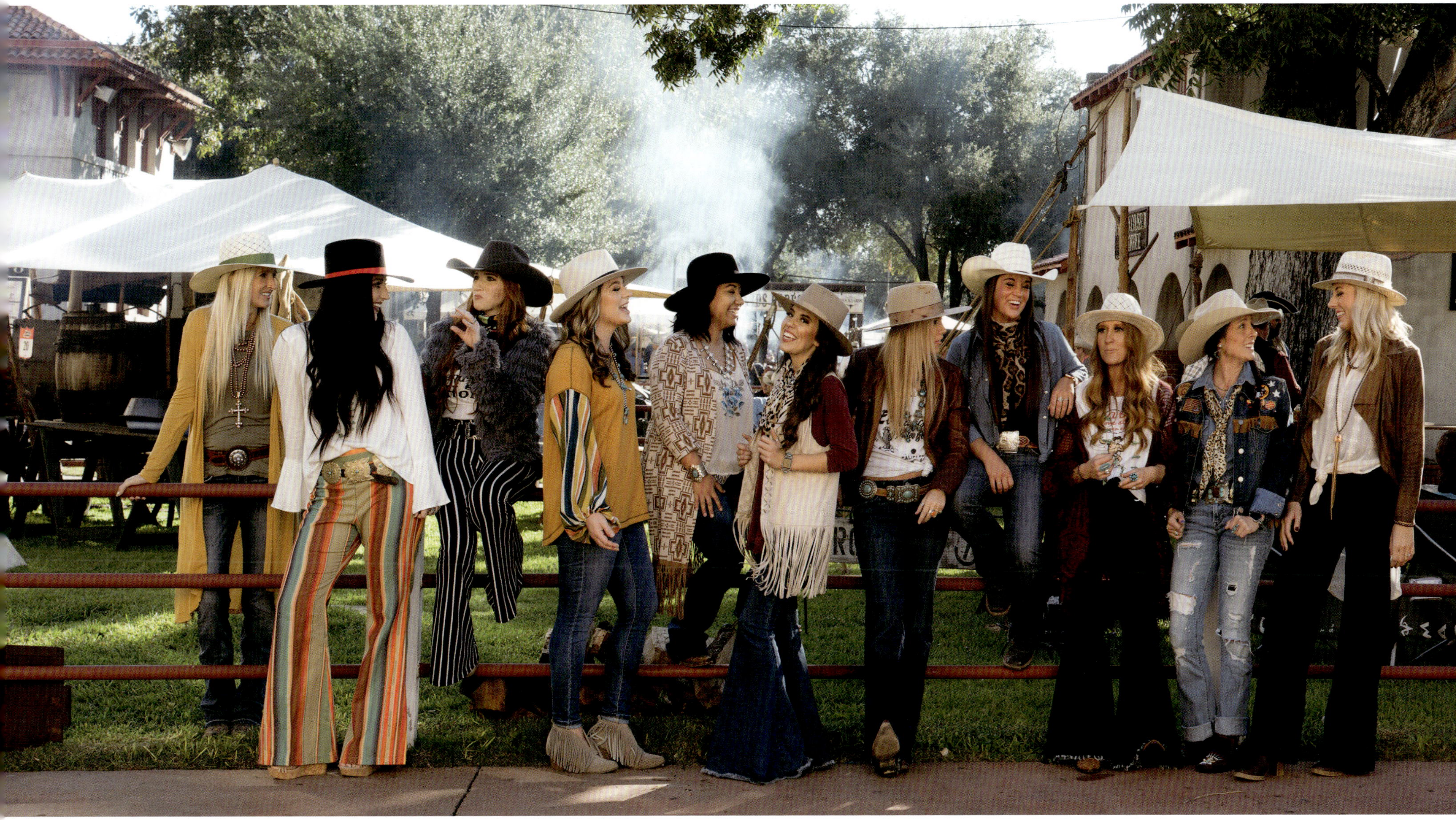

Tall, glamorous women appropriately dressed as cowgirls laugh and pose near a fence during an October event in front of the Livestock Exchange Building.

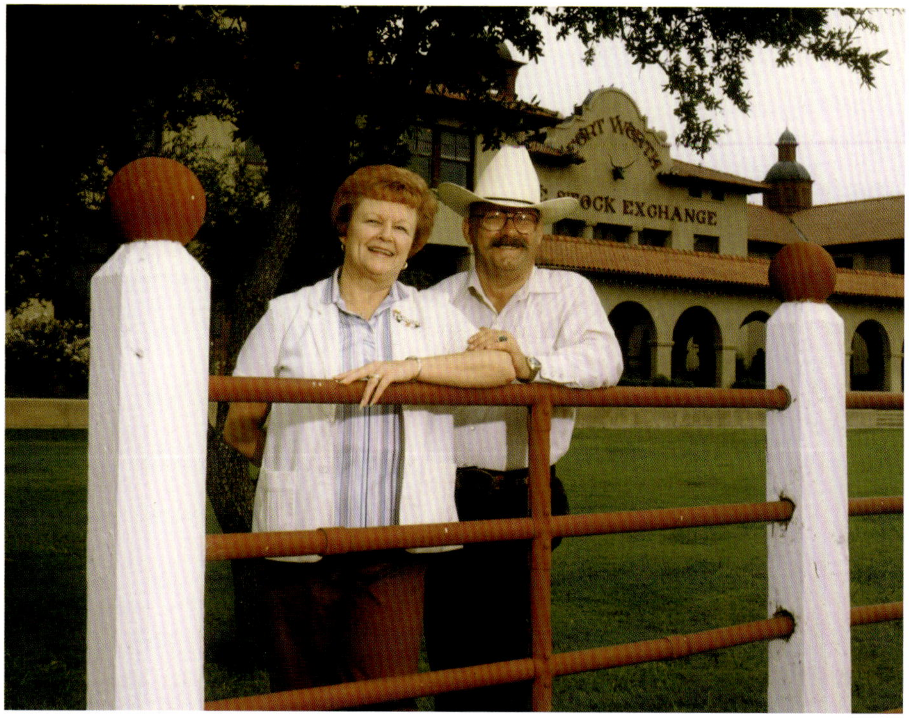

Sue and Charlie McCafferty are the visionaries who organized the North Fort Worth Historical Society. Courtesy of North Fort Worth Historical Society.

been for the livestock interests of the stockyards district. Charlie became president of the newly created North Fort Worth Historical Society first, but members the next year elevated his wife, Sue, and she served as president for twenty-three years. The society worked with the federal government to create a Fort Worth Stockyards Historic District in 1976, listed on the National Register of Historic Places. The city began efforts to acquire historical markers for various stockyard buildings and locations.

The Fort Worth Chamber of Commerce created the Chisholm Trail Roundup in 1977 to spark interest in developing the stockyards. Renamed Chisholm Trail Days, it was celebrated on the second weekend in June each year. Millions of Texas Longhorns traveled up the Texas Trail (which people in recent years mistakenly called the Chisholm Trail) through Fort Worth, actually bedding down north of downtown near the area that later became the stockyards. Northeast of the stockyards is Trail Drivers' Park, where many herds and their handlers also spent the night before continuing northward. Parking problems and other concerns caused Chisholm Trail Days to give way to many smaller events held more frequently in the stockyards.

These events brought hometown folks and visitors to the stockyards area. As a result, a few tourists started visiting in the 1970s, and Charlie McCafferty began a walking tour of the yards to accommodate them. Other members of the Historical Society volunteered their services in various ways, mostly on Saturdays, to call attention to the yards as well. Gary Havard created a slide presentation of the early days of the yards and showed it in the auction barn.

The Historical Society at first did not have a stockyards location in which to assemble, so they met in members' homes. When a lease ran out on the Cowtown Coliseum in 1975, Steve Murrin made a deal with the city of Fort Worth and took it over. Murrin let the society use the southeast corner of the building for its headquarters for a time. The group later moved into the northwest corner of the first floor of the Livestock Exchange Building, where

A tourist photographs his family against a huge Texas flag.

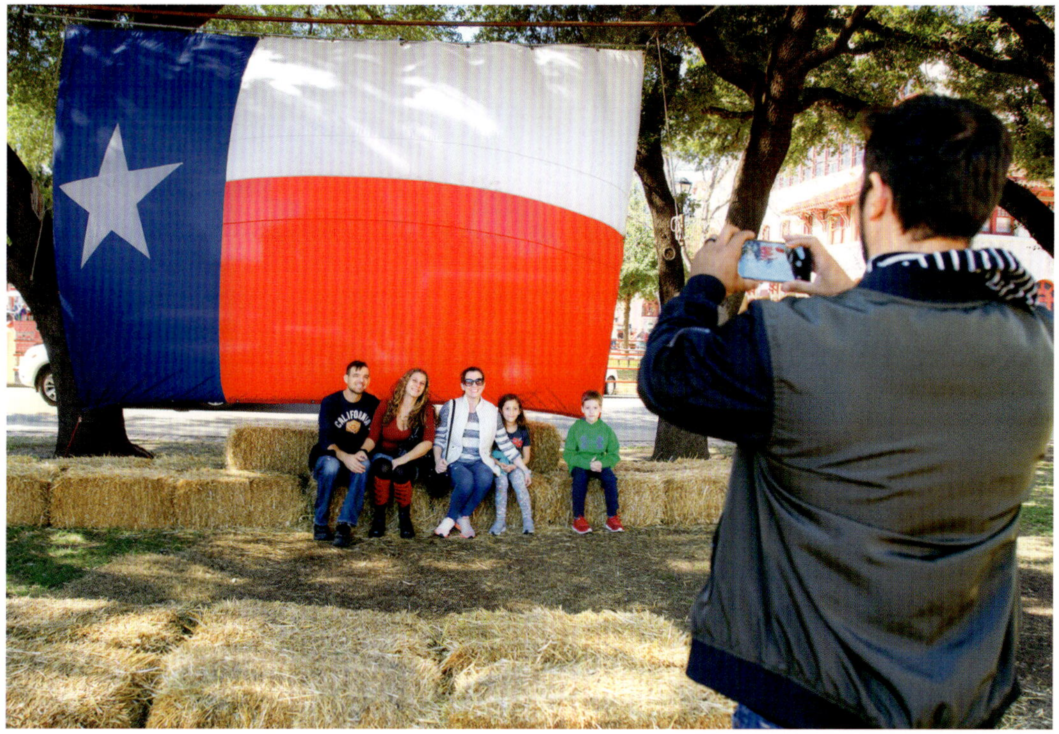

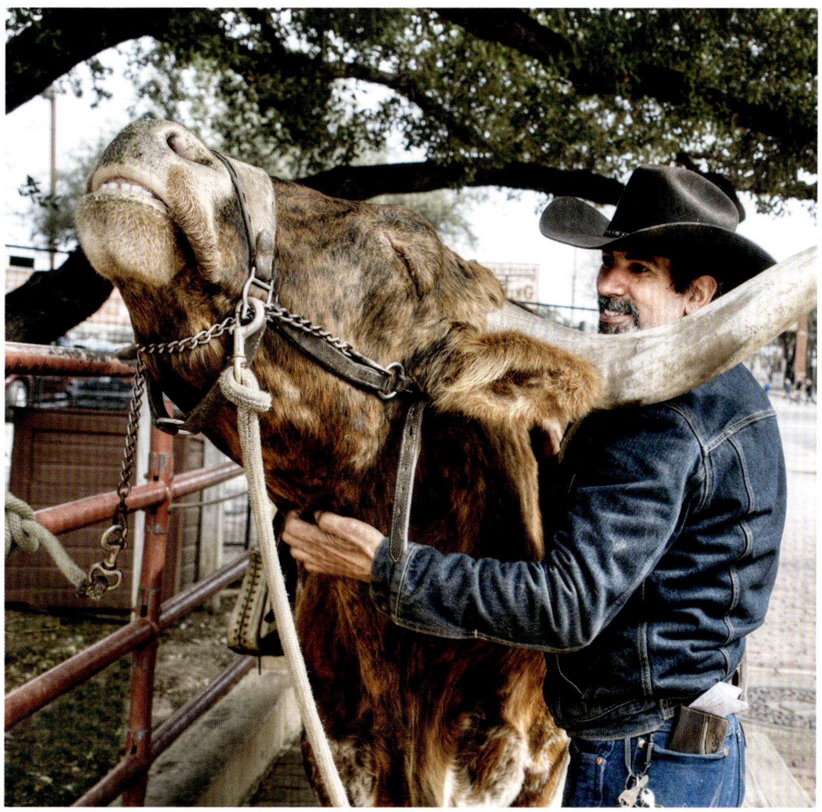

This Longhorn shows his pleasure as he gets a good scratch on his neck by a young cowboy.

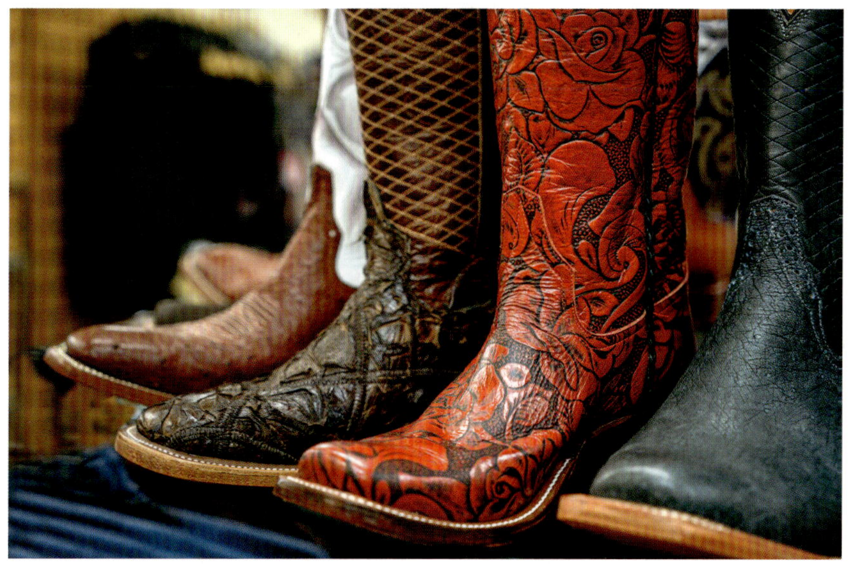

Expensive, handmade cowboy boots are in a special display at Fincher's White Front Western Wear, a long-standing Western clothing store that also sells gifts and souvenirs.

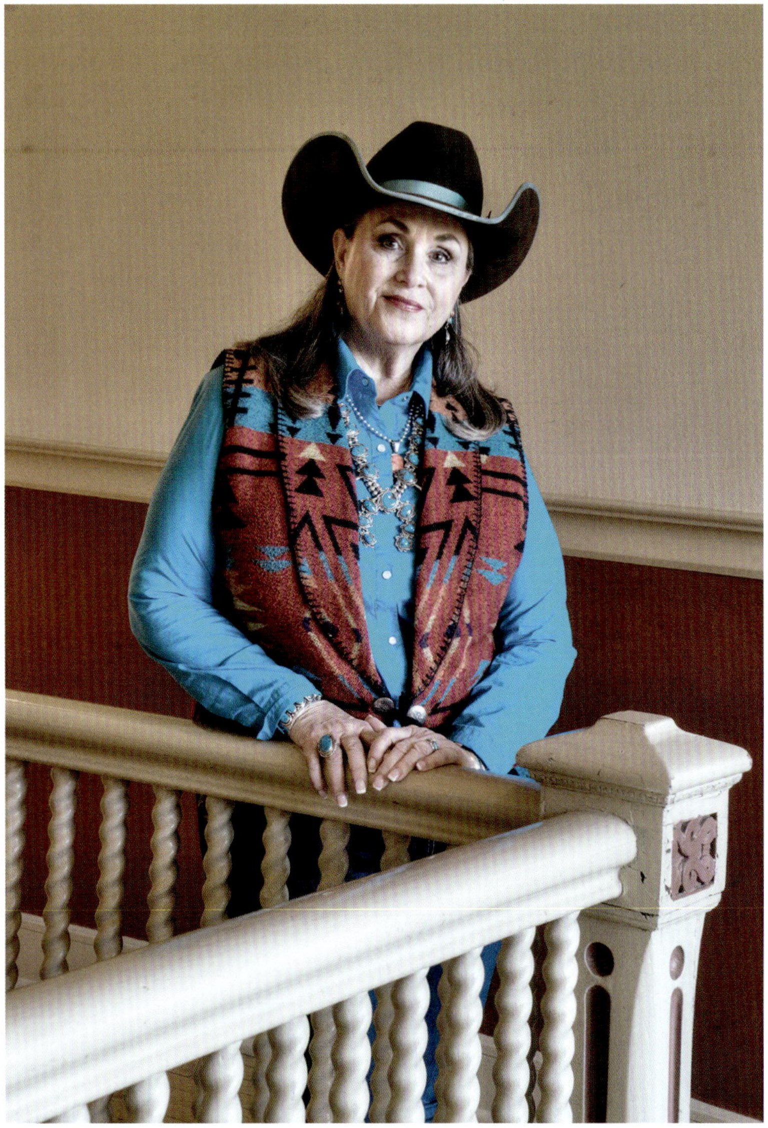
Teresa Burleson manages the museum in the historic Livestock Exchange Building. The museum was established and is overseen by the North Fort Worth Historical Society.

the society now operates its museum, which opened in 1988. There is a two-dollar entry fee for adults, and children under twelve are admitted free of charge.

Murrin, with partners P. K. Thomas, Whistle Ryan, and Harry Friedman, brought a weekly championship rodeo to the former North Side Coliseum, which they renamed the Cowtown Coliseum. Their first rodeo took place October 9–11, 1975. At first Murrin held a rodeo in the winter and a Wild West show during the summer. H. B. "Hub" Baker later became manager of the coliseum and for two decades into the twenty-first century produced the rodeo, every Friday and Saturday night year-round. The present coliseum manager is Clayton Cullen.

Tourists daily flock to the Cowtown Coliseum, located to the west of the Livestock Exchange Building. The building is open 8:00 a.m. to 5:00 p.m. Monday through Friday and 11:00 to 5:00 on Sunday and is free for tourists to visit on non-event days. Most tourists do not realize that the name "rodeo" originated there and that the popular event has taken place for more than one hundred years in its arena. The Fort Worth rodeo began in the coliseum in 1918 as the first indoor rodeo in the world. While for many years a rodeo did not take place in the stockyards, it currently is going strong.

Thousands of rodeo contestants from Fort Worth and elsewhere participate in rodeos at the coliseum each year, beginning at 8:00 p.m. each Friday and Saturday night. After all, many Texas folks grew up on farms or ranches. One of the locals who has participated and became World Champion is Trevor Brazile from Decatur, a small town near Fort Worth. The Fort Worth rodeo is unique in having performances every weekend year-round. Quite often all twenty-three hundred seats are sold out. Although the arena is small, in 1910 it was built for rodeo, stock shows, and selling cattle. It is close to the size of the National Finals Rodeo, so cowboys come to Fort Worth to practice for the event. Some of the cowboys who compete in Fort Worth also have become world champions through the years.

In the mid-1990s, Hub Baker, executive director and producer, added a Pawnee Bill Wild West Show with two performances each Saturday and Sunday, with shooting, trick riding, and other exciting events. Baker grew up on a farm and ranch near College Station. He arrived in Fort Worth in 1980, drawn by his friendship with Billy

Bob Barnett, whom he had known for many years. Along with Baker, board members of the coliseum include Steve Murrin, Joe Hickman, Don Jury, and Billy Minick. A group of Friends of the Cowtown Coliseum, who have fund-raisers and in other ways support it, include Baker, Betty Tanner, Douglas Harman, Bob Holmes, and Clara Ruddell.

The city of Fort Worth owns the coliseum and leases it to the directors. "The city of Fort Worth has been a great partner for us," Baker affirmed. The Cowtown Coliseum is a living museum for many reasons. Tourists visiting the coliseum when it is open during the day can see a pictorial timeline on the walls that tells its history. Inductees of the Texas Rodeo Cowboy Hall of Fame are listed on the west corridor of the coliseum, and the Bull Rider Hall of Fame, on the east.

The success of the stockyards in its revitalizing efforts as a business community dedicated to preserving its Western heritage depended almost entirely on the willingness of private businessmen and businesswomen to invest and get involved. People like Murrin and his friends realized that the North Side was an excellent business community, for it lay within five miles of both downtown Fort Worth and a municipal airport, Meacham Field.

Murrin had a love for the stockyards and was willing to take risks and spend his own money (or borrowed money) to try to save the area, as was his brother-in-law at the time, Joe Dulle. With other investors they purchased the White Elephant Saloon in 1976. Alice Walters became a financial partner with Murrin in several investments that saved older buildings on Exchange Avenue, including the Longhorn Saloon, the Maverick, General Store, and the White Elephant (with Dulle). Dulle became the major force at the White Elephant. He spent every day there for twenty-six years as its manager and became very good at promoting it. He arranged for an annual reenactment of the gunfight between Luke Short and Longhair Jim Courtright to take place each February 8 in front of the White Elephant to commemorate the actual fight that occurred in 1877 in downtown Fort Worth in the 300 block of Main Street. Other partners, at least part of the time, with Dulle at the White Elephant were Gene Miller and Jan Schlansker.

A couple of things helped Dulle make the White Elephant a success. He enjoyed the fortunate experience of inviting a singer named Don Edwards to perform cowboy songs in a small upstairs room in the evenings, which he called "Upstairs at the White Elephant." The upstairs room proved to be quieter than the floor below, where talking and dancing took place. Edwards gained his following at the White Elephant and even acquired a Warner Brothers' contract that lasted seven years. Dulle also made a deal with television shows such as *Dallas* and *Walker, Texas Ranger* to film some episodes at the White Elephant. He and his investors sold out to Tim Love in 2002. In the early 1960s and 1970s people who were down on their luck still lived in rooms at the hotel across Exchange Avenue from the White Elephant and sometimes would be drunk and set their mattresses on fire. Patrons at the White Elephant, while coming or leaving, sometimes saw a burning mattress being tossed out a window of the hotel.

Congressman for the Tarrant County area at the time, Jim Wright, sought and received federal funds for use in the stockyards to redo streets and take care of flooding in the area. This redevelopment in the 1970s helped persuade the city of Fort Worth also to take notice and spend funds for rejuvenation. This in turn convinced businesses and investors that the stockyards area was worthy of their support. Cleanup efforts slowly took effect. The city assigned more police, and folks soon felt less afraid to come to the stockyards at night. The city also spent $2.8 million to renovate the coliseum.

What early members of the North Fort Worth Historical Society only dreamed of in the late 1970s began to come true as economic activity in the form of tourism began to replace the loss of dollars in livestock activity at the Fort Worth Stockyards. Many things created the

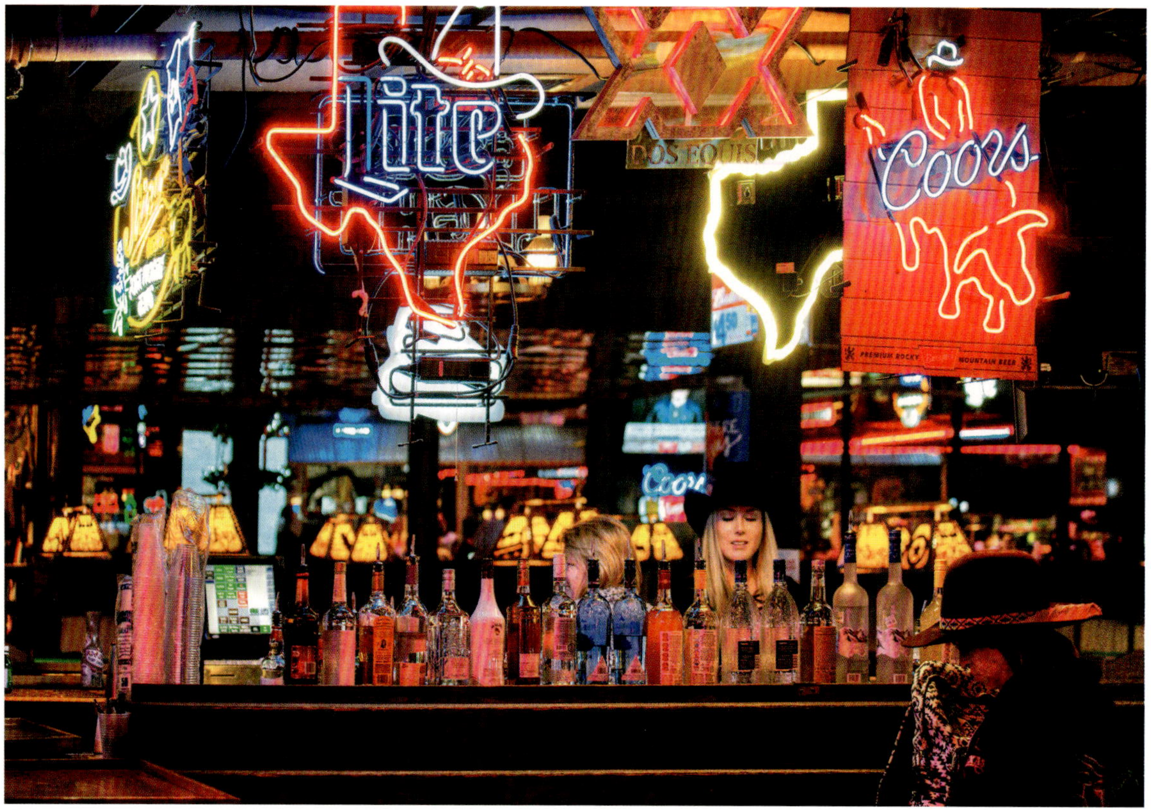

Billy Bob's Texas has a well-stocked bar and cheerful bartenders.

success story. In 1981 a group of developers that included Billy Bob Barnett, Steve Murrin, Hub Baker, and Don Jury created the "world's largest honky-tonk" in Fort Worth's vacant 127,000-square-foot exhibit building constructed in 1936 for the Fat Stock Show. The stockyards held its first auction in the same building in 1959. The nightclub, named after Barnett, is called Billy Bob's Texas and is located just north of the Cowtown Coliseum. It early on created an ambitious Western-style tourist attraction for the stockyards. The developers bought the building in 1980 and on April 1, 1981, opened it to enthusiastic crowds of five thousand to six thousand people a night. The first ninety days were booked heavily with big-name stars such as Waylon Jennings, Willie Nelson, and Larry Gatlin. With this popular talent performing, long lines appeared outside the building at the opening. The club became not only a national success but an international one, which brought attention to the stockyards area. Billy Bob's became so busy that five fire marshals kept track of the number of people inside so the club did not exceed the legal capacity. The building had a full house every night.

Determined to outdo a similar nightclub in Houston called Gilley's, instead of mechanical bull rides, Billy Bob's brought in live bulls for adventuresome folks to experience. The building also surpassed Gilley's square footage by a few hundred feet. Unfortunately, however, because of outside ventures not related to the stockyards or Billy Bob's, investors diverted money out of the club receipts, and the club went bankrupt January 8, 1988. A few months later on November 25, Steve Murrin, Don Jury, and Holt Hickman partnered to reopen the club, still named Billy Bob's because of its previous success under that name.

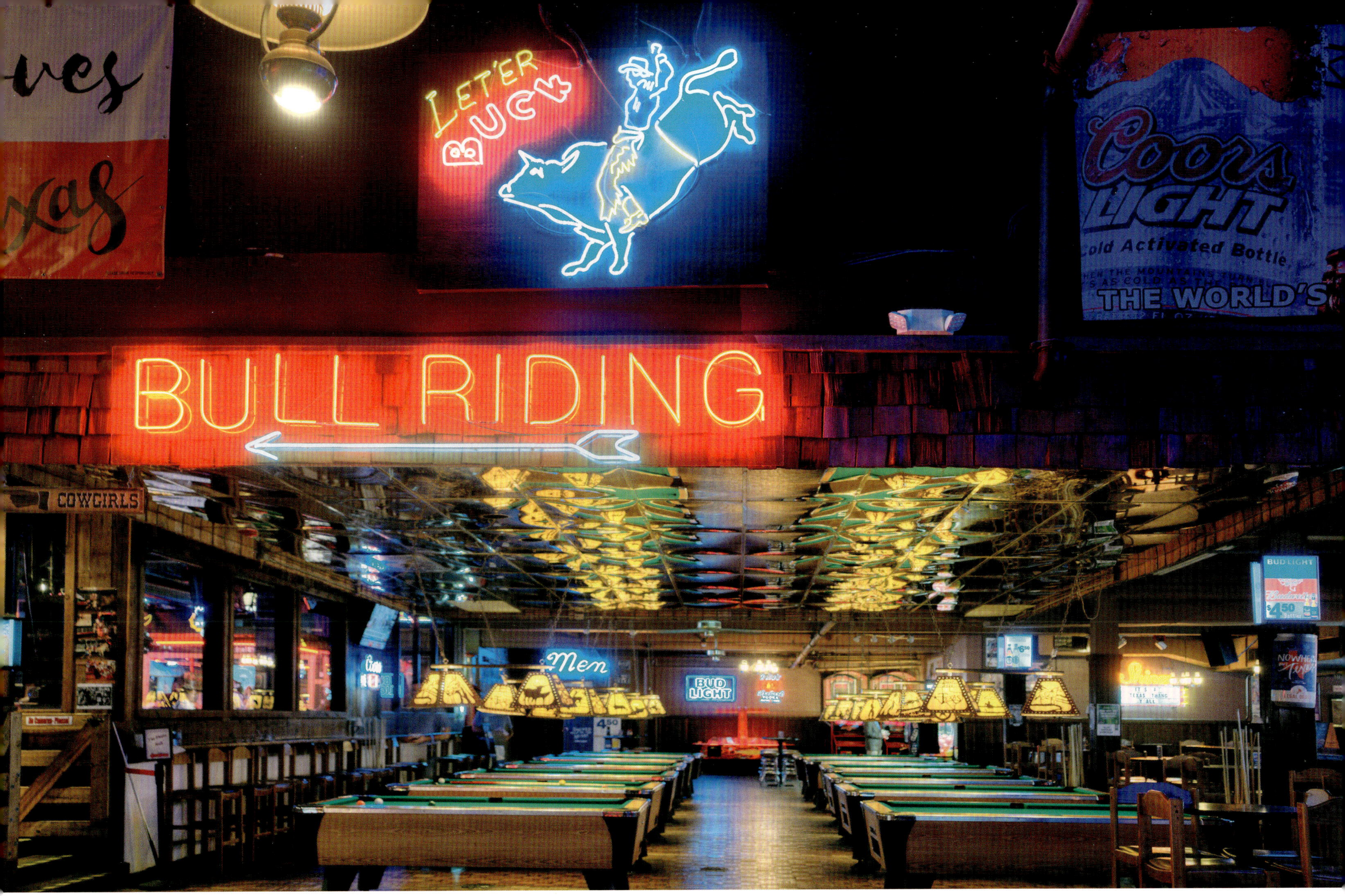

Bull riding and pool are two sports available for folks who visit Billy Bob's Texas. Bull-riding participants must be pro or semi-pro athletes with a valid rider's card from a recognized bull-riders' sanctioning organization. Billy Bob's can accommodate up to six thousand fun-loving folks at one time.

Billy Bob's won "Club of the Year" awards numerous times from the Country Music Hall of Fame because of its success in attracting all the major Western singers. The "world's largest honky-tonk" packs them in on weekends and in the twenty-first century still is going strong. Throughout the years, various partners have come and gone, but Billy Bob's lives on. Every major country-western star—and many others—have managed to play there.

Various ideas and plans surfaced in the 1970s and 1980s for a huge, modern Western entertainment complex in the stockyards area, but large investors for various reasons dropped out. Historians and many local people experienced sighs of relief because they wanted an authentic stockyards to remain, not a modern entertainment park. The value of the area is its Western authenticity, many locals emphasized. This grew when the Texas Longhorn Breeders' Association moved to the stockyards area in 1984 and dedicated the largest bronze statue in the world—at that time anyway—several Longhorn cattle located on Main Street just north of Billy Bob's.

The Texas Sesquicentennial Wagon Train, which traveled in a large circle around Texas for six months in 1986, also brought attention to the stockyards. Texas was celebrating its 150th birthday, and what a great place to end the train's successful jaunt around the state: the Fort Worth Stockyards, where it arrived on July 3, 1986, completing its successful journey.

The biggest investor of all in the stockyards area was entrepreneur Holt Hickman, who earned his money in an auto air-conditioning company. At first he wanted to tear down and modernize the area, but Sue McCafferty and others persuaded him that leaving the yards as much like they were in the beginning as possible is what attracts the tourists. Most other large stockyards throughout the country fell into disuse and were dismantled entirely. Fortunately, Fort Worth's major stockyards buildings remain mostly intact, including the Livestock Exchange Building, the coliseum, and the auction barn. Even the concrete covering over the hog and sheep pens and the brick building of the Horse and Mule Barns remain, with modern businesses operating inside, as well as the Swift Office Building. The area is unique.

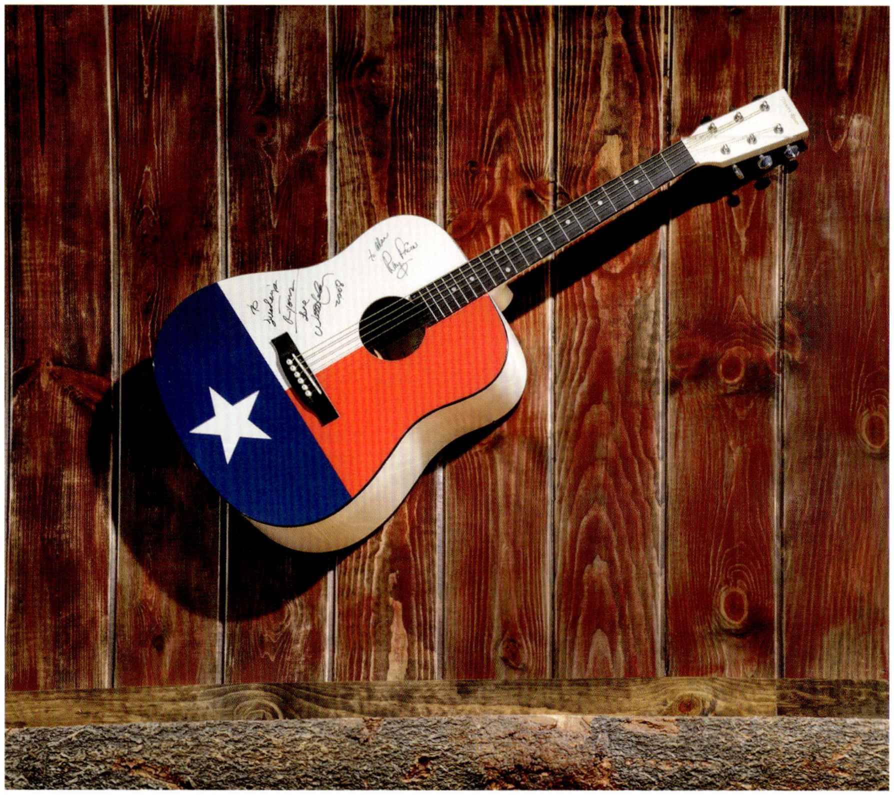

Musicians Willie Nelson and Ray Price signed this Texas-decorated guitar. It is on display at Cavender's Western Store (formerly Luskey's Ryon's Western Store).

Local enthusiasts persuaded Hickman to invest, and he did so heavily, beginning in the 1980s. He purchased the Livestock Exchange Building, Stockyards Station (formerly the sheep and hog area), the Texas Cowboy Hall of Fame and Museum in the mule barns, and the old Swift plant, torn down in 2016. Then he built a modern hotel, the Hyatt Place, and the former Visitors Center in 1992 on the south side of Exchange Avenue across from the Livestock Exchange Building. His purchases covered more than eighty acres.

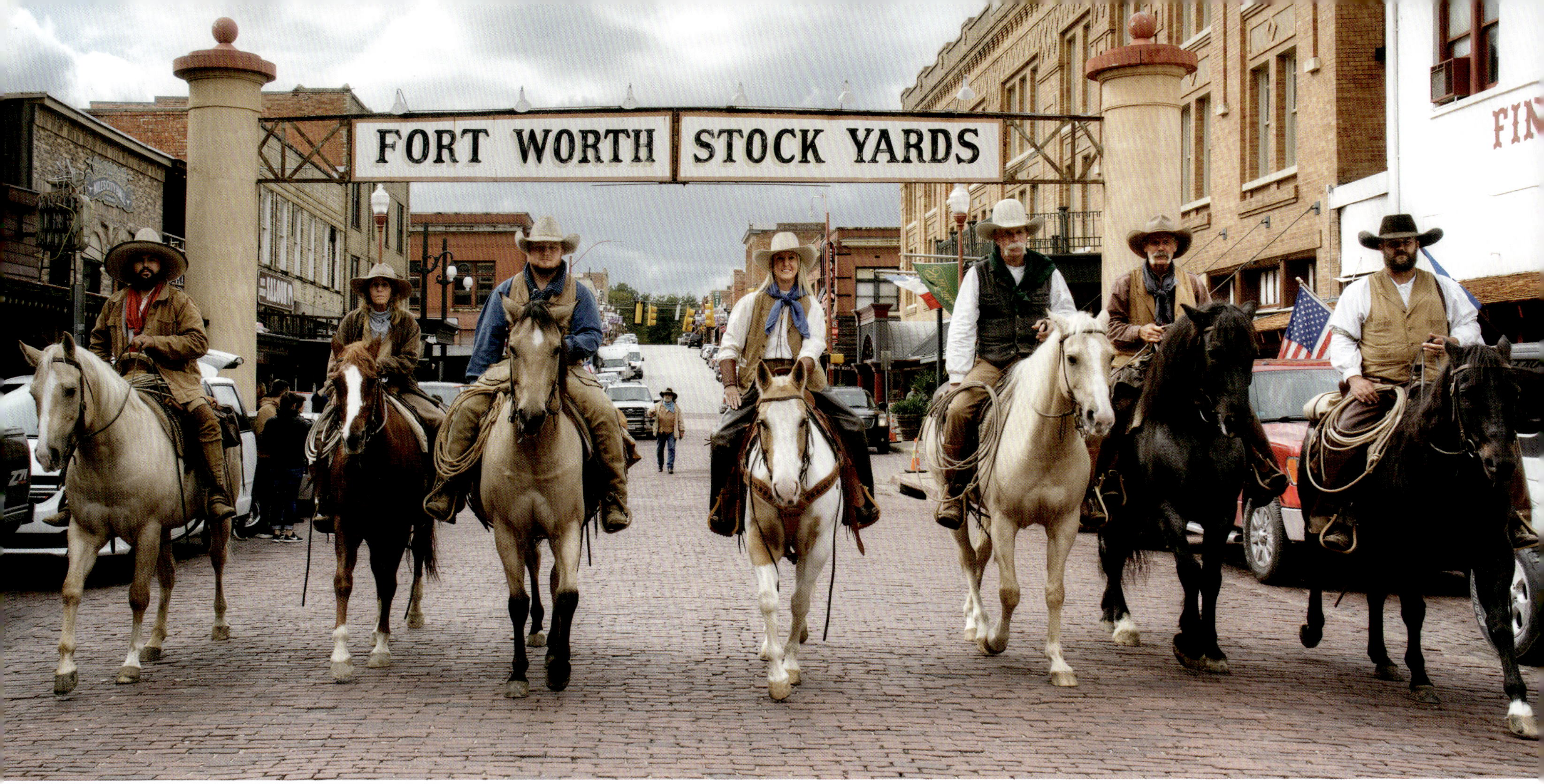

Drovers line up with Trail Boss Kristin Jaworski in the center. The Texas Longhorn and the American cowboy are two of the most enduring symbols of the Old West. They are a big reason that Fort Worth earned the nickname "Cowtown," and they formed the core of the great cattle drives of the late nineteenth century. The romance and mystique of cowboys and cattle drives can be seen every day with the Fort Worth Herd.

Being a Fort Worth property owner and developer, Hickman became easier to persuade to save the stockyards structures than outside investors would have been. He thus rescued much of the stockyards from both neglect and/or destruction. Much of the credit for the popularity of the stockyards for tourism that soon developed goes to Gary Brinkley, whom Hickman hired in 1998 as general manager. Brinkley became the businessman who kept spaces leased, hired people to maintain the lawns and sprinkler system, and managed employees whom he outfitted in spiffy uniforms. Brinkley also organized events such as "Cowtown Goes Green" on St. Patrick's day, Easter egg hunts, "Frontier Forts Muster" in May, and "National Day of the Cowboy" in July, Halloween events, and "Christmas in the Stockyards."

The Fort Worth Convention and Visitors Bureau helps attract tourists to Fort Worth and keeps a branch office in the stockyards. The bureau also urges visitors to see the Fort Worth Zoo, Six Flags over Texas, and the city's many museums.

Any history of the Fort Worth Stockyards cannot ignore the role of the politicians of city hall in helping make the area a popular success, even though some of its members at one time perpetuated the "Now Town, not Cowtown" slogan. Steve Murrin complained in the early days that the "downtown" people did not see the value of preservation. The people at city hall pushed for modernization of the yards, but Murrin and his friends pushed back. They wanted to preserve the integrity of the stockyards. The authenticity still remaining represented what the tourists wanted, he emphasized, as did others in the North Side.

Luckily for the success and popularity of the yards, a longtime resident of the North Side, Jim Lane, served for twelve years on the Fort Worth City Council. During that time, he figured that the stockyards needed a few live cattle for tourists to see and conceived the idea for the herd of Longhorns that now wander down East Exchange Avenue each day at 11:30 a.m. and 4:00 p.m. He spoke to the mayor of Fort Worth at the time, Kenneth Barr,

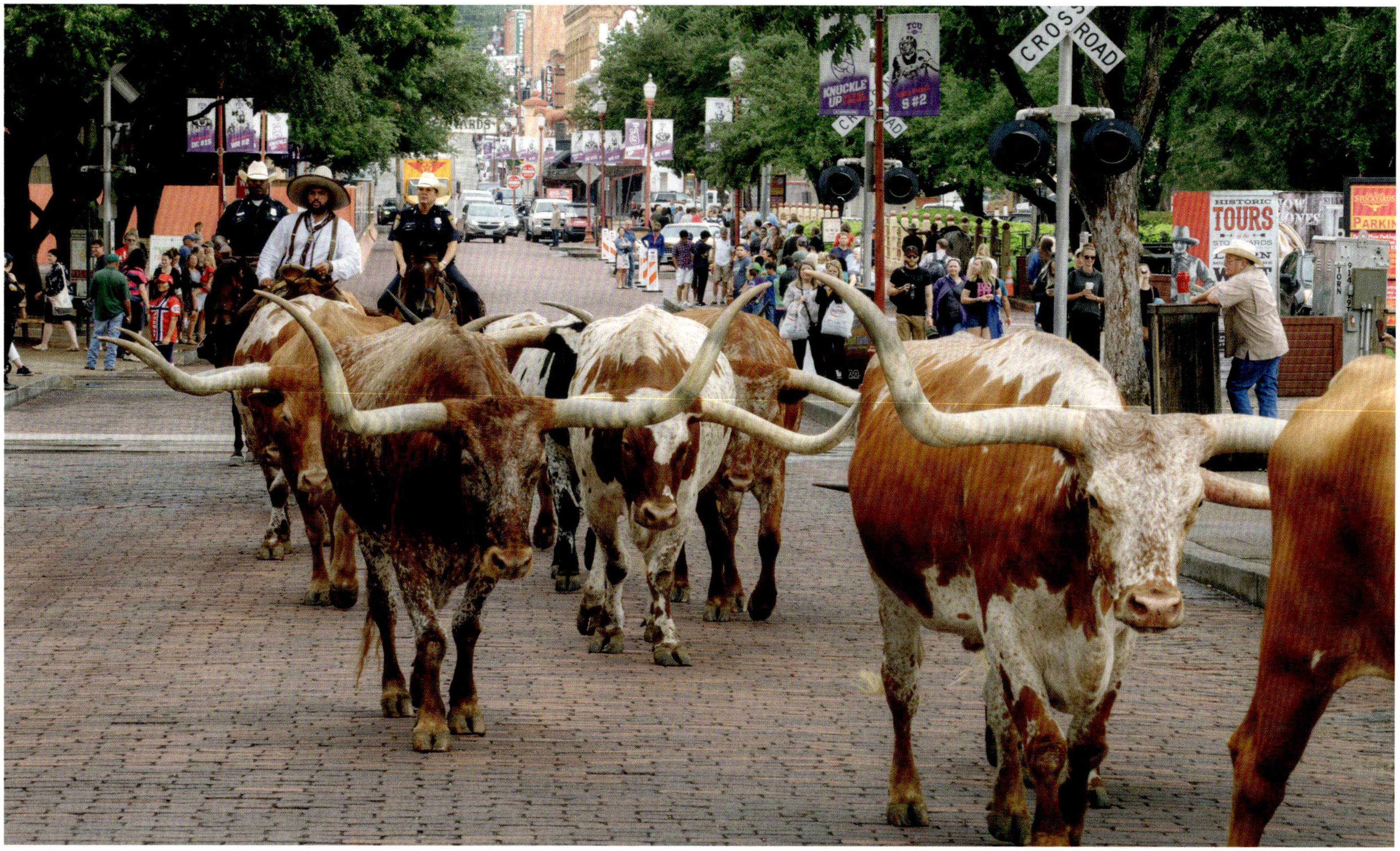

Drovers herd the famous Longhorns from one end of East Exchange Avenue to the other twice daily. Crowds watch from curbside as the herd passes by. Mounted security guards follow the herd on this September 11.

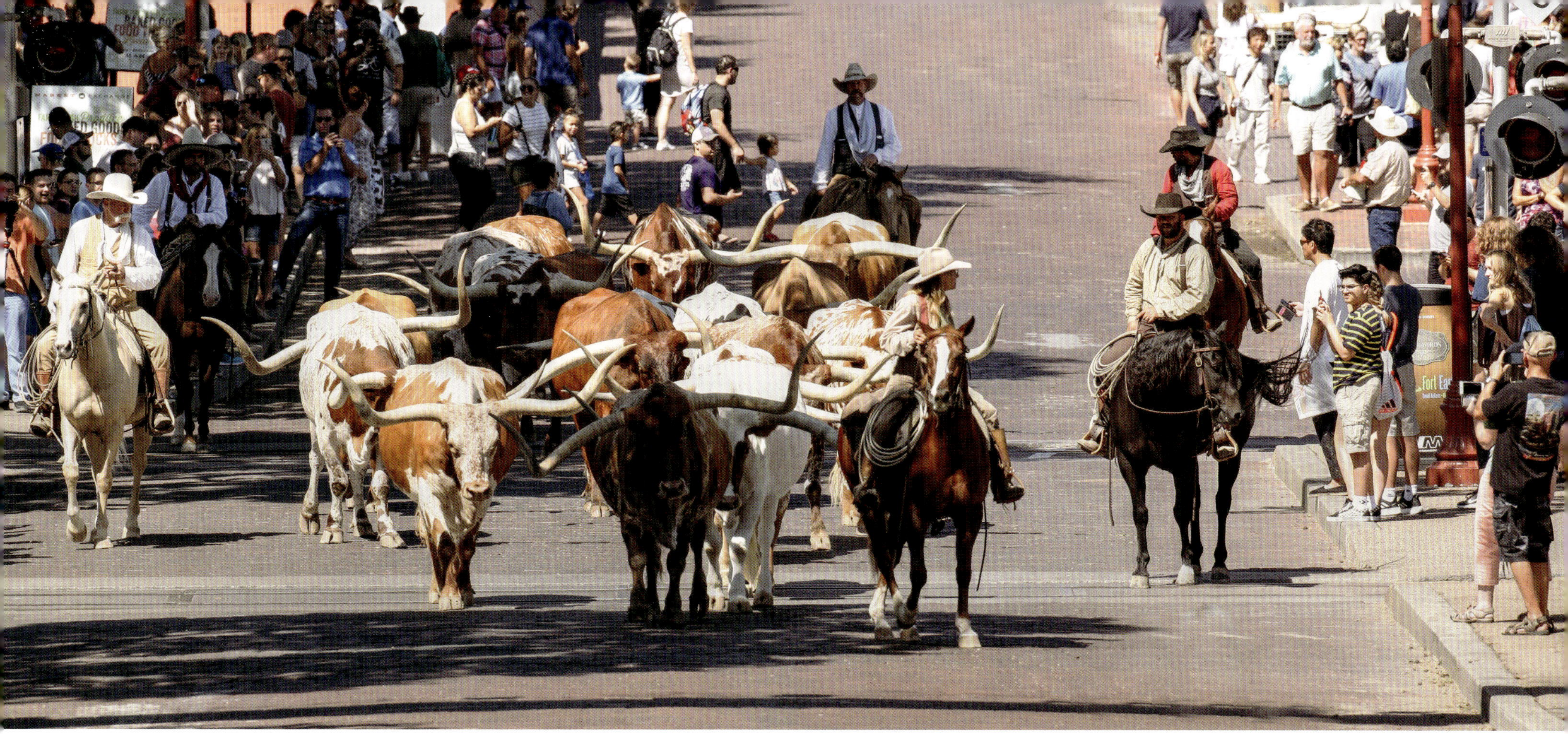

People crowd on the curb to get as close as possible to the herd and the drovers as they stroll down East Exchange Avenue.

fortunately a former fraternity brother at Texas Christian University, and both of them persuaded the city council to pay the cost for the "Fort Worth Herd" because of the excellent publicity it would bring. In addition, the timing of starting the herd in 1999 would be a way to celebrate the 150th birthday of Fort Worth (1849–1999).

To assemble the herd, promoters located Longhorns from major ranches in both Texas and Oklahoma. The very first herd boasted animals averaging eighteen hundred pounds and horn spans of approximately six feet. Organizers wanted the herd to be authentic. Dennis Merrell became the first trail boss. He explained that the animals were trained in ranches nearby to get them accustomed to horses and cowboys before they could become a part of the herd. They learned to follow a leader and each other in a specific order. Each Longhorn carries the brand of a previous owner, but the city added a "Running FW" brand as well. Tom B. Saunders IV, a descendant of a well-known family in Fort Worth, initially became historian for the herd.

The herd of fifteen to twenty animals began its appearance June 12, 1999. Not only did Lane suggest the herd; he also recommended that the Longhorn steer statue that appears at the top front of the Livestock Exchange Building be named Fort Worth's "mascot." It already had a name, because Charlie and Sue McCafferty called it "Molly." Wisely, the city council chose Molly as the mascot for Fort Worth. Also, instead of their previous "Now Town, not

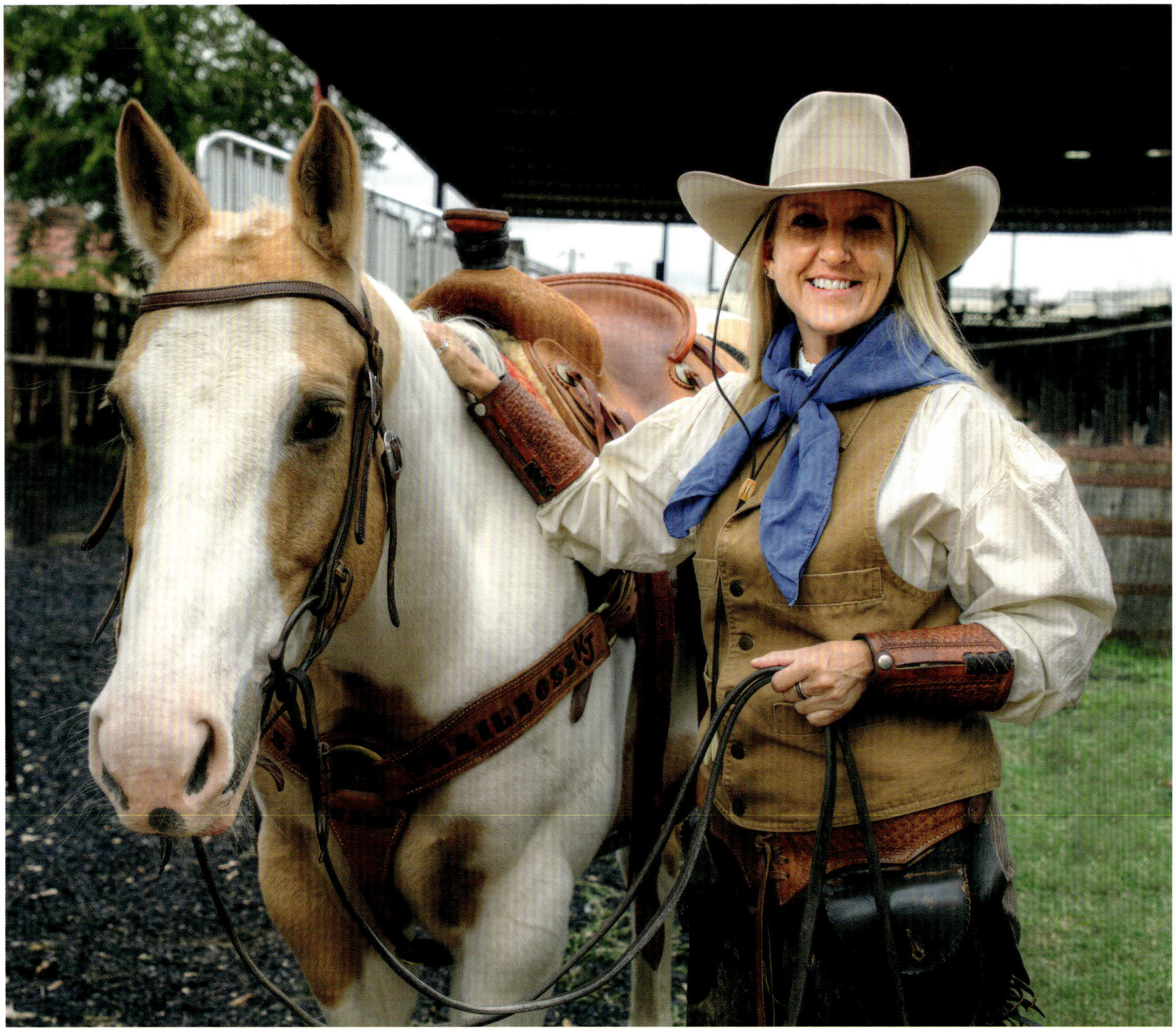

Kristin Jaworski, trail boss for the Fort Worth Herd, said at the herd's twentieth anniversary, "It is an amazing journey and one I am proud to be part of. We've touched so many lives over the years through our education programs, interacting with tourists and sharing the Fort Worth story with hundreds of domestic and international media outlets—we are excited [as] we continue to showcase this important piece of history." Kristin is shown with her horse, McCoy.

Cowtown" slogan, the term "Cowboys and Culture" now reigns as the new slogan, indicating a balance between the city's Western heritage of cattle and stockyards and its numerous cultural museums located in the west of the city, one of them the Cowgirl Museum. Currently, "Culture, Cowboys, and Commerce" is the slogan the Fort Worth Convention and Visitors Bureau uses to describe Fort Worth.

Kristin Jaworski has been trail boss for the herd since 2002. Around horses all her life while growing up in Flagstaff, Arizona, she came to Fort Worth when her father was transferred to Texas. Holding a master's degree in marketing and management, she won the job over ninety other applicants at age twenty-five. She took the Longhorns to New York City in 2005 after officials in New York extended the invitation. A group of Texas Longhorn cattle

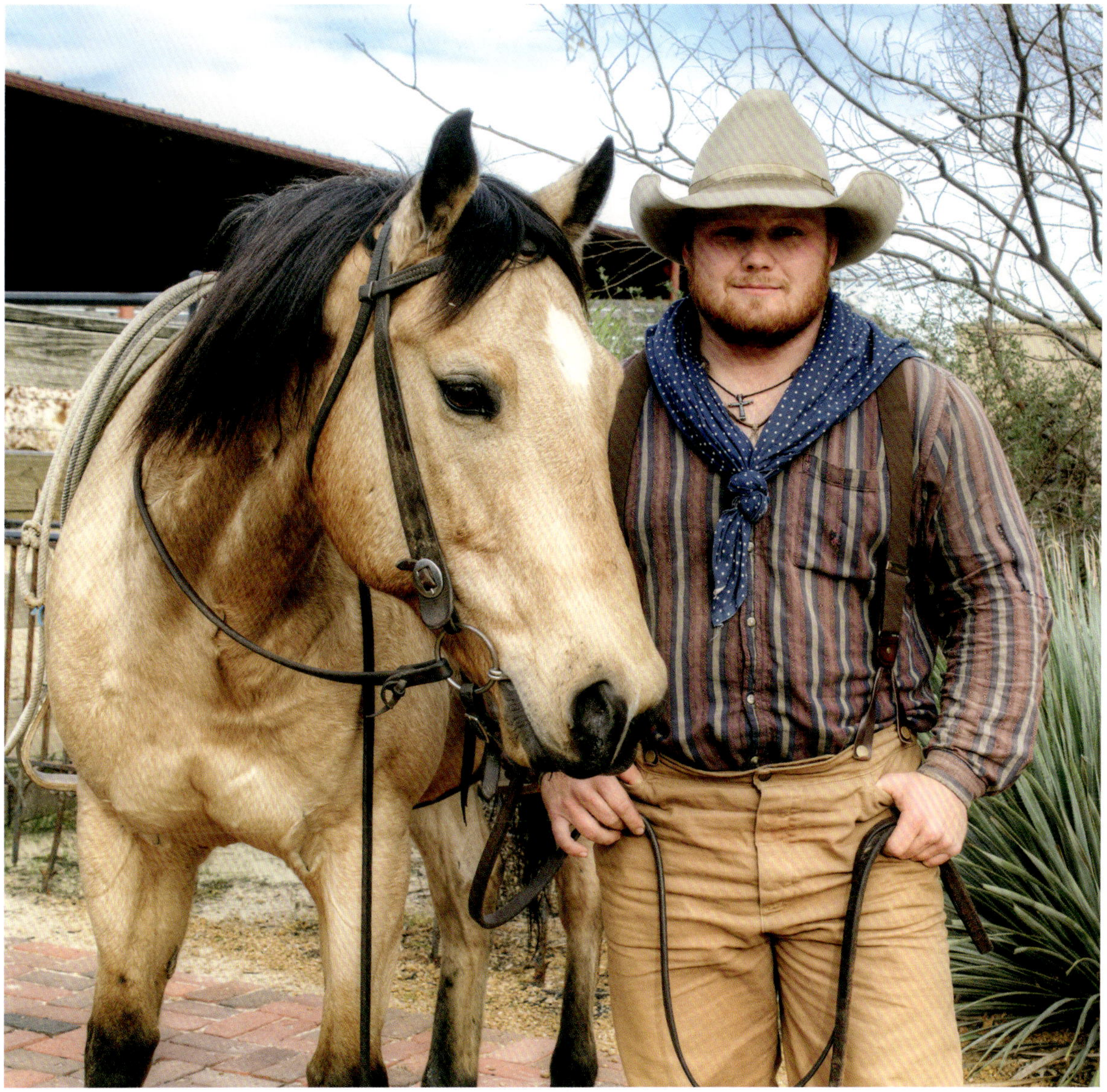

Drover Ethan Gustus poses with his horse, Parker. The drover's bandana is the most versatile piece of clothing he wears. It is called a "wild rag" because the first ones were made from old rags and it is the cheapest piece of equipment they use.

visiting the Big Apple drew crowds and created great publicity for Fort Worth and the stockyards.

Jaworski and the drovers involved with the herd do worry that spectators might get hurt. These are Longhorn cattle, after all. Visitors are urged to stay back on the curb and keep their distance. Tourists love the herd and begin lining up nearly an hour before each of the two daily appearances to see the twenty, long-horned animals slowly take their walk, surrounded by the wranglers who care for them and rub them down each day.

After the drive ends and the Longhorns go back to their pens, the wranglers return to Exchange Avenue to visit with tourists and answer questions. Tourists enjoy learning that similar Texas Longhorns going up the trail in the late 1860s began the long treks to those Kansas cowtowns.

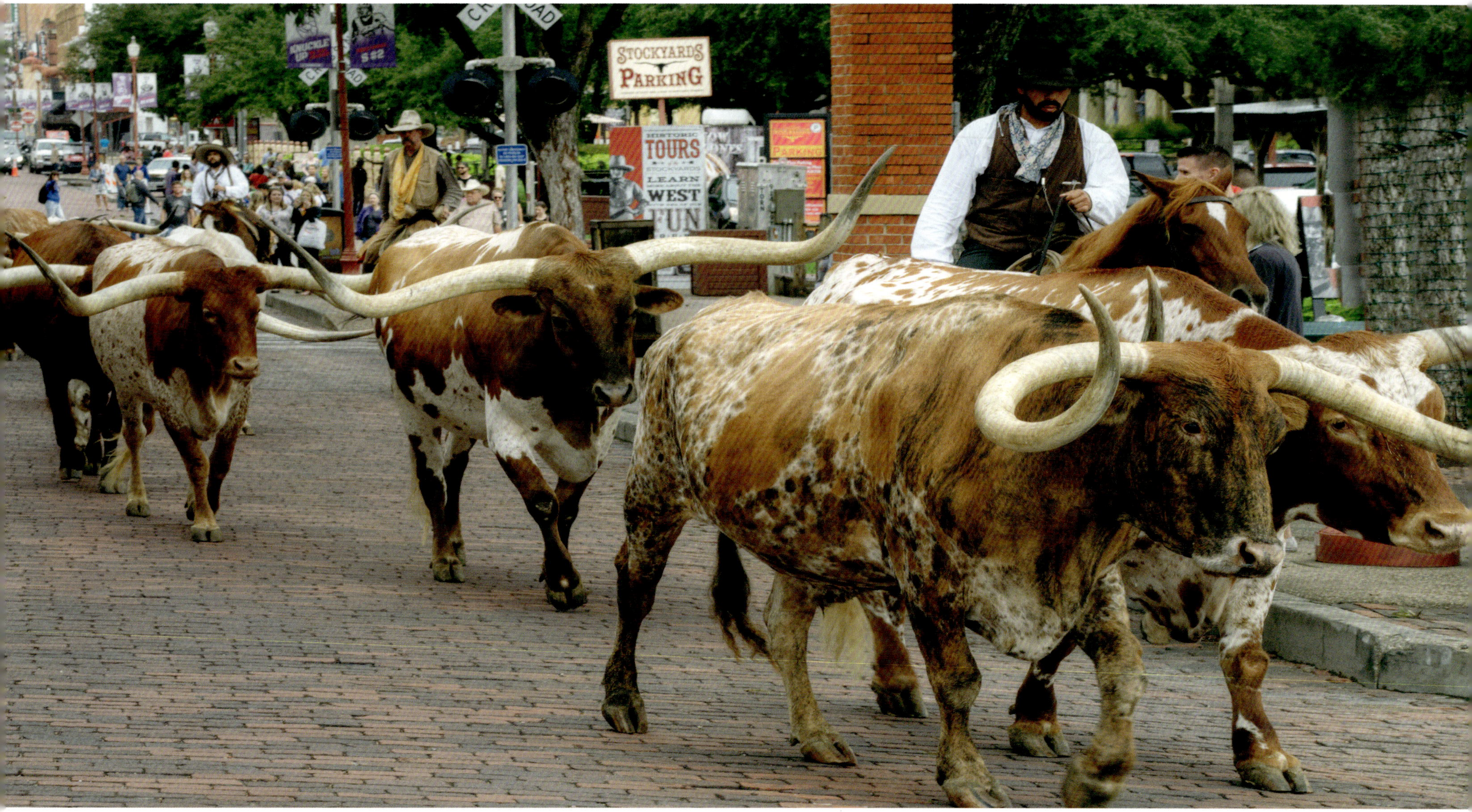

The Texas Longhorn is a breed of cattle known for its characteristic horns, which can extend to over seventy inches tip to tip for bulls and up to one hundred inches tip to tip for steers and exceptional cows.

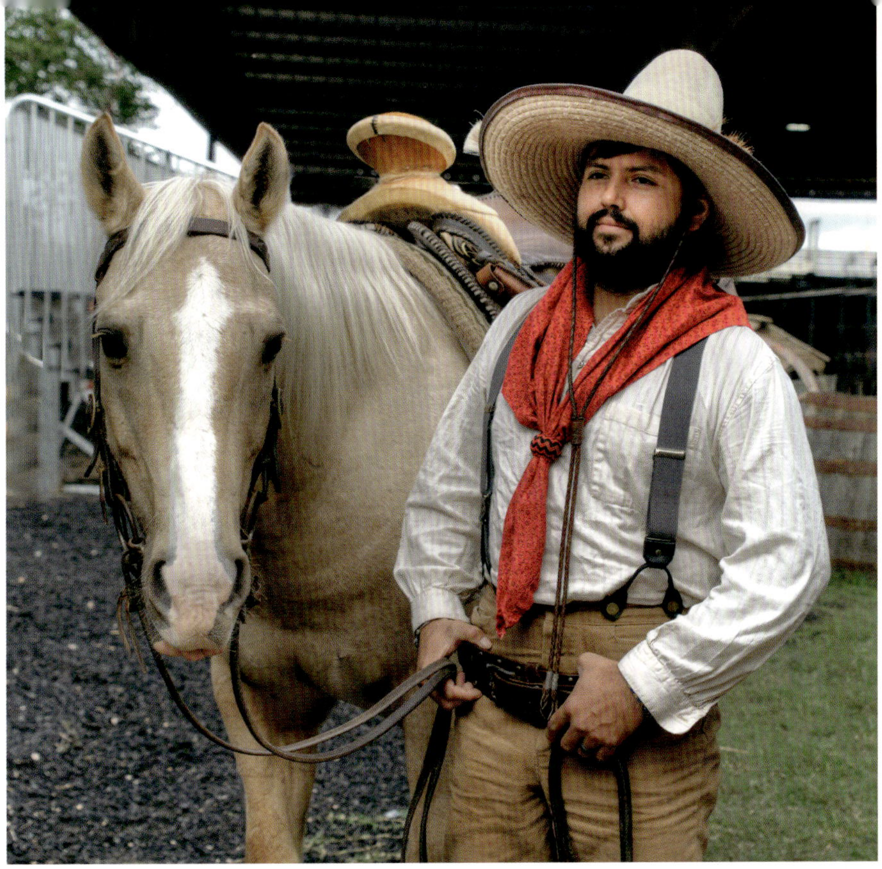

Drover José Hernandez stands with his horse, Charlie. José uses a Mexican vaquero saddle with the large saddle horn. The saddle is the most important piece of equipment a drover uses and is made of leather, rawhide, wood, and iron. It is designed to carry everything he needs, including tools.

Drover Tyler Peterson poses with his horse, Gotch. The cowboy hat evolved from the hats made of pressed beaver fur used during the Civil War. It cost about a month's salary.

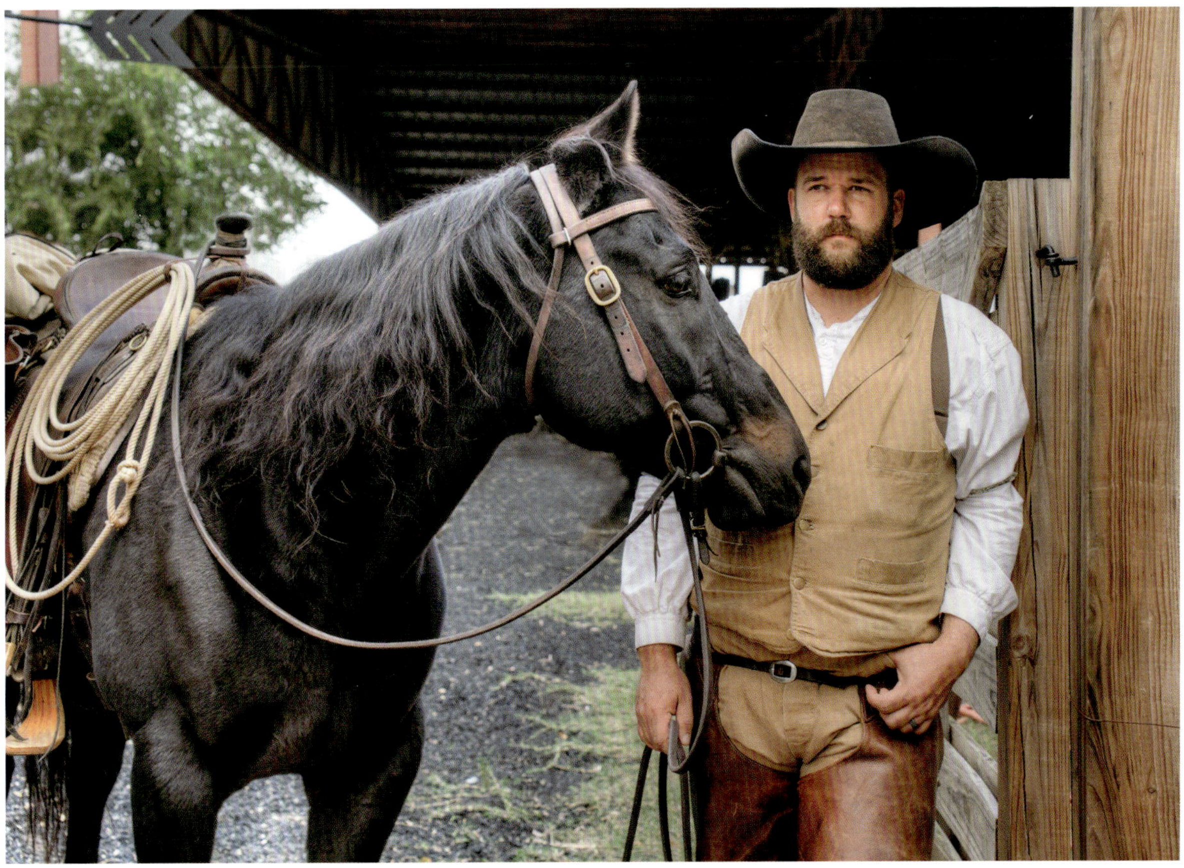

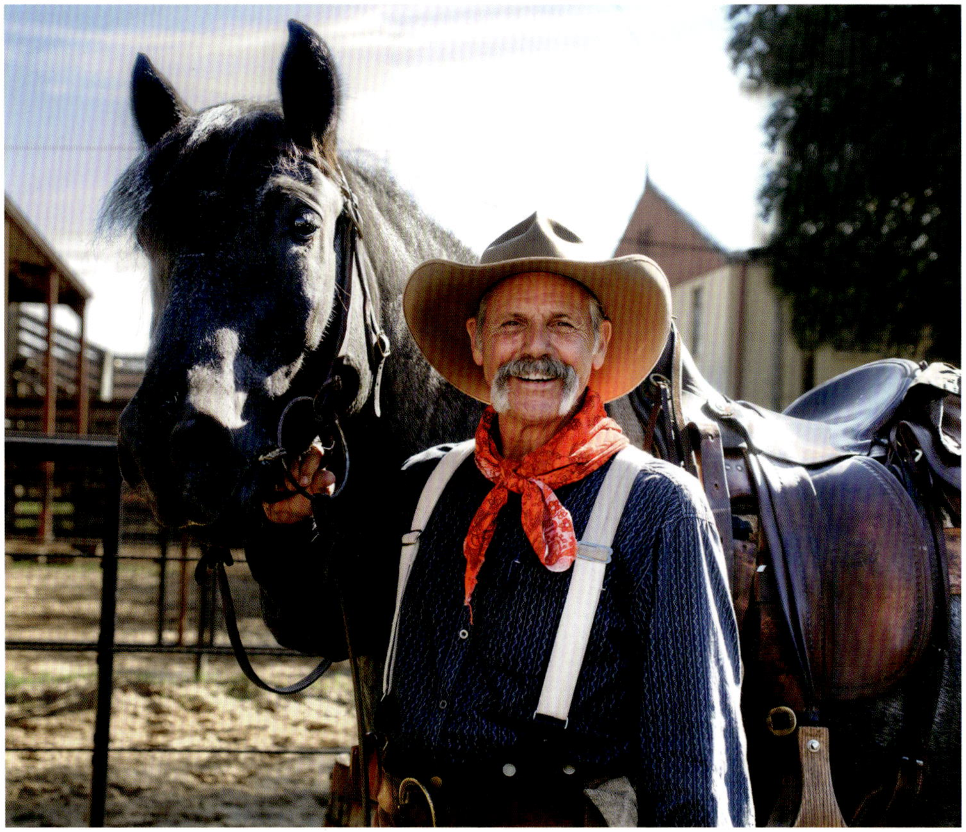

Drover Ken Burrill stands with his blue roan horse, Vaquero. On average, a herd of cattle could maintain a healthy weight moving about fifteen miles per day. Ken's suspenders stand out.

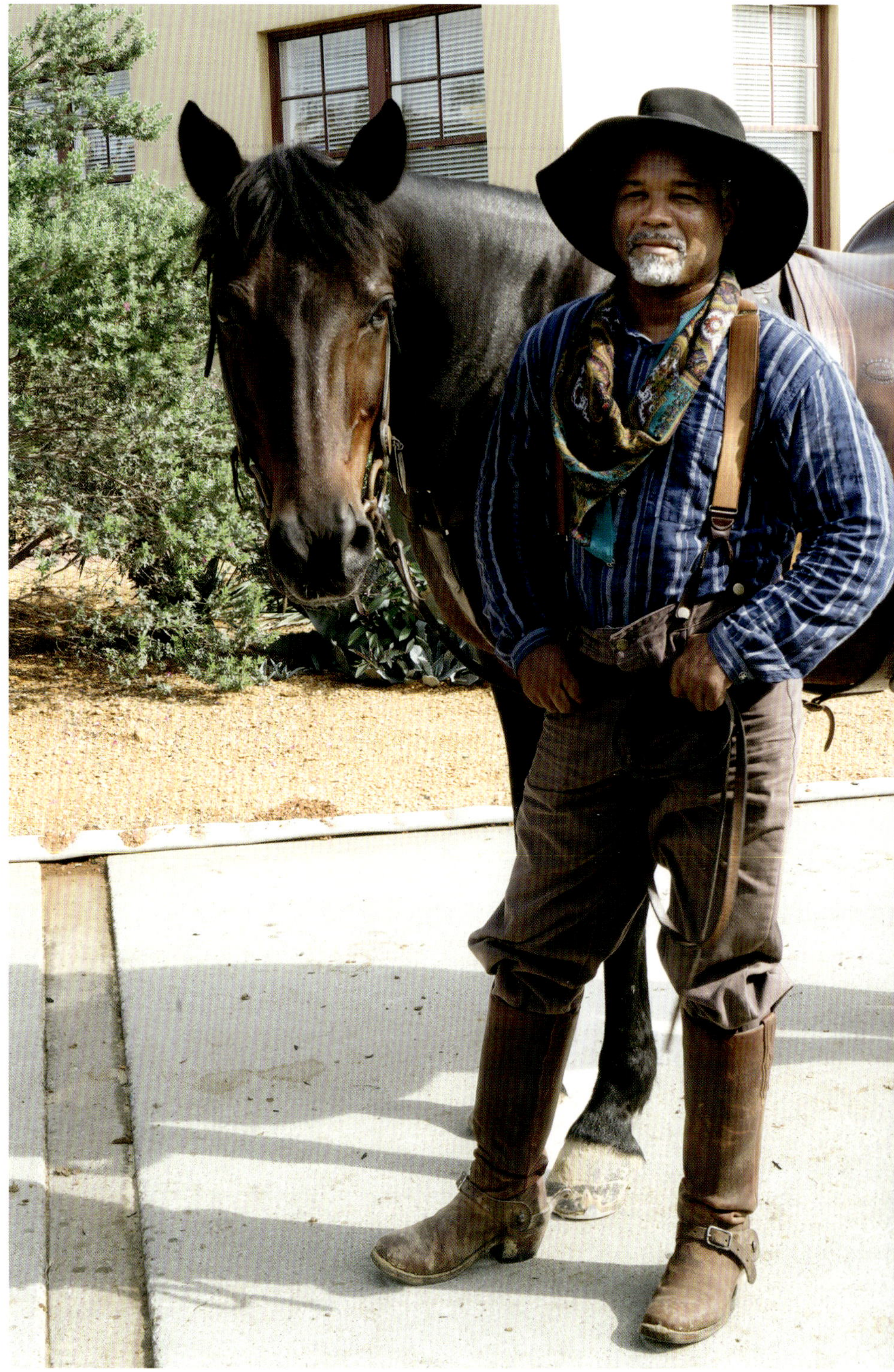

Drover Donald Lee stands beside his horse, Whiskey Pete.

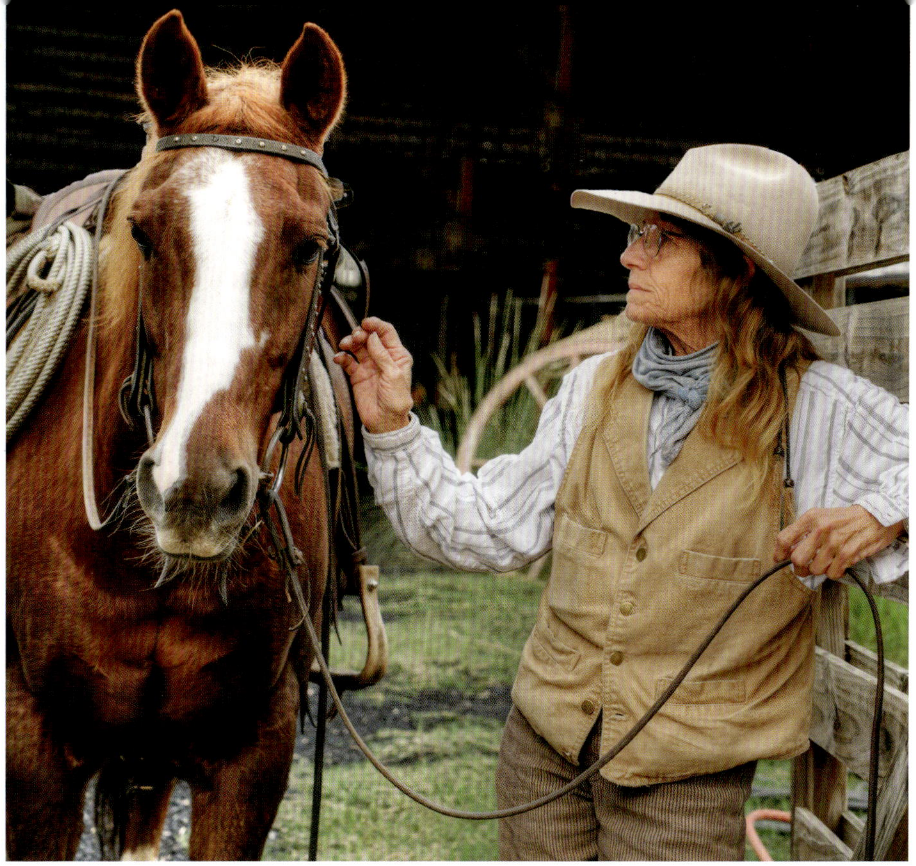

Drover Brenda Taylor poses with her horse, Little Texas. Brenda is unique, for few women accompanied the trails.

Brenda Taylor and Little Texas watch as the Longhorn herd happily head toward their pens.

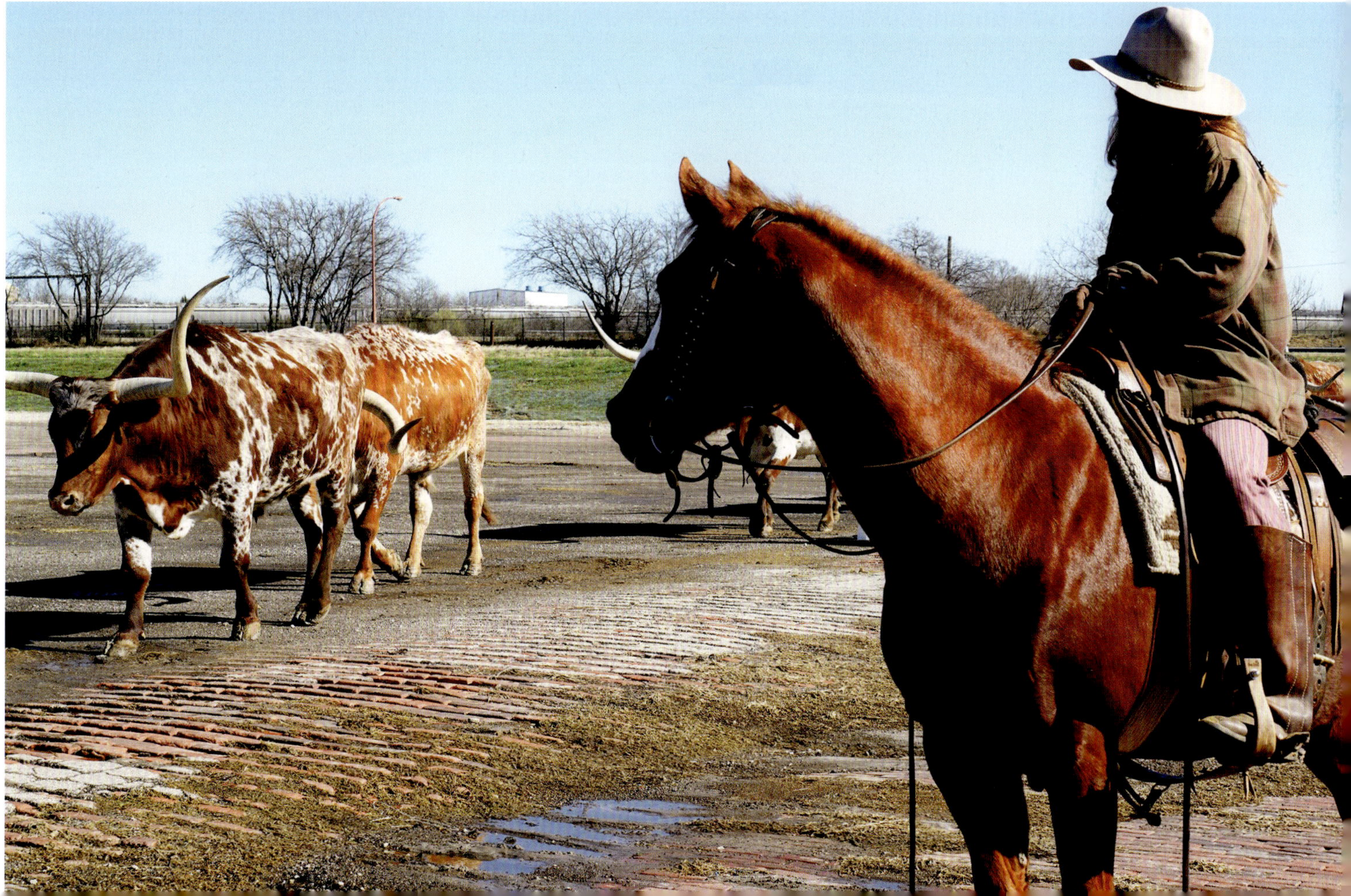

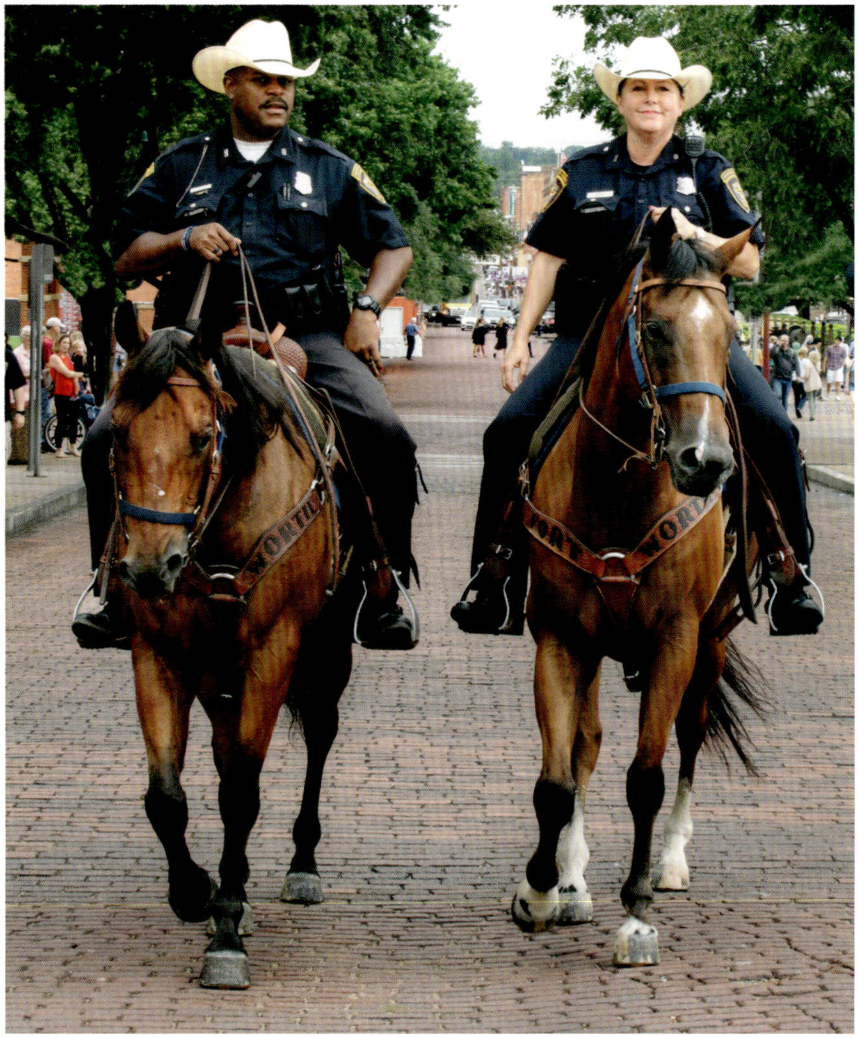

Officers Jorjana Urban (*right*) and Ivory Davis (*left*) help maintain public safety in the stockyards.

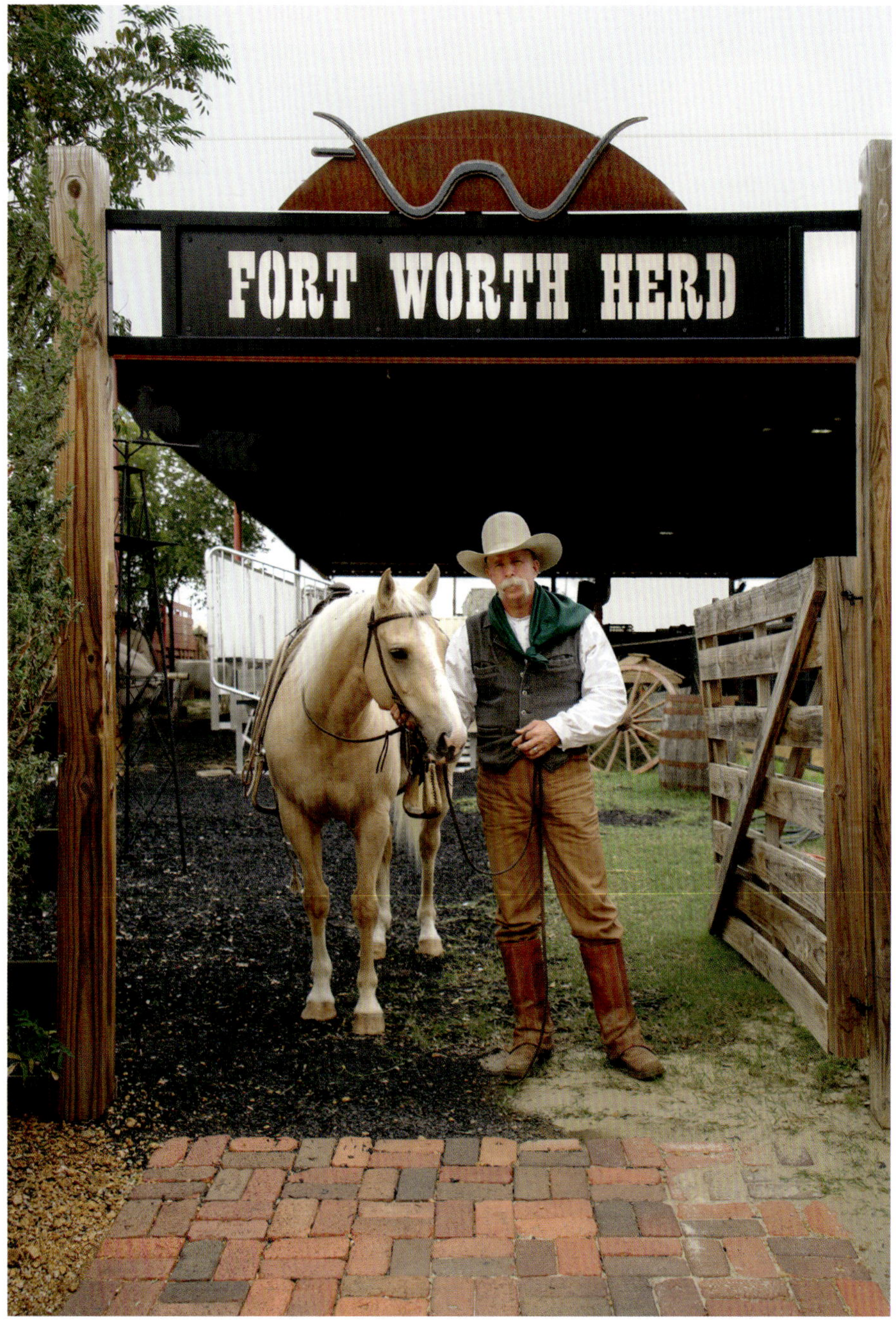

Drover David Mangold poses with his horse, Oliver. An individual owner of livestock cannot both take care of animals on his farm and take other stock on a long journey to market. So the owner might entrust this stock to an agent—usually a drover—who delivers the animals to market.

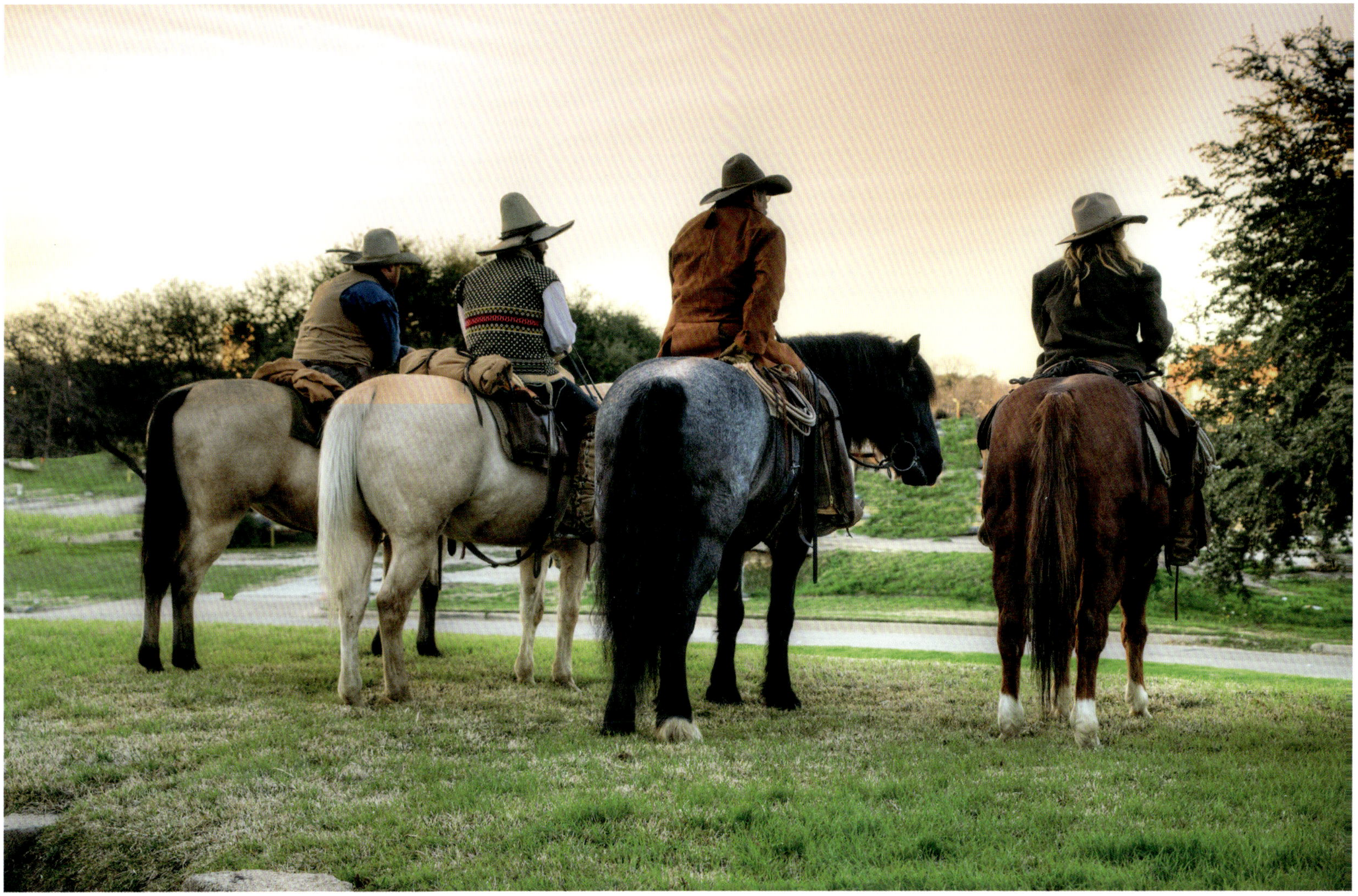

Four drovers on horseback look across the North Texas landscape as the sun sets.

Numerous buildings in the stockyards area on Exchange Avenue made up the original neighborhood of the couple of blocks nearest the Livestock Exchange Building and the Armour and Swift offices. Most of them still exist as homes for thriving businesses two decades into the twenty-first century. Each has its own story to tell.

The Maverick, a building on Exchange Avenue near the stockyards, once was a bar but presently is a store that draws many tourists to purchase its souvenirs and Western merchandise. It was built in 1905 as a hotel, but from 1928 to 1933 it operated as a hotel and bar. In the 1940s and 1950s it allowed gambling and became a bordello. During an expensive remodeling in the 1970s the Maverick became more respectable as a private social club and enjoyed members from throughout the city. During one of the early 1940s floods in the stockyards, a couple of horses were washed from the Horse and Mule Barns westward down Exchange Avenue and ended up in the lobby of the Maverick. Thanks to the efforts to save the original buildings in the area, the Maverick in the twenty-first century retains not only its name but its continued existence. As Maverick Fine Western Wear, the building still stands on the southeast corner of Main and Exchange, and its present owner is Gayle Hill. She arrived in the stockyards in August 1987 and has been in business at the Maverick ever since. She also started the General Store and Trading Post across the street on the southwest corner of Main and West Exchange.

Other businesses succeed in their role of keeping the stockyards area both Western and attractive to hometown folks and tourists. Wilson Franklin, owner of Leddy's Boots, located on the northwest corner of North Main and West Exchange, helped maintain stability in the yards through the years. Franklin's grandfather, M. L. Leddy, began the company in Brady, Texas, but three of his brothers, Frank, Silas, and O. C., sold an interest they had in the company back to M. L. and moved to Fort Worth in 1941. Leddy Brothers of Fort Worth later became the largest handmade boot and saddle company in the world. Franklin came to Fort Worth from San Angelo in 1972 at age twenty to operate the store that his three great-uncles started thirty-one years earlier. Of the dozen or so companies that fashion true handmade boots, Leddy's sells the largest volume. Franklin still follows the tradition of taking the foot measurements of each customer and making the person a pair of custom boots.

Fincher's White Front Western Wear, located on East Exchange Avenue, is in the first floor of a huge, white two-story building that has a large horse mannequin outside. The Western store has been in operation since 1902 in that location. Fincher's stocks a full line of Western wear for infants to adults. Third- and fourth-generation customers, as well as hordes of tourists, patronize the business. Fincher's has been in business at the stockyards for well over a century and has the motto of serving customers in the "old-fashioned way from hand-creased hats to properly fitted boots." Its unique telephone number is 1-877-HAT-BOOT.

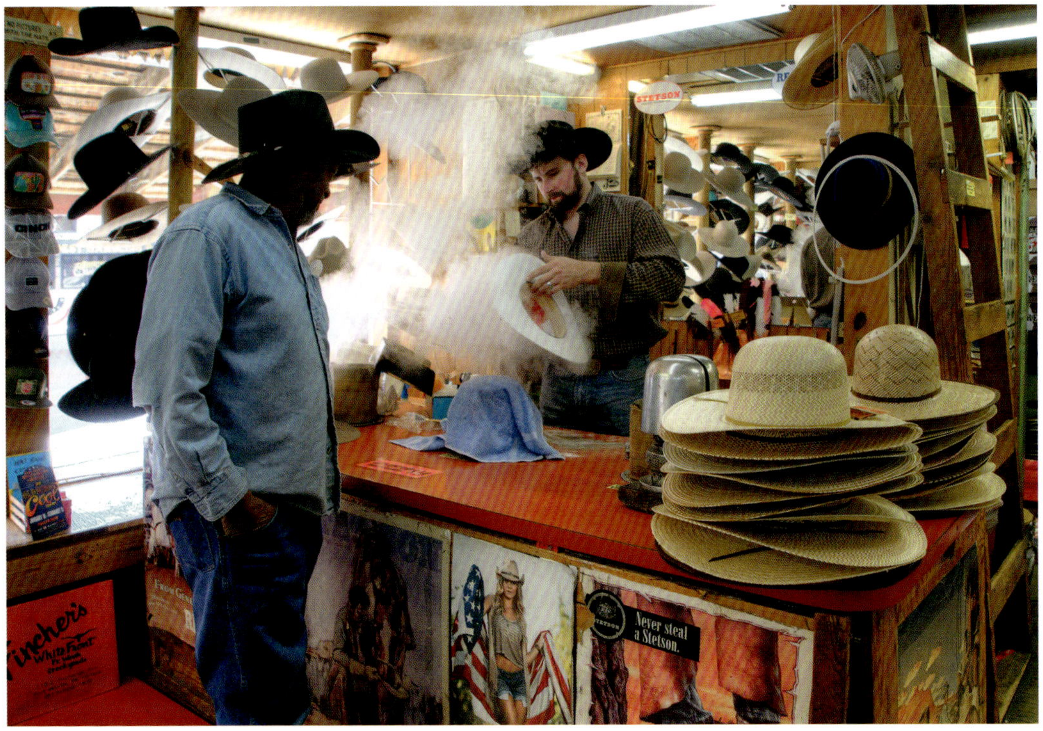

Cowboys and friends come to Fincher's White Front Western Wear to purchase their Western hats and have them steamed for an exact fit.

Red Steagall, a country-western singer who owns a ranch west of Fort Worth, moved his office from Nashville to the Livestock Exchange Building in 1977. He began making numerous appearances at the stockyards, including his Red Steagall Cowboy Gathering each October, beginning in 1990. A wagon train travels from fifty miles or more to the event each year, starting a day or two earlier. Once at the stockyards, the festivities include cowboy songs and poetry, a cook-off, bands, and camping out. Steagall donates the proceeds from the event to a charity that gives scholarships to working cowboys to attend college.

A Texas Cowboy Hall of Fame opened in 2001 in the former Barn A of the Horse and Mule Barns, but it has been moved to the exhibit building west of the coliseum temporarily until a better home can be located. Included is an outstanding exhibit of wagons called the Sterquell Wagon Collection: every kind of buggy or wagon one can imagine, carriages for funeral homes, milk wagons, fire wagons, and other antique, horse-drawn vehicles. Cowboys inducted into the Texas Cowboy Hall of Fame include Walt Garrison, Larry Mahan, Buck Taylor, W. R. Watt Sr., and even the Light Crust Doughboys.

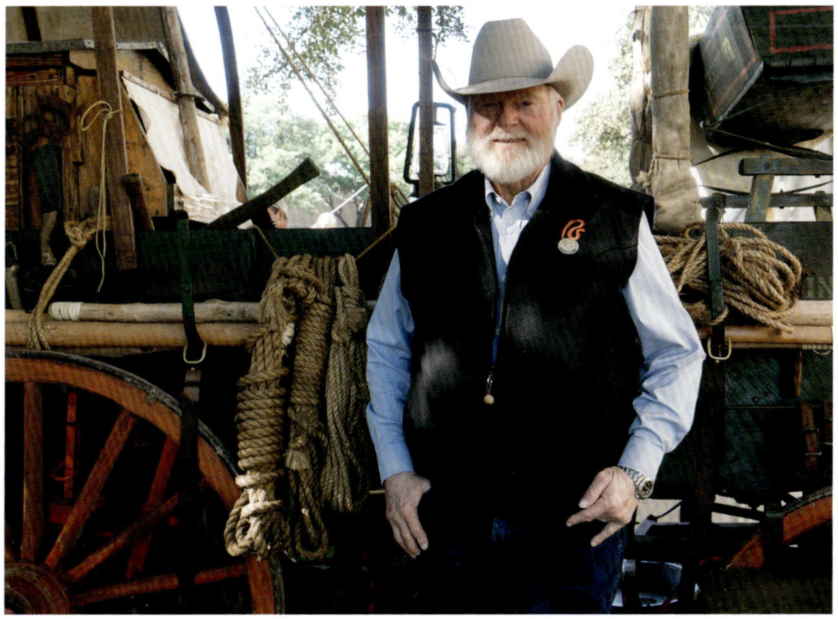

Red Steagall poses next to a well-supplied wagon on opening day of the Red Steagall Cowboy Gathering and Western Swing Festival.

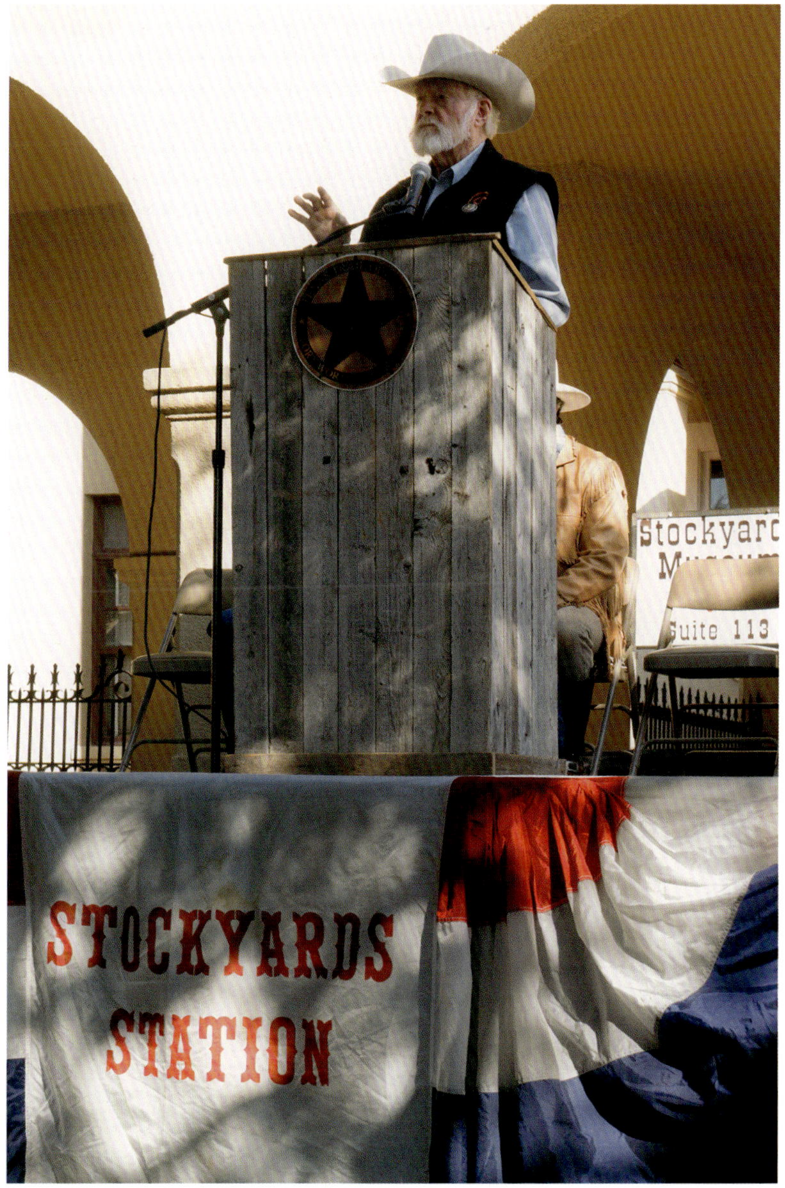

Speaking from the podium before a large audience, Red Steagall welcomes both cowboys and tourists to the annual Red Steagall Day celebration held in October of each year.

Other buildings near the stockyards, but not actually a part of the original yards, include the Stockyards Hotel, built in 1906. At the time, it housed an exclusive Stockyards Club and barber shop on the first floor and was called the Thannisch Building after its builder, T. M. Thannisch. He tore down the original two-story building in 1913 and constructed the three-story structure that still stands today. Stories are told that during the 1930s gangsters Bonnie Parker and Clyde Barrow stayed there and peeked out a two-story window to see if the law was watching the building. The Stockyards Hotel became run down by the 1950s and 1960s, and visitors to the area saw only people staying there who were down on their luck. Owners restored it in 1964, hoping to attract a better clientele. Eventually they did. By the twenty-first century the refurbished building again is an exclusive, sought-after hotel with fifty-two rooms, and a very welcoming and authentic lobby. Paul Gallaher is the manager.

Across East Exchange Avenue from the Stockyards Hotel and Fincher's is Riscky's Steakhouse. Joe Riscky came to the United States from Poland in 1911 and got a job at the Armour meatpacking company. He earned nine dollars per week. The next year he married a fellow Polish immigrant, Mary Bunkervitch, and opened a grocery store in the area in 1927. Their son, Pete, began management of the growing Riscky's Barbecue business in 1952. Their grandson, Jim, presently manages their chain of eight restaurants, which includes the steakhouse.

Among modern buildings constructed early in the twenty-first century in the area is the Hyatt, built in 2004

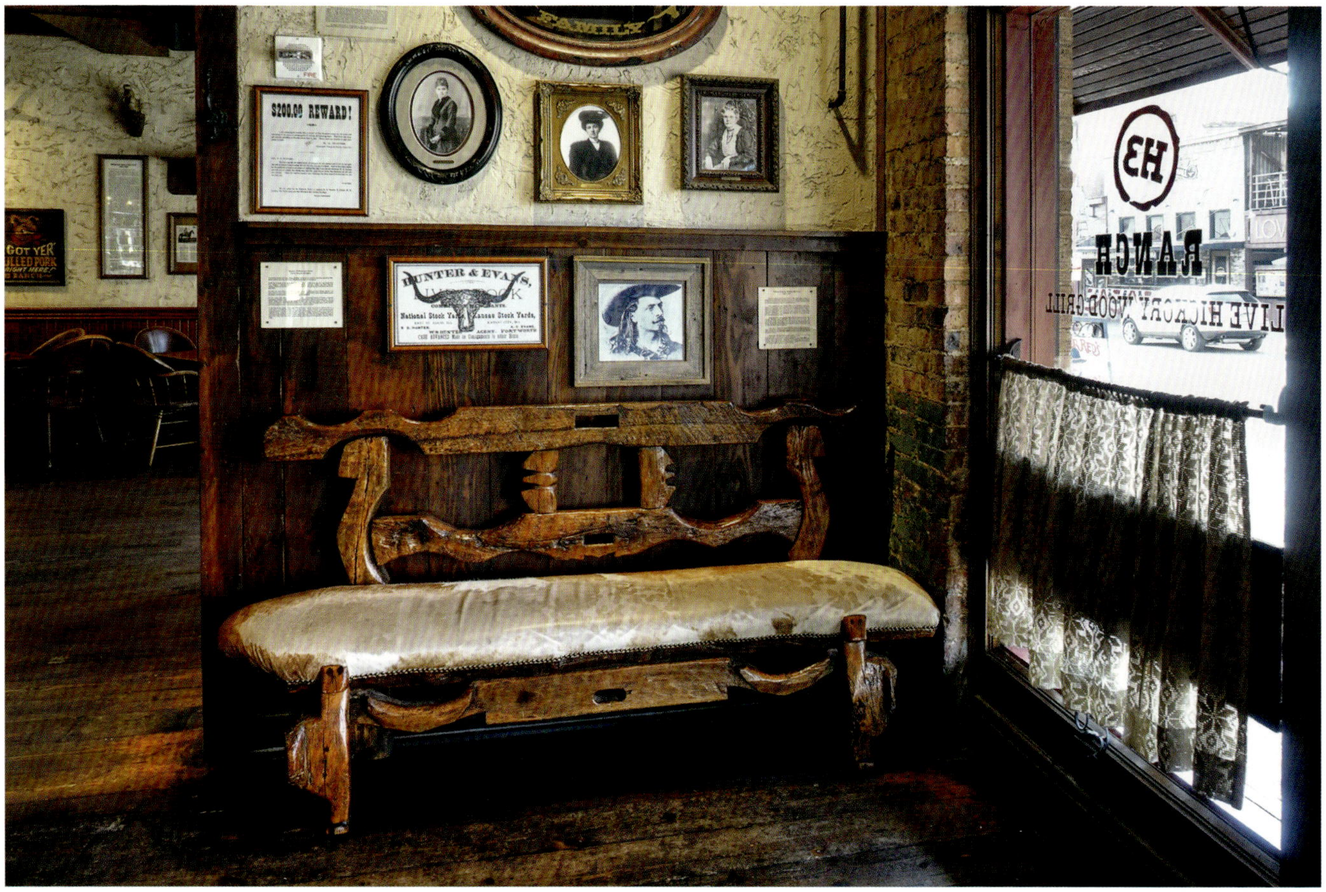

The lobby of the Stockyards Hotel Restaurant, H3 Ranch, is furnished with vintage furniture and memorabilia.

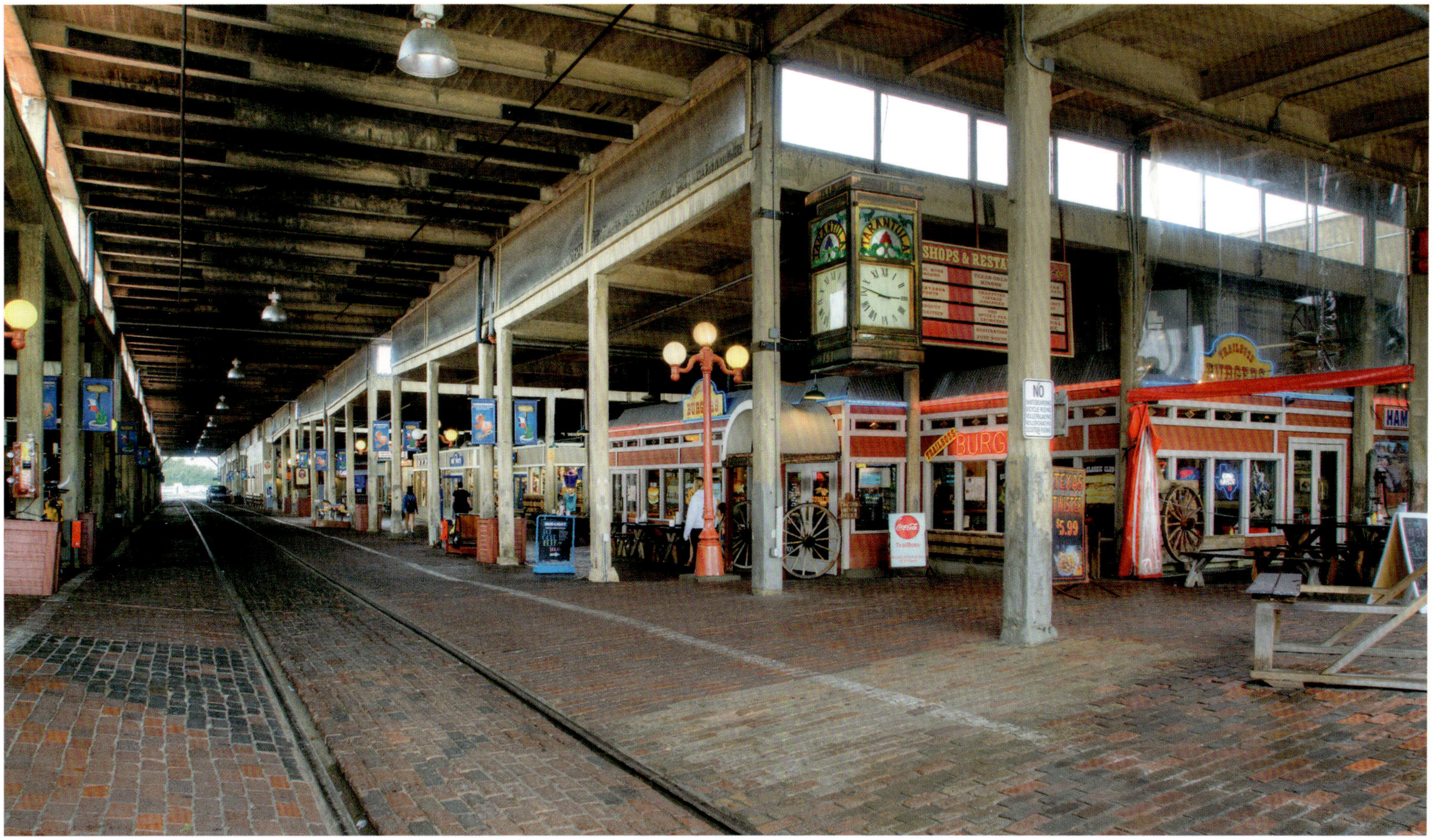

Stockyards Station at 200 East Exchange Avenue was originally constructed as a facility to house hogs and sheep. Presently it is a collection of small retail shops mixed with local restaurants, many with outdoor dining.

in a beige stucco style to match the Livestock Exchange Building. The Tarrant County Historical Commission dedicated a historical marker to Chief Quanah Parker near the Hyatt in 2008. New development plans at the stockyards in 2015 brought fears to stockyard old-timers that modern changes would alter the uniqueness of the yards. Editorials and letters to the editor appeared in the *Fort Worth Star-Telegram*. "Don't forget why tourists come here; if the stockyards do not remain real, then they won't come" became the oft-repeated fear. The Fort Worth Historic and Cultural Landmarks Commission received the proposal in January 2016 for new developments in the stockyards. Finding consensus was not easily achieved. The city in 2017 established the Stockyards Historic and Form Based Code District in an attempt to pacify worried historians and stockyards supporters as part of a compromise to allow more development in the stockyards.

There are at least three selling points to tourists about the Fort Worth Stockyards: it is old, authentic, and Western. In its busy days, the bars of Exchange Avenue separated the cowboy, or stockyard worker, from his money. By the mid-1980s, business establishments sought instead to relieve area residents and tourists of their cash. From a major cattle center, the stockyards transformed itself

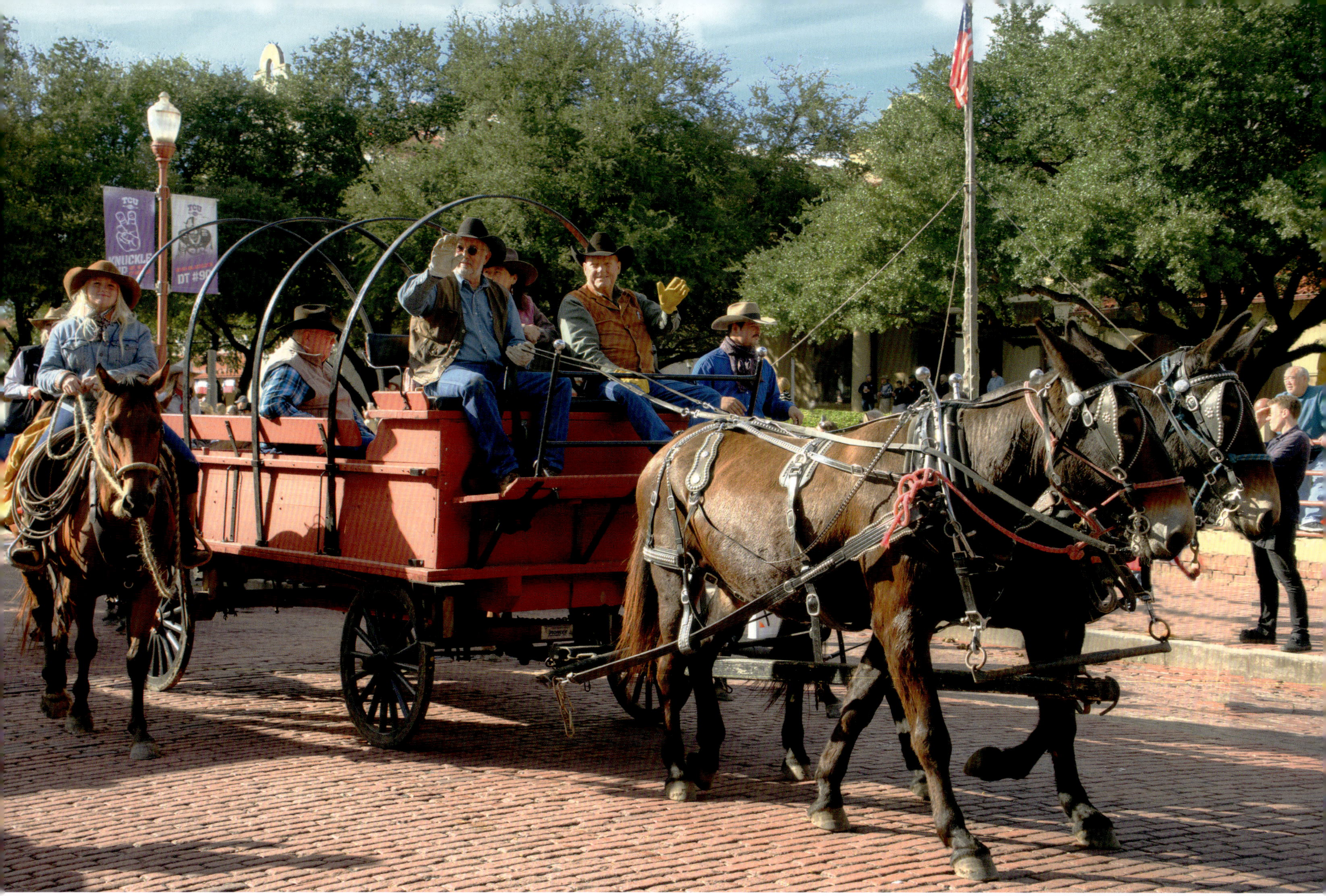

Every October, vintage wagons with wooden-spoke wheels drawn by horses and mules leave Jacksboro, Texas, for Fort Worth, where they camp and enjoy the annual Red Steagall Cowboy Gathering and Western Swing Festival. Cowboy hats and Western clothing are required.

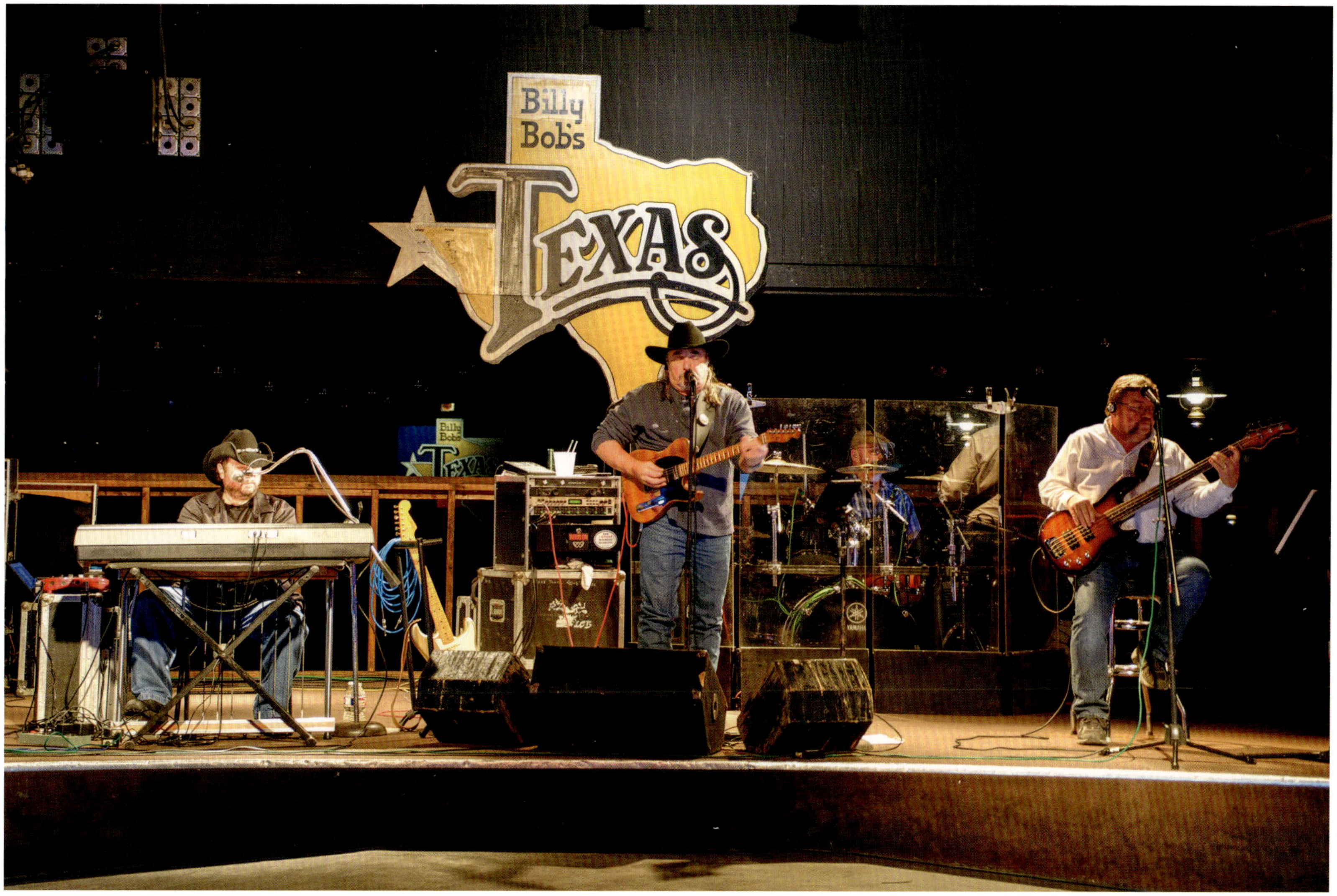

Famous musicians from all over the world play on the stage of Billy Bob's Texas. This group is the Honky Tonk Stage Dance Band.

into a major tourist attraction because of the real Western history that occurred in Fort Worth.

Of the more than dozen large stockyards in the heyday of their existence, only Fort Worth has turned its once-dying and rundown stockyards district into a vibrant, booming, tourist attraction and place of interest. The Portland Stockyards were torn down, and the land was nearly used as a garbage dump. Even the mighty Chicago Stockyards, which reigned as the largest market during the heyday of livestock marketing, was dismantled, and only its concrete entrance arch remains.

Fort Worthians, especially those who became concerned about the authenticity of the stockyards, did not want what happened in other former stockyards to occur in Fort Worth. City leaders assured the citizens this would not take place. Holt Hickman spent much of his money to save the stockyards. After his death, his son Brad partnered the Hickman interests with Majestic Realty to

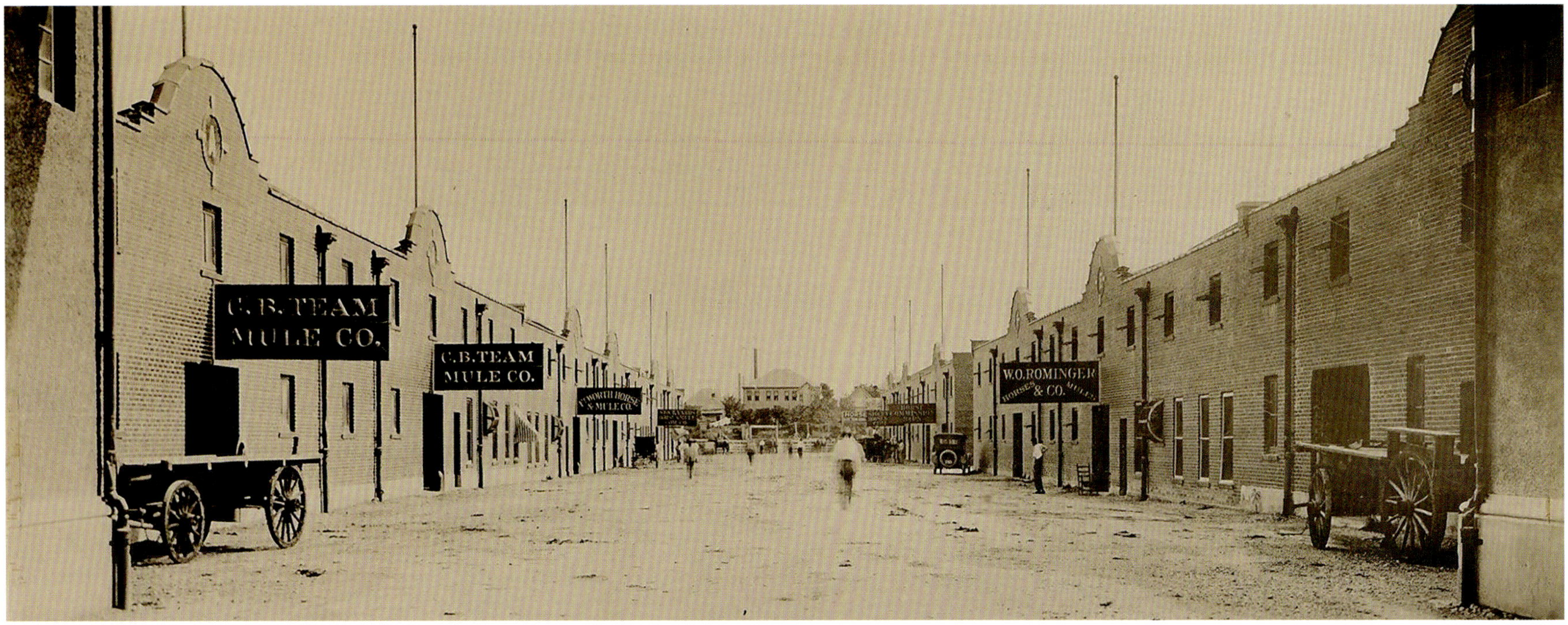

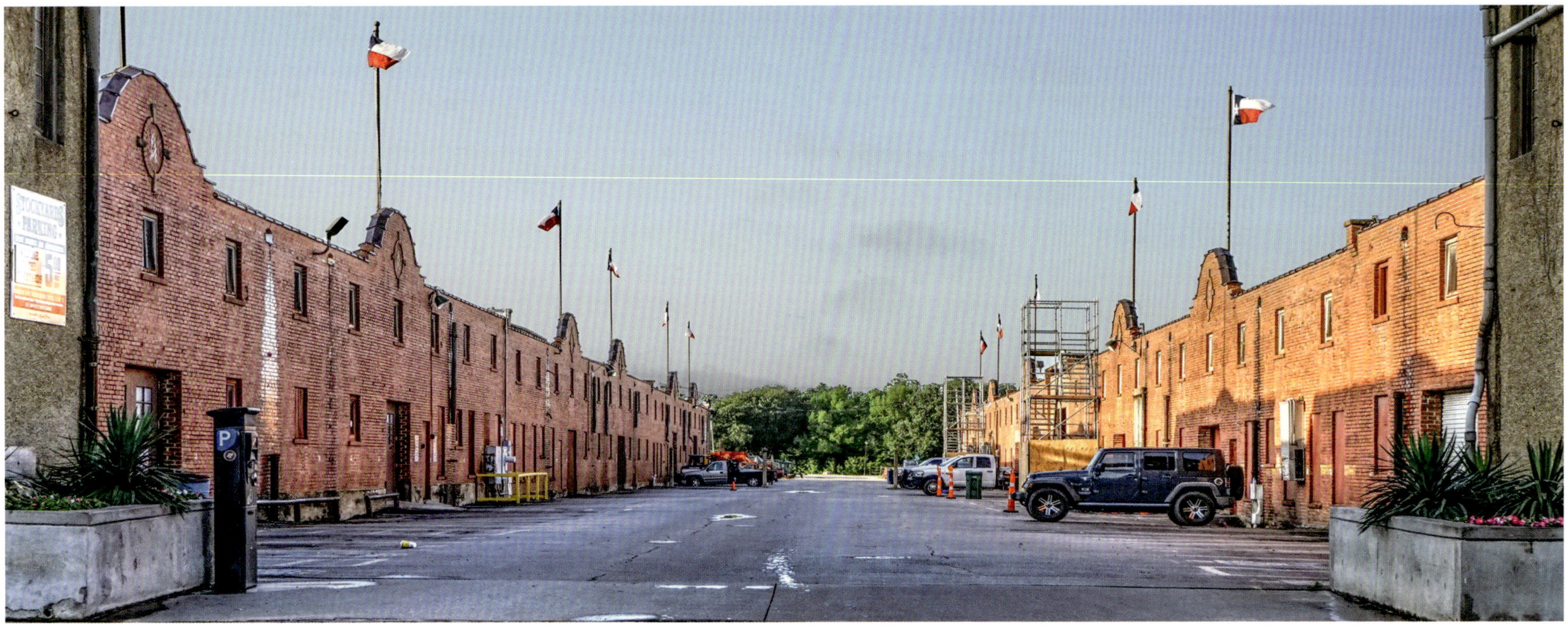

The Horse and Mule Barns were constructed by the Fort Worth Stockyards Company to serve the growing stockyard industry in Fort Worth after the turn of the twentieth century. At the top is an early photograph of what is now called Mule Alley; the scene below is taken from the same vantage point in 2016. Since that time, the horses and mules have been relocated, and Mule Alley is open with new retail shops and restaurants. Top photograph courtesy of North Fort Worth Historical Society.

create the Stockyards Heritage Development Company, Heritage Hickman.

"The plan is to revitalize an icon without changing the essence of what has always made it special," Brad Hickman affirmed. Craig Caviler is executive vice president of Majestic Realty Stockyards Heritage Development. He promises that their efforts will not "overly commercialize" the stockyards. The Majestic Realty project is a public/private partnership with the city of Fort Worth and Tarrant County. Ed Roski is chairman of Majestic.

The first phase of the $175 million project began in August 2018, when the company broke ground on the south side of East Exchange Avenue across from the coliseum in what always has been known as "Mule Alley." The name refers to the housing of horse and mule sales early in the twentieth century, especially during World War I. The brick walls of Mule Alley, constructed in 1912 after a fire destroyed the wooden stables for horses and mules, will stand. Inside those structures new businesses, including some restaurants, are emerging.

The world's second-largest international equine breed organization, the American Paint Horse Association, moved its headquarters to the stockyards. It has registered more than one million horses in fifty-nine nations. Executive Director Billy Smith affirms that his office is a paint-horse destination and a stop for visitors seeking the Western lifestyle. He said that the associations' members worldwide will want to visit. It includes offices, a theater, retail gallery, and museum.

RFD, "The Cowboy Channel" run by Patrick Gottsch, operates broadcast studios in the stockyards open to the public. It is located in the former auction barn behind the Livestock Exchange Building. An office, retail and entertainment, and broadcast facilities feature programing centered on the cowboy and cowgirl. The network reaches more than one hundred million homes worldwide and follows the mission to reconnect city with country.

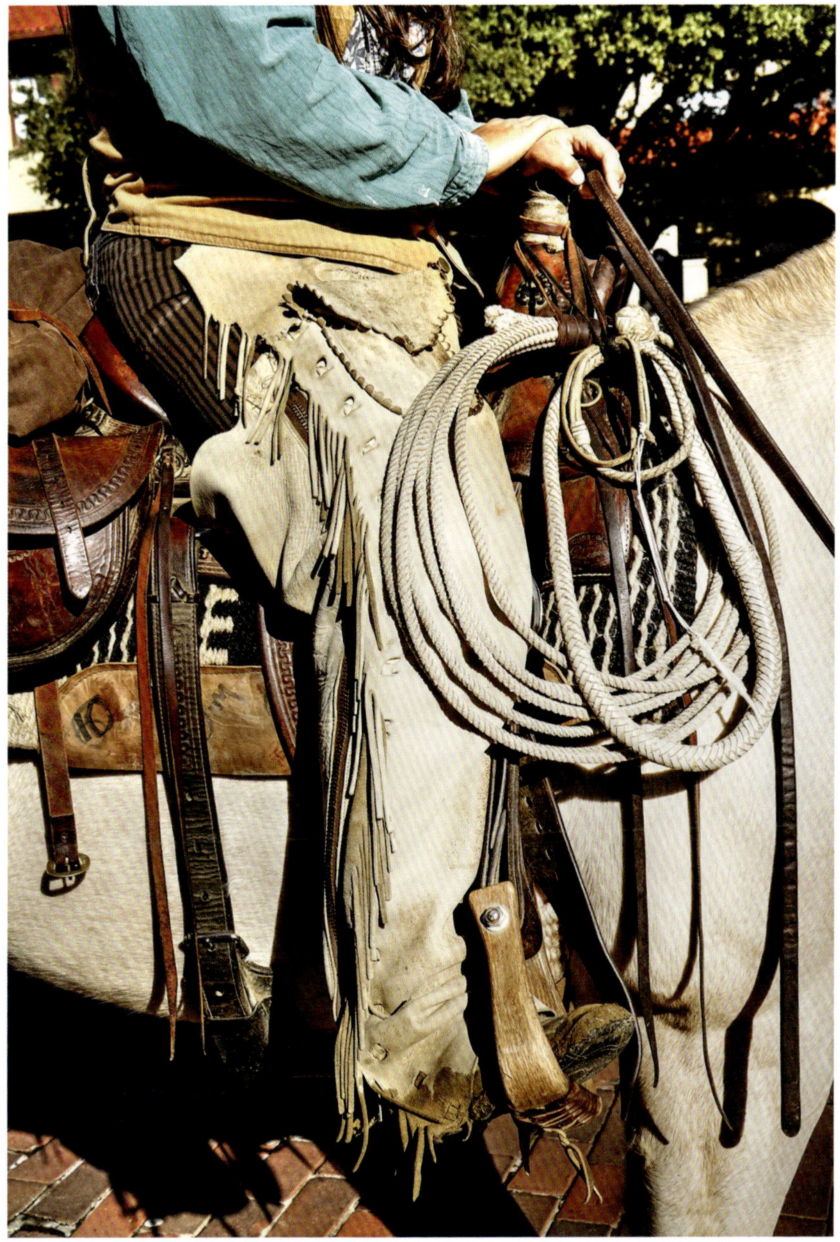

Drovers dress in historically accurate clothing, saddles, and lassos. Chaps are worn for protection, not fashion. They protect the drover from thorny brush, steer horns, and rope burns.

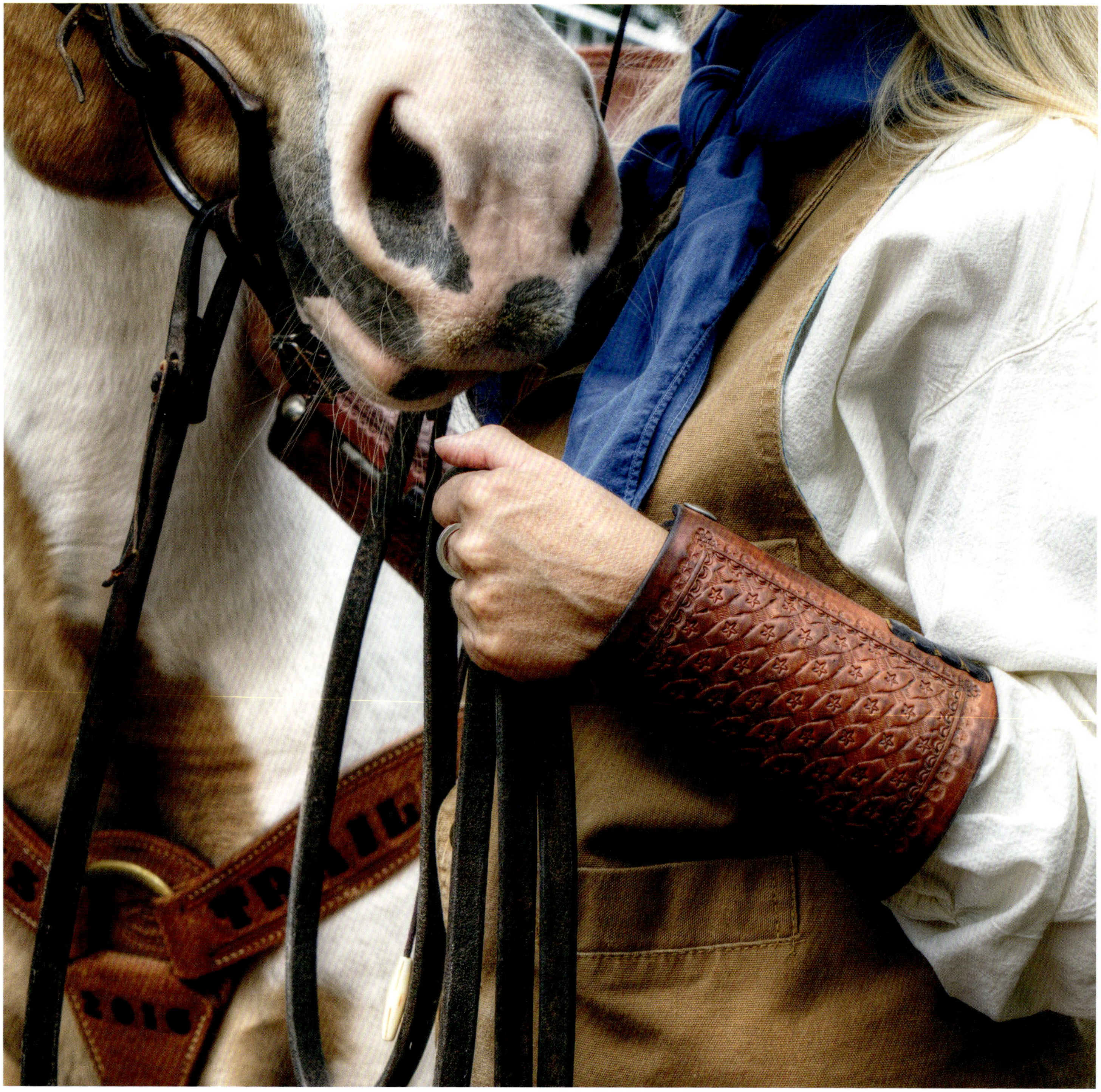

A close-up view of Trail Boss Kristin Jaworski and her horse, McCoy, shows colors of her clothing coordinated with those of her horse. She also wears hand-tooled brush cuffs and a blue bandana. McCoy wears a personalized breast collar. Kristin's dog, Tommy, is also tan and white.

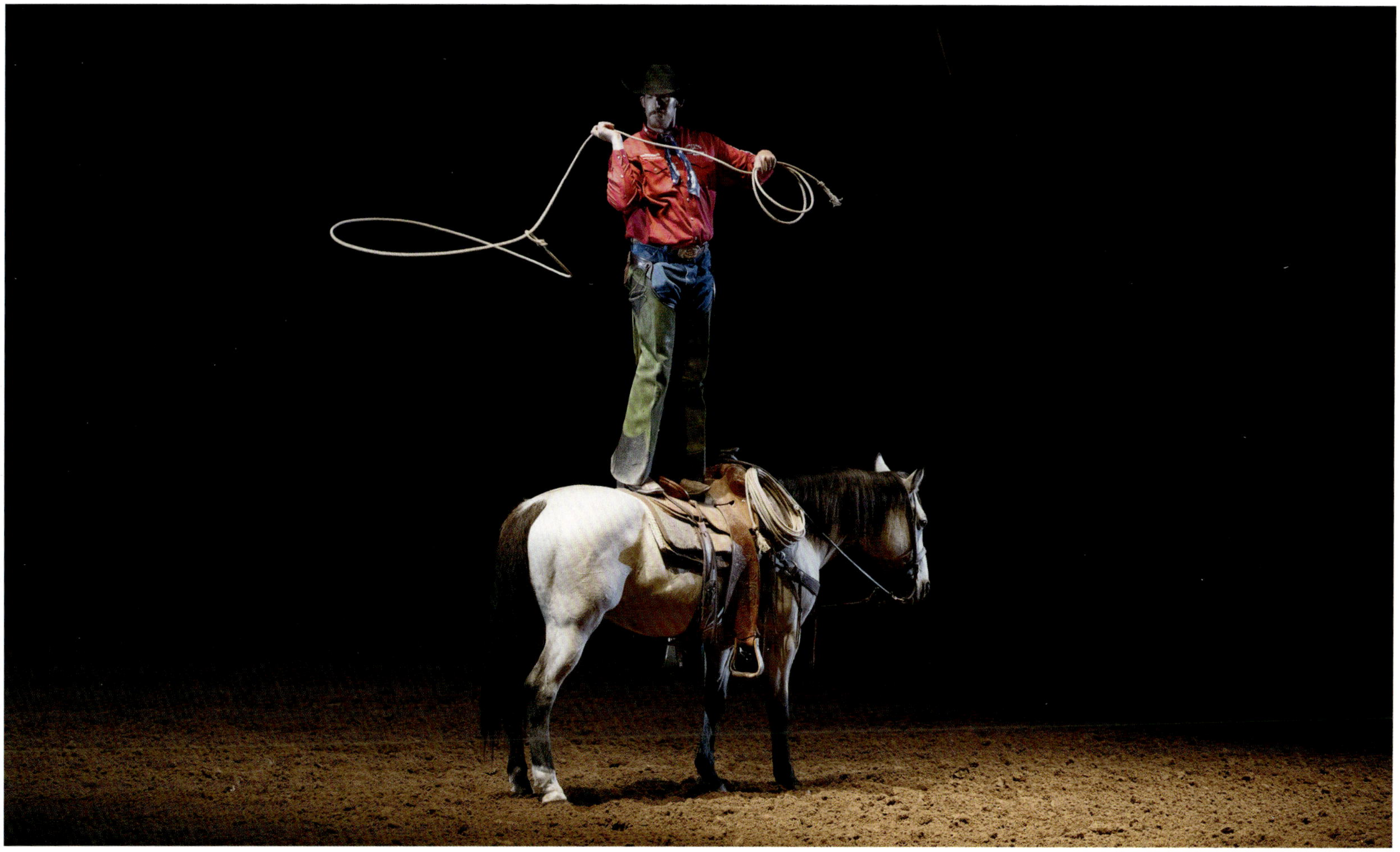

The world's only year-round rodeo is held every Friday and Saturday night at 8:00 p.m. in the historic Fort Worth Cowtown Coliseum. The two-hour Stockyards Championship Rodeo maintains a strong commitment to visitors looking for an authentic Western cowboy experience. The show features this talented lasso artist, Ketch Weaver, and his horse.

The flagship store of the former mule barns' new businesses is MB Mercantile and Supply, an emporium of merchandise that is "warmly rustic, charmingly vintage, and wonderfully western." The merchandise includes gifts, home decor, vintage finds, stationery, apothecary, books, artisan goods, and food.

The new Hotel Drover, part of the Marriott Autograph Collection of hotels, has two hundred rooms and suites, fifteen thousand square feet of meeting space, and a dramatic, elegant barn for weddings, meetings, and social events. The hotel's name refers to the drovers who represented the spirit of the West as they herded cattle along the trail through Fort Worth to areas farther north. Developers call the 155,937-square-foot hotel a "four star rustic resort."

Although sales of on-site animals ceased in 1992, Fort Worth was able to make a claim: "We are still selling livestock at the Fort Worth Stockyards" for the next twenty-eight years. This statement remained true because of Superior Livestock Auction, selling animals online in the Livestock Exchange Building from 1987 until September 2020, overlapping five years when the Fort Worth Stockyards remained in business. The company began in late 1986 and held its first auction in Denver at the same time as the Denver Stock Show. Its first Fort Worth auction took place in the Billy Bob's facility in the winter of 1987. Its offices eventually took up much of the Livestock Exchange Building. Although what few pens left at the stockyards were empty and silent (except for those that house the herd), Superior Livestock Auction posted that "millions of cattle still are being traded" at the Fort Worth Stockyards.

Beginning in September 2020, Superior Livestock Auction moved to a new facility built on land purchased due west of Fort Worth in the suburb of Hudson Oaks. Plenty of space for parking exists for patrons who wish to bid on animals at the live auction in person. These sales take place over the internet and Dish Network. Buyers in their own homes, offices, ranches, or in person at Superior's offices can view the cattle online and bid. Cofounder Jim Odle explained that it was "an innovative idea that worked." The company currently has four hundred representatives throughout the country. Their former offices in the Fort Worth Livestock Exchange Building broadcast the Dish Network 997 auctions from 1987 until September 2020, when they moved. The online auctions every other Thursday allow sellers to take videos of their animals and show them through Superior while the animals remain in their own pasture. Buyers then make the arrangements with the assistance of Superior to transfer their livestock purchases to their own land.

While Superior no longer operates from the Livestock Exchange Building in the Fort Worth Stockyards, it still remains in the Fort Worth area and gives local farmers and ranchers the opportunity to continue to come to the area for livestock sales and for buyers and sellers from all this and other countries to carry on their livestock operations online with the assistance of Superior Livestock Auction.

The company has a total of sixty employees in three locations. However, more than four hundred independent dealers are connected to the auction, which sells more than 1.5 million animals in a year. Although smaller companies, such as Western in California and one in Montana, sell livestock online, Superior is the largest such operation in the world. Cattle sales dominate, but the company has also sold hogs, elk, emus, and ostriches.

Fort Worth citizens and tourists are recipients of the efforts of the handful of stockyard enthusiasts who worked tirelessly to petition the city for help in preserving the stockyards area, updating infrastructure, and providing the herd. Success at the stockyards is also the result of private citizens risking their own money in creating businesses in a run-down and deteriorating part of town. Many pooled their resources in partnerships to make their dreams succeed. Their efforts ultimately drew visitors from all over the world. While more than five million tourists come to Fort Worth each year, fully half of them visit the stockyards.

Folks in the early 1970s, who looked at a decaying stockyards district and dreamed what might have seemed an impossible feat of turning it into a popular tourist attraction, would be surprised and gratified if they could see the success that hardworking Fort Worthians achieved a half century later. Surprisingly, many of those dreamers lived to see it happen. This writer is one who did.

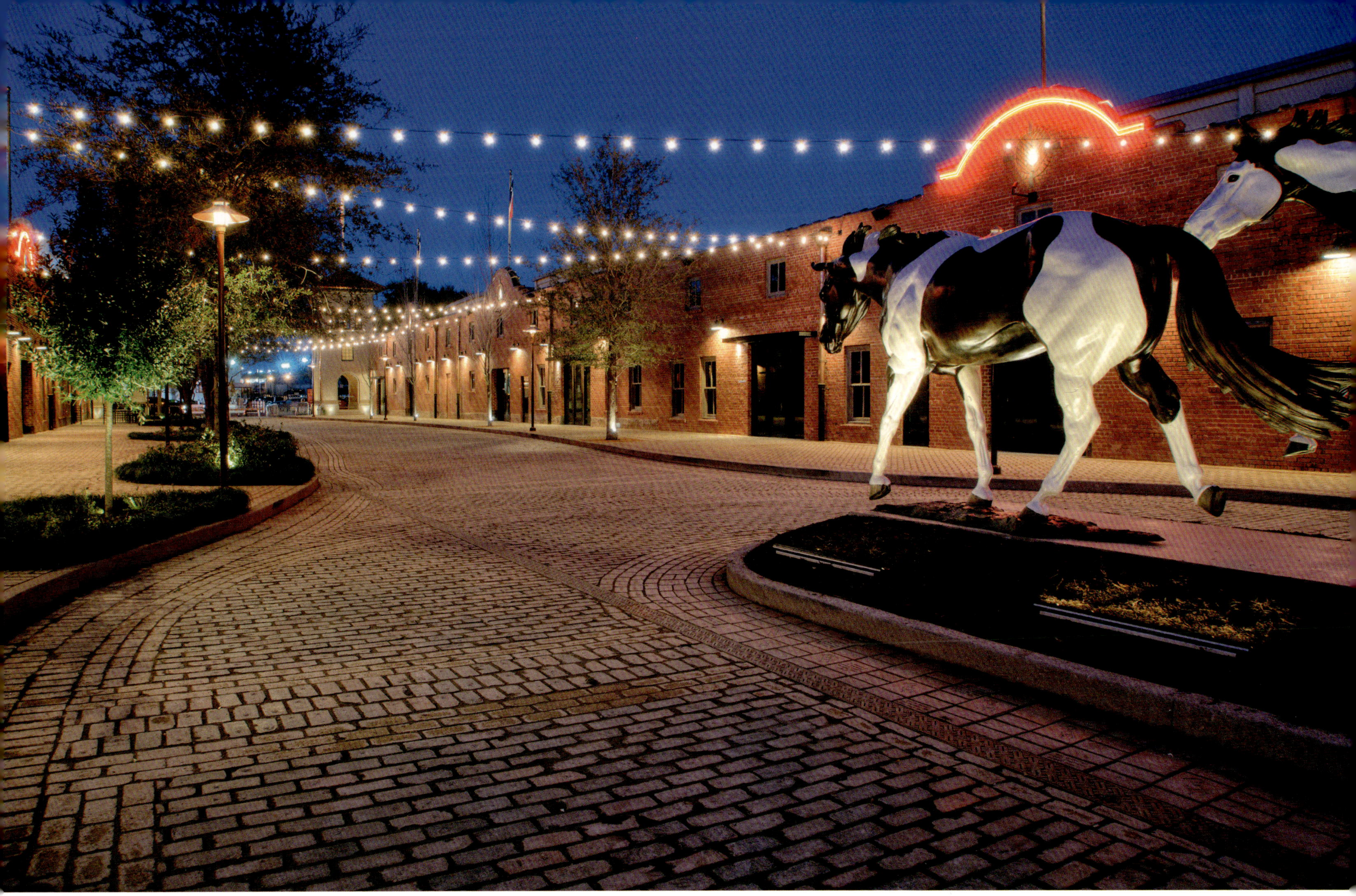

Harnessing the unique Western heritage of Fort Worth, the legendary Horse and Mule Barns of Mule Alley has reemerged as a beautifully restored destination within the Stockyards Historic District. A carefully curated collection of restaurants, eateries, entertainment venues, shops, heritage brands, creative workplaces, and a charmingly rustic four-star hotel will reimagine what a thriving market street can be. A huge statue of American Paint Horses is displayed on the one-hundred-year-old brick-covered street.

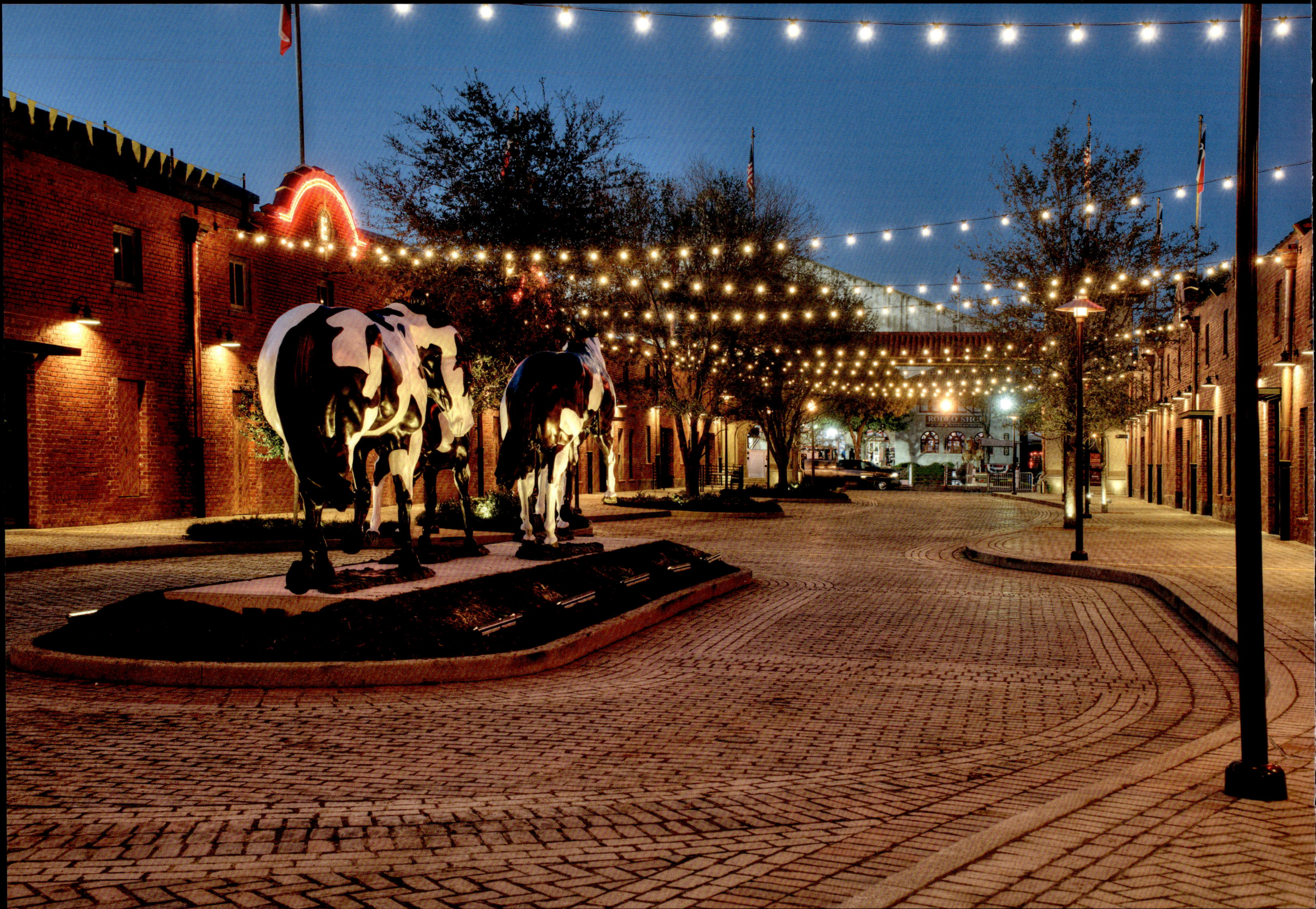

EPILOGUE

The Fort Worth Stockyards is a live and changing entity. New growth from the partnership between the city of Fort Worth and Majestic Realty / Stockyards Heritage Development Company, Heritage Hickman is ongoing. Other developments most likely will continue to occur. This and the unique existence of a real, former, major stockyards with its rodeo and the herd of Longhorns hopefully will keep tourists visiting Fort Worth and the North Side for many years to come.

This book began with the desire of talented photographer Carolyn Brown to capture images of the yards in glorious color. She began her career photographing ancient architecture while living in Cairo, Egypt, and traveling across Mexico photographing early architecture. Presently she specializes in projects such as Caddo Lake, the Fort Worth Swift Meat Packing Company Complex, and the Fort Worth Stockyards. This is her third book published by Texas A&M University Press. She exhibits at Craighead Green Gallery in Dallas.

This book represents a second major telling of the Fort Worth Stockyards story by author J'Nell Pate Barnes. The first, *Livestock Legacy: The Fort Worth Stockyards 1887–1987*, was published in 1988 by Texas A&M University Press. It won an award from the Texas State Historical Association as the best book on Texas history published that year. She has written nine other books, four of them on Fort Worth history, including *North of the River: A Brief History of North Fort Worth*, published by Texas Christian University Press in 1994.

To Fort Worth folks and tourists: Enjoy, and keep the story growing!

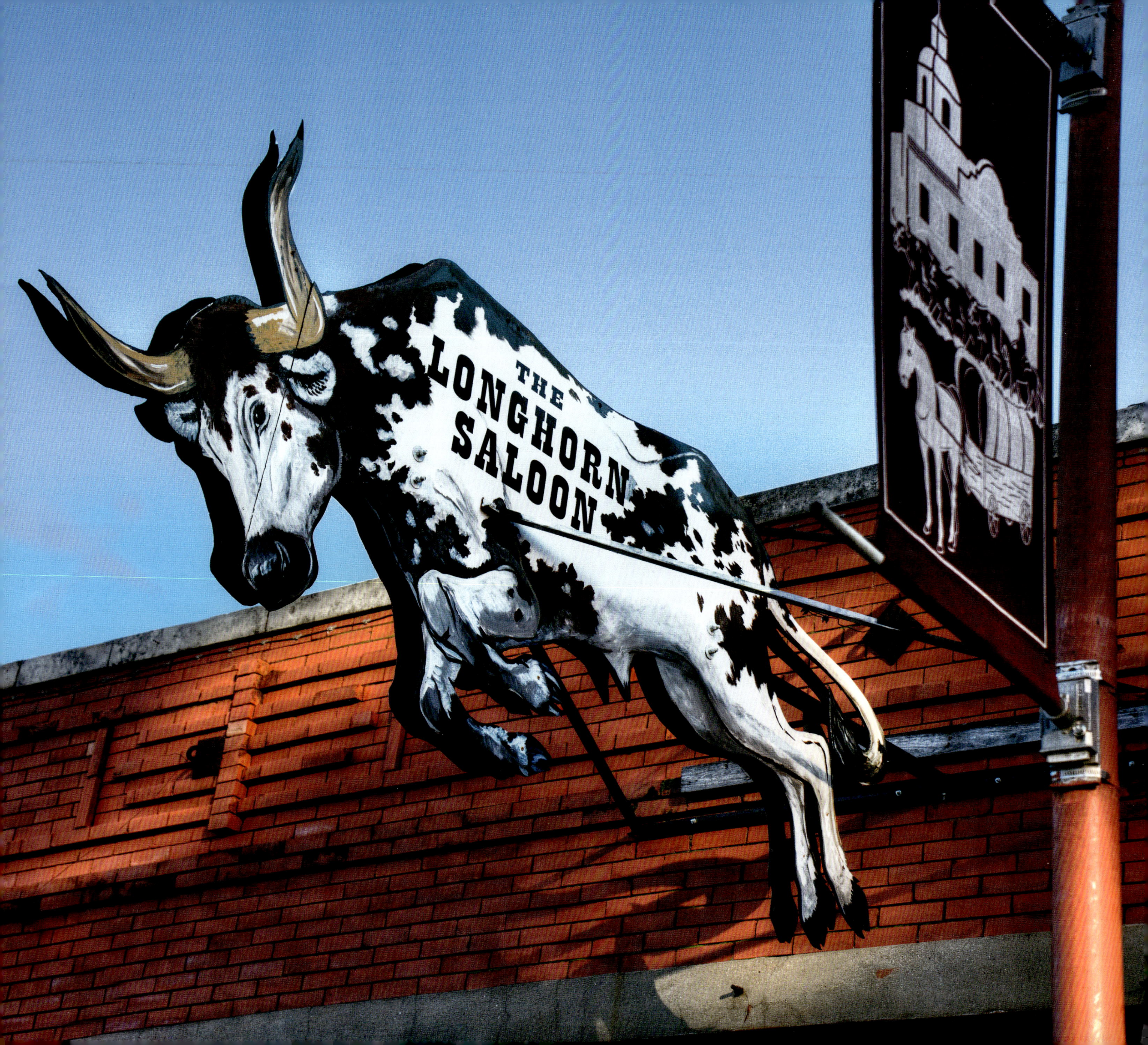
THE
LONGHORN
SALOON

INDEX

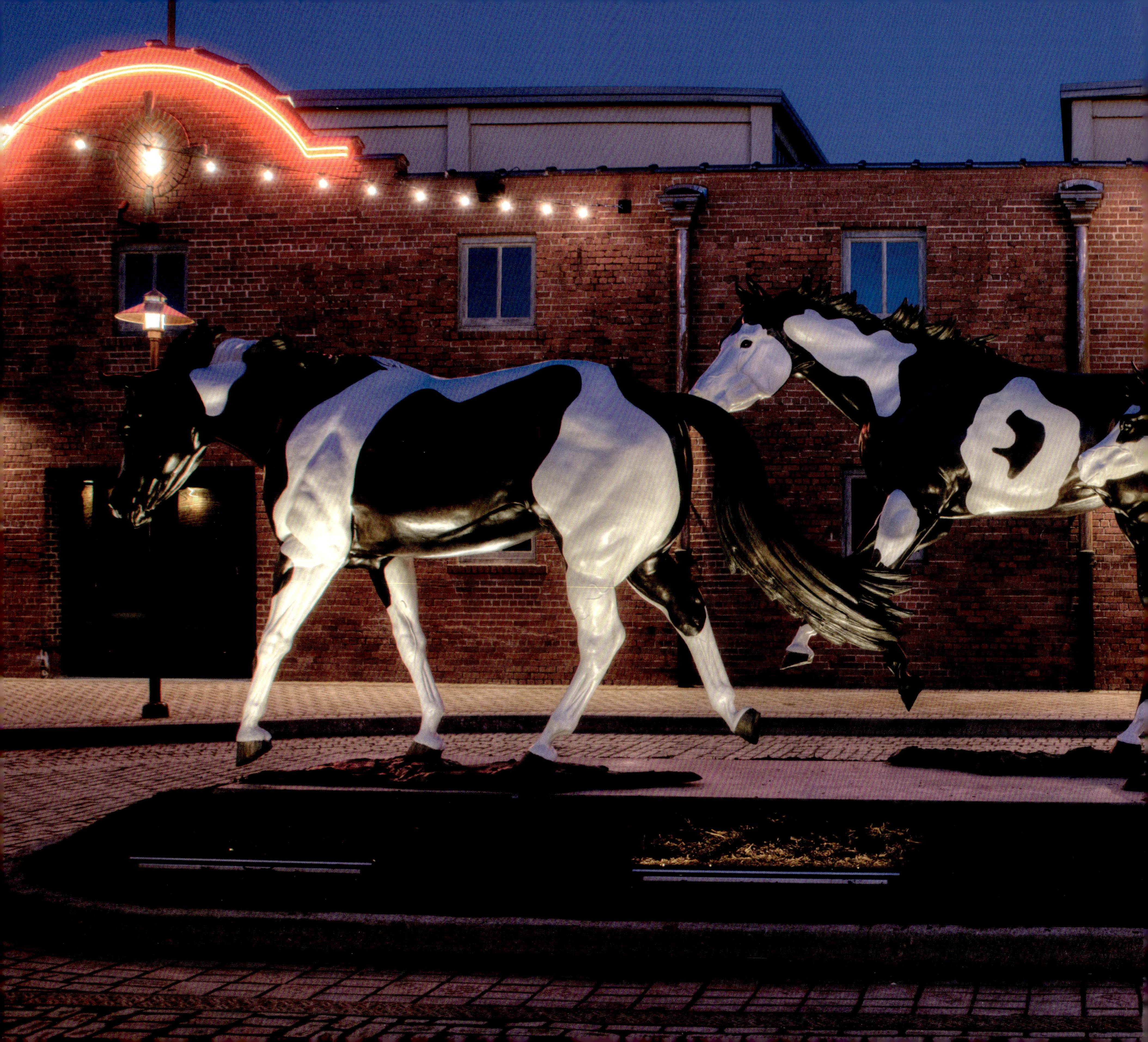

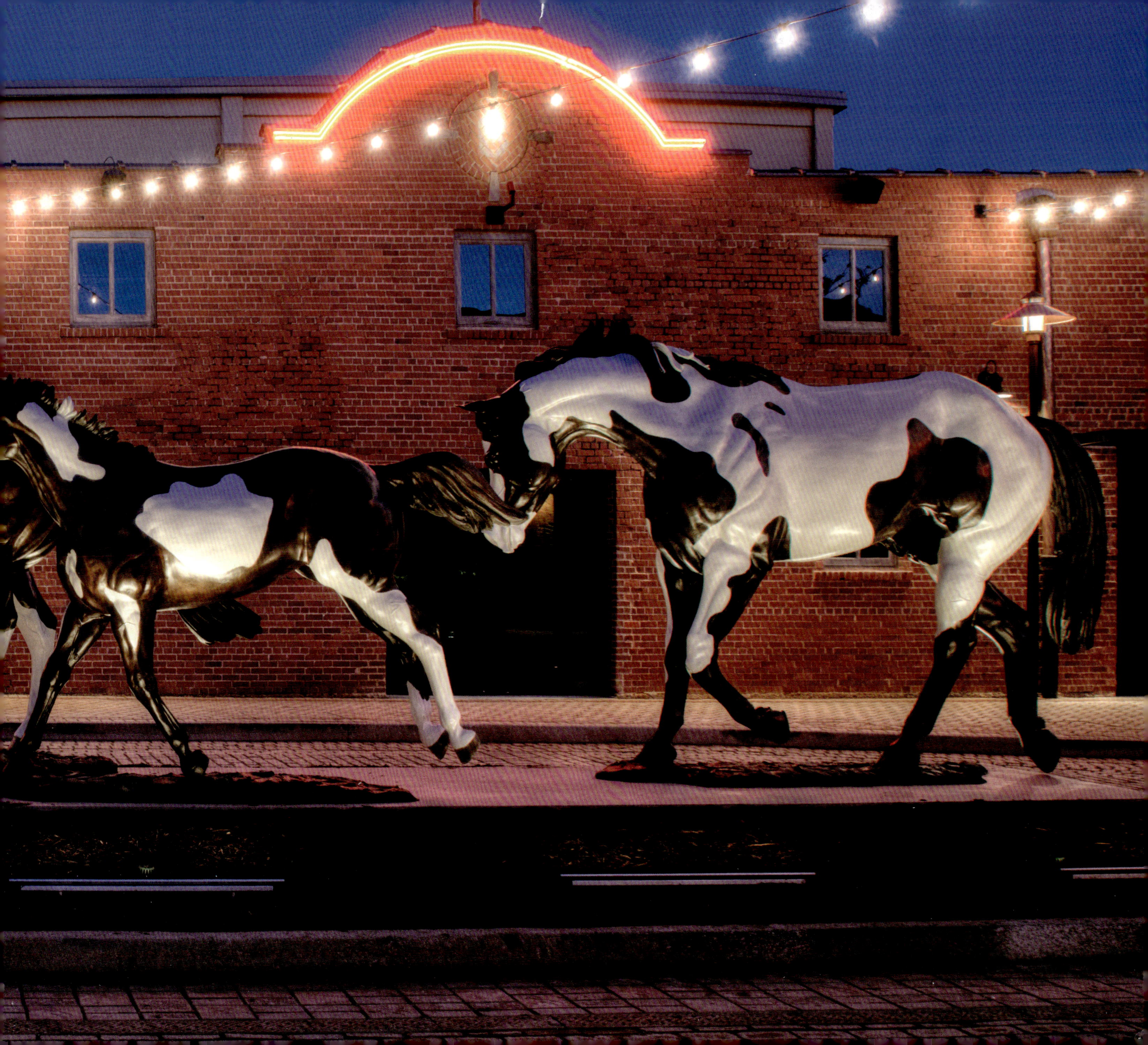